BEIJING
—THE TREASURES OF
AN ANCIENT CAPITAL

Yan Chongnian

BEIJING
—THE TREASURES OF AN ANCIENT CAPITAL

Translated by

Arnold Chao, Tan Aiqing,
Wang Xingzheng and Fang Zhenya

English text edited by
Arnold Chao

Morning Glory Press
Beijing, China

Editors: Wang Yanrong and Ma Yue
Photographers: Yan Zhongyi, Hu Chui, Liu Zhigang and Sun Guiqi
Designer: Wei Ming
Drawings by Yu Mei'er

First Edition   1987

Published by

　　Morning Glory Press
　　21 Chegongzhuang Xilu
　　Beijing, China

Printed by

　　Xinhua Color Printing House
　　3 Chegongzhuang Dajie
　　Beijing, China

Distributed by

　　China International Book Trading Corporation
　　21 Chegongzhuang Xilu
　　P.O. Box No.399
　　Beijing, China

ISBN 7—5054—0092—4

Printed in the People's Republic of China

AUTHOR'S
PREFACE

AUTHOR'S PREFACE

This book is the result of a pleasant surprise. In September 1984 an editor of the Morning Glory Press came to me with a proposal for a book on the history and culture of Beijing. I was told that the book would be illustrated with a great number of excellent photographs of our ancient city, and that it would have to be both entertaining and academically valuable.

While I was flattered by the offer, I could see that it was one of the most challenging jobs ever presented to a researcher in this field. But for two reasons I could not decline the offer. First, there were so many people who would like to know more about Beijing, including hundreds of thousands of tourists and other visitors from all over the world and ethnic Chinese coming back for home visits. And second, as a long-time resident of Beijing who had been studying it for years, I felt I was obliged to contribute my bit to the current understanding of the city.

A historical review of Beijing reveals that it is a giant cultural project accomplished through the efforts of many generations. The earliest inhabitant in this area, so far as we know, was Peking Man who made his home here some 700,000 years ago. The city was built and rebuilt through the centuries, but it was not until the 13th century, under the Yuan dynasty, that it became the national capital. Today's Beijing is largely the result of the work done under three dynasties — Yuan, Ming and Qing, during which the city attained its full glory and won recognition as a leading metropolis of the world.

The first characteristic of Beijing is, of course, its long history. If we leave aside the prehistoric times when the area was the settlement of Peking Man and his successors, the history of the city dates back at least to the 11th century B.C. when it became the city of *Ji,* which means "thistle," at the beginning of the Zhou dynasty. With a 3,000-year history, Beijing is one of the oldest cities in China and the world.

The layout of a city usually follows a philosophy. Historically dominated by a feudal monarchy, Beijing has a layout which makes a strict distinction between the principal sector and the auxiliary ones. Planners of the city under all dynasties acted on the principle which subordinated each and every person to the monarch and placed religious authority next to monarchical power. Under the Ming and Qing dynasties, designers of Beijing drew an axial line from north to south, placed the imperial palaces exactly at the center of the city, and symmetrically laid out the halls and palace walls, altars and temples, gardens and parks, government offices and civilian settlements on the two sides of the axial line. The palace complex, the imperial city, the inner city, and the outer city formed four square enclosures, each outside the other, even though the wall of the outer city remained unfinished because of a lack of resources. The whole design was based on the idea of seclusion and conformed to the socio-political hierarchy. The same philosophy applied to the layout of the gardens and parks, including the Imperial Garden in the Forbidden City, the Celestial Lake in the Imperial City, the altars and temples in the Inner City, and even the "Three Hills and Five Gardens" in the western suburbs. It may be interesting to compare the layout of imperial Beijing with that of Washington D.C. which grew out of the American War of Independence. Basing themselves on the concept of democracy and independence, designers of the American capital gave prominence to the Capitol and left the Lincoln Memorial open to the public on all sides. The second characteristic of Beijing, we may conclude, is a perfect integration of the feudalistic concept of monarchical supremacy with superb architecture and garden designing.

Beijing's long history as a capital city, particularly its 800-year experience as a dynastic capital from the beginning of the Jin (Jurchen) dynasty in 1115 to the end of the Qing dynasty in 1911, made it a colossal museum of art. The exhibits range from whole palaces and gardens, man-made hills and streams, towers and pavilions, corridors and terraces to rockeries and stone sculptures, trees and flower beds, rare books, paintings and calligraphy, jewels and silver and gold utensils. A huge treasurehouse of art — this may be considered a third characteristic of Beijing.

The fourth characteristic of Beijing has to do with its people. The city was built at a location joining the Central Plains dominated by a farming population with the regions north of the Great Wall, the domains of nomadic peoples. Beijing was often the scene of rivalry among China's different ethnic groups as well as a melting pot for all of them. The protracted struggles among them and their fusion were an important reason why China's economic, political and cultural center moved eastward, and why Beijing became the capital for the Yuan, Ming and Qing dynasties in the process. The buildings and gardens one finds in Beijing today represent a crystallization of the best in the culture of each and every ethnic group. Living together in the capital city, people from different ethnic groups have influenced one another in customs and habits with regard to clothing, the family menu, the style of housing construction, and even articles of daily use. One group became familiar with the religious beliefs of the others. In time, a festival for one of them changed into a common one for all.

I have tried to present a clear picture of Beijing's history and culture. Shi Tao, the famous Chinese painter of the 17th century, said that he usually surveyed a great number of grotesque peaks as raw material for his paintings. I am not a painter, but I too had to examine every interesting bit of material to put this book together, so that a panorama of Beijing could be composed through the pictures and the text. Historically the book starts from the dawn of the Stone Age and the rise of bronze culture and goes down to the initiation of the city of Ji as capital for the ancient state of Yan, the role of the city as an important military stronghold in North China during early dynasties, and its designation as capital city for three more states called Yan. Then it deals with the periods in which Beijing served as Southern Capital for the Liao dynasty, Middle Capital for the Jin (Jurchen) dynasty, Dadu (Great Capital) for the Yuan dynasty, Beijing (Northern Capital) for the Ming dynasty, and Jingshi (the Capital) for the Qing dynasty. The historical review is interspersed with accounts of interesting events and anecdotes about famous people. The palaces and halls, altars and temples, gardens and mausoleums are described in details, and special passages are devoted to education, science and technology, literature and art, the life of the imperial family, and the customs of the people.

The book is a joint creation. I borrowed extensively from the research done by my predecessors and contemporaries in history, archeology, cultural relics, traditional Chinese architecture, traditional gardening, and historical geography. My thanks are due to the editors, translators, photographers, artists and printers, whose hard work made this publication possible.

(Signed) Yan Chongnian

CONTENTS

BEIJING
—THE TREASURES OF AN ANCIENT CAPITAL

Sketch Map of China Showing Location of Beijing

Urumqi

XINJIANG UYGUR AUTONOMOUS REGION

GANSU

NINGXIA
AUTONOM
REGION

QINGHAI

Xining

Lanzhou

TIBET AUTONOMOUS REGION

Lhasa

SICHUAN

Chengdu

GU

Kunming

YUNNAN

G

★ National capital

Great Wall

Grand Canal

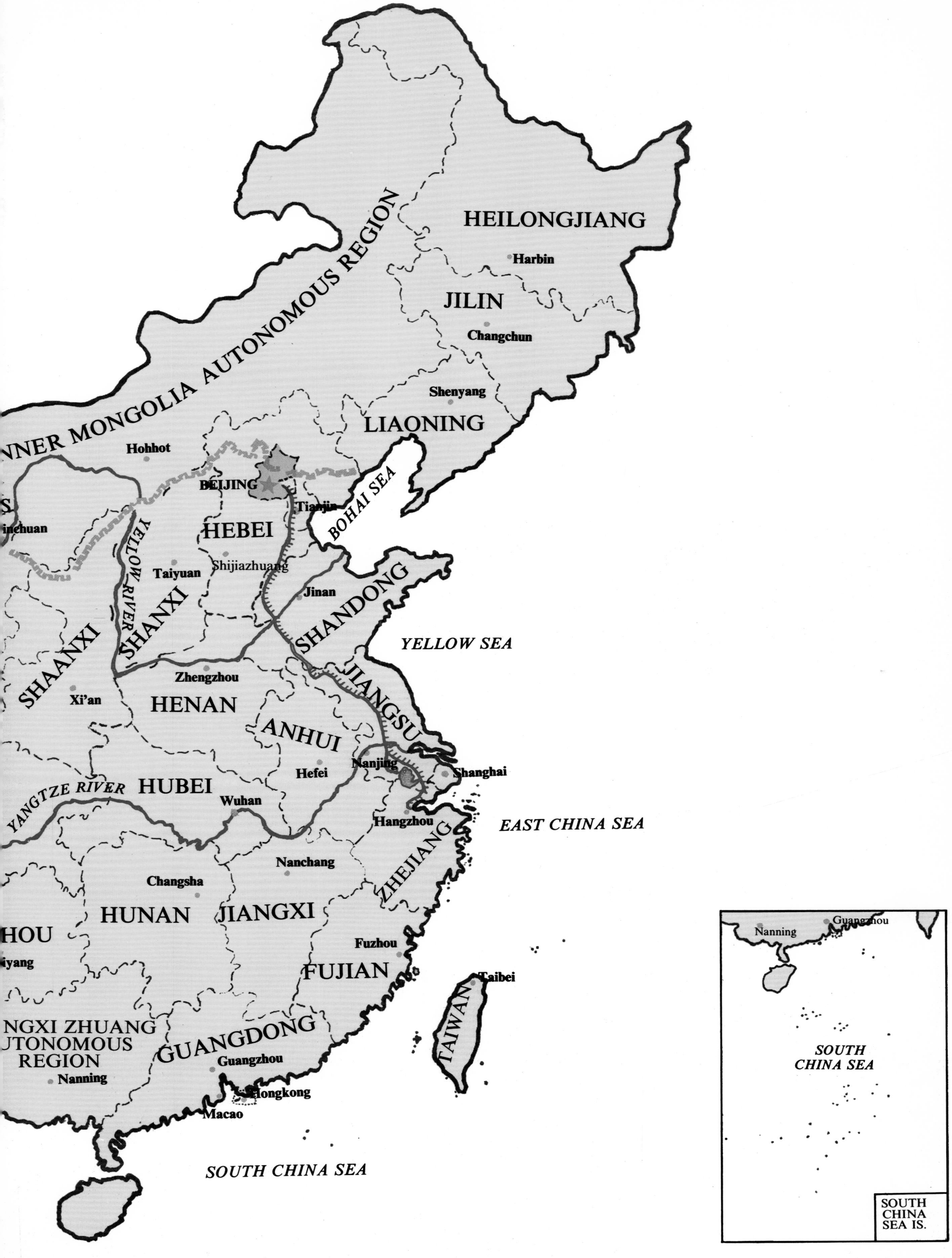

HEILONGJIANG

Harbin

JILIN

Changchun

Shenyang

LIAONING

INNER MONGOLIA AUTONOMOUS REGION

Hohhot

BOHAI SEA

BEIJING

Tianjin

HEBEI

inchuan

YELLOW RIVER

Taiyuan

Shijiazhuang

SHANXI

Jinan

SHANDONG

SHAANXI

YELLOW SEA

Zhengzhou

Xi'an

HENAN

ANHUI

JIANGSU

Yangtze River

HUBEI

Hefei

Nanjing

Shanghai

Wuhan

Hangzhou

EAST CHINA SEA

Nanchang

ZHEJIANG

Changsha

HOU

HUNAN

JIANGXI

iyang

Fuzhou

FUJIAN

Taibei

NGXI ZHUANG
UTONOMOUS
REGION

GUANGDONG

TAIWAN

Nanning

Guangzhou

Hongkong

Macao

SOUTH CHINA SEA

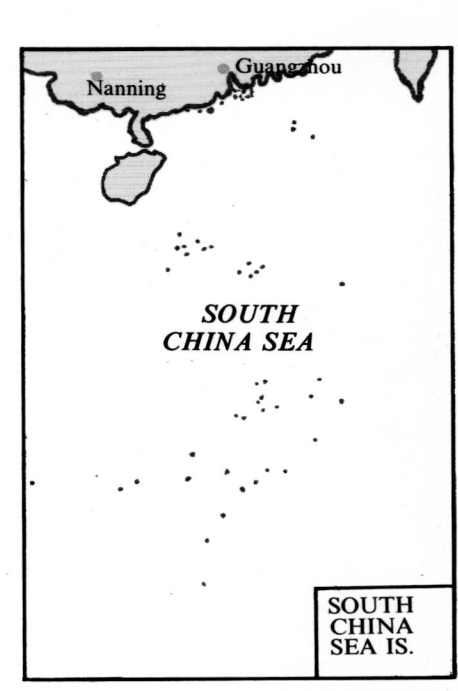

Nanning

Guangzhou

SOUTH
CHINA SEA

SOUTH
CHINA
SEA IS.

INTRODUCTION

If you look at a map of China, a vertical line and a horizontal one will catch your attention. The vertical line is the Grand Canal starting from Beijing in the north and terminating at the lake city of Hangzhou in the southeast. The horizontal line running in a east-west direction is none other than the Great Wall. The world boasts many historical relics, but few of them can compare with these two, in terms of age, size, significance and impact.

The Great Wall, for centuries a defence barrier against nomadic invaders, and the Grand Canal, a vital artery for bringing food grain from South China to the north, no longer perform their traditional functions. Yet they have acquired a greater cultural value and are being marveled at by visitors from all over the world in warm weather or biting cold.

The colossal relics are lined by cities and towns which remain part of the hustle and bustle of present-day China. One of them is Beijing, otherwise known as Peking, the national capital.

A wealth of myth and legend adorns the history of Beijing, giving the city a romantic tinge as a specimen of Oriental culture and intriguing all those who dream of the jade towers on celestial bodies so often visualized by China's classical poets.

One may ask: what is the motif of the city's layout? The answer is the predominance of monarchical and religious authority. The Forbidden City at the center symbolizes the immensity of power enjoyed by the emperor, who in turn must obey and carry out the Mandate of Heaven. An ascent to the Pavilion of Ten Thousand Spring Seasons in Jingshan Park (Prospect Hill or His Majesty's Hill Park) enables one to appreciate the magnificence of the imperial palaces: the Forbidden City skirted by the Tongzi River and covered by an ocean of shining glazed tiles.

Bird's-eye view of the Forbidden City, which covers an area of 720,000 square meters, with more than 9,000 rooms

With a powerful motif, the city's layout crystalizes China's heritage in capital city construction over a period of more than 3,000 years.

What did the earliest capital cities and royal palaces look like? The question remains unanswered to this day. Historians have identified the locations of the capitals of legendary kings in the remote past. They claim that Fuxi, father of the fishing and hunting professions, had his capital at Chen in present-day Henan Province. Shennong, who taught his people how to raise farm crops and discovered hundreds of medicinal herbs, operated in Lu, presumably somewhere in today's southern Shandong. The Yellow Emperor, revered as the ancestor of all Chinese, had his court in Youxiong, today's Xinzheng in Henan, while Emperor Shaohao, a renowned leader of the militant Yi people, wielded power from Qiongsang near present-day Qufu in Shandong. Emperor Zhuanxu was in Gaoyang in northeastern Henan, and Emperor Ku in Gaoxin, modern Yanshi in Henan. The highly prestigious Emperors Yao and Shun seated themselves in Pingyang in southern Shanxi and in Puban in southeastern Shaanxi respectively. But so far none of these assertions has been corroborated by archeological evidence. Until further excavations provide us with fresh information, the layout of any of these capital cities and the design of any of the palaces in these cities will be anybody's guess.

Documentary evidence and archeological findings do tell us, however, that beginning with the Shang dynasty (c. 16th-c. 11th centuries B.C.), the geometrical patterns of capital cities did not always agree with one another. The classic *Guanzi** contains the following passage:

The capital city of a state is usually established at the foot of a big mountain or on a vast plain. To ensure sufficient water supply, it should not be placed in a much too high and arid region. And to save the trouble of building ditches for the drainage of flood water, it should not be located too close to a river. Cities and roads should be built in light of the specific terrain shaped by mountains and rivers, and neither of them have to follow a set pattern.

Capital cities based on such a philosophy were quite different in layout and exhibited a variety of characteristics. The capital of an ethnic minority state in the Shang dynasty was built on a small peninsula. Rhomboid in shape, it rose and fell with the uneven terrain. The capital of the state of Zhao in the Warring States Period (475-221 B.C.), Handan in present-day Hebei Province, looked like the Chinese character *pin* (品) on a plane figure. The city of Chengdu, now capital of Sichuan Province, assumed a round shape in ancient times. Changle, present-day Fuzhou, resembled a peach in the days it served as capital of the state of Min (909-945). Visitors to Yinchuan, capital of the Ningxia Autonomous Region of the Hui Nationality, will be interested to know that the city looked something like the human body when it was known as Xingqing, capital of the West Xia dynasty (1034-1227).

The above examples are all taken from the days of a divided China, when the separate states were limited in their choice of capital cities. But even the central regime in a unified China was subject to

*The book *Guanzi*, though attributed to Guan Zhong (?-645 B.C.), an outstanding statesman and reformer of the Spring and Autumn Period, is actually a collection of works of much later times.

geographical and other limitations in capital city construction, an example being the seat of Yingtian Prefecture (present-day Nanjing) which served as the national capital in early Ming dynasty (1368-1644). With the Yangtze River in the north, the Qinhuai in the west, the Zhongshan Mountain in the east and Xuanwu Lake in the northeast, Nanjing has a winding city wall built according to terrain along an irregular course.

However, the main pattern of China's capital cities is a square one. The earliest advocacy of a square capital is found in the chapter called "The Artisans' Trades" in the Confucian classic, the *Rites of Zhou*:

> The artisan's concept of a capital city is a square measuring nine *li** on each side. Three gates on each side are open to traffic. There are nine vertical thoroughfares and nine horizontal ones in the city, each wide enough for nine chariots to run abreast. On the left is the Ancestral Temple of the royal family, and on the right, the Altar of Land and Grain for the sovereign to offer sacrifices to the God of Earth and the God of Five Cereals. The palaces are located in the front, while the noisy markets are pushed to the back.

Four inter-related principles are stated here: a square city, neat streets, placing the palaces in front of the markets, and maintaining a symmetrical balance between right and left. Such a strictly defined pattern of capital city construction fits in with the Confucian concept of a unified feudal empire. The Confucians believed in a round firmament and a square earth. The square in the Chinese character *guo* (国), meaning country, stands for its frontiers. The national capital, the political nerve center of the country, had to be surrounded by walls forming a square. Such a walled city was at once a military fortress for defense and a political symbol of the saying, "every inch of soil under heaven belongs to the emperor; all those living within the four seas are his subjects." Among the capitals of successive dynasties in Chinese history, Dadu (the Great Capital) of the Yuan or Mongol dynasty (1271-1368) was most typical of the Confucian concept of a capital city. Beijing, developed on the basis of Dadu during the Ming (1368-1644) and Qing (1644-1911) dynasties, is the only extant example of a capital built according to the requirements in "The Artisans' Trades" in the *Rites of Zhou*.

Beijing, as we see today, has become what it is in the course of an undetermined number of years or centuries. The palaces and mausoleums, gatetowers and pavilions, gardens and parks, shops and bazaars, the fabulous mansions of aristocratic families and humble courtyards of the common people may have a history of a few hundred years or several decades, but no less than 700,000 years have elapsed since the days of the Peking Man, and more than 3,000 years have gone by since the first city was built at Liulihe under the Shang and Zhou dynasties, the latter lasting from the 11th century to 256 B.C.

In the 11th century B.C., King Wu, the founding emperor of the Zhou dynasty, gave the Beijing area to Shi, the Duke of Zhao, as his fief. Beginning then, Beijing served as the capital for 11 states or dynasties before it became the capital of the People's Republic of China in 1949. The 11 regimes were:

The state of Ji in the early Zhou dynasty, believed to be the fief of the descendants of the legendary Emperor Yao;

The state of Yan in the Warring States Period (475-221 B.C.);

The state of Former Yan (A.D. 337-570);

The state of Great Yan founded in 756;

The state of Yan founded by Liu Shouguang in 911;

The Liao dynasty (916-1125);

The Jin or Jurchen dynasty (1115-1234);

The Yuan or Mongol dynasty (1271-1368);

The Ming dynasty (1368-1644);

The Qing or Manchu dynasty (1644-1911); and

The Republic of China founded in 1912 in its early period.**

The city acquired an ever higher status through a succession of dynasties. Beginning as the capital of an ethnic minority state under the Western Zhou dynasty (c. 11th century-771 B.C.), it became an important North China stronghold of a unified Chinese empire under the Qin (221-207 B.C.) and Western Han (206 B.C.-A.D. 24) and Eastern Han (A.D. 25-220) dynasties. It served as a capital city on three occasions during the Northern Dynasties (386-581) and the Five Dynasties (907-960), and as the auxiliary capital of the Liao dynasty under the name of Nanjing (Southern Capital) or Yanjing. It was given the name of Zhongdu (Middle Capital) in the Jin dynasty, during which it became the royal capital for the first time and functioned as the political center of North China. Finally, it was upgraded as the national capital in the Yuan dynasty, and enjoyed the same status in the Ming and Qing dynasties.

To trace the history of Beijing, we will have to go back to the days of the Peking Man in the next few pages.

---

*One *li* is half a kilometer.

**The Republic of China was a product of the Revolution of 1911 led by Sun Yat-sen. On January 1, 1912, Dr. Sun took office in Nanjing as Provisional President of the republic. Under domestic and international pressure, however, he had to yield the post to the warlord Yuan Shikai, who assumed the title in Beijing on March 10 the same year.

Chapter I

A CRADLE OF CHINESE CIVILIZATION

Physical Features of the Beijing Area

Beijing nestles at the foot of the Yanshan Mountains on the northern tip of the North China plain. Located at 116°23'17" east longitude and 39°54'27" north latitude, it is just about halfway between Mohe, the northernmost town of the country, and Haikou, an important port city along the northeastern coast of Hainan Island.

Beijing is favorably positioned some 140 kilometers from the Gulf of Bohai to its southeast, and protected by the Taihang Mountains to its west. It is in the path of a natural corridor connecting the Songliao Plain in the northeast and the Mongolian Plateau in the north with the Yellow River valley in the south. The area is semi-enclosed by the Yanshan Mountains and Taihang Mountains, which meet each other in the northwest of Beijing. The eastern ranges of the Yanshan Mountains extend to Shanhaiguan Pass, the eastern end of the Great Wall, which pushes its way westward like a dragon to terminate at Jiayuguan Pass in Gansu Province. The precipitous Jundu Mountain forms the western section of the Yanshan Mountains. South of the Yanshan Mountains and east of the Taihang Mountains is an alluvial plain which geographers call the Beijing sub-plain or the "Gulf of Beijing." The two mountain ranges combine as a strategic barrier for Beijing's protection, supplemented by a number of important passes created by the rivers cutting through the valleys. As the lines go:

> The city lies astride the passage to the Great Desert;
> By the will of Heaven, a formidable mountain stronghold serves
> as a lock on its gate.

The city is provided with roads leading to all parts of the country. Its vital position makes it a hub of communications and a potential center of military operations for regions north and south of the Great Wall and the Yanshan Mountains.

However, the rivers in the Beijing area were less than a boon to the local people. The city is sandwiched between two tributaries of North China's Haihe River — the Yongding River and the Chaobai River. The former comes down from the mountains in the northwest, the latter from a hilly region in the northeast, reminding one of the Euphrates and the Tigris and the ancient kingdom of Babylonia lying between the two. Like the Tigris, the Yongding and the Chaobai used to cause floods in the Beijing area. The Yongding, which means "eternal peace," was previously known as the Hun River (Turbid River) and the Wuding River (Capricious River) because its waters carried much silt and often became a source of flood disasters. In 1698 Emperor Kangxi of the Qing dynasty bestowed the auspicious name of Yongding on the river in the hope of changing its unruly character. Instead of submitting to the royal wish, it continued to submerge farmland and houses in a rainy season. This was why, from the very beginning, the city of Beijing was built far away from the Yongding and Chaobai rivers. It was not until the days of the People's Republic that reservoirs were constructed to divert flood water and bring the rivers under control.

On the other hand, Beijing had an ample water supply in the old days. Names like Western Glory Pond, Jar Mountain Pool, White Bubble Spring and Jade Spring mentioned in historical records point to an abundance of water resources and scenic spots around the city.

Located in a semi-humid, warm temperate zone, Beijing has a continental climate of the monsoon type. The annual average temperature is 11.8 degrees centigrade, and the annual precipitation 637 milimeters, which makes it one of the rainiest areas in North China. The wind comes from the northwest in winter and from the southeast in summer. The weather is neither as cold as that in regions north of the Great Wall, nor as hot as that in areas south of the Yangtze. The congenial climate and adequate rainfall favor plant growth. Spring is heralded by swallows returning in pairs from the south, followed by a riot of winter jasmines, magnolias, apricot flowers and peach blossoms. In summer there is a concentration of rain, which lowers the temperature in the mornings and evenings. The air is sweetened by the fragrance from the lotus ponds and enlivened by the singing of migrants and orioles. In autumn the sky is clear and the air crisp, and the city comes under the domination of chrysanthemums which present themselves in a variety of shapes and colors with a refreshing aroma. In winter the city is ice-bound but suffers from no scathing cold. A heavy snow would clothe the evergreen pines and cypresses in white robes and put a silvery layer on top of the yellow glazed tiles above the red palace walls.

The favorable environment of Beijing accounts for the early start of human life in this area as well as its rise as the political center of a unified multi-national state.

Dawn of the Stone Age

Beijing was one of the cradles of Chinese civilization. It was also one of the earliest homes of the human race.

On December 2, 1929, the fossil of the skull cap of a Peking ape was found in a natural cave on Dragon Bone Hill at Zhoukoudian in Fangshan County 50 kilometers to the southwest of Beijing. A C^{14} test (radioactive carbon test) proved the skull cap to be some 700,000 years old. Reconstructed on the basis of the fossil, the bust of the Peking ape showed low, flat and receding forehead, heavy brow bones, a prominent ridge over the eyes, and protruding jaws. The ape could already walk upright, make tools for manual labor, and communicate with fellow apes in a common language. As the fossil was unearthed in Beijing and resembled both ape and man, archeologists gave it the name of Peking Ape, or Peking Man. Further excavations led to the discovery of the fossil bones of more than 40 men and women, some 100,000 stone articles, and a great number of paleontological fossils.

In the days of Peking Man, Beijing was inhabited by many more species of animals in a warmer and more humid climate than at present. In daytime Peking Man went out to hunt for game and gather fruits and berries. By night he returned to his cave home. Archeologists found in the caves several layers of ash deposits and quite a few burnt animal bones, an indication that Peking Man was already using fire for various purposes. The importance of such an advance can never be overestimated. The employment of fire enabled him to cook his food and thus accelerate his physiological development as never before. With fire he could also illuminate his environment, protect himself from cold, and frighten away the beasts of prey. The fire lit by Peking Man on the Chinese continent meant the dawning of human civilization in this part of the globe. He was the real Prometheus, in addition to perhaps a few others in other parts of our planet.

Archeologists call the era of Peking Man the early period of the Paleolithic age, corresponding to the early period of primitive society in terms of socio-economic development. The rise of Peking Man assigned the ape a proper place in the history of human progress and revealed the earliest origin of the Chinese nation.

In 1977, the fossil of a man's molar tooth was discovered at Site 4 of the Peking Man caves in addition to stone implements, animal fossils and polished pieces of bone. He is believed to have lived in the Beijing area some 200,000-100,000 years ago, and is called New Cave Man by archeologists. His tools are more sophisticated than those used by Peking Man, and his features closer to those of Modern Man. He lived in the middle period of the Paleolithic age, a period in which the art of polishing began.

Previously, in 1933, fossil bones of eight primitive men and women, including three complete skull caps, fragments of the lower jaws and some teeth, were discovered in a cave on top of Dragon Bone Hill at Zhoukoudian, the home of Peking Man. These early inhabitants of Beijing lived some 18,000 years ago and are known as Upper Cave Man to students of archeology. Physiologically and morphologically they were almost the same as Modern Man. Ornaments discovered at the site include perforated animal teeth, clam shells, pebbles, stone beads, carved tubes made of bird bones, and the eye-socket bones of black carp. These early men and women already knew how to make themselves look better. They wore necklaces consisting of perforated animal teeth and shells strung together with a piece of leather, sometimes colored red with hematite powder. Apparently they had mastered the skills of drilling, abrading and perforation, an indication of a relatively high level of intelligence.

Covering his privates with a piece of animal skin and making clothes with bone needles and awls, Upper Cave Man put an end to his nudity. He also learned to strike fire with flint. The red hematite powder sprinkled over the bodies of the dead and signs of relatives coming together to weep for the deceased reveal the rudiments of a primitive concept of religion. The times of the Upper Cave Man are known in archeology as the late period of the Paleolithic age.

Reconstructed bust of Peking Man

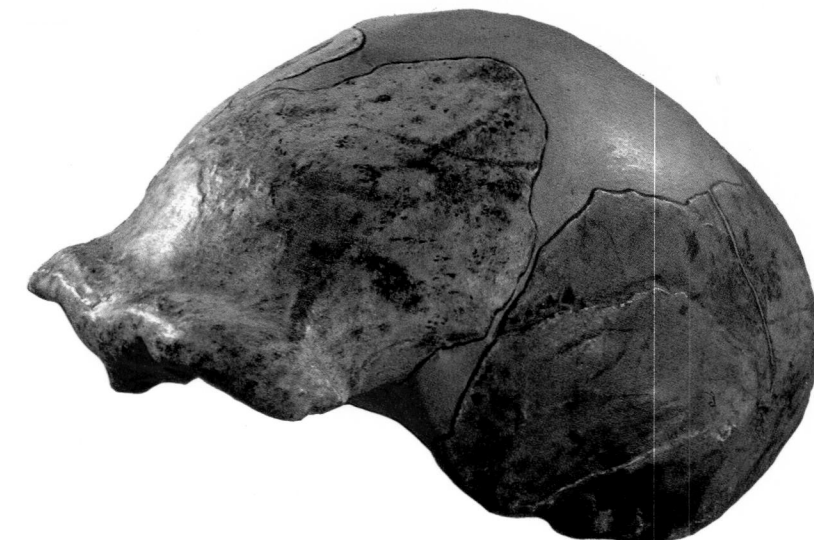

Fossil of Peking Man's skull cap found at Zhoukoudian in 1966

Fossil teeth of Peking Man

What was society like in the days of Peking Man, New Cave Man and Upper Cave Man? Was there any family? Lewis H. Morgan, the American authority on the history of primitive society, and other paleoanthropologists point out that primitive people, who had only just separated themselves from the animal kingdom, lived in groupings and followed a system of group marriage. The consanguineous family, or a family based on ties of blood, appeared later. In such a family, promiscuity was limited to men and women of a certain generation, i.e., to grandfathers and grandmothers, fathers and mothers, sons and daughters, etc., while sexual intercourse between parents and children was forbidden. In the text of *The Ring of the Nibelungen*, a masterpiece by W. R. Wagner, the famous German composer, one of the lines reads, "Whoever heard of a brother embracing his sister as his bride?" Such a practice, however, was not regarded as immoral in primitive times. The practice came to an end with the rise of the Punaluan Family, a family consisting of *punaluas*, which means intimate companions. Under this system, the males of a certain clan married the females of another clan, and vice versa. From the Punaluan Family emerged the matrilineal clan and thus a society based on matriarchal communes, in which descent could be traced only through the female line. The ancient Chinese classic, *Zhuang Zi*, part of which was written by the philosopher Zhuang Zhou (c. 369 B.C.-286 B.C.), also refers to a time when people "knew their mothers, but not their fathers." It is logical to assume that Peking Man, New Cave Man and Upper Cave Man experienced more or less the same process of evolution in mankind's marriage and family systems.

The Neolithic age lasted still longer for the early inhabitants of Beijing and brought them more trials and tribulations.

Some of them are known today as Donghulin Man, named after a tomb discovered in 1966 on a loess terrace west of Donghulin Village on the banks of the Qingshui River, a tributary of the Yongding River, in Beijing's Mentougou District. The fossil bones of two men and a young woman, believed to be some 10,000 years old, were interred in the tomb. A necklace consisting of some 50 conch shells, evenly sized and neatly arranged, and strung together with a strip of leather, adorned the breast of the young woman. She also wore a bracelet on her wrist, which had been made from seven pieces of bones cut from the ribs of an ox.

Having left the caves and settled down on a plain, Donghulin Man fared better than Upper Cave Man ever had. The ancient book *Huainanzi*, compiled under the editorship of Liu An, Prince of Huainan under the Western Han dynasty (206 B.C.-A.D. 24), refers to the building of palaces and chambers with wood and earth in early

Home of Upper Cave Man

Stone implement discovered in a Peking Man cave. It belongs to the early period of the Paleolithic Age.

Replica of a bone needle used by Upper Cave Man. Being 82 mm. long, it has a sharp point at one end and a hole at the other.

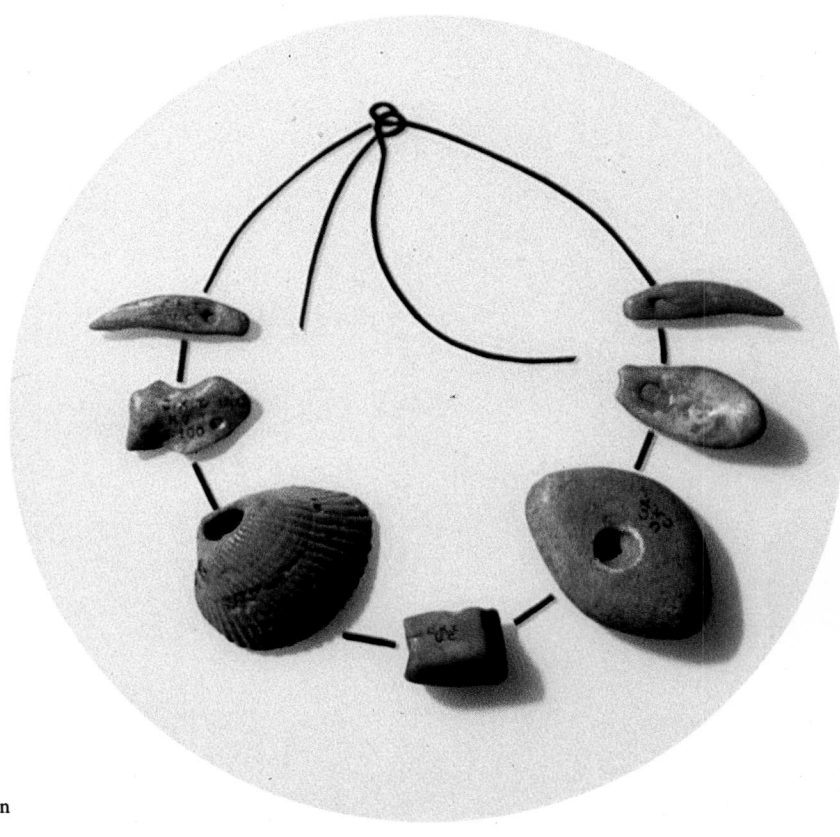

Necklace of Upper Cave Man

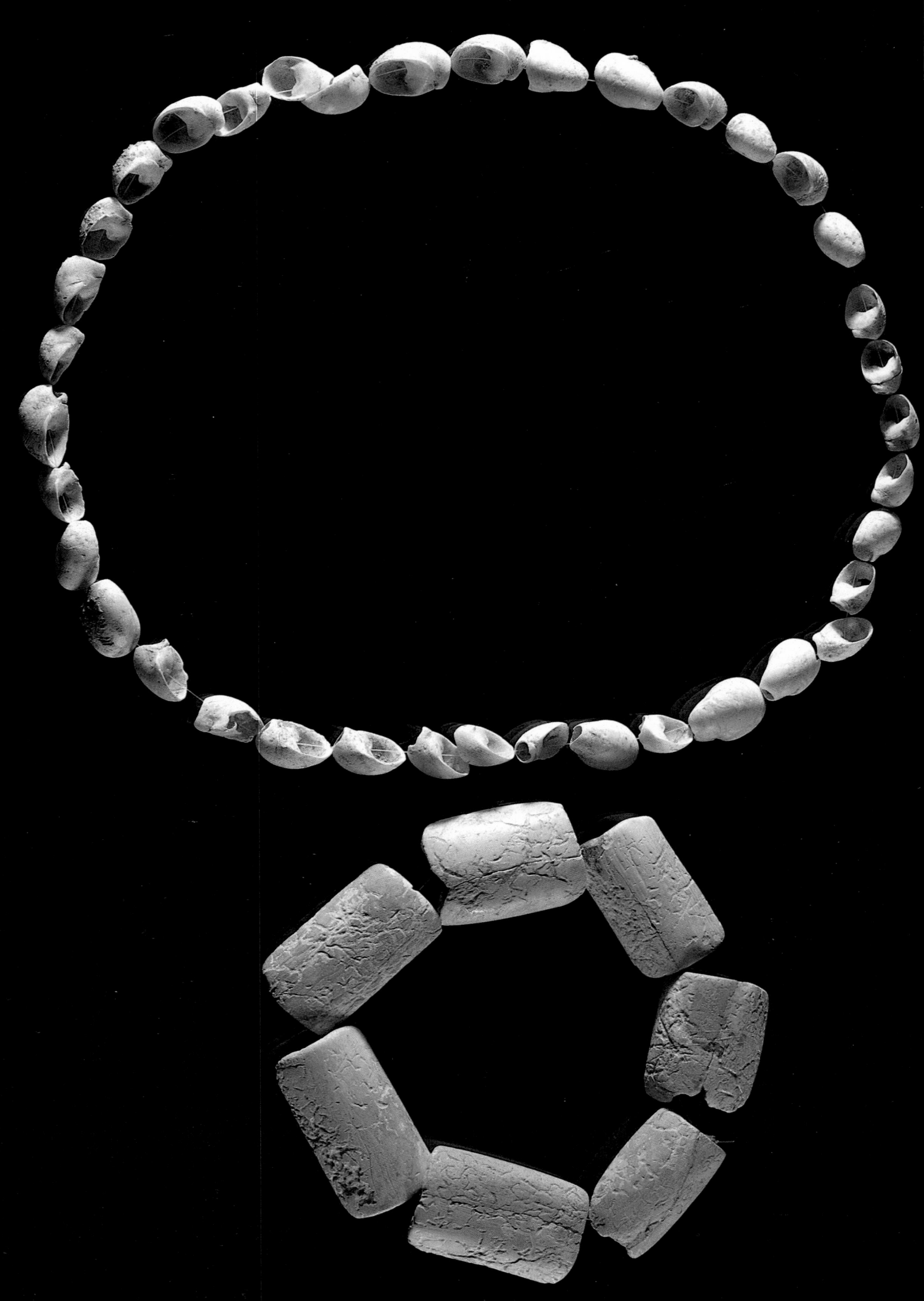

Black pottery basin from the second period of Xueshan culture

times, an indication of the kind of housing which sheltered Donghulin Man from wind and rain, severe cold and scorching heat, and protected him from insects, snakes, and wild beasts.

The residents of Beijing of a much later time, i.e., about 6,000 years ago, are known as Xueshan Man, named after an archeological excavation made at Xueshan Village in Beijing's suburban Changping County in 1961. The site is located in front of the Yanshan Mountains on the northern apex of the Beijing plain. The village is favored with fertile soil, much grassland, and a network of streams and brooks. It was here that Xueshan Man lived in compact communities to graze herds of animals and develop crop farming.

Geologically the area is marked by clear stratification, which accounts for an easily distinguishable type of relics found on each layer of earth. Archeologists identify the relics with three periods of development of Xueshan culture, but pottery-making seems to be common to them all. At first the clay was rolled into cords by hand and coiled into embryonic shapes. Vessels made by this method include double-handled pitchers, basins to carry food in, and bowls used at meals. Produced at a low heat, they have a red-brownish color. Utensils from a later period show much better skills. Made by the potter's wheel, they have a fine texture, a well-polished surface, and a shining black coating. One black jar measures 34.5 cm. in height and 28.5 cm. in diameter at the opening. The beautifully decorated rim is matched by symmetrical lobes, a prominent, glistening belly, and a flat, steady base to produce a gem of the potter's art. A black basin, 23.4 cm. in height and 32 cm. in diameter, has a wide opening and a receding body. The decorations are well-balanced, and the style shows good taste. It is identified as one of the better products from the second period of Xueshan's pottery culture.

Neolithic cultures have also been found at two other sites — at Beiniantou and Shangzhai in Pinggu County. Beiniantou, located in the northwestern part of Pinggu, has an area of some 6,000 square meters and lies on the southern bank of the Cuohe River along the

southern slopes of the Yanshan Mountains. Remains of the dwellings of Beijing's early inhabitants discovered here are irregular in size and unevenly distributed, and seem to be halfway between houses and caves. The stone implements used by them include axes, chisels and mills. The other site, Shangzhai, is situated in the northeastern section of Pinggu. Some 300 pottery articles and 200 stone implements have been unearthed here, and it is particularly interesting to look at the finely carved miniature stone monkeys which almost come to life, an evidence of the genius and skill of the ancient sculptors.

The Beijing area is associated with myth and legend dating to a late period of the Neolithic age. Three big wars are said to have taken place in the course of evolution from clan tribes to the birth of China's majority ethnic group, historically known as Huaxia but generally referred to as the Hans today, and all three of them are believed to have been fought in the neighborhood of the Beijing area. The best known of them is the Battle of Banquan waged between a tribe headed by Emperor Yandi and another one with Emperor Huangdi (the Yellow Emperor) as its chief. Having prevailed over his opponent on three occasions, the Yellow Emperor led his men in a march toward the Yangtze and Han river valleys and conquered the larger part of the country after 52 battles. The wars made possible the migrations of the various tribes and intermarriages among their members, and eventually an alliance took shape between the tribes under the leadership of Emperor Yandi and the Yellow Emperor. This tribal alliance is regarded as the earliest origin of the Han nationality. For this reason, the Chinese living at home and abroad, including those who have become citizens of other countries, call the two emperors their ancestral fathers.

Having experienced the arduous life of the Stone Age, the early men and women in the Beijing area found themselves on the threshold of civilization or, more specifically, at the door of a bronze civilization.

Necklace and bone bracelet of Donghulin Man

Chapter II

THE BRILLIANCE OF ANCIENT YAN CIVILIZATION

Bronze Civilization

Round about the 22nd century B.C., the Xia dynasty was founded in China just as the Euphrates and Tigris valleys came under the domination of the Kurds. And sometime in the 17th century B.C., King Tang founded the Shang dynasty after defeating Jie, the last king of the Xia dynasty, just as Egypt was overrun by the Hyksos. A bronze civilization flourished in the Beijing area and other parts of China under the Shang dynasty.

Residents of Beijing cultivated millet and other types of cereals, turning up the soil with stone hoes and harvesting the crops with clamshell sickles. They diversified their economy by domesticating animals, gathering fruits and berries, hunting for game, and fishing with a net. Particularly noteworthy, however, were their skills in producing bronze and gold ornaments.

The bronze smelters mixed malachite with a certain amount of tin and lead. Then they heated the mixture at no less than 1,000 degrees centigrade to produce molten bronze. Before making any bronze utensil, the workers had to build a clay model, marking the design in vermilion lines by which they carved out the concaves with a knife and attached the convexes. The clay model was only a medium for making a pottery mold. Molten bronze was poured into the pottery mold, which was withdrawn after the metal cooled off. The whole process involved mining, preparation of the mixture, smelting, making the clay model and the pottery mold, pouring molten metal into the mold, and the finishing touches, which could not be accomplished without a proper division of labor among skilled workers.

A tomb dating to the middle period of the Shang dynasty was discovered at Liujiahe Village in Beijing's suburban Pinggu County in 1977. It contained 16 bronze utensils, four gold ornaments, plus a bronze battle ax with an iron cutting edge. The battle ax as well as two other articles — a bronze jar decorated with three ram heads and a bronze bowl with bird designs on its stem — are of high historical and artistic value, and so are some of the gold ornaments.

The jar, a wine vessel, measures 26.8 cm. in height and 19.9 cm. in diameter. The ram heads rest on its shoulder. The eyes are directed downward, and the mouths slightly drawn back, giving a calm and meek appearance to the rams. These are matched by their weapons for defense — the curved horns pointing upward. The belly of the jar shows a finely carved and vigorous-looking ogre mask. The bottom part is also elegantly designed. The ancient craftsmen knew how to combine dignity with charm.

The bronze bowl with a bird design on its stem has a thin body, a wide rim, a solid base, and a gradually receding interior leading to a tortoise motif in the middle, which again is surrounded by a number of fish designs. When the shallow bowl is filled with water, it looks as though the tortoise were hiding itself at the bottom and the fish were sporting beneath the surface. The rim is decorated with two symmetrical marine birds, so lively that they seem to be singing or taking off.

The bronze ax with an iron blade was an important weapon in ancient times. The blade was cast from siderite and molded together with the bronze part of the ax. There are only two such axes in China,

the other one having been unearthed in Gaocheng County, Hebei Province, in 1972. Both were produced about the time the Hittites began to smelt iron in Asia Minor. In other words, iron came into use in the Beijing area under the Shang dynasty more than 3,000 years ago.

A gold eardrop and a gold bracelet have been found among the Shang dynasty relics in the Beijing area. The eardrop is shaped like an awl in its upper part, followed by a hook and a bell 2.2 cm. in diameter. Weighing 6.8 grams, it glitters with the ingenuity and fine workmanship of the producer.

The bracelet, made from round pieces of gold, has a circumference of 12.5 cm. and weighes 173.5 grams. Each end looks like a seedpod of lotus.

Gold was presumably even more valuable in those days than it is today. One can imagine how graceful it was for an ancient lady to walk around in colorful dress with a gold clasp on her glossy black hair, gold eardrops above her shoulders, and gold bracelets on both arms.

Under the Shang dynasty, the Beijing area was already dotted with clusters of houses forming a number of villages. People had made much headway in developing agriculture and handicrafts, which corresponded to a fairly high level of ancient culture, science and technology.

Bronze jar decorated with three ram heads

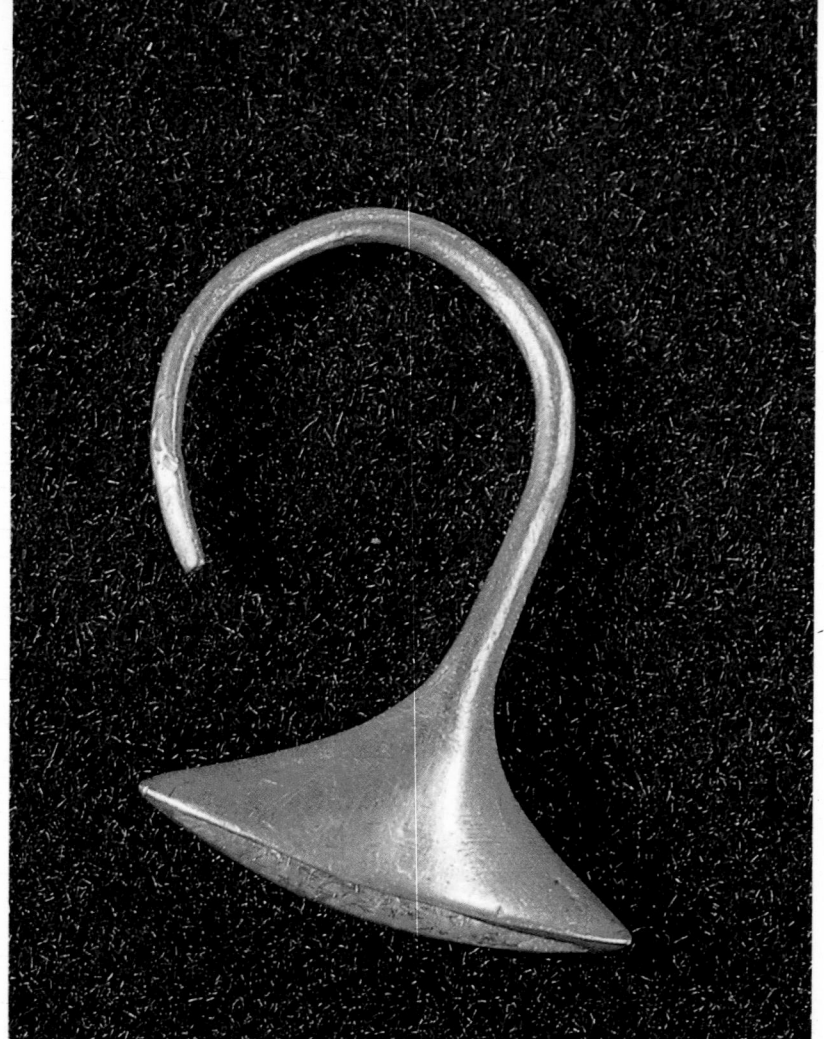

Gold eardrop

Bronze ax with an iron blade

Gold bracelets

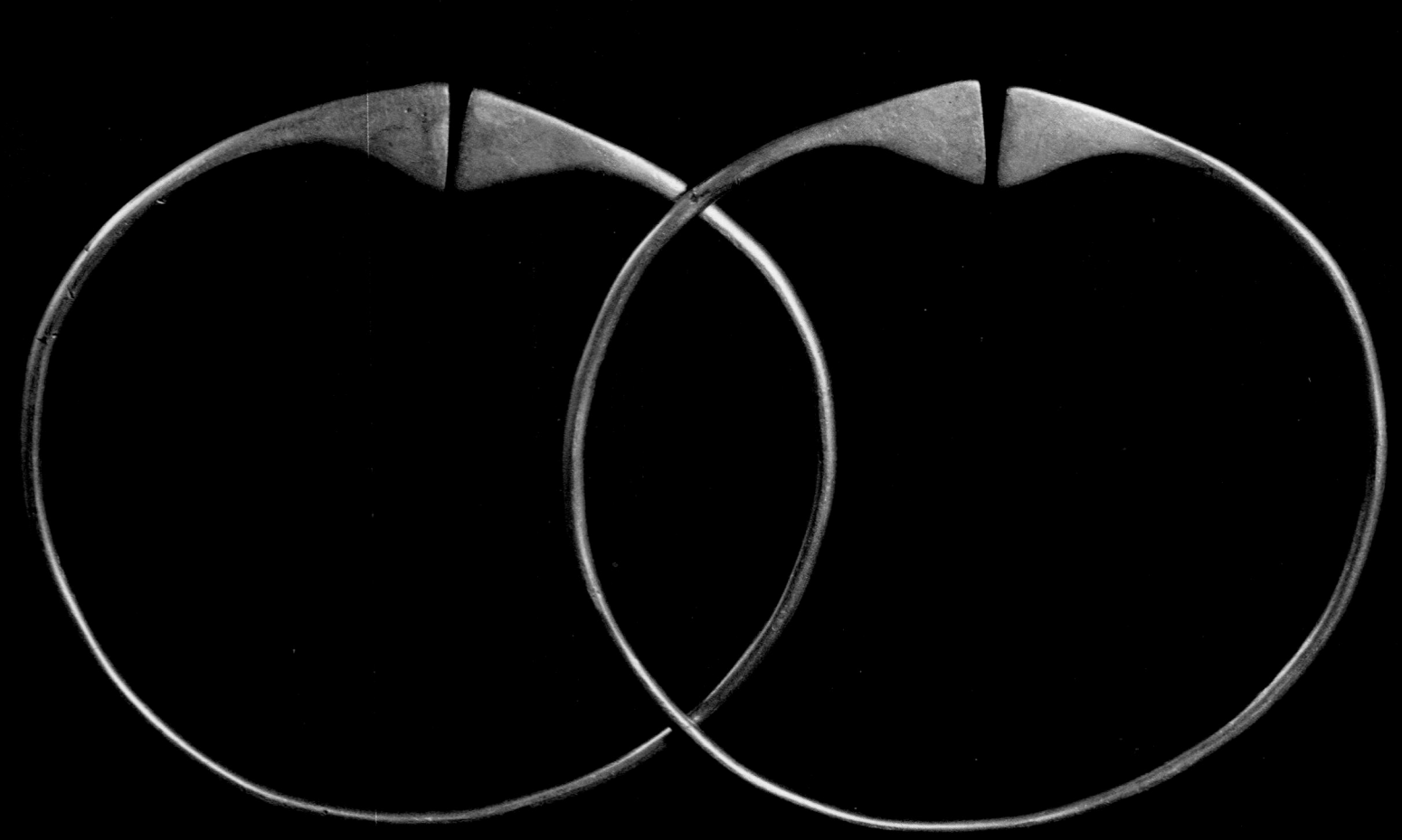

Ji—Capital of the State of Yan

Toward the end of the Shang dynasty, or in the 11th-10th centuries B.C., states of ethnic minorities known as Ji and Yan emerged in the Beijing area. The name of Ji is attributed to a local plant which may be translated as "thistle" and which grows erect and bursts into purplish flowers in early summer. The neighboring state was called Yan, which means "swallow." Some historians claim that the name was inherited from the ancestors of the Yan people, who had used swallow as the totem of their tribe. Both Ji and Yan were subordinate to the court of the Shang dynasty.

The earliest ruler of the Beijing area that we know of was the Duke of Zhao, a half-brother of the first king of the Zhou dynasty.

Around 1027 B.C. King Wu of the state of Zhou, which had built up its strength in Northwest China, crushed the armed forces of the Shang dynasty, put an end to its rule, and founded the Zhou dynasty. He distributed fiefs to members of his family and other nobles, and so created vassal states all over the country which served as barriers against any invasion of the royal domain. According to *Records of the Historian,* written by the Han dynasty historian Sima Qian (c. 145-90 B.C.), King Wu designated Yan as the fief of the Duke of Zhao, who was his half-brother, and granted the neighboring area of Ji to the descendants of the Yellow Emperor. While the state of Yan grew ever stronger, the Ji regime kept declining. The former annexed the latter and built a capital city in its urban districts.

These urban districts were located in today's municipality of Beijing. In the past few years archeologists have discovered a whole zone of relics of the state of Yan at Liulihe in Beijing's suburban Fangshan County. Among them are foundations of city walls dating back to the Shang and Zhou dynasties, several state of Yan tombs, and quite a few bronze vessels bearing inscriptions related to the Duke of Yan. All these are evidence that the capital of Yan was located here. The site of a capital city is often indicated by the remains of surrounding walls and ditches used for defensive purposes.

The Dongjialin remains of an ancient city are located on a terrace on the left bank of the Dashi River (now Liulihe River) in Fangshan County. The rectangular city measures 830 meters from east to west and about 600 meters from north to south. The city walls built with rammed earth are four meters thick and are composed of the main walls, the inner walls and the protective ramps, surrounded on the outside by ditches. All these form a structure of considerable proportions. This is the earliest city that we know of in the history of Beijing. In fact, it is one of the two earliest ancient cities discovered in China so far.

Some highly valuable articles have been unearthed at the site. Among them are:

Minister Jin's tripod: A bronze cooking vessel with three legs, it measures 62 cm. in height and 48 cm. in diameter and weighs 41.5 kilograms. The style is highly dignified, the designs have a typical antique flavor. The two sturdy handles are each decorated with a dragon, the one dancing toward the other. The belly shows a clear-cut ogre-mask pattern all round. The legs all have vigorous but elegant animal designs. Significantly, 26 characters in four lines are carved on the inside of the wall. From the characters we know that the tripod was cast on the orders of a high official by the name of Jin in memory of his reception by the Duke of Zhao in the national capital. As mentioned earlier, the Duke of Zhao was a half-brother of King Wu,

Minister Jin's tripod

Inscription on Minister Jin's tripod

Remains of the northwestern corner of an ancient city discovered at Dongjialin

Glazed blue jar

founder of the Zhou dynasty. *Although he had been given the Yan area as his fief by order of the king, the duke continued to live in the national capital, Zongzhou (present-day Xi'an), where he served as Prime Minister of the central government. Meanwhile, he made his eldest son the actual ruler on his fief with the title of Duke of Yan. The inscription states that the young Duke of Yan sent one of his ministers, Jin, to the national capital to present choice food to his father. Pleased at Jin's mission, the Prime Minister received him courteously and gave him a handsome reward. Returning home, Minister Jin had a bronze tripod built to honor the occasion. The inscription is corroborated by historical records and provides further proof that the fief of the Duke of Yan was today's Beijing and that Beijing, first built around the 11th century B.C., has a history of more than 3,000 years.

Boju's cauldron: The bronze cauldron, often used to cook meat or cereals, was named after Boju, a member of the aristocracy in the state of Yan who had it built in memory of the reward granted him by the Duke of Yan. The vessel is 32.5 cm. high and 24 cm. in diameter. It shows exquisite workmanship and has ox-head designs on the cover, the body and the legs.

You's food container: The bronze vessel was named after You, another member of the aristocracy in the state of Yan, who had it cast also for the reward given him by the Duke of Yan. It has two handles, a round rim, a round body, and a lid with a phoenix design.

Glazed blue jar: This relic is 29 cm. high and 14 cm. in circumference. Its discovery shows that porcelain was made in China over 3,000 years ago, corresponding to the early period of Homer's times in Greece.

The state of Yan relics excavated at Liulihe enables us to visualize the religious and moral concepts of its people. It was widely believed that the soul of a person did not die with his or her body, but ascended to a heavenly paradise to enjoy a life of eternal happiness. In the temporal world, the barriers between the high and the lowly, the superior and the inferior, the nobles and the commons were regarded as immutable. The tombs already excavated make it perfectly clear that the chief occupant of a tomb had considered his burial a means of continuing his life and an embodiment of his values. Thus a tomb became an epitome of social life based on the prevailing religious and moral outlook. The size of the mound depended on the rank of the deceased. While the corpse of a noble person was interred in a certain number of inner and outer coffins, depending on his or her title, the

*Both King Wu and the Duke of Zhao, whose personal name was Shi, were sons of King Wen of the state of Zhou in Northwest China, which finally attained national power under King Wu. King Wu's mother was the queen, while the mother of the duke was one of the royal concubines.

You's food container

You's food container (detail)

26

Boju's cauldron

Chariot and horses unearthed at Liulihe (detail)

Chariot and horses unearthed from a tomb of the Western Zhou dynasty at Liulihe

sacrificial slaves were placed in between the coffins or simply in the earth underneath. A slaveowner always lay in a supine position, symbolizing his ascendancy to heaven where he would continue his life of pleasure, while the slaves were made to lie on their sides or with their faces downward, their bodies coiled, their limbs flexed, indications of their obedience to their master after death.

Certain principles governed the placement of burial objects. Important ritual objects were put in front of the head of a noble man's corpse, and articles of a common run were placed by his sides. The jade ornaments he had used adorned the upper part of his breast. Shells, an ancient form of money, were kept in his hands.

The pet dog of the deceased was often buried under his coffin to keep him company. Also buried with him were his chariot and its driver, his horses, and his servants. Since he had been served by male and female attendants at home and by a chariot driver whenever he went out, he couldn't dispense with their services after death.

At the Liulihe site, a chariot, six horses and two dogs were found buried in front of Tomb No. 53. In addition, the remains of a young slave were discovered behind the chariot. It is almost certain that the young man had been cruelly tortured because his skeleton shows only the bones of his palms but not those of his fingers. A chapter on the punishment of crimes in the ancient classic, *Rites of Zhou,* lists five ways of punishment: tattooing the face, cutting off the nose, cutting off the feet, castration and decapitation. The books contains 3,000 provisions on the Five Punishments. They were systematic, comprehensive, and most inhuman.

The state of Yan remained a weak and small one among the duchies and principalities in the Spring and Autumn Period (770-476 B.C.) and the subsequent period of the Warring States (475-221 B.C.) It was accorded the status of a principality. However, once the troops of the state of Qi stormed into the capital of Yan , killed the sovereign

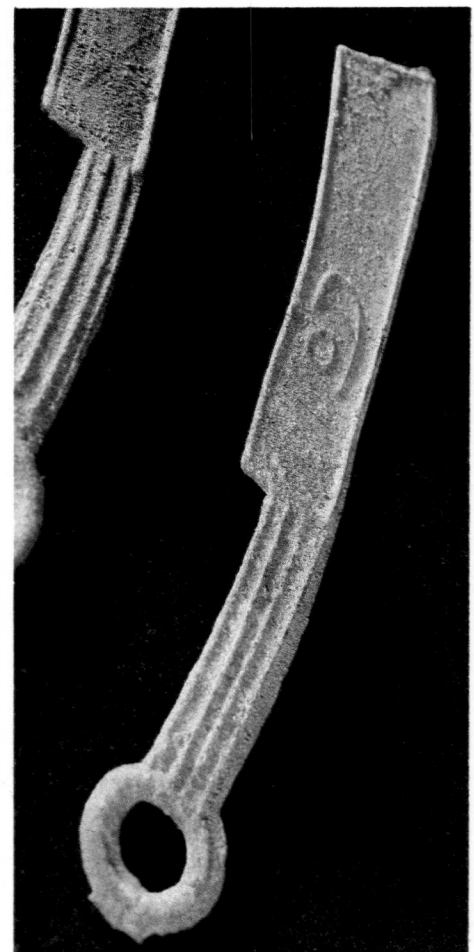

Sword-shaped coins of the state of Yan. Coins used in the various ducal states of ancient China varied in shape.

Bronze helmet. In ancient China, helmets used in battle were made of rattan, leather, iron or bronze. This helmet, 23 cm. high and 24 cm. wide, was discovered in 1975 in a Shang-Zhou tomb in Baifu Village, Changping County in Beijing's suburbs.

prince Kuai and the prime minister Zezhi, and took practically all the valuables they could find in the city. Following this humiliating disaster Prince Zhao came to the throne with the resolve to avenge his countrymen. He had a high terrace built, on which he placed gold as a token of his appreciation of services any talented person was willing to offer at his court. Prominent statesmen and generals like Guo Wei and Yue Yi came to Yan and helped rebuild its strength. In 284 B.C., or a decade before Asoka of the Maurya dynasty was enthroned in India, an allied army of Yan and four other states (Chu, Zhao, Han and Wei) vanquished the army of the state of Qi, thanks to Yue Yi's able commandership. The Yan army under him captured Linzi, capital of Qi, and no less than 70 towns of the principality. Prince Min of Qi was killed during his flight. The Yan warriors did to their enemy what he had done to them, taking home Qi's treasures and exhibiting them in the royal palace. The *Strategies of the Warring States,* a collection of the arguments of itinerant politicians and military experts in those days, has a chapter called "The Strategies of Yan" which describes the booty of General Yue Yi's army. It says that the pearls, jade ornaments, money as well as armors, vehicles, and rare utensils captured during the campaign were all taken back to Yan. A huge bell and a tripod dating to times immemorial, plus a number of valuable artifacts, were displayed in the chambers of the royal palace. The victors from Yan even planted saplings from their homeland on Qi soil.

To fortify its defenses, Yan constructed several sections of the Great Wall to the north and south of its territory. The colossal undertaking marked the heyday of its glory.

Prince Zhao, who had achieved Yan's revival, died five years later and was succeeded by his son, Prince Hui. Unfortunately, the young sovereign was jealous of talented people and became suspicious of Yue Yi. The enemy state of Qi successfully sowed discord between the two, and the prince eventually replaced the general with another officer, Qi Jie. General Yue Yi, who had gone into exile, offered his services to the court of Zhao, a state lying to the west of Yan, because he would probably be executed if he returned to Yan. The change of the commander for the Yan army gave the state of Qi a golden opportunity to fight back. In a counter-offensive, the Qi army inflicted a crushing defeat on the Yan troops under General Qi Jie, recovered the towns they had occupied, and installed their sovereign in the capital city of Linzi. The state of Yan never recovered from this blow. By the end of the Warring States period, the state of Qin in the west had become the leading power while the state of Yan was in its twilight. Crown Prince Dan of Yan sent a dauntless warrier, Jing Ke, to assassinate the Prince of Qin, who later became the celebrated First Emperor or the Qin dynasty. The assassin went to the court of Qin on the pretext of presenting to the prince the head of a Qin general who had defected and a military map of the state of Yan. As he unrolled the map, however, the prince spotted a dagger hidden in it, and Jing Ke died a martyr to his state at the court of Qin. In 226 B.C. the Qin general Wang Jian attacked Yan and occupied its capital city of Ji in present-day Beijing. Four years later Prince Xi, the last sovereign of Yan, who had escaped to present-day Liaoyang in Liaoning Province, was taken prisoner by the Qin army. This marked the end of the state of Yan and the history of the city of Ji as Yan's capital.

Chapter III
IMPORTANT STRONGHOLD UNDER THE QIN, HAN, SUI, AND TANG DYNASTIES

North China Stronghold

Under the Qin, Han, and Western Jin dynasties, the city of Ji was an important stronghold in North China in a unified Chinese empire.

The First Emperor of the Qin dynasty put an end to the separatist regimes of the Warring States period and unified China in 221 B.C., which was the 26th year of his reign or the year when King Antigonos III died and was succeeded by his son Philip V in Macedon. The First Emperor abolished the system of enfeoffment followed ever since the Western Zhou dynasty, under which a whole ring of vassal states were created around the royal domain, and replaced it with a two-level administration consisting of prefectures and counties under the central government. The prefects and county magistrates were appointed by the emperor himself. The empire was divided into 36 prefectures, and the city of Ji was made capital of Guangyang Prefecture.

Building a highly centralized government structure was one of the First Emperor's main concerns. Thus he gave instructions for the construction of broad highways extending from his capital, Xianyang, to all parts of the country. The ancient version of the modern freeway leading to the northeast terminated at the city of Ji. It was 50 meters wide and planted with pines at every 10 meters.

By order of the First Emperor, the northern chain of walls built for defense in the times of the separate states of Qin, Zhao, and Yan were connected, renovated, and extended both eastward and westward to form a 5,000-kilometer wall beginning at Lintao (present-day Minxian County, Gansu Province) in the west and ending at Liaodong (present-day Liaoyang, Liaoning Province). This was how the Great Wall took shape.

Many folk stories are associated with the Great Wall, the best-known among them being the tragedy of a young woman by the name of Mengjiang Nu. The pretty girl was betrothed to a young scholar, Fang Xiliang. On the day of their wedding, however, the bridegroom was pressganged for the Great Wall project. After he was taken away, Mengjiang worried about him day and night, and finally decided to look for him and send him some badly-needed winter clothes. She travelled on foot across mountains and rivers but, when she arrived at the construction site, her husband was nowhere to be found. Sitting by the Great Wall, she cried for three days and nights, giving such a violent shake to the earth that the Great Wall collapsed along a distance of 400 kilometers. Only then did she know that her husband had been buried under the bricks and earth of the wall. She covered him with the winter clothes she had brought and died on the spot to keep him company.

The place where the admirably pathetic young woman died is said to be Gubeikou Pass in Beijing's suburban Miyun County, where a temple was built to her memory. The temple has disappeared for unknown reasons. The present Temple of Mengjiang Nu, built in the

The Gubeikou section of the Great Wall. Gubeikou, a strategic gateway north of Beijing and an important pass of the Great Wall, was built in the Ming dynasty.

Ming dynasty, is located near Shanhaiguan Pass, the eastern end of the Great Wall, where visitors pay respects to her the year round.

In 202 B.C. Liu Bang, founding emperor of the Han dynasty, came to the throne. His dynasty is known as Western Han because he made Chang'an (present-day Xi'an) in Northwest China his capital city. This was the year when the Roman general Scipio Africanus defeated the Carthaginian general Hannibal in a battle at Zama south of Carthage, during which Hannibal had a narrow escape.

Departing from the practice under the Qin dynasty, rulers of the Han dynasty coupled the prefectures with a number of vassal states. The Yan area was a prefecture at certain times and a state at others, but the city of Ji always remained the capital city.

It was in the early period of the Western Han dynasty (206 B.C.-A.D. 24) that the Beijing area produced its first great scholar, Han Ying, who devoted himself to research on the *Book of Songs*. The earliest collection of Chinese poetry, the book contains 305 poems based on folk songs and ballads. In ancient times officials in charge of the collection of folk poetry toured the country every spring, using a bell fitted with a wooden tongue and a bronze lip to signal their arrival and ask people to contribute their literary resources. Han Ying's writings were collected as *Han Ying's Commentaries on the "Book of Songs,"* in which he compared ancient events with the accounts in the *Book of Songs* and which remains to this day an important guide to the study of this classic. On account of his academic achievement, he was appointed Chancellor of Historical and Literary Studies by Emperor Wendi (r.180-157 B.C.).

Emperor Wudi (r. 141-87 B.C.) of the Western Han dynasty made one of his sons, Liu Dan, the Prince of Yan. The prince built magnificent palaces in the city of Ji, including a Ten-Thousand-Year Palace and a Hall of Brightness. Although Emperor Wudi was an outstanding monarch with civil and military successes to his credit, he indulged in sensual pleasures in his late years and disliked such people as Liu Dan, leading to a tragic struggle over succession to the throne after his demise. The empress hanged herself, while the crown prince committed suicide. A blood bath in the capital cost thousands of lives. The coronation of Fuling, an eight-year-old son of the late emperor, angered Liu Dan and other princes, but their rebellion was crushed by the forces of the court. Returning home, the Prince of Yan gathered his ministers and consorts and sang in despair:

> The capital city is so deserted.
> The dogs are not barking, the cocks not crowing;
> Why do the streets look so spacious?
> Because there are few inhabitants.

His wife, Lady Huarong, chimed in as she rose to do a dance:

> Our homeland is in disorder,
> Mothers weep for their sons, wives for their husbands;
> A nobleman wanders about,
> Unable to live in peace.

The songs brought tears to the eyes of all present. Seeing that he could not escape capital punishment, the prince strangled himself, followed by some 20 others. The court exempted his son Liu Jian from death, but relegated him to the status of a commoner. Eventually he was reinstated as Prince of the Guangyang Region and returned to the palaces in the city of Ji.

While it is difficult to trace the palaces of the Yan princes, some of their tombs have been excavated in the Beijing area. The No.1 Han tomb was discovered at Dabaotai in Beijing's Fengtai District in August 1974, and the No.2 Han tomb to the west was found a little later. While the former is a large vertical earth pit containing a wooden coffin, the latter, which is parallel to the former and has a similar structure, is presumably the tomb of a Yan prince and his wife. Both tombs had been plundered and seriously damaged. Even so, however, a total of over 400 articles have been unearthed, including pottery vessels, bronzes, iron articles, jade ornaments, lacquerware and silks. Among the rare artifacts are gilded bronze brackets for door rings, weapons inlaid with gold and silver, gilded pillows with dragon-head designs and jade inlays, ivory chess pieces, iron axes carved with inscriptions, jade ornaments with hydra and tiger designs, jade unbinders with phoenix designs, and jade figurines waving their sleeves in a dance, all of which make the tomb an underground museum.

The No.1 Han tomb at Dabaotai measures 18 meters from east to west and 23.2 meters from north to south. It is 4.7 meters deep, and has an underground space of 417.6 square meters. The whole structure consists of a tomb passage, a covered walk, an outer corridor, inside walls composed of yellow-pith cypress wood blocks, the front chamber, and the back chamber. Three chariots, painted elegantly with vermilion speckles, are found along the tomb passage

Gilded bronze bracket used as a door handle in the No.1 Han tomb at Dabaotai

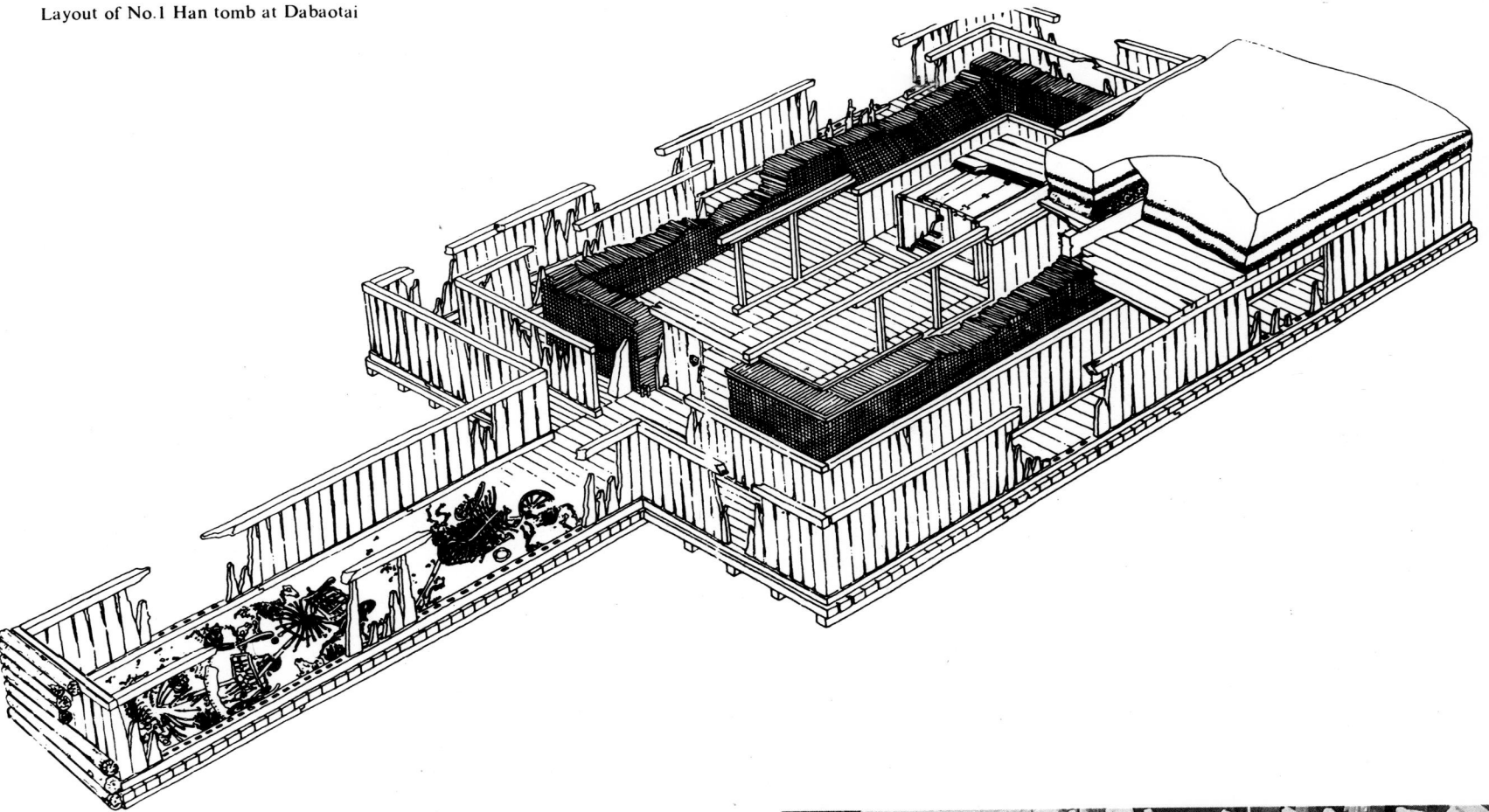

together with the remains of 11 horses, presumably the means of transportation used for the burial of the occupant of the tomb.

The outer corridor of the tomb leads directly to the cypress walls. A special privilege developed under the Western Han dynasty, they could be erected only in the tombs of emperors, vassal lords, and the upper echelons of the nobility. The cypress wood blocks are all fresh with yellow pith in the center, placed with one end inboard and the other end toward the rammed earth. Enclosing a rectangular space, the walls in the No.1 Han tomb are composed of a total of 15,880 blocks. Each block was cut to a uniform size of 90 cm. in length and 10 by 10 cm. in cross section. Each wall consists of 30 stands of blocks, piled tightly one against the other without being joined by tenons and mortises. The 108 blocks making up each stand in the north wall were piled from south to north. The 160 blocks making up each stand in the east and the west wall were piled from east to west. The 34 blocks making up each stand in the southern wall, which has a doorway in the middle, were also piled from south to north. Buried for over 2,000 years, the yellow-pith wood blocks emit a unique fragrance even today.

An inner corridor connects the cypress walls with the coffin chamber, where the coffin rests on a platform in the middle. On a closer look, one finds a set of five coffins. This conforms to the burial system described in *Zhuangzi,* an ancient classic on philosophy, which says that there must be seven coffins, including the inner and outer ones, for the emperor, five for a vassal lord, three for a minister, and two for a common official. The Prince of Yan, a vassal lord, was entitled to five coffins according to the ritual stipulations. As to the material, the two inner coffins and the middle one are made of *Phoebe nanmu,* and the two outer ones, of *Catalpa bungei.* While the innermost one is painted black on both sides, all the rest are vermilion on the inside and black on the outside. The tomb is protected against dampness by the use of charcoal and white clay, which are found under the planks on the floor of the coffin chamber. The panels on the walls of the coffin chamber are coated with charcoal, and the ceiling consists of a layer of white clay between two layers of charcoal. The horizontal purlins of the tomb rest on the tops of the cypress walls and are supported by three beams running in a north-south direction. Covered under a mound which is at least a dozen meters high, all this turns the tomb into an underground palace.

The Western Han dynasty eventually declined. Wang Mang, a nephew of Empress Dowager Wang, usurped the throne in A.D.9. His misgovernment aggravated the prevailing socio-economic contradictions and triggered off peasant risings all over the country. Liu Xiu, a scion of the Han house, joined the peasant insurgents, became one of their leaders, built up his prestige by his military successes, and founded the Eastern Han dynasty in A.D.25. Historians call the dynasty Eastern Han because its capital, Luoyang,

Yellow-pith cypress wood blocks used for the inside walls of the No.1 Han tomb at Dabaotai

Pottery storied house unearthed in an Eastern Han tomb in Linhe Village, Shunyi County, in Beijing's suburbs

was located to the east of Chang'an, capital of the Western Han dynasty.

The Beijing area was a prefecture under Eastern Han. By the early years of the dynasty, nomadic tribes known as Xiongnu (the Huns) in northern China had split into two sections, the Northern and Southern Xiongnu. While the Northern Xiongnu remained on the Mongolian highlands, the Southern Xiongnu migrated to the Yellow River Bend and the northwestern parts of Shaanxi and Shanxi and its cavalry often invaded the territory under Han control. The Beijing area was called Yuyang Prefecture, and the prefectural government had its seat in a town southwest of today's Miyun County in suburban Beijing. When more than 10,000 mounted troops of Xiongnu swooped down on Yuyang, the prefect, Zhang Kan, met them at the head of a cavalry force of a few thousand and dealt them a staggering blow. The victory gave the prefecture years of peace and security.

The prefect also created a life of affluence for his people by initiating the planting of rice paddies. For the first time, the crop was grown in the Beijing area over some 53,000 hectares of land in Hunu, present-day Shunyi County in Beijing's suburbs.

Growth in national production under the Eastern Han dynasty gave rise to a prosperous landlord economy. The big landowners built mansions on their plantations, surrounded by citadels, watchtowers, high walls and ditches. These plantations are nowhere to be found today. In April 1975, however, a tomb of the Eastern Han dynasty was excavated at Linhe Village in Shunyi County, the place where Prefect Zhang Kan introduced rice paddies, and a number of funerary objects found in the tomb give some idea of life on a landlord's plantation in those days.

A pottery lamp found in the Eastern Han tomb throws light on the life of the plantation owner. The painted lamp has three parts. The upper part, a plate, has a pointed stick in the middle, presumably the candle stick. The middle part shows vivid dragon-head and flame designs. The base, shaped like a bell, is decorated with figurines stuck onto it: five at the top — two pipe musicians, an acrobat standing on his hands, another acrobat juggling with balls, plus a dancer; two in the middle — a pipe musician and a percussion instrumentalist; and a group of equestrian figurines at the bottom. Clearly, the plantation owner wanted to enjoy his pleasures even after death.

The Eastern Han empire had a counterpart in the west, the Roman Empire, with which it had some contact. The Eastern Han territory extended to the dessert in the north, the South China Sea in the south, the Pacific in the east, and Congling* in the west. The Roman Empire reached the middle and southern parts of Britain and the Danube valley in the north, the Sahara in the south, the Euphrates in the east, and the Atlantic in the west. In A.D. 97, during the reign of the Eastern Han emperor Hedi, General Ban Chao (A.D. 32-102) who served as Governor of the Western Regions sent Gan Ying on a mission to Rome. Even though the emissary never reached his destination, the Roman Emperor (believed to be Marcus Aurelius Antoninus) sent an envoy to the Eastern Han capital by the sea route to present ivory and other gifts to emperor Huandi. This was the earliest contact between China and a European country. But the Eastern Han empire broke up before the Roman Empire did, and China was divided among the Three Kingdoms —Wei, Shu and Wu.

Beijing was still called Guangyang Prefecture in the period of the Three Kingdoms (A.D. 220-280). The battlefields used by the states of Wei, Shu and Wu in their rivalry for national hegemony were generally located between the Yellow River and Yangtze River valleys. The city of Ji, which lay within the state of Wei, served as a military base for its ruler's eastern expeditions as well as a granary from which his army received provisions for a march on the Yangtze valley. Cao Cao (155-220), the all-powerful prime minister in the last years of Eastern Han who laid the framework for his son's founding of the Wei dynasty, used Ji as his base during one of his military conquests and went as far as the Jieshi Mountains near the Bohai Bay. He built a Conquer-the-Enemy Canal connecting the Hutuo River in today's western Hebei with the Lushui River to the north so that the rice harvested in the Yangtze River and Huaihe River basins could be sent up to North China for his army. In particular, the Wei authorities developed farm production in the area around Ji and recruited peasant vagabonds for land reclamation and the building of water conservancy projects. The city of Ji was skirted by Leishui River (today's Yongding River) on the north and by Gaoliang River on the south. The former often flooded, while the latter dried up frequently. Liu Jing, Conquer-the-North General under the Wei who was garrison commander for Guangyang Prefecture, organized the construction of a weir across Leishui River at Liling in today's Shijingshan District. The Liling Weir was 2.42 meters high, 72.36 meters from east to west, and 70 meters from north to south. Sluice gates were installed to regulate the flow. General Liu also had a canal dug to lead the water of Leishui River into Gaoliang River and then into Lushui River along a 50-kilometer course through today's Changping, Shunyi, and Tongxian counties. The canal, called Chexiang, was used to irrigate the fields in a dry season and drain

---

*Congling was the general name for the Pamirs and the western sections of the Kunlun Mountains and Karakoram Mountains.

The Chexiang Canal and the Liling Weir

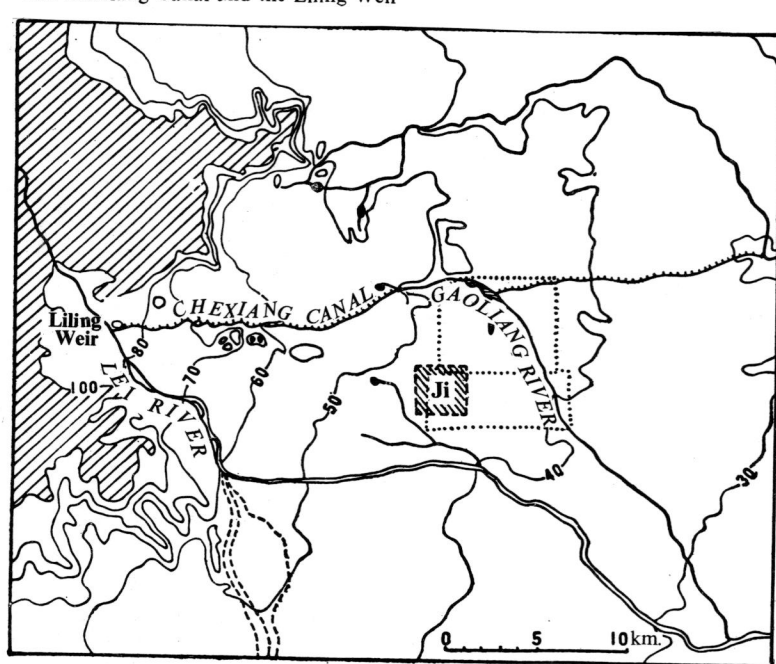

water during a flood, benefitting 13,000 hectares of land from the very beginning and 260,000 hectares after it was linked with a network of smaller canals. The Liling Weir and the Chexiang Canal were the first major water conservancy projects ever built in the Beijing area. They made possible faster advances in agriculture and added to the strategic importance of the city of Ji.

In 265 Sima Yan, a powerful minister at the Wei court, usurped the throne and founded the Jin dynasty, historically known as Western Jin. The state of Shu had been vanquished by the Wei dynasty. Operating from his capital, which remained in Luoyang as under the Wei, Sima Yan sent troops to wipe out the state of Wu and so ended the division of the country into the Three Kingdoms. A period of peace and order ensued, and the people fared better. The court of Western Jin first designated the city of Ji as the fief of a member of the imperial family, again called the Prince of Yan, and then made it the capital of an administrative region known as Youzhou.

The Western Jin emperors and the nobility led an extravagant, decadent life. Sima Yan, referred to posthumously as Emperor Wudi, put in his palace no fewer than 10,000 young maidens — at first some from the families of officials and army officers of high and middle ranks, then 5,000 from the families of lower officials and landed aristocrats, and finally some from the palaces of the extinguished state of Wu. Emperor Huidi, i.e., Sima Zhong, enfeoffed 1,081 family members and relatives as vassal lords. One noble spent 20,000 coins on food in his house everyday, and enjoyed drinking wine from a basin with one of his pigs. The nobility subscribed to a philosophy described in the following lines:

In vain I tried to be an immortal by taking elixirs of life;
Tasty wine, fine silk, and comfortable bedding —
Aren't they far more enjoyable?

The life-styles of the wealthy also affected society at large.

Meanwhile, more and more people were converted to Buddhism. Burning incense before the statue of Buddha, they prayed for their happinese and the avoidance of evil. The Temple of the Pool and Wild Mulberry, the oldest Buddhist temple existing in Beijing today, was built in the Jin dynasty.

Nestling in the hills of Mentougou District in the western suburbs of Beijing, the temple was called Temple of Auspicious Fortune when it was completed some 1,600 years ago. It became Dragon Spring Temple under the Tang dynasty and Great Temple of Longevity under the Jin (Jurchen) dynasty, acquiring a different name almost every time it was renovated. But residents of Beijing have always referred to it as the Temple of the Pool and Wild Mulberry because of the Dragon Pool behind its halls and the wild mulberries on one of its hills. People used to say that the temple was older than the administrative region of Youzhou to which Beijing belonged, which testifies to the long history of the temple.

"Pagoda Forest" at the Temple of the Pool and Wild Mulberry. Under the pagodas are buried the bodies of high priests and abbots who lived during the 1,000 years from the Liao and Jin (Jurchen) dynasties to the Ming and Qing.

Temple of the Pool and Wild Mulberry. It was first built in the Jin dynasty and expanded and rebuilt in the Ming and Qing dynasties.

"Imperial Tree" in the Temple of the Pool and Wild Mulberry. The 1000-year-old gingko tree, about 30 meters high and seven meters in perimeter, is said to have been planted in the Liao dynasty. The Qing emperor Qianlong gave it the name of "Imperial Tree."

Capital of Three Yan Regimes

The founding emperor of the Jin dynasty, Sima Yan, passed away in A.D. 290. His demise was followed by a fratricidal struggle for power among eight princes of the Jin house which historians call the "Disturbances of the Eight Princes." After a turmoil of more than two decades, Sima Rui became emperor in 317, making Jiankang (present-day Nanjing or Nanking) his capital. The dynasty is known as Eastern Jin because Jiankang was to the east of Luoyang, capital of Western Jin.

The internecine struggle had caused so much bloodshed that there was no political and social stability to speak of, and the country suffered for 300 more years from the incessant wars fought among separatist regimes. While Eastern Jin controlled the south, 16 regimes established mostly by five ethnic groups — Xiongnu, Xianbei, Jie, Di and Qiang, ruled the north and a few other parts of the country. Murong Jun, chief of a Xianbei tribe, made the city of Ji (present-day Beijing) the capital of his state, known as Former Yan.

The Xianbei people had always inhabited the banks of Liaohe River in today's Northeast China beyond the Great Wall. Members of one of their tribes, with the common surname of Murong, looked attractive with their white skin and fine features. Many of the women were bought as maids and concubines by influential families of the Western and Eastern Jin dynasties. Lady Gou, mother of Emperor Mindi (Sima Shao) of Eastern Jin, came from the Murong tribe. The Western Jin court had given the titles of general or military governor to the successive chiefs of the Murong tribe. Having built up their strength, the Murongs embarked on military expansion. Led by

Murong Jun, sovereign of their state called Former Yan, they invaded the Youzhou region in North China and occupied the city of Ji. Then Murong Jun moved his capital from Longcheng (present-day Chaoyang in Liaoning Province) to the newly acquired Ji. He planned to organize an army of 1.5 million men for a march on the south, but died before he could fulfil his task.

The would-be conqueror of South China is known for the story of his beloved horse, a heirloom of his family. Colored russet and white, the powerful steed had been used by his grandfather, Murong Wei, and his father, Murong Huang, who founded the state of Former Yan. In Murong Jun's time it remained as brave and loyal as ever, and served its master splendidly in the battles that made him a North China ruler. Aware of his indebtedness to the horse, Murong Jun ordered the building of a bronze statue for it and personally wrote a eulogy to be inscribed on it. Just as craftsmen were putting the finishing touches on the statue, however, the horse died after 49 years of service to the Murong family.

It may be recalled that Beijing had twice been a capital city — first for the state of Ji and then for the state of Yan. Under Former Yan it became a capital city for the third time, this time for a powerful ethnic minority dynasty.

In the period of the Sixteen States, dominated mostly by ethnic minorities, one ruler replaced another in a merry-go-round taking place in the city of Ji and its neighborhood. In 386 Touba Gui, known as Emperor Daowudi (r.386-409), founded the Northern Wei dynasty by ending the turmoil created by the Sixteen States and

Taihe Statue. The oldest stone statue in Beijing, it was carved after the image of Emperor Xiaowendi, a Xianbei ruler of the Northern Wei.

Group of statuettes behind the Taihe Statue. They represent officials loyal to Emperor Xiaowendi.

The court of Sui abolished the prefecture of Yan while keeping the administrative region of Youzhou. Then it changed Youzhou to Zhuo Prefecture. The city of Ji was the seat of both the regional government of Youzhou and the prefectural government of Zhuo. The economic and cultural development of Beijing was speeded up by two events — the building of the Grand Canal and the carving of Buddhist scriptures on the rocks of present-day Fangshan in Beijing's suburbs.

To facilitate the transportation of grain from South to North China, Emperor Yangdi (r. 604-618) of the Sui dynasty decided to build the Grand Canal from Beijing to Hangzhou in Southeast China. The canal system consisted of four sections: First, the Jiangnan channel which linked Zhejiang (Qiantang) River with the Yangtze. Second, the Han canal dug in the time of King Fuchai of the state of Wu in the Spring and Autumn Period, which linked the Yangtze with Huaihe River. Third, the Tongji channel, for the construction of which more than 1,000,000 workers were recruited in areas north of Huaihe River to direct water from Gushui and Luoshui Rivers at Luoyang's West Park to the Yellow River which again was linked with the Huaihe River. The channel was 40 meters wide and lined with "royal paths" on both banks, which were planted with willows. And fourth, the Yongji channel, for the construction of which more than 1,000,000 men and women were recruited in areas north of the Yellow River to direct water from Qinshui River at Luokou south to the Yellow River and north to the city of Ji in Zhuo Prefecture. It took more than six years to complete the Grand Canal, which extended over nearly 2,000 kilometers from Yuhang (present-day Hangzhou, Zhejiang Province) to the city of Ji on the northern apex of the North China plain.

In 611, seven years before the fall of his dynasty, Emperor Yangdi boarded a dragon boat at Jiangdu (present-day Yangzhou, Jiangsu Province) to sail to Ji along the Grand Canal. The four-decked boat was 106 meters high and 471 meters long. A main chamber, an inner chamber, a east court, and a west court were laid out on the upper deck. The two decks in the middle were divided into 120 cabines. The lower deck provided accommodation for the eunuchs. The dragon boat was dragged forward from the banks by several hundred people dressed in colorful robes. The boats of the entourage — the princes, court ladies and officials — followed the emperor's. Extending over 100 kilometers or more, the royal fleet was protected by foot soldiers and cavalry units marching on the banks. The gorgeous boats on the canal were matched by a forest of colored

unifying North China. Under Northern Wei the Beijing area became the Yan Prefecture belonging to the administrative region of Youzhou. The city of Ji provided the seat for both the regional and the prefectural government. The Northern Wei period saw a spectacular rise of Buddhism, accompanied by the building of temples, the erection of Buddha statues, and the excavation of grottoes. Northern Wei contributed to the construction of the famous grottoes at three sites — the Mogao Grottoes southeast of Dunhuang, Gansu Province; the Yungang Grottoes at Datong, Shanxi Province; and the Longmen Grottoes south of Luoyang, Henan Province. A 10-meter-high statue of Sakyamuni in standing position was built with 50 tons of bronze and 0.3 tons of gold. A well-known Buddha statue was built in Ji city during the Taihe reign of Northern Wei.

The statue of Buddha, known as the Taihe Statue, was completed in 489, the 13th year of the Taihe reign of Emperor Xiaowendi (r.471-499) of Northern Wei. It was built in today's Che'erying Village west of Hot Spring in Beijing's Haidian District. Located in a stone hall, it is 2.2 meters high and shows a plump face and a natural, calm composure. It is the oldest stone sculpture of Buddha existing in Beijing today.

Northern Wei was the first of the Northern dynasties which, along with the Southern dynasties, ruled China for more than 160 years. In 589 Yang Jian, later known as Emperor Wendi of the Sui dynasty, unified China by ending the state of division which had caused so much suffering to the people since the period of the Sixteen States. It may be recalled that the First Emperor of the Qin dynasty ended the history of national split which had existed for more than 500 years through the Spring and Autumn period and the period of Warring States, but the Qin dynasty maintained its rule for only 15 years (221-207 B.C.). The Sui dynasty was also a short-lived one which existed for only 29 years (A.D. 581-618).* In spite of its brief history, however, the dynasty contributed a good deal to the development of the Beijing area.

---

*Yang Jian proclaimed himself emperor and founded the Sui dynasty in 581, but he did not eliminate Chen, the last of the Southern dynasties, until 589.

The Grand Canal in the Sui dynasty

Zhuojun

Yellow River

Qinshui River

Yongji Channel

Chang'an

Guangtong Channel

Luoshui River

Luoyang

Banzhu

Luokoucang

Tongji Channel

Shanyang

Huaihe River

Han Canal

Jiangdu

Jingkou

Yangtze River

Zhejiang River

Yuhang

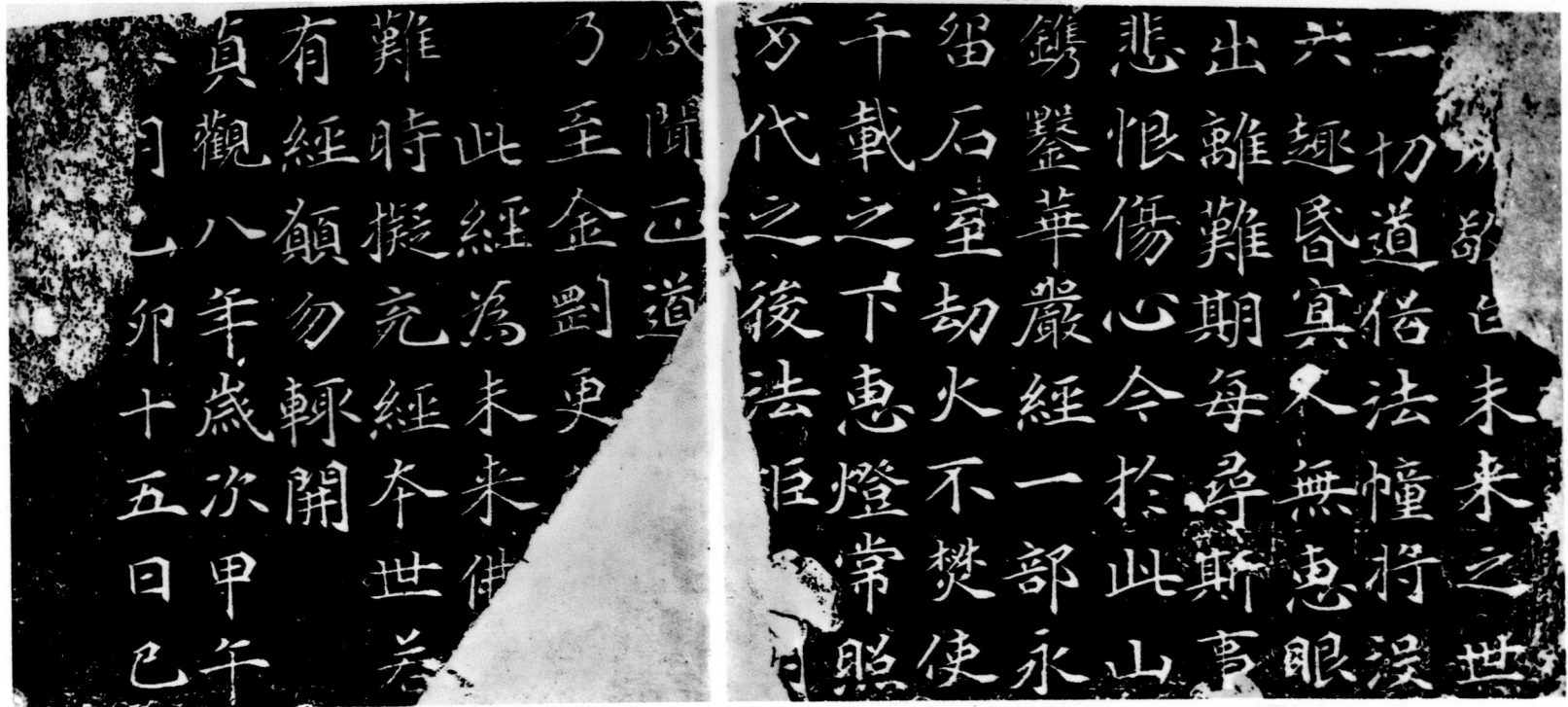

Buddhist scriptures in Monk Jingwan's handwriting carved on a rock in 634, the eighth year of the Zhenguan reign of the Tang dynasty

flags on land to create a panorama of imperial grandeur. The emperor arrived at Ji after a voyage of more than 50 days and put up at the Linshuo Palace.

However, Emperor Yangdi regarded Ji not just as the terminus of his pleasure trip, but the transit station for his conquest of Liaodong. In 612 all his recruits arrived at Ji, and he grouped them into 24 armies, 12 for the left route and 12 for the right route, for a march on Liaodong. Headed by a senior general, each army had 40 cavalry detachments and 80 infantry detachments. One hundred men and horses made up a cavalry detachment, and 10 detachments made up a regiment. Twenty infantry detachments were grouped as a regiment. Four ordnance regiments marched between infantry units. The total strength was 1,133,800 men, but claimed as 2 million. The number of civilians carrying food grain and fodder was double the number of men in active service.

The first army set out on the ninth day of the second moon, followed by one more army everyday at a distance of 20 kilometers. The six armies under the emperor's personal command brought up the rear. The whole procession extended over 500 kilometers or more, dotting the hillsides with flags and filling the valleys with the sound of drums.

An innovation developed for Emperor Yangdi's eastern expedition was a prefabricated city designed by He Chou, a master craftsman. The city measured four kilometers on each of the four sides, and the walls were 20 meters high. It was erected overnight with warriors, weapons and flags on the walls to overwhelm the enemy. Based in the city of Ji, Emperor Yangdi's expedition was bigger than any previous one in Chinese history, and is regarded as a spectacular military game by historians.

Buddhist scriptures were carved on the rocks in today's Fangshan in suburban Beijing in the time of Emperor Yangdi when Buddhism flourished throughout China.

Buddhism was introduced into China under the Eastern Han dynasty. It expanded its influence under the Wei dynasty, the Jin dynasty, and the Northern and Southern dynasties to become one of the three main religions in China, the other two being Confucianism and Taoism. The three religions influenced one another, and each was given a higher or lower status in different times. Until the Sui dynasty, however, Buddhism had never been the state religion of any dynasty controlling the whole of China.

A change took place under the Sui dynasty because of the personal background of the founding emperor. Yang Jian, later known as Emperor Wendi, was raised in a nunnery until he was 13. When Emperor Wudi (r.561-578) of Northern Zhou suppressed Buddhism, the nun who had been Yang Jian's guardian, Zhixian (Intelligent Goddess) by her religious name, went into hiding at Yang Jian's house and told his parents that someday the boy would be the emperor destined to revive Buddhism. After Yang Jian became

emperor in 581, he declared, "I owe my ascension to the teachings of Buddha." Both he and his successor, Emperor Yangdi, made it legitimate for people to become Buddhist monks and nuns, built temples, had Buddhist scriptures copied for circulation, and ordered the erection of statues of Buddha. Thus Buddhism rose to the status of state religion and flourished as never before under the Sui dynasty. This provided the political basis for the carving of Buddhist scriptures on the rocks in Fangshan.

Monk Jingwan, who initiated the project, also saw it as a precaution against any further suppression of Buddhism. Although the emperors of several dynasties were avowed Buddhists, contradictions often arose between monarchical authority and religious authority, leading to suppression of the religion and persecution of the preachers and followers. A case like this is known as a "calamity for the Dharma" in Buddhist history. Such calamities occurred twice before the Sui dynasty and twice after it. Before the Sui dynasty, the

Thunder Cave in the Dwelling-in-the-Clouds Temple

The 1000-Buddha Pillar in the Thunder Cave

first calamity for Buddhism took place under Emperor Taiwudi (r. 423-451) of Northern Wei, when the court was alarmed at the emergence of over 30,000 Buddhist temples, the increase of the number of monks and nuns to 2 million, a good number of court ladies becoming novices in nunneries, and relatives of the royal family pulling down their mansions for the building of temples. Worse still, a stupa built in front of the imperial palaces towered 240 meters, surpassing the height of the palace buildings and suggesting the supremacy of religious authority over imperial power. Thus in 444 the emperor issued a decree by which all Buddhist practices were forbidden. The next calamity came in 574 under Emperor Wudi of Northern Zhou, when Buddhism was banned as totally illegal, Buddhist scriptures and statues of Buddha were destroyed, and the monks' and nuns' profession was abolished. Three million monks and nuns were ordered to return to secular life, and 40,000 temples were converted into residential houses for princes and dukes. The calamities were repeated after the Sui dynasty. In 845, under Emperor Wuzong (r. 840-846) of the Tang dynasty, 40,000 temples were destroyed, 260,000 monks and nuns were returned to secular life, millions of hectares of land belonging to temples and nunneries were confiscated, and 150,000 male and female laborers in Buddhist institutions were transferred to other trades. Then in 955, under Emperor Shizong (r.954—959) of the Later Zhou dynasty (the last of the Five Dynasties), 33,336 temples were destroyed. These were the four major calamities in the history of Chinese Buddhism. No wonder that Jingwan, the far-sighted monk of the Sui dynasty, wanted to have Buddhist scriptures inscribed on the rocks in the hills of Beijing in order to preserve them forever.

The hills of Fangshan are 75 kilometers to the southwest of Beijing. Surrounded by clouds which looked like white bands from a distance, they used to be called the White-Band Mountain. With its towering peaks, shady trees, and gurgling springs, the secluded mountain velley became a holy place of Buddhism after the scriptures were carved on its rocks.

Buddhist scriptures carved on the rock walls of the Thunder Cave

Stupa for the Enshrinement of Buddha Relics in the Dwelling-in-the-Clouds Temple. Built in the Liao dynasty, it is 30 meters high and has three parts. The upper part is cone-shaped and decorated with circular bands, the middle part is a two-storied brick pavilion, and the base is a square with a small Tang-dynasty pagoda in each corner.

High-relief sculptures on the stupa

Small Tang-dynasty pagodas in the corners of the base of the stupa

The Liao-dynasty Southern Pagoda in the Dwelling-in-the-Clouds Temple. A total of 10,082 stone slabs carved with Buddhist scriptures lie underground by its side.

Flying deva in bas-relief on the base of the Southern Pagoda

It took 30 years to complete Jingwan's project, which was carried further ahead over a period of more than 1,000 years under the Tang, Liao, Jin (Jurchen), Yuan and Ming dynasties. More than 1,000 Buddhist sutras were carved on the rocks, equivalent to more than 3,000 Chinese *juan* (thread-bound volumes). Today we see complete inscriptions on 14,620 rocks and incomplete ones on 420 rocks, plus inscriptions on 420 steles. These are the largest reserve of early Buddhist scriptures on rock in China and anywhere. They are unparalleled in several respects — the scale of the project, the time taken to complete it, the abundance of material, and the magnificence of the sight.

The vault for keeping Buddhist scriptures is divided into two decks, with seven caves on the upper deck and two on the lower one. Cave No.5 is the Hall of the Buddhawatamsaka Sutra (Sutra of the Adornment of Buddha), generally known as Thunder Cave. The ceiling of this spacious cave is supported by four octagonal pillars with the carvings of 1,054 Buddha statues, called the Pillars of a Thousand Buddhas. Buddhist scriptures are carved on the rock walls on the four sides. The other caves vary in size, and some are surrounded by elegant stone balustrades.

A Dwelling-in-the-Clouds Temple was built in the Tang dynasty (A.D. 618-907) among the hills with Buddhist rock carvings. Facing the east, the temple had six main buildings: the Davaraja Hall (the Hall of Heavenly Kings) right inside the main gate, followed by five halls placed each higher than the other along the ascent of the stairs — the Vairocana Hall (the Hall of All-Pervasive Buddha Truth), the Hall of Sakyamuni (Sakyamuni, or "the Sage of the Sakyas," being the commonest title of Gautama Buddha), the Chandana Hall (Sandalwood Hall), the Bhaaisajyaguru Hall (the Hall of the God of Medicine), the Maitreya Hall (the Hall of the Buddha of the Future), and finally, the Hall of Universal Mercy. These were supplemented by buildings on the two sides: a bell tower and a drum tower, the Manjusri Hall (the Hall of the Bodhisattva of Wisdom), and living quarters for the monks, plus a bamboo garden and a special courtyard for the abbot of the temple. The temple was destroyed during the Anti-Japanese War of 1937-45. What remains today includes a stupa for the enshrinement of Buddha relics in the north and a Tripitaka pagoda (library of Buddhist scriptures) in the south, matched by a unique pagoda in the northwest. The last one, measuring only three meters in height, has a delicate stone pagoda on each of the four corners. The pagoda, like the rest of the temple, was built in the Tang dynasty, but the Liao dynasty (A.D. 916-1125) added its own innovation by erecting a stupa within the pagoda, creating a Diamond Throne Pagoda or a Sarira-stupa which is one of the most valuable relics of Chinese Buddhism.

Since the rock carvings in Beijing's Fangshan County are probably the only reserve of Buddhist scriptures of the sixth and seventh centuries in relatively complete texts, they are a rare historical relic for China and the world, comparable to the Buddhist murals at Dunhuang in Gansu Province.

In 618 Li Yuan founded the Tang dynasty which replaced the Sui dynasty. The new dynasty changed the name of the Beijing area from Zhuo Prefecture to Youzhou region. The city of Ji remained the capital, but was sometimes referred to as Youzhou city.

As a great empire in Chinese history, the Tang was marked by abundant resources, a prosperous economy, a thriving culture, and a vast territory. Its territory extended to the Pacific in the east, the Balkash Lake in the west, the Outer Hinggan Range beyond the Heilongjiang River in the north, and the islands in the South China Sea in the south. The empire found its parallel in the Arab empire in the west. Mohammed (570-632), the founder of Islam, extended his influence throughout southwest Arabia. His successors, the caliphs, fought a series of battles and built an empire across parts of Asia, Africa and Europe, which spread to the Indus River in the east, Spain in the west, the Caspian Sea in the north, and North Africa in the south. Amid the cultural interchange between the Tang empire and the Arab empire, the compass, paper-making techniques, gunpowder, and firearms invented in China were introduced to the West through the Arabs, while the sciences of astronomy and medicine of the Arabs and their Islamic faith found their way into China.

Operating from the national capital of Chang'an, the court of the Tang dynasty regarded the city of Ji, also called Youzhou city, as an important stronghold in the country's northeast. A Tang dynasty manual of prefectures and counties says that Youzhou city had a circumference of 12.5 kilometers and was surrounded by solid walls of rammed earth. People familiar with present-day Beijing might be interested to know that the eastern walls of Youzhou city were located west of today's Xuanwumen Street (the street along the former Gate of Military Virtue), the western walls were east of Lianhuachi, the northern walls were just south of Xinwenhua Street,

and the southern walls were to the south of Baizhifang Street. There were a total of 12 gates on the four sides, according to the Tang manual. The streets were neatly laid out. The Yanzhou Administrative Office, which handled the affairs of ethnic minorities, had its premises in the western part of the city at a site called Yanzhou Corner. A street which has been kept intact for more than 1,000 years since the Tang dynasty is today's Sanmiao Street outside Xuanwumen (site of the former Gate of Military Virtue), which was called Tanzhou Street in those days. It is, so far as we know, the oldest street in Beijing. Like the Tang dynasty's western capital Chang'an and its eastern capital Luoyang, Youzhou city was divided along a number of thoroughfares each leading to a city gate, which was open during the day and closed at night and was patrolled by guards on schedule.

Youzhou city served as a strategic base for the Tang regime's expeditions against Liaodong beyond the Great Wall. In fact, it was associated with the desire of so many emperors for military aggrandizement. As mentioned earlier, Emperor Yangdi of the Sui dynasty made the city the starting point of a march on Liaodong, but his defeat hastened the fall of his dynasty. Forgetting this lesson, Emperor Taizong (r. 626-649) of the Tang dynasty launched another expedition in spite of the warnings of his advisors and took personal command of the expeditionary army. He directed a march on Liaodong by both land and sea, placing General Li Jie at the head of a cavalry force of 60,000 and Admiral Zhang Liang in command of a naval fleet of 500 boats with 40,000 officers and men on board. In 645 the emperor himself led his imperial army from Luoyang to Youzhou and then to the vicinity of Liaodong city. Both the imperial army and the forces under General Li and Admiral Zhang won a number of battles. But the Tang army had to face the scathing winter cold outside the Great Wall before it could capture Liaodong. It suffered heavy casualties because it was running out of food grain and fodder. Seeing the plight, the emperor regretted his action. He is quoted to have said that he would not have launched the expedition if Grand Censor Wei Zheng, who had always offered him unsparing criticism, were still living. As he led his army back through the city of Youzhou, he ordered the construction of a Buddhist temple in memory of those who had died during the expedition. The temple was completed in 696 under the reign of Empress Wu Zetian and was named Temple to Mourn the Loyal Ones by an imperial decree. Renovated over the centuries, it was renamed Temple of the Source of Dharma in 1734 when a major reconstruction project was accomplished under Emperor Yongzheng of the Qing dynasty.

Located outside the Gate of Military Virtue, the Temple of the Source of Dharma faces the south. Two stone lions guard the vermilion gate of the temple. Shaded by pines and cone-shaped cypresses (*Sabina chinensis*), the first courtyard welcomes visitors with its antique tranquility and has a bell tower and a drum tower on the left and right. The Devaraja Hall stands in the north. The four devarajas (heavenly kings) gave a fierce stare to all evils. The second

Platform to Mourn the Loyal Ones in the Temple of the Source of Dharma. This platform was built in place of the Tang-dynasty temple of the same name which had been destroyed.

Bronze statue of Buddha Piluzhena in the Temple of the Source of Dharma. Cast in the Ming dynasty, it is 4.5 meters high and has three parts. The upper part is a statue of Piluzhena, the middle part is a square with an image of Buddha on each of the four sides, and the lower part is a huge drum-shaped base with a pattern of lotus leaves, on each of which is a carving of Buddha.

The lotus-leaf pattern on the base of a stone pillar in the Mahavira Hall of the Temple of the Source of Dharma. There are two such pillars in the temple, which must be relics of early Tang because the patterns are identical with other Tang-dynasty patterns in the temple.

courtyard is dominated by the Mahavira Hall (Hall of the Fearless Hero) built on a vast terrace. Tall and spacious, it looks magnificent with pillars and beams decorated with carvings and paintings. Inside the hall are enshrined the "Three Sages of Huayan." In the middle is Buddha Piluzhena (Vairochana). In Sanscrit "pi" means "high and distinguished" while "luzhenna" means broad vision. Piluzhena is also known as Buddha of the Great Sun. He is flanked by his two disciples, with Manjusri, the Bodhisattva of Wisdom, on the left and Samantabhadra, the great Bodhisattva of Universal Benevolence, on the right. The dignified images are presented in exquisite carvings on the gilded and lacquered statues of wood. Carved steles from the Tang, Liao, Jin (Jurchen) and Qing dynasties are inlaid on the outside of the eastern and western walls of the hall. Two steles from the Tang dynasty, with inscriptions entitled "Eulogy of the Spotlessly Clean Pagoda" and "An Account of the Re-enshrinement of Buddha Relics in the Tang Dynasty's Temple to Mourn the Loyal Ones," bear the earliest stele carvings discovered in Beijing. "Eulogy of the Spotlessly Clean Pagoda" was carved in 757, the second year of the Zhide reign of the Tang dynasty. The stone stele was erected by Shi Siming before his surrender to the Tang emperor. Later he revolted against the Tang court but was finally murdered by his son. Thus the inscriptions were rubbed off and restored at several places. "An Account of the Re-enshrinement of Buddha Relics in the Tang Dynasty's Temple to Mourn the Loyal Ones" records how Fu Yan, a priest of the temple, re-enshrined Buddha relics in front of the statue of the God of Mercy in 893, the sixth year of the Huichang reign. He had the event recorded on a stele as a precaution against the eventuality of damage. Also preserved in the hall are Buddhist scriptures translated and annotated by Hsuan Tsang or the Great Tripitaka, high priest of the Tang dynasty who brought back the scriptures from India. The Buddhist library is located in the last courtyard. The two-storied building has vermilion walls and a bluish-grey roof. It is decorated with colorful paintings on the purlins and eaves, and owes part of its elegance to the balustraded corridors. Preserved in the library are such rare relics as Buddhist scriptures from India written on Pattra leaves, a Ming dynasty edition of the *Avatamsaka Sutra* recorded in gold paint, and an edition of *The Tripitaka in Chinese* of the same dynasty.

The Reclining Buddha in the Temple of the Source of Dharma. Carved in wood in the Ming dynasty, this 7.4-meter-long sculpture was originally placed in the Temple of Reclining Buddha in the Chongwen District of Beijing.

Statue of Avalokitesvara in the Temple of the Source of Dharma

The Temple of the Source of Dharma is a famous monastery of the longest history in Beijing. Emperor Qinzong, the last sovereign of the Northern Song dynasty, was imprisoned here by Jurchen invaders. The Jurchen rulers gave examinations here for candidates for the highest academic honors from their own nationality. In modern times a major event took place in May 1980, when a sitting statue of Jian Zhen, a high priest of the Tang dynasty who made outstanding contributions to the cultural exchange with Japan, was brought to the temple for exhibition in different parts of China. The temple also provides the premises for the Chinese Buddhist Academy.

To be sure, events connected with the construction of the temple, initially called Temple to Mourn the Loyal Ones, hurt the pride of the Tang emperor Taizong who had won practically all his battles except those in Liaodong. The frontiers of the Tang empire once extended to the Caspian Sea on the borders of the Arab empire in the northwest through a victory over the West Turks and to the Gobi Desert in the north through a victory over the East Turks. The expeditions in the northeast, however, were ill-devised and unsuccessful and led to serious consequences. Finally, An Lushan staged a rebellion against the Tang court in Fanyang (Youzhou). This mutiny, launched by a militarist of an ethnic minority, heralded the rise of other nationalities — the Qidans (Khitans), the Mongols, and the Manchus, all of whom used Beijing as a springboard for their conquest of power throughout China, a feature of China's socio-political history for 1,000 years.

An Lushan's parents came from an ethnic minority in Northeast China, but he was raised in the house of a Turk to whom his mother was remarried. He started his career as a broker in the market places and later joined the army. As he rose from post to post, he came into contact with the emperor and soon learned to curry the royal favor. Once when Emperor Xuanzong joked about his big belly and asked what was in it, he replied. "Nothing but a heart loyal to Your Majesty." He was also liked by Yang Yuhuan, the emperor's most favorite concubine. Once the imperial consort ordered her attendants to wrap him up in silk and satin and smuggle him into the palace, and drank with him all night. Trusting him, the emperor appointed him military satrap for the three important strongholds of Fanyang, Pinglu and Hedong, placing in his hands military command and civil administration over vast regions north of Yellow River. An Lushan built a new city north of Fanyang where he recruited troops, stored army provisions, and gathered a number of cohorts in preparation for rebellion.

In 755 An Lushan rose in Fanyang at the head of 150,000 men, who swept through prefectures and counties and soon took Luoyang, the eastern capital of the Tang court. The next year he proclaimed himself Emperor of Great Yan with his capital in Fanyang. As his army advanced on Chang'an, Emperor Xuanzong, the imperial consort Yang Yuhuan, and their entourage fled the capital. After the party arrived at Maweiyi, the imperial guards refused to go any further, declaring that they would not resume the journey until the imperial consort was put to death. The emperor ordered the attendants to give her a white scarf, with which she strangled herself.

Meanwhile, an internecine struggle for power broke out within the ranks of An Lushan's army. An Lushan was murdered by his son, An Qingxu, who proclaimed himself Emperor of Yan. On the side of the Tang dynasty, the crown prince ascended the throne to become Emperor Suzong, while the old emperor, who had lost much of his prestige by his debauchery and neglect of duty, was relegated to the background as Emperor Emeritus. The Tang army was eventually revitalized under General Guo Ziyi, and recovered Chang'an and Luoyang. An Qingxu was murdered, after his retreat from Luoyang, by Shi Siming, a general in his army, who called himself Emperor of Great Yan and changed the name of the capital, Fanyang, to Yanjing. This is the origin of the name of Yanjing for Beijing, which is widely used by hotels and other business establishments in the city today. Shi Siming managed to recapture Luoyang but, like his former superior An Lushan, he was murdered by his son Shi Chaoyi who made himself emperor of Yan. Defeated by the Tang army, Shi Chaoyi retreated to Fanyang, where he was killed in 763 by the garrison commander, Li Huaixian, who surrendered to the Tang court. This ended the eight-year turmoil caused by the An Lushan-Shi Siming rebellion, which started in Fanyang and was finally suppressed in the same city. The Tang court changed the name of Fanyang back to Youzhou. Right up to the time of its downfall, however, the dynasty was never able to put an end to the separatist regimes of military governors in outlying areas, and the city of Youzhou was always controlled by one local warlord or another.

Some relics of the period of the An Lushan-Shi Siming rebellion have been found in Beijing. In addition to some steles from those years preserved in the Temple of the Source of Dharma, a tomb of the Tang dynasty period was excavated in 1966 at Linjiafen in Beijing's Fengtai District. The jade records unearthed there bear the words of "Emperor Chaoyi," an obvious reference to Shi Chaoyi. Among the rare relics found in the tomb is a bronze ox which looks vigorous and sturdy with a protruding nose, bright eyes, slanted horns, raised shoulders, a muscular body and solid legs. The artist seemed to have given it some of the moral features of the common people in China: honesty, industry, ingenuity and tenacity.

By a custom originating most probably in the Han dynasty, ox is one of the 12 animals matched with the 12 Earthly Branches by which the lunar calendar years are numbered. The animals are, in the order of the Earthly Branches, mouse, ox, tiger, rabbit, dragon, snake, horse, sheep, monkey, chicken, dog and pig. Thus a person born in the year of the first Earthly Branch is also one born in the year of the mouse, and a person born in the year of the 12th Earthly Branch is also one born in the year of the pig. A person born in 1947 belongs to the year of the pig, and so does one born after a cycle of 12 years, in 1959. At a tomb of the Tang dynasty excavated in Beijing's Xuanwu District, 12 stone statues were discovered, each with the head of one of the 12 animals matched with the 12 Earthly Branches and the body of a human being. They are all dressed in the comfortable, broad-sleeved robes of the Tang dynasty and come to life.

With the An Lushan-Shi Siming rebellion as the turning point, the once prosperous and powerful Tang empire began to decline. Coincidentally, the three great empires of the world split up around the same time. The Arab empire became three caliphates with capitals in Bagdad, Cordova in Spain and Cairo. By the Treaty of Verdun of 843 the Charlemagne Empire was divided into three principal states which later became Italy, Germany, and France. And the first half of the 10th century saw the disintegration of the Tang empire, which was replaced by a total of 15 states existing at different times, known historically as the Five Dynasties and Ten States (907-960).*

During the early years of Later Liang of the Five Dynasties period, Liu Rengong, who had been commander of the Lulong Army in the frontier region of Youzhou under the Tang dynasty, occupied the region of Northern Yan and stationed his troops at Youzhou. Liu was greedy, extravagent and brutal. One historical record says that on a hill west of the city he "lavishly decorated his mansion in a palace style, assembled beautiful women, and indulged in luxury and debauchery." He cheated the people by circulating clay coins in the districts under his control and selling grass leaves for tea at an exorbitant price. He flogged his son, Liu Shouguang, who was found to have sexual relations with one of his concubines. In 907, the first year of the Kaiping reign, the Younger Liu rose against his father, took Youzhou, imprisoned his father and murdered his elder brother. In 911 Liu Shouguang ascended the throne, calling his dynasty the Great Yan and making Ji his capital. But his regime collapsed only three years later.

During the Five Dynasties, except for the three years during which Beijing was the capital of Great Yan under Liu Shouguang, the area was called Youzhou, with its capital city remaining at Ji, under the first two of the Five Dynasties, Later Liang and Later Tang. But Shi Jintang (r. 936-942), founder of Later Jin, the third of the Five Dynasties, ceded Youzhou and other districts to the Qidan (Khitan) tribes, which thus used the Beijing area as an important base for their conquest of part of North China.

To recapitulate, for about a thousand years from the conquest of the ancient state of Yan by the First Emperor of the Qin dynasty to the cession of the Beijing area to the Qidans by Shi Jintang, the city of Ji maintained its position as a North China military stronghold, a commercial metropolis, and a center of national fusion. Whenever the ruling dynasty on the Central Plains was strong, it used the city of Ji as a base for the conquest of the frontier regions in Northeast China. But whenever one ethnic minority or another became a formidable power in Northeast China, it made Ji an advance post for a march on the Central Plains. Beijing acquired increasing significance in the course of fusion and conflicts among China's various ethnic groups or, to put it another way, in the course of evolution of the Chinese nation. In about 500 years from the Eastern Jin dynasty to the Five Dynasties, Beijing served as capital for a state called Yan on three occasions. This marked its transition from a North China stronghold to a national political center.

---

*The period of the Five Dynasties began in 907, when Zhu Wen, a frontier commander under the Tang dynasty, usurped the throne and proclaimed himself emperor of Later Liang. The period ended in 960, when Later Zhou, the last of the Five Dynasties, was replaced by the Northern Song dynasty. However, it was not until 979 that Northern Song conquered the last of the Ten States.

Chapter IV

THE ETHNIC MINORITIES MAKE BEIJING THEIR CAPITAL

Southern Capital Under the Liao Dynasty

Toward the end of the Tang dynasty, tribes known as Qidans became increasingly strong in the eastern parts of the Mongolian highlands. In 907, the last year of the Tang dynasty, Yelu Abaoji (r. 916 — 926), an outstanding leader, was elected Khan of these tribes. Taking advantage of the turmoil on the Central Plains in the period of the Five Dynasties and Ten States, he founded the state of Qidan and extended his influence into North China. He was succeeded by his son, Yelu Deguang (r. 926 — 947),who changed the name of his state to Liao in 947.

When Shi Jintang, a frontier commander for the Hedong region under the Later Tang dynasty, staged a rebellion against the court and was in danger of being suppressed by the latter, he appealed to the Qidans for aid, promising allegiance to them after victory. The Qidan'troops swept south, eliminated Later Tang, and installed Shi Jintang as emperor of the Later Jin dynasty. In 938 Shi, who called himself a "filial emperor" in relation to the Qidans, ceded Youzhou and 15 other districts to them. The acquisition of these strategically important districts, particularly the city of Ji, strengthened the position of the Qidans immeasurably and enabled them to pose a direct threat to the Central Plains.

After entering Youzhou, Yelu Deguang elevated it to Southern Capital in 938 in keeping with the Qidans' custom of maintaining five capitals. The Southern Capital was simultaneously known as Yanjing.

The Qidans had always led a nomadic life, obtaining their food by hunting and fishing, clothing themselves in animal hides and fur, and possessing no domicile except their horses, chariots and tents. They settled where they could find water and grass, knowing how to avoid heat in summer and cold in winter. The emperor also moved his tent from season to season. In spring he started his journey early in the first moon on the lunar calendar and, after a travel of 60 days, put up his tent on ice. His party broke ice to obtain fish and often spent the whole day on a hunting trip. As soon as the mounted men startled a swan, the emperor would release an eagle to seize it. One of the courtiers would pierce the head of the swan with an awl and feed the eagle with its brain, whereupon a band would strike up cheerful music and the ministers would rejoice by inserting the feathers of the swan into their hats. The summer journey started in the middle of the fourth moon. A cool and auspicious environment would be chosen by divination before the royal party settled down for the administration of state affairs and took hunting trips. In autumn the emperor and his men started moving in the middle of the seventh moon to a place called Tigers-Lying-in-Ambush Forest, where they put up their tents along the Luoshui River. At midnight, the time when deer came out to drink water, hunters would be ordered to imitate the cries of deer by blowing horns. When the flocks grew larger, the royal party would hunt them down with arrows. The destination for the winter journey, which started in the middle of the tenth moon, was a place called Guangpingdian where luxurious tents were put up for the emperor. With felt covers, satin on the walls, and carpeted floors, they were supported by wooden pillars painted in a variety of colors and guarded by several thousand Qidan soldiers going on day or night duty.

The itinerant nature of the Qidan tribes and their rulers was perhaps the origin of their system of maintaining several capitals. The Liao dynasty had five capitals: an Upper Capital at Linhuang (south of today's Bairin Left Banner in Ju Ud League, Inner Mongolia), an Auxiliary Capital or Middle Capital (east of Ningcheng, Inner Mongolia), an Eastern Capital (Liaoyang, Liaoning Province), a Western Capital (Datong, Shanxi Province), and a Southern Capital (Beijing). But the Southern Capital was the largest in terms of both scale and population. It had an outer city enclosing a royal city. With a circumference of 13 kilometers, the outer city had walls measuring 9.2 meters high and 4.6 meters thick, which were provided with parapets on top and surrounded by three moats. The eight gates were each accessible by a suspension bridge. To all intents and purposes the Southern Capital was a fortified city of a feudal lord. The royal city, located in the southwest, was a complex of palaces, towers and pavilions and had seven gates. There was an open ground for polo games outside the south gate. To the east of the royal city was the Pavilion of Eternal Peace where the emperor received envoys from the court of the Song dynasty and gave banquets for officials and members of the nobility.

The Southern Capital had neatly laid-out streets. The Chinese word for "city" consists of two characters, one meaning "city" and the other, "market place." The cities were separate from the market places during and before the Tang dynasty. The barrier between the two gradually disappeared in the Song dynasty amid the growth of industry and commerce. For instance, there was no apparent distinction between them in Bianliang (present-day Kaifeng in Henan), the Eastern Capital of the Song dynasty, where shops lined the streets and alleys and business continued deep into the night. The Southern Capital of the Liao dynasty was not as prosperous as Bianliang, but the city was more developed than before. The *Record of the State of Qidan* says:

> The city has a population of 300,000. In addition to the magnificent palaces, there is a market in the northern district where you see every description of merchandise brought in by land or sea. The city leads the northern regions of the country in the number of monasteries and monks. The silks and satins available here are the best under the sun. Edible oils, vegetables, fruits, hemp, and rice and other cereals are found everywhere, and so are sheep, pigs, chickens and rabbits. The soil is fertile, the water sweet, and the people endowed with a variety of skills.

The above passage shows the abundant human and material resources of the Southern Capital as well as its thriving economy. Besides the market in the northern district, there was another business section known as the Six Streets which teemed with people during every festival. Even the emperor changed into civilian attire to mix with the merrymakers and have a look at the gorgeous displays in the brightly-lit shops at night.

Multiple-Treasure Pagoda. Located in Liangxiang Township in Beijing's suburban Fangshan County, it is a five-storied octagonal building of the Liao dynasty, the only pavilion-style pagoda remaining in Beijing.

Boy-Chanting-Scripture Pot. Unearthed from under the base of a Liao dynasty pagoda in Beijing's suburban Shunyi County in 1963, the pot is in the shape of a boy sitting in a chair. The back of the chair is the pot's handle, and the rolled-up book in the boy's hands is the spout. In the center of the boy's coiled-up hair is an opening for pouring in water.

As believers in Buddhism, the rulers of the Liao dynasty erected temples and gave special treatment to Buddhist monks. Four of the temples remain to this day as Beijing's scenic spots.

The Temple of Great Awakening is located at the foot of the Yangtai Mountains some 30 kilometers to the west of Beijing. The mountains are sometimes called Lion Mountains because they look like a squatting lion. A spring gushes down one of the hills like a strip of white cloth. When the apricot trees are in blossom, they turn the hillsides into a vast sea of pink waves. A Clear Water Temple was built here in 1068 under the Liao dynasty. Domiciles for monks were put up with 300,000 strings of cash contributed by Buddhist followers; *The Tripitaka in Chinese* was printed, and a Tripitaka Pavilion built, with additional donations of 500,000 strings of cash. The name was changed to Temple of Great Awakening when the premises were enlarged under the Ming dynasty. Renovation under the Qing dynasty gave the temple its present shape. Leaning against a mountain, the temple has the following structures in an ascending order: the main gate, the Devaraja Hall, the main hall, the Hall of the Buddha of Infinite Longevity, and the Hall of the Dragon King. The bronze statue of Avalokitesvara (the Goddess of Mercy) and those of the 32 devas in the Hall of the Buddha of Infinite Longevity are among the finest Buddhist relics in Beijing, like the mural paintings in the Fahai Temple and the clay sculptures in the Temple of Great Wisdom. A sarira-stupa built by the late High Priest Jialing rivals the White Dagoba in the Beihai (North Sea) Park in dignity and delicacy. The *sumeru* base of the stupa has elegant designs in bas-relief.

The garden of the Temple of Great Awakening delights visitors with towering ancient trees and the surrounding network of springs converging into a blue pool. It is said in an inscription on a 1,000-year-old stele that "the best-known pool in the Ji area is located at the foot of the Yangtai Mountains, and the most enjoyable environment is provided by the garden of the Clear Water Temple."

Clay statues of devas in the Temple of Great Awakening

Stupa in the Temple of Great Awakening. Built in the Qing dynasty, it enshrines the remains of Monk Jialing, abbot of the temple.

The Ordination Terrace Temple is situated at the foot of the Ma'anshan Mountain (Saddle Hill) in the Mentougou District 35 kilometers west of the urban area of Beijing. Under the Tang dynasty, a Temple for the Gathering of Wisdom was built here in 622, the first year on the Moslem calender in which Mohammed moved from Mecca to Medina. A terrace was founded at the site in 1069 under the Liao dynasty by High Priest Fajun for the ordination of novices into Buddhist priesthood. The buildings were reconstructed or renovated under the Ming and Qing dynasties. The Ordination Terrace of the temple is larger than that in any other Buddhist temple in China.

An ordination terrace is the place where novices pledge to observe one of several codes of monastic commandments. There are the Five Commandments against the killing of living beings, stealing, lust, telling lies and drinking; the Eight Commandments which include the Five Commandments as well as refrainment from sitting or lying on a luxurious couch, from watching dances and listening to songs, and from eating at improper times, i.e., after noontime; the Ten Commandments which include the Eight Commandments as well as refrainment from the use of balms and the hoarding of gold, silver and other treasures; and the Cardinal Commandments which include 250 rules for male novices and 348 rules for female novices, both aged between seven and 20 and ordinated on the Ten Commandments. According to the Ordination Law, male and female novices ordinated on the Cardinal Commandments qualify as monks and nuns. The ordination ceremonies vary according to the different types of commandments. The ceremonies held in the Ordination Terrace Temple are those based on the Cardinal Commandments. In the Hall of the Ordination Terrace is a large three-layered altar of carved bronze-colored rocks with a seated statue of Sakyamuni putting his palms together. There used to be 10 carved sandalwood chairs in front of the statue of Sakyamuni, seats for the three masters and seven witnesses at an ordination ceremony. The three masters

The main gate of the Ordination Terrace Temple

The ordination terrace in the Ordination Terrace Temple

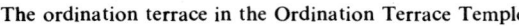

The Nine-Dragon Pine in the Ordination Terrace Temple

were the Ordination Monk, the Karma Monk and the Instructor. The Ordination Monk would preside over the ceremony. The Karma Monk would announce the commandments to the novices three times and would accept them as monks or nuns if they voiced no objection. The Instructor was the one who taught the novices how to perform Buddhist rituals. Apart from the Ordination Terrace, the temple also has a Devaraja Hall, a Mahavira Hall, and many other structures. A pagoda of the Liao dynasty and another of the Yuan dynasty are well-preserved in the pagoda courtyard. The ancient pines in the garden take grotesque forms. A poet writes, "each has its own posture, as if to compete with sentient beings." The five best-known ones are the Circling-the-Pagoda Pine, the Recumbent-Dragon Pine, the Carefree Pine, the Nine-Dragon Pine, and the Sensitive Pine. The last one was named by Emperor Qianlong (r.1735-96) of the Qing dynasty. If you touch any of the branches, the whole tree quivers. A stele under the tree is inscribed with three poems by Emperor Qianlong.

Located outside today's Guanganmen (site of the former Gate of Pervasive Peace), the Temple of Celestial Tranquility was built as the Temple of Shining Woods in the fifth century. A towering pagoda was erected behind the temple under the Liao dynasty. The temple was destroyed during a war that ended the Yuan dynasty, but the pagoda remained. Reconstruction was carried out under the Ming dynasty which gave the temple the present name.

The pagoda of the temple is a solid brick structure. It is octagonal and has 13 stories with a total height of 57.8 meters. Resting on a square terrace, the *sumeru* base has three layers of lotus petals supporting the body of the pagoda. There is a semi-circular gate on each of the four sides, and each gate is decorated on the right and left with the portraits of guardian deities, Buddhisattvas, and designs of dragons and clouds in bas-relief. The guardian deities have broad shoulders and a muscular body, giving people a powerful stare with wide-open eyes. The eaves of the different stories become narrower from bottom to top. Shining in the sun, they cast a succession of shades on the ground. Standing against the red walls and green tiles of the temple, the pagoda must have added much grandeur to the Southern Capital of the Liao dynasty.

The Temple of Great Awakening, the Ordination Terrace Temple, and the Temple of Celestial Tranquility described above are all Buddhist monasteries. Islam, another major religion of the world,

High-relief sculptures on the pagoda in the Temple of Celestial Tranquility

The Prayer Hall in the Ox Street Mosque

The *Minaret* in the Ox Street Mosque

Arabic inscriptions on two tombstones in the Ox Street Mosque. The tombstones were erected in memory of two Arabic priests who came to China to preach Islamism. They built the mosque in 996 under the Liao dynasty and were later buried in the mosque.

found its way into China during the Tang dynasty whose territory was contiguous to the Arab empire. The Liao dynasty had close ties with countries of Central Asia. Historical records refer to envoys of the Arab empire paying tribute at the court of Liao. In 1020 the monarch of the Arab empire sent an emissary to Liao, presenting elephants and special products to the Liao emperor and proposing a match between an Arab prince and a Liao princess, a request which was granted the following year. At the time China was divided into three states—Song, Liao and Western Xia. Merchants and imams from the Arab countries came to China through Kaxgar in today's Xinjiang and went to the three states by way of Yarkant and Hetian, also in Xinjiang, and by Shazhou which is today's Dunhuang in Gansu Province. The religious teachings and architectural art of Islamism eventually reached the Southern Capital, where buildings appeared in a combination of Arab and Liao styles. A typical example is the mosque on Ox Street in Beijing.

The mosque has a concentrated and symmetrical layout. The main buildings include the Prayer Hall, the *Minaret*, the Tower for Observing the Moon, and two Stele Pavilions. The roof of the Prayer Hall consists of three sections, and the overlapping parts are decorated with carved murals. A hexagonal structure at the far end of the hall, called the *mihrab*, contains a niche which points out the direction of Kaaba* at Mecca. A *mimbar* by the side of the *mihrab* provides a seat for the preacher who leads the prayer service on Friday and various festivals. The spacious hall accommodates at least 1,000 people, looking solemn and impressive. A wooden structure built by traditional Chinese methods, it is nevertheless distinctively Arabic in architectural style. The *Minerat*, a square, double-eaved tower, stands in front of the Prayer Hall. This is the place from where a *muezzin* cries out the prayer hours for followers of the Islamic faith. The Tower for Observing the Moon, situated between the first and second gates of the mosque, is ascended by Moslems before they break their fast. The two Stele Pavilions are found on the sides of the Moon Terrace in front of the Prayer Hall. The steles, erected in 1496 under the Ming dynasty, are inscribed with Chinese and Arabic texts. In the southeastern section of the mosque are two tombs dating to the 13th century. The Arabic inscriptions on the tomb stones, the oldest in Beijing, give the names of the two imams buried here, who had come from Iran and Bokhara to preach Islamism in China during the reign of Kublai Khan.

Buddhism reached its heyday under three emperors of the Liao dynasty—Emperor Shengzong (r. 983—1031) who built a large

---

* Kaaba is the sanctuary at Mecca which encloses the Black Stone, the most sacred object of Islam.

---

number of monasteries, Emperor Xingzong (r. 1031-55)who was accepted as a novice, and Emperor Daozong (r. 1055-1101) who achieved proficiency in Sanskrit. Yanjing led the whole country in putting up pagodas and Buddha's statues and in printing Buddhist sutras. The wood blocks for the *Tripitaka in Chinese* were completed under the Liao dynasty. This is why the book is also known as the *Liao Tripitaka* or *Qidan Tripitaka*. The wood blocks for all the 579 cloth-wrapped sets of the Buddhist classic were cut in Yanjing. An account of the publication of the book, kept in the Temple of Great Awakening, states that 500,000 strings of cash were contributed by Buddhists for the project, and that the 579 cloth-wrapped sets were enshrined in a niche. The statement was colloborated by no visible evidence until 1974, when some volumes of the classic dating to the Liao dynasty were discovered in the belly of the statue of Sakyamuni in the Buddhist Palace Temple in Ying County, Shanxi Province. The Chinese characters are done in powerful, elegant calligraphy, and the printing and binding are both of a high quality, showing the excellent workmanship of Yanjing's printers. Also discovered were other Buddhist classics printed in Yanjing, including two volumes of the *Commentary on Mahayana Philosophy* and the fourth volume of the *Lotus Sutra*. The imprints show that the publications were sponsored by monasteries or influential families.

The mosque is located on Ox Street near Guanganmen in Beijing. The Ox Street, which used to be called Pomegranate Street because of the many pomegranate trees there, was a settlement of visitors from the Arab world. Their custom of eating a lot of beef changed the street name to the present one. The mosque is believed to have been built by Nasr Ud-din, an imam from the Arab world, in 995 under the Liao dynasty. The oldest and largest mosque in Beijing, it was renovated under the Ming and Qing dynasties and after the founding of the People's Republic.

Mahayana sutra carved and printed in Yanjing in the Liao dynasty. This was also discovered in the belly of the statue of Sakyamuni in 1974.

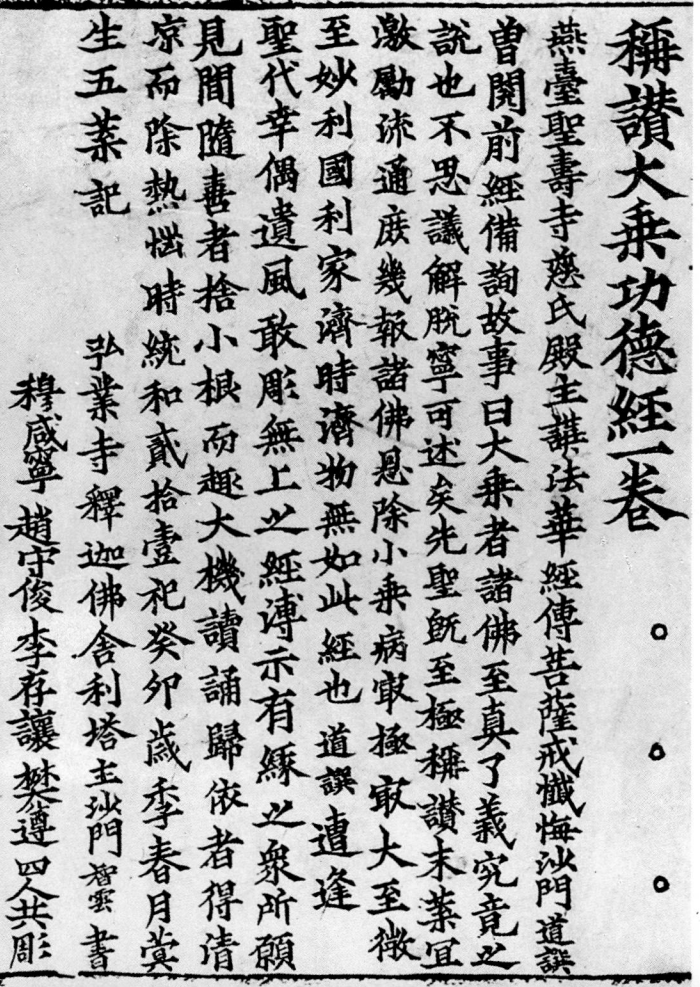

Portrait of Sakyamuni carved and printed in Yanjing in the Liao dynasty. The relic was discovered in 1974 in the belly of a statue of Sakyamuni in the Buddhist Palace Temple in Ying County, Shanxi Province.

Middle Capital Under the Jurchen Dynasty

As the power of the Liao dynasty declined, the Jurchen people in Northeast China gained in strength. In 1115 their leader Wanyan Aguda founded the Jin (Jurchen) dynasty with an Upper Capital in today's Acheng County, Heilongjiang Province. The Jurchen dynasty in the north and the Song dynasty in the south entered into an alliance for a joint attack on the Liao regime. In 1122 Jurchen troops penetrated Liao territory and captured Yanjing, which was turned over to Song in exchange for a huge quantity of rice and cash. The Song court renamed Yanjing as Yanshan Prefecture. Three years later, in 1125, the Jurchens wiped out the state of Liao. The next year they invaded Song and seized Yanshan Prefecture. In the third year, 1127, the Northern Song regime collapsed under Jurchen attacks, and a Southern Song dynasty was founded in south China under Emperor Gaozong. Thus China came under the rule of two rival dynasties — the Jurchen dynasty occupying the vast regions north of Huaishui River and the Southern Song dynasty in control of those south of the river. To facilitate military actions against the south, Wanyan Liang, the fourth emperor of the Jurchen dynasty who was also known as the Prince of Hailing, moved the seat of his regime from Upper Capital to Yanjing, which was named Middle Capital. For the first time, Beijing became the main capital of an empire as well as the political center of North China.

The Middle Capital of the Jurchens followed Bianliang (present-day Kaifeng), capital of the Northern Song dynasty, in planning and layout and was constructed on the basis of the Southern Capital of the Liao dynasty. It had an outer city enclosing an imperial city which in turn enclosed the palace complex.

While the northern wall of the outer city from the Liao period was preserved, the walls on the three other sides were pushed further toward the suburbs. The outer city was a square one with a circumference of 18 kilometers. The 12-meter-high city walls had 910 watchtowers and were surrounded by three rings of ditches.

The southeastern corner of the outer city was located to the southwest of today's railway station at Yongdingmen (site of the former Gate of Everlasting Stability). The northeastern corner coincided with Cuihua Street within the Gate of Military Virtue. The northwestern corner was at Huangtingzi south of the Military Museum. And the southwestern corner has become Fenghuangming Village in Beijing's Fengtai District. The outer city had 12 gates, three on each side, with the middle gate on the north and that on the south forming the city's axis. The yellow earth used for building the city walls were brought in from Zhuozhou dozens of kilometers away. Thousands upon thousands of people stood in a line to pass the baskets of earth all the way to the city. No less than a million civilians, artisans and soldiers were recruited for the construction of the Middle Capital.

Located a little to the south of the center of the outer city, the imperial city had four gates and a circumference of 4.5 kilometers. A broad imperial path lined with willows led from the southern gate to the palace complex. Inside the gate were a bell tower on the east and a drum tower on the west. There were also two long, covered walks leading to the palaces. Located on the east and west, they were each divided into three sections with a gate for each. But one could not approach the palaces without going through two additional sections flanked by the premises of the Chancery for Civil Administration, the Board for Ethnic Minority and Foreign Affairs, and other important offices.

The palace complex, which was inside the imperial city, had a 24-meter-high gate tower on the south. This was the main gate, and one had to go through two more gates before coming to the Hall of Great Peace where the emperor of the Jurchen dynasty presided over major ceremonies. The place where he gave audiences to his ministers was called the Hall of Benevolent Rule, which had the Gate of Benevolent Rule in front of it and which was flanked by two side halls with high towers. The whole complex had 34 halls and 68 towers and pavilions. It was neatly laid out and full of color and splendor.

The buildings were tall, spacious and elegant. The gates on the four sides were named after the sun, the moon, and heaven and earth and were the terminals of broad roads lined with a double row of willows on each side over a distance of some 50 kilometers. In scale and dignity the city of Beijing, as Middle Capital of the Jurchen dynasty, surpassed its former self as Southern Capital of the Liao dynasty.

Along with the construction of Middle Capital and the palaces, emperors of the Jurchen dynasty built quite a number of imperial villas and gardens. The biggest of these was the Palace of Tranquility started under Emperor Shizong in 1179 on the basis of the Jade Flower Islet which had been built out of a swamp in the Liao dynasty. The palace was reconstructed and expanded under successive dynasties, and is known as Beihai (North Sea) Park today.

A lake was dug and a Jade Flower Islet created by soldiers, civilian laborers and artisans. Some people claim that the Jurchen emperors built the islet to counterbalance an imposing mountain in Mongolia which was considered a threat to their authority. This cannot be true because the palace was built at a time when nobody could possibly predict the rise of the Mongols. After the Jurchens put an end to Northern Song in 1127, they moved the rockeries in Bianliang, capital of Northern Song, to the Jade Flower Islet, built a hill on the islet, and erected a Hall of Pervasive Cold on top. The name of the hall is attributed to Emperor Xuanzong of the Tang dynasty. On the 15th of the eighth moon, as the story goes, the emperor visited a palace in the moon in his dream, where the crystal stairs made him feel as though he were walking in a mirror, and where he saw a board inscribed with the words:"The Land of Pervasive Cold and Pure Voidness." The Hall of Pervasive Cold on Jade Flower Islet looked like a fairyland created by nature itself. Emperor Zhangzong (r. 1213-23) of the Jurchen dynasty spent almost six months here every year before returning to his palace in the city in autumn.

The gardens in Beijing were initiated in the Jurchen dynasty, given a solid foundation by the Yuan, and expanded during the Ming before enjoying their heyday under the Qing. What was done by the Jurchens laid the framework for later development. In addition to the Palace of Tranquility, Middle Capital boasted a East Garden, a West Garden, a North Garden, and a South Garden. It was in the West Garden that the emperor reviewed his troops. The Jurchens, including their nobility, were good fighters known for their horsemanship and marksmanship. On the fifth day of the fifth moon the emperor would gather the princes and officials in a garden where they played polo and vied to shoot an arrow through a willow leaf. The emperor rewarded the winners and gave a banquet for all participants. Imperial villas were built in the northwestern suburbs — on today's Longevity Hill, Fragrant Hills, and Jade Spring Mountain. Emperor Zhangzong went fishing in spring at the site of today's State Guest House known as Fishing Terrace. The gardens enhanced the natural beauty of Middle Capital.

It was during the Jurchen dynasty that the "Eight Views of Yanjing" took shape. They were:

The Celestial Lake, which has become the Central-South Lake at the center of the city.

The Jade Flower Islet, which remains in the Beihai Park.

The Golden Terrace Shining in the Setting Sun, which has become Jintai Road (Golden Terrace Road) in the eastern section of the city.

Clouds over the Trees at the Northern City Gate, a site to be found on Xueyuannanlu in the northern suburbs of the city.

The Snow-clad Western Hills, which are known as Fragrant Hills today.

Stone tablet carved with characters meaning "The Moon over Reed Gully Bridge at Dawn" in the handwriting of Emperor Qianlong of the Qing dynasty

Reed Gully Bridge (Marco Polo Bridge)

The Rainbow Spring, referring to the spring flowing down Jade Spring Mountain which looks like a rainbow in the sun and which can still be seen at the foot of the same mountain.

The Moon over Reed Gully Bridge at Dawn, a view which can still be enjoyed by travellers at the same bridge.

The Greenery at the Pass of Recruited Laborers, which refers to the green woods at one of the passes of the Great Wall.

It took three years to complete the Reed Gully Bridge, otherwise known as Marco Polo Bridge, in 1192 under Emperor Zhangzong of the Jurchen dynasty. Being 266.5 meters long and 7.5 meters wide, the stone bridge has 11 arches. Renovated under the Yuan, Ming and Qing dynasties, it was the longest stone arch bridge in North China in those days and remains the oldest one in Beijing today.

The bridge appeared as one of the best for China and the world. It was an important undertaking for the Jurchen dynasty in every sense — political, economic and military. The Jurchen regime controlled a vast territory extending from areas beyond the Outer Hinggan Range in the north to the northern banks of the Huai River in the south. Like the Liao dynasty, it had five capitals. However, the Reed Gully River (now Yongding River) lying to the southwest of its Middle Capital presented a barrier to communication with its Southern Capital (present-day Kaifeng in Henan), and the bridge was built to lift this barrier. Economically the Middle Capital needed no less than a million piculs (50,000 tons) of food grain every year to feed its population, and grain transportation from the south would be speeded up if the bottleneck at the Reed Gully River ferries could be removed by a bridge, which became all the more necessary after the failure of a canal project linking the Middle Capital with Tongzhou. Strategically the Jurchen rulers found their main enemy in the regime of the Southern Song dynasty until the rise of the Mongols. To handle the heavy south-bound traffic, they decided to replace the original ferries, wooden bridge and pontoon with a large stone bridge.

The piers of the bridge were ingenuously designed. For each pier, the side facing upstream is pointed and is fitted with a triangular piece of iron which parts the flow and breaks up ice in winter, while the side facing downstream is dented so as to reduce the pressure of the flow inside the arches. The widest arch has a span of 13.42 meters, and the piers and arches are linked by iron bracings so that they can withstand flood water.

The bridge has on both sides a total of 140 balusters, each of which is decorated with lotus and pearl designs and has a marble lion on its square top. The balusters are linked by slabs of stone averaging 85 cm. in height and showing ornamental patterns on the inside. The lions on the bridge may be regarded as masterpieces of human imagination.

For centuries, people have been saying that it is impossible to count the lions on the bridge. Is this true?

The biggest pair is found at the eastern end of the bridge. Each 90 cm. high and 1.73 meters long, the two lions support the balusters with their powerful heads. The western end of the bridge is guarded by two stone elephants. The lions squatting on the balusters impress visitors with a variety of postures. One raises its head to gaze at the sky; another watches the traffic on the bridge; a third one listens to the flow underneath with pricked ears; and a fourth greets pedestrians with a courteous look. One of the lions seems to keep an eye on the water level, while some others simply neglect their duty and play hide-and-seek. A mother lion is fondling its cub. A dormant lion rests its head on one shoulder, and a couchant one is absorbed in thinking.

The naughty cubs, however, are not so easy to count. Measuring only a few centimeters, they have climbed onto the heads or backs of the big lions, or are playing in their embraces, or are sporting with their bells and ribbons. One of these cubs shows only part of its head, and another only its mouth.

A thorough count places the number at 485, including 198 cubs crawling on the adults. But one can usually count only 481 because four are squatting on the ornamental pylons, two at each end of the bridge. Proud and carefree, each of them gazes into the distance from the top of a towering column.

The whole bridge shows traditional Chinese architecture at its best. In his *Travels,* Marco Polo describes it as a beautiful stone bridge, a unique one and the best in the world at the time.

As stated above, China was split between two antagonistic regimes along the Huai River at the time. The Middle Capital of the Jurchen dynasty in the north was rivalled by Lin'an (present-day Hangzhou, Zhejiang Province), capital of the Southern Song dynasty, in the south. Ever since the Eastern Jin dynasty (317-420), the center of gravity in China's economy had been moving southward from the Yellow River basin to the Yangtze River basin. Located in a most fertile area between the lower reaches of the Yangtze River and of the Qiantangjiang River, Lin'an was a focus of economic growth and commercial prosperity. There were three business sections in the northern, central, and southern parts of the city. The thoroughfares and alleys were lined with shops, and business had become almost as important as government affairs. Nevertheless, the high city walls remained as defense works and a symbol of imperial authority.

The Middle Capital of the Jurchen dynasty was quite different from Lin'an. It was located on the northern tip of the North China Plain which was economically less developed than areas south of the Yangtze. In economic development the Jurchens had lagged behind the Han people, and they remained so in spite of their absorption of Han culture after their conquest of the Central Plains. Thus the Middle Capital was less developed than Lin'an in an economic sense. For the Jurchen dynasty, it served the triple purpose of being a site for offering sacrifices to gods and ancestors, a military stronghold, and an administrative center. The population was divided into 62 communities, 20 in the eastern section of the city and 42 in the western section. These communities were separated by walls fitted with gates. The two capitals were similar in their role as a site for sacrificial ceremonies and a military stronghold, but different in that commerce was far more important in Lin'an than in the Middle Capital. As Middle Capital for the Jurchen dynasty, the Beijing area had undoubtedly made much economic and social progress as compared

with the days when it served as Southern Capital for the Liao dynasty, but essentially it was the biggest feudal military fortress in North China in the second half of the 12th century.

However, the Middle Capital was the cultural center of North China. The Jurchens established here the Imperial College, the highest institution of learning under their regime, to give civil examinations. They devised a Jurchen script and a revised one, and conducted examinations in the Jurchen language for high academic honors. An astronomical observatory was set up in the city. Theatrical art also flourished in the Middle Capital, *Story of the Western Chamber Set to Tunes* by Dong Jieyuan was an outstanding work. It presents the love story of a young scholar, Zhang Gong, and the beautiful maiden Cui Yingying who dared to marry the man of her own choice against feudal convention. Drama in the Middle Capital, known as *za ju* (poetic drama set to music), gradually spread from the imperial palaces and the mansions of the nobility to the general public, paving the way for a major development under the Yuan dynasty.

As the Jurchen rulers were Buddhist devotees, they erected hundreds of temples and pagodas in the Middle Capital, leaving us a rich heritage of architectural art. One of the relics is known as the Pagoda of the Venerable Wansong. A high priest, Wansong was a respected guest in the imperial palace and exercised much political influence in the later period of the Jurchen dynasty. He was the teacher of Yelu Chucai (1190-1244), an outstanding scholar and politician of Qidan origin active during the reigns of Genghis Khan and Ogdai Khan in the early period of the Yuan dynasty. The remains of the Venerable Wansong were buried at the site of the pagoda which was built in his honor. The seven-story brick pagoda is an exquisite and delicate structure constructed in the style of concentrated eaves. It is located at the eastern end of the Zhuanta (Brick Pagoda) Alley in Beijing's Western District, which obviously acquired its name from the historical relic.

Located at Yungang Village in Beijing's Fengtai District, the Protect-the-Mound Pagoda is associated with folklore. Once it was believed that a dragon's cave could be found in a mound in the village, and a descendant of someone buried in the cave would

Marble lions on the Reed Gully Bridge

Illustration of a scene from the play *The Western Chamber*. On the right is Hongniang, Cui Yingying's maid, and on the left, Zhang Gong. Zhang is writing a love letter to Cui, which the maid promises to deliver.

Buddhism. The pagodas in China, however, took on the features of indigenous architecture. The building material used could be stones, bricks, pottery, wood, gold, silver, iron or glazed tiles. The shape may be square, round or multiangular. The number of stories may be seven, 11, 12, or 15. The style may be lamaistic, that of concentrated eaves, bouquets, towers, pavilions or that of vajrasana (Buddha's seat). The body can be solid or hollow, and the color white, yellow, grey or black. Historically the pagodas date from various dynasties. The first one to be built in Beijing was the Princess Jinxian Pagoda in the Dwelling-in-the-Clouds Temple, which remains to this day. Many more were erected under the Liao and Jurchen dynasties, but few of them exist today. Most of them have been destroyed during

Protect-the-Mound Pagoda

become a most prominent figure, perhaps an emperor. The rich families kept looking for the cave, but couldn't locate it. When rumor had it that the mound was going to collapse, they all contributed money to build a pagoda on it in the hope of protecting it by some supernatural power. With elaborate designs on its upper part, the pagoda looks like a huge bouquet. Thus it is also known as Flower Pagoda. The 13-storied, octagonal pagoda is three meters long on each side and 18 meters in height. In the upper part are base brackets carved out of bricks with patterns of potted flowers at the points of support. Short eaves project from the pagoda body, on which are *sumerus* or carved platforms supporting seven niches, one on top of the other. These structures combine into a huge cone-shaped bouquet.

Buddhist images are carved on the pagoda. Some raise one hand, others two hands, and still others put their palms together. Arrayed in good order, they all come to life. Pearls are placed on top of the pagoda, a rare relic from the Jurchen period.

The Silver Hill Pagodas are located at the southern foot of Silver Hill of Haizi Village in Beijing's suburban Changping County. They are one of the Eight Views of Changping. It is said that in the Liao and Jurchen periods there were 72 Buddhist monasteries and nunneries on the Silver Hill and at the hillsides. The largest monastery was Longevity Temple, also known as Splendor of Dharma Temple, which was built in 1125, the third year of the Tianhui reign of the Jurchen dynasty. The pagodas on the hill are stupas built in memory of the high priests of the monastery. Two of the seven existing pagodas date from the Yuan dynasty, the five others from the Jurchen dynasty. All of them are brick pagodas. The ones from the Jurchen period are in the style of concentrated eaves, showing delicate bas-reliefs and vigorous patterns.

Pagodas and similar structures are an important form of human civilization. Among the best-known ones are the Egyptian pyramids, Burma's gold-spired Shwe Dagon in Rangoon and *Tour Eiffel* of France. No such structures existed in China until the stupa was introduced into the country from India along with the teachings of

Niches for Buddhist statues on the Protect-the-Mound Pagoda

Pagoda in honor of Princess Jinxian. The ninth daughter of Emperor Ruizong of the Tang dynasty, Princess Jinxian helped in the carving of Buddhist scriptures in Monk Jingwan's handwriting by obtaining the emperor's permission and by contributing money to the project.

◁ Silver Hill Pagodas

natural or human disasters. But while the invaders of Beijing committed arson against palaces and civilian houses, they were more or less afraid to destroy Buddhist structures. The solidity of the brick pagodas built by the Jurchens is another reason why they remain to this day. In contrast, the magnificent palaces in the Middle Capital were crushed under the iron heels of the Mongol troops.

The city came under Mongol attacks in January 1212. Two years later Genghis Khan led his cavalry units right to the city walls. Emperor Xuanzong of the Jurchen regime pursuaded the Mongol troops to withdraw by giving them large quantities of gold and silver in addition to men and women and horses. The same year he moved the capital to Bianliang, putting an end to Beijing's 62-year history as capital of the Jurchen dynasty. The next year the city fell into Mongolian hands. Fan Chengda, an envoy of the Southern Song regime, had been impressed by the grandeur of the palaces in the Middle Capital. In a poem he compared them to the colossal Epang Palace of the ancient Qin dynasty which was reduced to a cinder by Xiang Yu, the Hegemonic King of Western Chu. And sure enough, the palaces in the Middle Capital were burnt down by the Mongolian cavalry. The royal city, once powerful and prosperous, lay in ruins, lonely and desolate.

Chapter V
CAMBALUC OF THE MONGOL EMPIRE

The Great Capital of Kublai Khan

A world figure emerged on the Mongolian grasslands early in the 13th century. Initially known as Temujin, he was taken by his father at the age of nine to a fraternal tribe to find a fiancee. Unfortunately his father was poisoned on the way back. His mother raised him and the other children by gathering berries and edible wild herbs. The boy turned out to be an excellent rider, archer and fighter. But once he was taken prisoner by members of an enemy tribe, who imposed a cangue on him and paraded him before the public. Eventually he managed to escape at night.

As a young man Temujin united various tribes, organized an army, and built up his strength through military expeditions. In 1206 he was elected Great Khan for the whole of Mongolia at a conference of noblemen held on the bank of the Onon River. His reign title,

Genghis Khan, meant a khan as large as an ocean. By now he had gained control of a vast territory extending from the Hinggan Ranges in the east to the Altai mountains in the west and bordering on the Jurchen empire in the south.

An envoy arrived from the court of the Jurchen dynasty to proclaim a decree of the new emperor to the Mongols. When he asked Genghis Khan to kneel before the imperial decree, the Mongol ruler said, "What's the point of kneeling before a good-for-nothing emperor?" By this statement he announced his split with the Jurchen regime. He launched an expedition against it and laid siege to its Middle Capital in 1214. But he withdrew his troops after the Jurchen emperor, Xuanzong, sued for peace and gave him a princess, who became his fourth wife. The next year Mongol troops sacked the Middle Capital, carried away large quantities of valuables and presented them to Genghis Khan. The celebrated Mongol ruler died of illness at the age of 66 while conducting another expedition in 1227. He was succeeded by Ogdai, Guyuk, Mangu and, finally, Kublai, who was inaugurated as Great Khan at Kaiping (northwest of modern Duolun in Inner Mongolia) in 1260.

In 1264 Kublai Khan proclaimed Yanjing the Middle Capital or the second capital of his Khanate. In 1271 he named his empire "the Great Yuan," basing on the term "qian yuan" in the Confucian classic, the *Book of Changes*, which means the male origin of the universe as distinguished from "kun yuan," the female origin of the universe. The adoption of such a cosmopolitan term explained his concept of the empire as a continuation of the feudal dynasties based in the Central Plains and not as the state of a single ethnic group, the Mongols. The next year his trusted Han Chinese advisor, Liu Bingzhong, recommended changing Middle Capital to Dadu (Great Capital) because the city "occupies a commanding position where a tiger crouches and a dragon curls, is contiguous to the Great Desert in the north, and facilitates control over the Yangtze and Huai river basins in the south." Kublai Khan adopted the proposal, and moved his court from Kaiping, the summer capital of the migratory Mongol rulers, to the newly designated Dadu.

Thus Beijing became the political center of the multi-national empire of the Yuan dynasty, and remained the national capital under the Ming and Qing dynasties. Its construction as Dadu of the Yuan had a far-reaching significance.

The Mongols called the city *cambaluc*, meaning "the city of the Khan." With its neat and extensive layout, magnificent buildings, and thriving economy, it was the largest city of the world and, for a time, politically the most important.

Portrait of Genghis Khan

The Emperor and His Entourage on a Trip (painting of the Yuan dynasty)

Some Features of Dadu

As the Great Capital of the Yuan dynasty, Beijing became the political center of the most powerful empire of the world. While conquering the whole of China, the Mongol army conducted expeditions against Japan in the east and reached Java in the south, occupied Persia in the southwest, and invaded Poland in the west via the neighborhood of Moscow.

As the largest capital city of the world, Dadu was built to the northeast of the Middle Capital of the Jurchens, at a site near the Jade Flower Islet in today's Beihai Park. This was because the former Middle Capital, reduced to ruins in war, could hardly be restored. Hydrologically it was necessary to choose a site far removed from the Yongding River, which often caused floods, and near the Gaoliang River system which could provide the capital with an abundant water supply. The Jade Flower Islet and the surrounding lake offered a beautiful environment for the palaces. And of course the Mongol rulers wanted to build a capital which would be bigger and more impressive than that of the previous dynasty.

It took some 20 years to complete the building of Dadu, from 1264 when the Jade Flower Islet was rebuilt to 1285 when residents of the old city moved into the new.

Dadu had a greater city, an imperial city, and a palace complex. The greater city, also called the outer city, faced the south, was rectangular in shape, and had a periphery of 28.6 kilometers. Its southern walls were located to the south of the present East and West Chang'an Boulevard of Beijing. Its northern walls were near Xiaoguan beyond today's Deshengmen (site of the former Gate of Victory) and Andingmen (site of the former Gate of Stability), where one can still see the ruins, and its east and west walls roughly coincided with the bases of the city walls in modern times. All the walls were built with rammed earth and were reinforced with vertical pillars and horizontal bars of wood. The ratio between the width of the base, the height, and the width of the top was 3:2:1. A sewage system was installed on top of the walls for the drainage of water. The walls were not inlaid with bricks or stones, but covered with reed mats to resist wind and rain. There were 11 city gates and citadels outside

Remains of a wall of Dadu (Great Capital) of the Yuan dynasty

66

Plan of Dadu (Great Capital) of the Yuan Dynasty

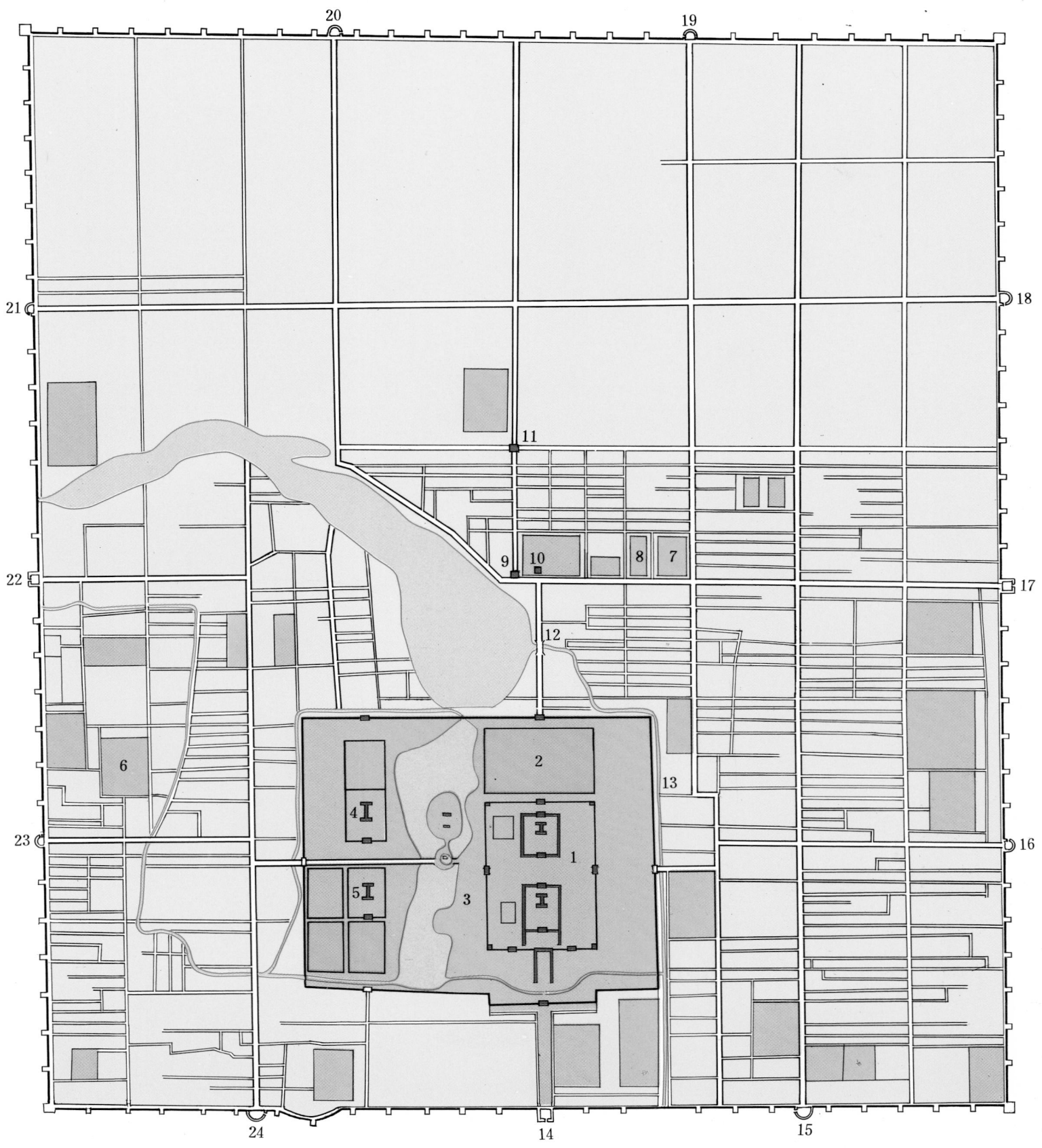

1. Palace complex	9. Drum Tower	17. Gate for Upholding Benevolence
2. Imperial Garden	10. Central Tower	18. Gate of Splendor
3. Imperial City	11. Bell Tower	19. Gate of Peace and Integrity
4. Palace of the Rising Monarch	12. Bridge of Peace	20. Gate of High Virtue
5. Palace of Prosperity	13. Tonghui River	21. Gate of Respect and Purity
6. Altar of Land and Grain	14. Beautiful Main Gate	22. Gate of Harmony and Righteousness
7. Confucian Temple	15. Gate of Culture	23. Gate of Just Rule
8. Imperial College	16. Gate of Homogeneous Civilization	

Site of a citadel outside Dadu's Gate of Harmony and Righteousness

Stone tablet inscribed with four characters meaning "Trees in Mist at the Ancient City of Jizhou" in the calligraphy of Emperor Qianlong of the Qing dynasty. Situated northwest of the former Gate of Victory, the site is one of the "Eight Views of Yanjing (now Beijing)." There used to be many trees and buildings shrouded in mist in this area, but they have disappeared. The remains shown in the picture date back to the Liao and Yuan dynasties.

the gates for defense purposes. The barbican entrance to the Gate of Harmony and Righteousness of Dadu was discovered in 1969 when workers were pulling down the Arrow Tower (embrasured tower) of the Straight West Gate of the Inner City of the Ming-Qing period. An inscription on the wall of the covered passage of the barbican entrance tells us that the entrance was built in 1358, the 18th year of the Zhizheng reign. The remaining gate of the entrance is 22 meters high and the covered passage is 9.92 meters long. Lined with bricks, the gate of the barbican entrance looks magnificent, giving a general idea of the 11 gates of the Yuan capital. A big watchtower stood on each of the four corners of the city which was surrounded by a moat of considerable depth and breadth.

Located in the central-south part of the greater city, the imperial city had a periphery of nearly 10 kilometers. The main purpose in marking out an imperial city was to confine the palace complex, the Celestial Lake, the Palace of the Rising Monarch, and the Palace of Prosperity within another wall. The central gate on the southern side of the imperial city led to its counterpart for the greater city via a square which had a "Thousand-Step Corridor" on either side. The premises of important government offices were located in this area. A stream ran through the central-south gate of the imperial city. It was spanned by a stone bridge, and the towering willow trees planted on the banks added dignity to the environment.

The palace complex was situated in the southern part of the imperial city. It was slanted toward the east instead of being centrally located because it was constructed by the side of the Celestial Lake to its west. Rectangular in shape, it had a periphery of over four kilometers. There were four gates, one on each side. The southern gate, called the Gate for the Worship of Heaven, measured 51 meters from east to west, 16 meters in depth, and 26 meters in height, and had a tower above it. Two of the buildings making up the palace complex were the most important — the Welcome-to-Spring Tower in the north and the Hall of Great Light in the south.

A gate led to the Hall of Great Light which was flanked by a bell tower on the left and a drum tower on the right. This was the place where the emperor was enthroned and where he presided over New Year celebrations, received greetings on his birthday, and held sessions with his ministers. The imposing hall measured 61.44 meters from east to west, 36.85 meters from north to south, and 27.64 meters in height. By the order of Kublai Khan, grass from Mongolia was planted along the red stairs of the terraces in front of the hall to remind the royal descendants of the grasslands where their ancestors had come from. The emperor's seat in the hall was decorated with patterns of dragons and clouds and with the Seven Valuables listed in Buddhist scriptures, including gold and silver. A parallel seat was provided for the empress in the Mongolian tradition. As a unique practice unknown to any other feudal dynasty in China, the Yuan emperor and his empress jointly presided over court sessions with top officials.

Another innovation in the Hall of Great Light was a lamp which served as a timepiece. In former times the Chinese divided the day into 12 two-hour periods instead of 24 hours and named each period after one of the 12 Earthly Branches, which again were represented by 12 different animals. Twelve wooden puppets were installed in the lamp and were driven by a mechanism motivated by water power. At the first quater of each time period, a wooden puppet would appear from a door to report the time to the emperor, holding a particular animal in its arms. The lamp was 5.22 meters high, divided into four decks sustained by gold brackets, and decorated with the Seven Valuables and pearls. It was designed and built by Guo Shoujing (1231-1316), the great astronomer, water conservancy expert and inventor of the Yuan dynasty.

The Welcome-to-Spring Tower was even higher than the Hall of Great Light, measuring 30.72 meters from tip to base, and had three layers of eaves. There were bedchambers in the rear sections of both buildings. The imperial consorts lived in the Palace of Eternal Spring and the Palace of Delightful Coolness. It is said that Genghis Khan had 500 wives and concubines, and he placed them in four palaces, each under the charge of one of his wives. The system was inherited by Kublai Khan, who organized his harems by the same method.

Lotus flowers grew all over Celestial Lake to the southwest of the palaces. Located centrally between the east and west banks of the lake was a hall which is known as Round City today. In a pavilion in the elevated citadel one finds the oldest and largest jade article existing in China today — a 3,500-kilogram jade wine-container made in early Yuan dynasty. In the north was the Ten-Thousand-Year Hill, or Longevity Hill, which has reverted to its old name of Jade Flower Islet. Shaded by pines and Chinese junipers, the artificial hill and its grotesque rocks looked, as they look today, like a creation of nature. In the Yuan period water was siphoned to the top of the hill from where it flowed into a square pond through a Stone Dragon Mouth. An undercurrent was channelled to the Hall of Benevolence and Wisdom, spurted through the mouth of a coiled stone dragon, and directed into Celestial Lake in an east and a west subcurrent. Emperor Shundi, the last sovereign of the Yuan dynasty, once sailed on the lake with his concubines in a dragon boat, which was 36 meters long and six meters high. As the artificial dragon plied the waters, its head, eyes, mouth, claws and tail all moved.

The Palace of Prosperity and the Palace of the Rising Monarch were both built to the west of Celestial Lake. The former was positioned in the south and surrounded by a brick wall with six gates. Its main structure was the Bright Sky Hall which had stately eaves, engraved ceilings, carved windows and vermilion balustrades. The enclosed rear section provided accommodation for the empress dowager, the crown prince, and other members of the royal family. The Palace of the Rising Monarch was located in the north right in front of the Longevity Hill. It was also surrounded by a brick wall with six gates. The main structure was the Hall of the Rising Monarch. At its back was the Hall of Perpetual Brilliance, a square building with a cross ridge, an eastern hall balanced with a western one, a covered veranda in front and a round pavilion in the rear. The palace was the emperor's harem. During the reign of Emperor Shundi a beautiful maiden from Korea won imperial favor and gave birth to a boy. Both mother and son lived in the palace.

The whole city was as neatly laid out as a chessboard. It had several thoroughfares running from east to west and from north to south. The thoroughfares were 24 meters wide, and the other streets 12 meters. The former were provided with sewers and ditches for the drainage of water, and were paved with stone slabs. Archaeological excavations revealed the name of a stonemason inscribed on one of the stone slabs. It gives the name, Liu San, as well as the day and month in 1328, the first year of the Zhihe reign, presumably the date on which the sewers were built. The residents were placed in 50 communities, each of which had a gate bearing the name of the community.

The design for Dadu was a classical one. We have quoted earlier a passage from the chapter "The Artisans' Trades" in the *Rites of Zhou* which defines the concept of a capital city as a square. The city walls of Dadu were almost equal in length. The palaces were in the southern section, while the business area was in the north. The Ancestral Temple of the royal family was east of the palaces, and the Altar of Land and Grain was to the west. As stipulated in the same Confucian classic, there were nine thoroughfares, each wide enough for nine chariots to run abreast. But Dadu was the first capital city that had an axis running from the central southern gate of the outer city to its counterparts for the imperial city and the palace complex and right up to a centrally positioned pavilion in the Temple of Universal Tranquility in the north.

Dadu was perhaps the most prosperous and impressive city of the world at the time. Marco Polo said in his *Travels* that its beauty and clever layout was beyond description.

Jade wine-container

Flourishing Commerce

As a thriving commercial center, Dadu had a dense population and over 30 markets. In line with the ancient principle of placing the business area behind the palaces, the markets were set up around the drum and bell towers, the center of the city north of the palace complex. The docks of Dadu, where freight boats from South China dropped anchor, were located at Waterpool west of the drum and bell towers. Here one would find many restaurants and bars where sing-song girls offered entertainment to customers. These were the haunts of wealthy merchants and members of the nobility. Everybody seemed to be in business — officials, army officers and civilians. The drum tower and bell tower area boasted a variety of markets specializing in silks and satins, fur hats, pearls, poultry, ironware, rice and flour or coral. At a place called Sheep Horn Market, also in the western part of the city, one could buy sheep, horses, oxen, camels, and mules and hinnies.

Commercial prosperity in Dadu was promoted by the efficient transportation of goods along the Great Canal, maritime navigation, and a courier service. The Great Canal opened under Emperor Yangdi of the Sui dynasty had become clogged during the long period of confrontation between the Song and Jurchen dynasties. And Luoyang, the hub of the canal network under the Sui dynasty, no longer suited the needs of the Yuan rulers based in Beijing. Thus they opened two channels in Shandong to shorten the course of the canal by more than 400 kilometers and linked it directly with Dadu by digging another channel from the city to Tongzhou. This made it possible to ship grain and other goods to the capital all the way from Hangzhou, the southern terminus of the canal, resulting in much closer economic ties between North and South China and accelerating commercial growth in Dadu. The freight service along the canal was supplemented by one along the coast. The cargo ships sailed from Liujia harbor at the mouth of the Yangtze River and were unloaded at Zhigu, prototype of the modern port of Tianjin. The government once controlled a merchant marine of over 900 boats, which sailed along various navigation lines and brought as much as 3,300,000 piculs (165,000 tons) of grain and large quantities of other goods from South China to the capital every year. The courier service was conducted by both land and sea, and the means of transport included sledges pulled by dogs in Northeast China. Under the Yuan dynasty there was a network of over 1,400 courier posts across the country, which primarily served political and military needs. But the official

messengers also brought back to the capital a great variety of goods to add to its prosperity.

Dadu was also a hub of international trade. The four Mongol khanates stretching over Asia and Europe became ever more independent of one another, but they always served as a medium of contact between merchants of the East and the West and promoted the interflow of goods.

Dadu was the center of trade by land. Merchants travelled westward along three routes. First, they could follow the route along the northern banks of the Aral Sea and the Caspian Sea, cross the Kipchak steppe, and reach the banks of the Volga, from where they could go to the East European countries, to Constantinople via the Crimean peninsula and the Black Sea, or to Asia Minor via Caucasus. Second, they could also reach Asia Minor by way of Samarkand and Bukhara in today's Soviet Union and via Iran. As a third alternative they could go to Hetian in present-day Xinjiang, cross the Pamirs, and arrive in Persia via Afghanistan. Dadu was visited by merchants from many countries, including those from Persia and the Arab peninsula.

A sea route led from Shanghai or Hangzhou to Japan. From Quanzhou, Guangzhou, and other ports along the southern coast merchants could sail to Java and Sumatra via the South China Sea, or to India, Ceylon, the Arab peninsula, and East Africa. They imported goods like lilac, round cardamon, spices, diamonds, pearls, hauksbill turtle, rhinoceros horns, elephant tusks, coral and medicine, which were unloaded at Guangzhou, Hangzhou, Shanghai, and other ports and then sent to Dadu by courier service, boats on the Great Canal, or boats plying the coastal waters.

Referring to the commercial boom in Dadu, a historian wrote with some poetic license: "Here you can see the rare products from the mountains and seas, the choice goods made in heaven or on earth, those created by human or supernatural beings, and everything loved by gods or monsters." The docks along the canal were crowded with freight boats from South China, and some of the suburban districts were inhabited by whole communities of business people from other parts of the country or from foreign lands. Marco Polo stated in his *Travels* that the Cambaluc population included a large percentage of Chinese and foreign merchants who had turned the city into a huge bazaar. At least a thousand cartloads of silk fabrics were sent into the city everyday, he said, and the abundance of goods was to be seen in no other city in China or abroad. And no other city of the world could compare with Dadu in the quantity of imported goods, particularly the valuables, he declared.

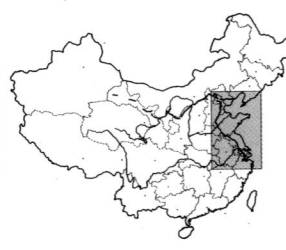

Sketch Map of Freight Service Routes Along the Great Canal and the Sea Coast in the Yuan dynasty

Coin of the Yuan dynasty

Science, Technology and Culture

Dadu was also the cultural center of the Yuan empire. At the time, China was quite advanced in science and technology by world standard. Guo Shoujing, the scientist mentioned earlier, was a great astronomer and calendar-maker. Both astronomy and calendar-making required the aid of an observatory. The first observatory in Beijing was established under the Jurchen dynasty. Another one was set up under the Yuan dynasty in 1279, and a third one under the Ming and Qing dynasties. The observatory we see today was built under the Ming, but the instruments were made under the Qing.

Guo Shoujing (1231-1316), an outstanding scientist, improved on the astronomical instruments developed by his predecessors and built an "abridged armilla" for measuring equatorial and horizontal coordinates. He also built a colossal gnomon for measuring the shadow of the sun. One ancient record describes an early gnomon:

> On the day of summer solstice an eight-feet-high* pole is erected above a one-and-half feet template to measure the shadow of the sun, which turns out to be the same length as the template. This is how people find the center of the earth.

The gnomon was also called a "sky-measuring scale." During the Yuan dynasty the shadow template was usually a stone one, while the vertical indicator or scale could be stone or bronze. According to historical records, the giant gnomon built in Dadu consisted of a bronze vertical scale which was 50 feet high, 2.4 feet wide, and 1.2 feet thick, rising 36 feet above the template. The upper part of the scale was decorated with two coiling dragons half-attached to the column, which supported a cross-bar six feet in length and 0.3 feet in thickness. The center of the bar was four feet above the tip of the scale and 40 feet above the stone template, which was 128 feet long, 4.5 feet wide, and 1.4 feet thick, and was graduated along the center and the two sides of the surface. The whole structure was mounted on a 2.6-feet-high base. This was the biggest gnomon in China prior to the advent of modern times.

On the basis of extensive astronomical observations, a highly accurate *Time-Telling Calendar* was compiled under Guo Shoujing's direction, according to which 365.2425 days constituted a tropical year, only 26 seconds more than its true duration. The *Time-Telling Calendar* was just as accurate as the Gregorian Calendar in use today, but it was adopted some 300 years before the latter.

Guo Shoujing also located over 1,000 stars, increasing the number of recorded stars from 1,464 to 2,500, and compiled a new star catalog.

Jamal al-Din, an astronomer from Persia, was credited with the invention of seven astronomical instruments, including an early terrestrial globe. The "Annals of Astronomy" in the *History of the Yuan Dynasty* contains the following description:

> The globe is made of wood. Seven-tenths of the surface are painted green to represent water, and three-tenths colored white to show the land area. Contours are marked out to indicate rivers and lakes. The entire globe is divided into small squares for the measurement of width and length.

The passage shows that Jamal al-Din's terrestrial globe, the first recorded in Chinese history, had a grid which gave people an idea of longitudes and latitudes.

As for clepsydras, an inventive mind was found in the royal family of the Yuan dynasty. The biography of Emperor Shundi (r. 1333-68) in the *History of the Yuan Dynasty* refers to a "time-telling palace drip-vessel" built by him, last ruler of the Mongol dynasty. It says that the water-driven clock measured "six to seven feet in height and half as much in width" and that "water was circulated through a number of jars placed in a wooden box." The upper part of the box was occupied by the Temple of the Three Sacred Beings of the Western Heavens. The middle part was fitted with jade maidens who held graduated time scales and who rose with the water at designated times. Two armored gods stood on the left and right, one holding an ordinary bell and the other, a long-handled one. When they struck the bells on schedule at night, lions and phoenixes danced to the rhythm. The sun palace and moon palace on the west and east sides of the box were each guarded by six fairies, who sailed in pairs across the Heavenly Bridge and through the Temple of the Three Sacred Beings at noon and midnight before returning to their normal positions. The originality of the water-driven timepiece showed the mechanical genius of its inventor, who nevertheless was a poor sovereign indulging in sensuous pleasures. His corrupt regime was finally

---

* The "feet" used in this context refers to the Chinese *chi*, each of which is 1.0936 English feet.

subverted by peasant insurgents, and he had to flee to the Gobi Desert.

An Imperial College devoted to the study of the Confucian doctrine was established under the Yuan dynasty as the highest institution of learning in the country. The premises, built in 1306, are to be found on Chengxian Street within Beijing's Andingmen (site of the former Gate of Stability). The advanced students enrolled at the college belonged to many ethnic groups — Mongolian, Hui (Moslem), Han, Jurchen, etc., and quite a few came from Korea, Siam (Thailand), Annam (Vietnam) and Japan. The buildings we see today have been reconstructed under the Ming and Qing dynasties.

The Confucian Temple, which honors the memory of the great ancient philosopher and educator, is located to the east of the Imperial College. The Mongol troops under Genghis Khan committed looting and arson as they swept across China proper. Yelu Chucai, however, advised the khans to follow the teachings of Confucianism and give official posts to Confucian scholars. Confucianism eventually acquired the status of state learning under the Mongol rulers. The Confucian Temple was completed in 1302 under the Yuan dynasty and renovated and expanded under the Ming and Qing dynasties. The temple consists of three courtyards, and the three gates on the central axis all have names which pay tribute to Confucius as the great master who summarized the best in ancient Chinese learning. There are stone balustrades on the four sides of the main hall in which visitors can see the musical instruments and other articles used during ceremonies for offering sacrifices to Confucius. A temple built within the Confucian Temple, located behind the main hall, is dedicated to the ancestors of Confucius, in which tablets inscribed with the names of five generations of his ancestors are placed on the altar. Towering ancient pines create an atmosphere of dignity and solemnity in the main courtyard where some highly valuable relics are preserved — 198 steles carved with the names of 51,624 scholars who passed the metropolitan examination under the Yuan, Ming and Qing dynasties, complete with the names of their native towns and their places in the competitions.

While considering themselves Confucianists, the emperors of the Yuan dynasty also assigned an important place to Taoism.

Taoism is a religion native to China. The main classic of Taoism, *Dao De Jing*, sometimes translated as *The Way and Its Power*, is attributed to Lao Tse who is known under the surname of Li. As the emperors of the Tang dynasty had the same surname, one of them, Emperor Gaozong, identified Lao Tse as the ancestor of the royal family, gave him the posthumous title of "Supreme Emperor of the Profound Heavens," and issued an order for the construction of a Taoist temple in every prefecture and county. Emperor Huizong of the Song dynasty gave much impetus to the growth of Taoism by calling himself an emperor who was concurrently the "Supreme Master of the Taoist Religion." Meanwhile, China's traditional Confucianism and Buddhism introduced from India continued to prevail. Under these circumstances, Wang Chongyang (1113-1170) of the Jurchen dynasty founded the Quan Zhen Dao (Comprehensive True Religion) which incorporated some elements of Confucianism and Buddhism into Taoism and which became an important Taoist sect. Wang's disciple, Qiu Chuji (1148-1227), known as the Immortal Man of Eternal Spring, practised Taoist self-cultivation by living in a cave and going around as a mendicant in a straw rain cape. In 1221 Genghis Khan received him in his camp by the side of Amu River. They discussed Taoist teachings for three days, during which the Mongol conquerer asked the friar about the secret of achieving immortality. Resenting the murder, looting and arson committed by Mongol troops, Qiu Chuji presented his view on sound government and healthy life by saying that, to achieve peace and order in the country, one must revere heaven and love the people, and to attain immortality, one must rid oneself of unworthy desires. Convinced, Genghis Khan gave him the title of an "Immortal" and put him in charge of Taoist undertakings across the country. Two years later the Khan made him head of the Palace of the Supreme Being, known today as White Cloud Taoist Temple outside Xibianmen (the site of the former West Informal Gate) in the western section of Beijing.

The White Cloud Taoist Temple was built under the Tang dynasty as the Everlasting Temple and was changed to Palace of the Supreme Being under the Jurchen dynasty. Then it was changed to Palace of Eternal Spring after Genghis Khan placed it in the hands of Qiu Chuji who was known as the Immortal Man of Eternal Spring. After Qiu's death his remains were buried here, and the temple was renamed White Cloud Temple. His birthday, the 19th of the first moon on the lunar calendar, was celebrated as a Taoist festival, during which Taoist followers came to the temple to offer sacrifices to the deceased Immortal Man and see if they could meet some living ones. Dressed in fancy robes, they arrived in an endless stream of

Wooden archway at the White Cloud Taoist Temple. Renovated in the Qing dynasty, the temple is a famous structure of the Comprehensive True Religion, located outside the West Informal Gate which no longer exists.

Inside the Hall of the Jade Emperor in the White Cloud Taoist Temple. The Jade Emperor, the supreme god in Taoism, is the counterpart of the emperor in the temporal world.

Portrait of Qiu Chuji, the Immortal Man of Eternal Spring

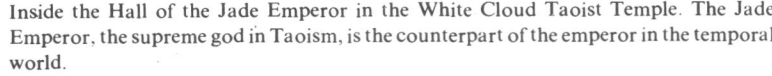

Accepting a Mission at the Foot of the Snow Mountains, a painting of Qiu Chuji and his 18 disciples accepting a sacred mission from Genghis Khan, who summons them to his tent on the banks of the Amu River at the foot of the Snow Mountains and instructs them to visit regions west of China

decorated carts and horses, held archery contests, sang to the accompaniment of flutes and percussion instruments, and didn't disperse till after sunset.

As the best-known Taoist site in Beijing's history, the White Cloud Temple has been renovated and expanded over the centuries. It has several square courtyards with buildings on all sides, and the main halls are located along the central axis. The gate is guarded by stone lions and decorated with a wooden arch. The halls, arranged in an ascending order, include the Hall of Divine Inspiration; the Hall of the Jade Emperor, the supreme god of Taoism; the Hall of Seven Immortals, which honors Wang Chongyang, founder of the Comprehensive True Religion, and his six disciples; the Hall of Master Qiu, an obvious reference to Qiu Chuji; a two-story hall dedicated to the Four Heavenly Emperors; and finally, the Tower of the Taoist Trinity — the God of Primeval Being, the God of Sentient Being, and the God of the Way, who are considered superior to the Four Heavenly Emperors. The Taoist library located by the side of the Tower of the Taoist Trinity was built in 1445 under the Ming dynasty. The *Taoist Tripitaka* kept in the library consists of 5,305 *juan* (thread-bound volumes) grouped in 480 *han* (cloth-covered boxes with open ends), and this is the earliest collection of Taoist scriptures found anywhere to this day. Like Buddhism, Taoism is characterized by pantheism and adherence to a variety of sutras, whereas in both Christianity and Islam there is a single God and only one sacred book.

The emperors of the Yuan dynasty were at once Taoist and Buddhist devotees. Temples were built by emperors and empresses generation after generation and by members of the aristocracy and bureaucracy. Every emperor started his reign by building a new temple. Thus the temples in Dadu surpassed those of the previous dynasties in number, scale and magnificence. The Yuan emperors also bestowed the title of "Teacher of the Nation" on high priests of the Buddhist faith and granted them jade seals. For generations, the Mongols had no written script, and the troops of Genghis Khan had to keep records by tying knots and carving wood marks. Under Kublai Khan a written script was created on the basis of the Tibetan script by Phatspa, a high priest. He was the fifth-generation master of the Shajia sect of Lamaist Buddhism. In 1253 Kublai Khan, impressed by his reputation, summoned him to court and accepted the Buddhist Commandments. In 1260 Kublai Khan granted him the title of "Teacher of the Nation" and a jade seal. In 1269 Phatspa presented his new Mongolian script to the emperor, which was adopted for use throughout the nation. The next year he received the titles of "Imperial Teacher" and "Great Venerable Lamaist." Buddhists received much favor from the court. Phatspa was worshipped by the emperor, the empress, the imperial consorts, and the princes and princesses, all of whom were ordained by him. The Buddhist priesthood enjoyed enormous privileges, so much so that whoever beat a priest would see his hands cut off and whoever cursed him would lose his tongue. Some of the priests became so truculent that they beat up court ladies and stopped at no evil.

Temples in Dadu had magnificent buildings and a good number of pagodas. Each had a large number of monks, and worshippers kept the incense burning day and night. The foremost one was the Temple of Imperial Peace and Longevity. As part of his plan for the construction of the imperial capital, Kublai Khan had an imposing White Dagoba built inside today's Fuchengmen (site of the former Gate of Great Tranquility) and, for that purpose, brought over the architect Arnico from Nepal, who introduced into China the shape and style of Nepalese dagobas. It took eight years to complete the White Dagoba, around which the Temple of Imperial Peace and Longevity, modelled on the imperial palace, was built in another 10

Statue of Avalokitesvara (the Goddess of Mercy) with a thousand hands and a thousand eyes in the Temple of Divine Response

years. The temple served as the site for rehearsing the emperor's coronation and New Year reception. The temple was burnt down toward the end of the Yuan dynasty, but the dagoba survived. Reconstructed under the Ming dynasty, it acquired its present name of Temple of Divine Response.

The White Dagoba in the Temple of Divine Response is a brick and stone structure in the Lamaist style. The dagoba is called the White Dagoba because of its color. Rising to a height of 50.9 meters, it is composed of three parts — the base, the body and the top. The base is nine meters high and has an area of over 800 square meters. It consists of three *sumerus* (carved square platforms) one upon the other, all of which have folding corners. On top of the base are 24 lotus leaves forming a Buddha's seat. On the seat are five tapering bands serving as a transition from the square base to the circular body, which takes the shape of an inverted almsbowl, measures 18.4 meters in diameter, and is reinforced with seven iron hoops. A small *sumeru* above the circular body supports a conical structure provided with 13 iron rings in an ascending order. On top of the cone is an umbrella-like bronze disc, 9.7 meters in diameter, which has a thick wooden base and a bronze-tile cover. Thirty-six openwork strings of bronze, each two meters long and fitted with a small bell at the end, hang from the rim of the bronze disc. A gilded bronze top, also in the form of a dagoba, is mounted on the bronze disc. At the very top are eight iron chains which hold the bronze strings in position.

Construction of the White Dagoba added to the beauty of the Yuan capital and enhanced its dignity. Many important relics are enshrined here, but one of them was not discovered until 1978, when maintenance workers found, on top of the dagoba, a Pure-Gold Sarira Buddha of Longevity. The Buddha, inlaid with 44 precious red stones, holds in his hands a shining piece of sarira, one of the most valuable relics found in recent years.

The Cloud Terrace at the Pass of Recruited Laborers is another Yuan relic related to Buddhism. It was located along the passageway between Dadu and Shangdu (Upper Capital) in present-day Inner Mongolia. Emperors of the Yuan dynasty spent half of every year, from the fourth to the ninth moon, in Shangdu, making it their summer capital, and handled military and political affairs from there. Writing about the frequent trips made by the emperors and their messengers through the Pass of Recruited Laborers, a Yuan dynasty priest said in a poem that even the birds flying over there could recognize the emperor and his officials. Pagodas were erected here by imperial order in the hope that Buddha would ensure the safety of travellers along the precipitous path. The Cloud Terrace was built in 1345 along with three stone pagodas overlooking the archway through which chariots, horses and pedestrians would pass. The elephants, lions, dragon gods, and birds with gold wings in bas-relief decorating the border of the arch come to life, and so do the images of

White Dagoba at the Temple of Divine Response. A Lamaist structure located inside the former Gate of Great Tranquility, it was designed and built with the help of a Nepalese architect in 1271, the eighth year of the Zhiyuan reign of the Yuan dynasty.

Statues in bas-relief decorating the border of the arch of the Cloud Terrace at the Pass of Recruited Laborers

Cloud Terrace at the Pass of Recruited Laborers

Statues in bas-relief on the inside wall of the arch of the Cloud Terrace at the Pass of Recruited Laborers

the four devarajas and attendants carved on the inside wall of the arch. But the most valuable relics are the inscriptions of *dharani* (charms) in six languages — Sanskrit, Tibetan, Phatspa (Mongolian), Uygur, West Xia and Han, which are well-preserved on the inside wall of the arch and which provide an important source for the study of these old scripts.

As a matter of policy, the Yuan emperors revered Confucianism, Taoism and Buddhism alike, leaving us a rich heritage of monasteries and pagodas, a monument to the cultural achievements of the Mongol period in Chinese history. In addition to progress in science and technology, culture in Dadu was distinguished by fresh developments in poetry and prose-writing, a flourishing theatre, a return to the ancients in calligraphy, excellent painting, and new levels reached in sculpture and porcelain art.

Freed from the unhealthy styles of the late years of the Jurchen and the Song dynasties, prose and poetry produced in Dadu manifested a rediscovery of literary purity and elegance, as one can see from the works of Yuan Haowen (1190-1257) and Hao Jing (1223-1275) of the early Yuan period, Zhao Mengfu (1254-1322) and Yu Ji (1272-1348) of the middle period, and Saidula (c. 1300-?) and Ouyang Xuan (1274-1358) of the late period. All these men of letters lived in Dadu at one time or another and wrote about life in the city. Mongols, Uygurs, Hui Huis (Moslems) and other ethnic minorities also produced some of the best works. The cultural interchange among different ethnic groups added to the splendor of Yuan literature and art. Meanwhile, the intricacy of contradictions in Yuan society found expression in the sorrows of the writers. In his poem, *The Tomb of Lord Yue,* Zhao Mengfu paid tribute to the memory of Yue Fei, famous patriot of the Song dynasty who died at the hands of a traitorous minister. Depicting the wild grass growing around the lonely West Lake in Hangzhou, he wrote:

Do not sing this song to the West Lake,
The waters and hills bring me nothing but grief.

Another poet, Zhou Chi, wrote a dirge for the regimes vanquished by the Mongols which contained the lines:

In vain you would look for
    Historical sites in the city of Ji;
All of them are buried under
    Sky-kissing grass at Golden Terrace.

Quite a few poems satirized the decadent life of the ruling class in Dadu which subjected scholars to cruel persecution. Doctors often prescribed earthworm pills with a wax coating for wealthy people, who washed them down with wine. Fan Zhong, a native of the city, wrote in a poem:

Only the wealthy know the taste of wax
    —they chew it before taking a bowl of earthworm soup;
Paper has become expensive in the capital city
    —it is being used for more prescriptions, not poems.

Perhaps this state of affairs had something to do with the idiosyncrasies of Kublai Khan, an excellent horseman and archer who nevertheless scorned poetry, a specialty of Han scholars. He considered it absolutely useless to the country and to the writers themselves. Paradoxically, however, the emperors and scholars of the Yuan dynasty were fond of stage art, particularly *zaju*, which means poetic drama set to music.

Dadu was the cradle of *zaju*. The four great dramatists of the Yuan dynasty were Guan Hanqing (c. 1213-1297), Wang Shifu (dates unknown), Ma Zhiyuan (?-1321?) and Bai Pu (1226-1312 or a later date). The first three were natives of the city, while the last one also did his writings there. A book giving the biographies of Yuan dramatists and a catalogue of their works, called *A Manual of Those in the Nether World,* describes Guan Hanqing as "a leader of theatrical circles, the dean of script writers, and the head of a *zaju* troupe." He is said to have written more than 60 plays, but only about a dozen are extant. The best-known ones include *Snow in Midsummer, Rescued by a Coquette,* and *Lord Guan Goes to the Feast.*

Snow in Midsummer is the tragedy of Dou Eh, a girl who has lost her mother at the age of three. Her father, an impoverished scholar, has to give her to Mrs. Cai, a widow, as a child bride for her son, when she is only seven. When Dou Eh grows to 17, her husband dies. One day when Mrs. Cai goes out alone, she meets Lu, a wicked doctor, who attempts to strangle her and seize her money. She is rescued by Old Zhang and his son, Donkey, who subsequently move into her house on the excuse of having saved her life. Their purpose is to molest her and her daughter-in-law, Dou Eh. The helpless Mrs. Cai yields to Old Zhang, but the brave Dou Eh refuses Donkey. When Mrs. Cai falls ill, Donkey tries to poison her so that he can have Dou Eh, but by accident he poisons his father. When Dou Eh turns him down a second time, he takes her to court and accuses her of murder. Cruelly tortured, she has to plead guilty. Facing execution, she sings:

The good are poor, and die before their time;
The wicked are rich, and live to a great old age.
The gods are afraid of the mighty and bully the weak;
They let evil take its course.
Ah, Earth! you will not distinguish good from bad,
And, Heaven! you let me suffer this injustice!
Tears pour down my cheeks in vain.*

After the innocent young woman is executed, a heavy snow falls in midsummer as if to protest the utter injustice. A drought continues for three years, withering all trees and grass.

This masterpiece of realism is a scathing critique of the inhuman despotism of the Yuan regime. It remains one of the best traditional plays in China today.

Equally well-known is *West Chamber* by Wang Shifu, which is the story of love between a young scholar and a beautiful maiden who marry each other in defiance of feudal conventions.

---

* Quoted from *Selected Plays of Guan Hanqing,* translated by Yang Xianyi and Gladys Yang, Foreign Languages Press, Beijing, second edition, 1979, p. 27.

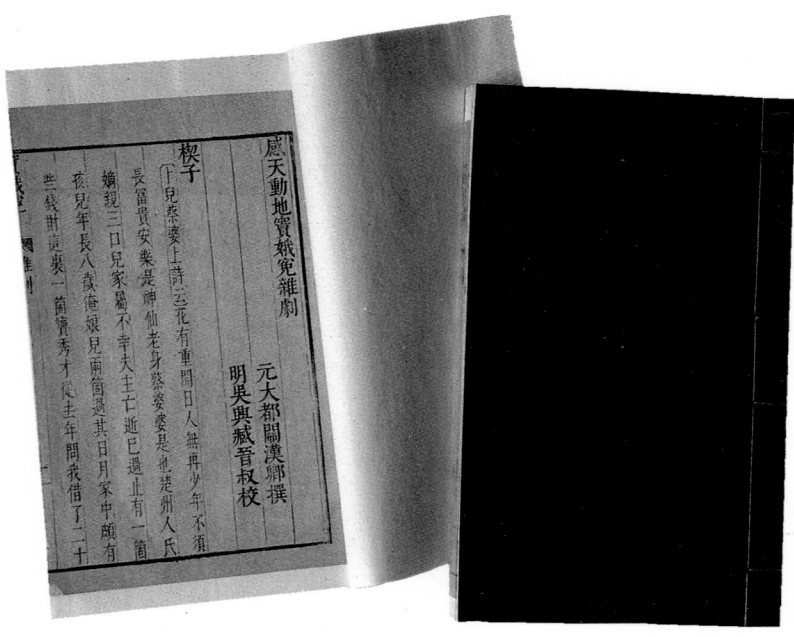

Guan Hanqing's play, *Snow in Midsummer*

Calligraphy by Zhao Mengfu

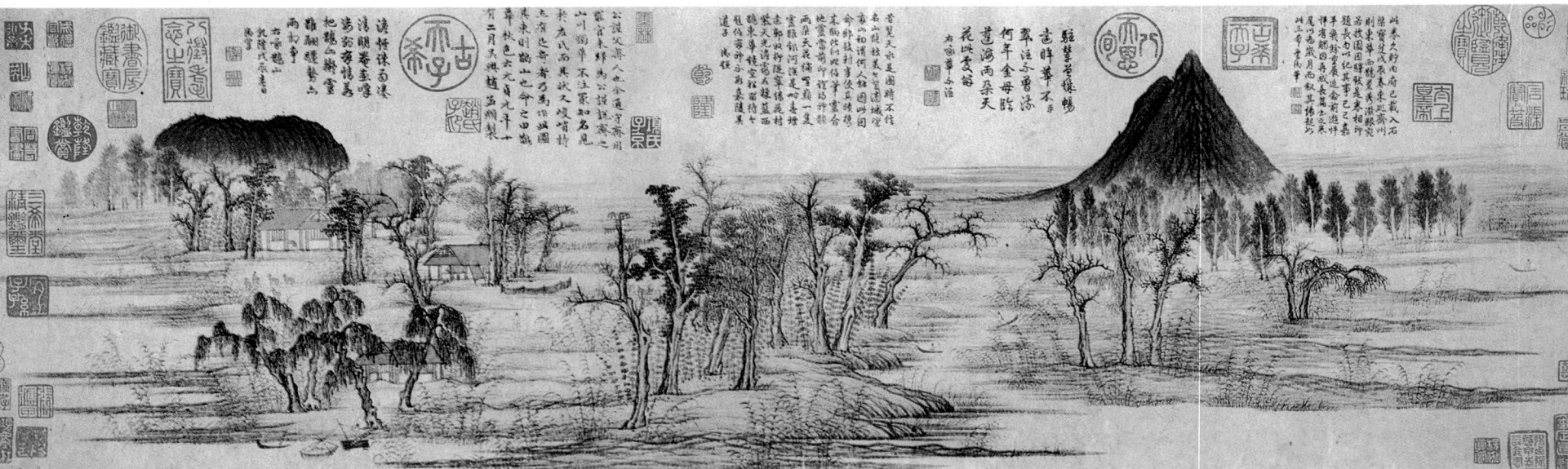

Autumn Scene, a painting by Zhao Mengfu

The times of the great playwrights also produced a galaxy of stars of musical drama, among whom were five actresses whose names ended with the character *xiu* (elegant). The Five Elegants, as people called them, had the capital city at their feet because of their melodious singing and touching performances. They enriched the cultural enjoyment of the residents.

Dadu boasted a number of outstanding calligraphers. Ouyang Xiu, (100-72), celebrated statesman and man of letters of the Song dynasty, once remarked that Chinese calligraphy had reached its acme under the Tang dynasty but declined more sharply than ever under the Song. Some critics even held that Song calligraphy showed little more than a beginner's skill, while Yuan calligraphy represented a revival of the ancient legacy. Such revival stemmed from the change from Han to Mongol rule, especially from the self-contradictory state of mind of intellectuals at the time. Scholar-officials who had served at the Song court were nostalgic about the defunct dynasty while working for Mongol rulers. Those who refused to cooperate with the conquerors lived in unhappy hermitage. Both found consolation in calligraphy, a traditional hobby of better-educated Chinese, particularly in a return to the ancient styles of brush work. The chief exponent of this trend was Zhao Mengfu.

A descendant of the Song house serving at the Yuan court, Zhao Mengfu was a prose-writer and poet, an expert on music and, above all, a painter and calligrapher. In calligraphy he stood for taking the ancient masters as one's models. He was skilled in all the four scripts — official, regular, cursive and semi-cursive, and was best known for his regular and semi-cursive characters, particularly small

ones. He is known to have written 10,000-20,000 small, regular characters in a day, a rare achievement for any calligrapher, ancient or modern. He was particular about every character and every stroke, always seeking a way to give it dignity and charm. And yet his solid training enabled him to work fast. Yu Ji, another calligrapher who was his contemporary, noted that some calligraphers relied mainly on their talent and others on their training, and he who combined both could be superhuman. Zhao Mengfu was, in fact, a superhuman artist exhibiting a unity of genius and hard work. This was how he became a giant of Chinese calligraphy. High priests of India came to China to acquire his works, regarding them as a treasure. The Zhao Mengfu script became extremely popular under Emperor Qianlong (r. 1735-96) of the Qing dynasty and remains a principal school of Chinese calligraphy today.

Dadu also witnessed a golden age of Chinese painting. This branch of art had already flourished under the Song dynasty, which left behind a rich heritage of paintings of mountains and rivers, rocks and woods, flowers and bamboos, birds and fish. Most of the rulers of the Yuan dynasty, particularly the last few emperors, were keenly interested in painting. Some Mongol aristocrats dabbled in the art to join the ranks of cultured men. A book written toward the end of the Yuan dynasty, the *Treasury of National Painting*, lists some 200 outstanding painters, many of whom were born in the capital or worked there. The attainment of Yuan painters can be seen from the mountains and rivers depicted by Zhao Mengfu and Gao Kegong (1248-1310), the horses and equestrians by Zhao Mengfu and Zhang Yanfu, the bamboos and woods by Li Kan (1245-1320) and Wang

Towers and Balconies Mirrored in Water, a painting by Xia Yong

綠窗仙人學道成欲乘

駕鶴親三清月明獨

立天壇上雪殼承裳玉

珮聲 唐扇

和靖門前雪作堆多少

滿身苦珠草簡閣冰玉蕊沁吹

他不下來笈已夏五會稽王元章

白南焦

Mian (1287-1359), the human figures by Li Xiaoyan and Chen Zhitian, and the architectural paintings by He Cheng and Wang Zhenpeng. Chinese painters had always cherished a tradition of stressing the meaning of a painting rather than its resemblance of the object depicted. This tradition became all the stronger under the Yuan dynasty because of the pent-up fury of the literati under Mongol domination. Thus Yuan paintings are characterized by the depth of the message instead of formal likeness, an important reason accounting for the towering achievements in philosophical paintings as well as those done in the architectural style. Being a great calligrapher, Zhao Mengfu also excelled in putting across political-philosophical messages through his paintings.

Paintings in the architectural style grew out of designs for buildings, on the basis of which painters began to delineate halls, towers and pavilions with the aid of the architect's rulers and pens, founding a new school of painting. Any such painting could also carry a political or philosophical message. In fact, painters of this school in the Yuan dynasty often expressed their nostalgia about the extinct Song dynasty by presenting towers and balconies mirrored in water with the mystic tinge of a fairyland. Wang Zhenpeng's *Sketch of Halls and Pavilions in Dadu* has long been lost, but we still have the *Album of Towers and Balconies Mirrored in Water* by Xia Yong, done on silk by line drawing in the traditional ink-and-brush style. In this picture the stately buildings on the right, resting on a rock foundation surrounded by water, are linked with the bank by a rainbow-shaped stone bridge on the left. The lotus on the water is matched by the green hills in the distance. A poem accompanying the painting says:

Early Spring, a painting by Wang Mian

Celadon pot with a spout shaped like the head of a phoenix

Without resting on land
The buildings are suspended in mid-air;
The spirit is majestic, the impact great;
The trees on distant hills are turning green,
Vying with the pinkish lotus nearby.

A well-known architectural-style painting of the Yuan dynasty, called *Rafting on the Reed Gully River*, recreates the intoxicating scenery in the area of the Reed Gully Bridge to the southwest of Dadu. It is one of the treasures of Chinese painting.

The capital city was a museum of stone and clay sculptures preserved in its palaces and mansions, temples and altars. The traditional Chinese style was modified through the influence of Lamaism. The Nepalese architect Arnico played no small part in this process. It was he who brought in the Nepalese style of Buddha's statues, known as "Buddha's statues from the Western Heavens." Liu Yuan, a Taoist monk who later became a sculptor, learned Nepalese techniques from Arnico, incorporated them into the traditional Chinese style, and built excellent statues of Buddha in the capital's famous temples toward the end of the 13th century and early in the 14th century. One of the alleys in Beijing today is named after him.

The porcelain of Dadu was among the best produced under the Yuan dynasty, typical of which was celadon or blue-and-white porcelain. Using cobalt as pigment, the craftsman painted blue designs on the biscuit, coated it with a thin layer of transparent glaze, heated it at a temperature of 1300 degrees centigrade, and produced porcelain with light blue designs against a white background. Light-colored and elegant, such porcelain was difficult to make, but the accomplished craftsman was always rewarded with success for his skill and labor. The manufacture of celadon on a wide scale represented a significant advance in Chinese ceramics. It also raised Jingdezhen, a porcelain-producing town in Jiangxi Province which abounded in *Kaolin (terra alba)*, to the status of China's "porcelain capital."

Celadon produced under the Yuan dynasty exhibits a style inherited from the Song period as well as Tibetan and Central Asian influences. But it remains characteristically Chinese, being refined, properly glazed, serene and pleasing to the eye. A dozen flat-shaped vessels bearing blue dragon designs have been unearthed, mostly in Indonesia and the Philippines. In the Beijing area, a flat celadon pot has been discovered in a cellar dating to the days of Dadu. The mouth of the pot is painted like the raised head of a phoenix, the belly represents its body, and the handle its upturned tail. The whole piece is full of vigor, resembling a richly-plumed phoenix ready to take off.

Artware produced in Dadu included vase with an attached stand, technicolored furnace, red and white chess pieces made of agate, and the famous lacquer plate with mother-of-pearl inlay. In a riot of color, the shells form on the plate a picture with the Palace of Pervasive Coolness, the mythical palace in the moon, in the background. There is also a two-storied, double-eaved tower in the *Xieshan* * style surrounded by balustrades. An osmanthus tree stands by the tower, a misty cloud hovers above it. The mother-of-pearl offers a whole spectrum of color — blue on the balustrades, red on the pillars, yellow on the tiles, green on the leaves, deep-blue on the ridges of the buildings, purple on the clouds, etc. The inlaid work surpasses any product of nature.

Entertainment in the city ranged from acrobatics and ballad-singing to Chinese wrestling and puppet show. An acrobat could scale a 100-feet pole at a royal banquet, winning a smile from the emperor. When he displayed his skill in an open-air theatre, the sound of the accompanying drums and flutes were drowned by the thunderous cheers of the spectators. The ballad-singers were great story-tellers who attracted big crowds in the streets. Both wrestling and puppet shows were performed in market places in town and country, and maintained their popularity through the decades.

---

* *Xieshan* refers to a roof in the traditional style of Chinese palace architecture. It is fully hipped on two sides and half-hipped at the ends so that an upper gable is left exposed.

Rafting on the Reed Gully River, a painting of the Yuan dynasty in the architectural style

Celadon statue of the Goddess of Mercy. It was built in Mongolian style in the Yuan dynasty with a round face, a broad forehead, and a sturdy body.

Cultural Exchange with Other Countries

The Yuan period saw an expansion of cultural exchange with countries of Asia, Africa and Europe. Scientists, medical doctors and missionaries of foreign countries came to Dadu in increasing numbers, while Chinese scholars, officials and priests went abroad. The capital city became a center of international cultural activities.

The Yuan empire had much contact with Korea. Emperor Renzong (Ayurbadrabal, r. 1311-20) presented Korea with more than 4,300 volumes of authentic editions of Chinese classics kept in the imperial library since the Song dynasty, in addition to the books exchanged between the two countries through commercial channels. Korean paper found a ready market among Chinese scholar-officials. Quite a number of Korean students came to study at the Imperial College in the Yuan capital. Neo-Confucianism* was introduced into Korea in the early Yuan period. The Korean scholar An Sang acquired the *Complete Works of Zhu Xi* in the Yuan capital in 1289, and lectured on "the teachings of Master Zhu" at the Korean imperial college after his return. He was followed by Bek Rizeng, another Korean scholar, who took back many copies of the Neo-Confucianist works by the Cheng brothers and Zhu Xi and lectured on them at the imperial college. The *Collected Commentaries on the Four Books*** compiled by Zhu Xi was published in Korea, and Neo-Confucianism spread wide in the country. In 1312 the Korean poet Ri Chihien came to Dadu and lived there a long time. He was a great friend of Zhao Mengfu and other men of letters.

China and Japan are separated only by a strip of water. The two countries remained in close contact during the Yuan dynasty. Economic and cultural exchange was promoted by the visits of

merchants and priests. Chinese books, paintings and calligraphy were introduced into Japan. In particular, Yuan priests visiting Japan did much to spread Neo-Confucianism in that country.

China expanded its ties with Southeast Asia during the Yuan dynasty. Envoys from Indo-Chinese states, Burma and Siam came to the Yuan court, which sent its envoys to Siam on three occasions and also to India. Kublai Khan sent his envoy to Ceylon (Sri Lanka) in search of Buddha's tooth. He did receive it and some of Buddha's hair.

Four khanates appeared during the western expedition of the Mongol troops — the Kipchak Khanate which once extended its territory to the lower reaches of the Danube, the Jagatai Khanate

---

* Neo-Confucianism was the dominant school of Confucian philosophy from the Song dynasty onward, and its chief exponent, Zhu Xi (1130-1200), was the most influential Confucian scholar after Confucius himself and Dong Zhongshu of the Western Han dynasty. The school was founded by Zhou Dunyi (1016-1073) of the Northern Song dynasty. Combining Confucianism with Buddhism and Taoism, he stated that "the Absolute" was the essence of the universe transcending all material things. His theory was inherited by the Cheng brothers — Cheng Hao (1032-85) and Cheng Yi (1033-1107), who advanced the idea of "reason" as the essence of the universe existing before anything else. Zhu Xi, who lived under the Sounthern Song dynasty, also believed that "reason" in things existed before things themselves, but added that all changes in things were governed by it, and "reason" was nothing but man's nature which was inherently good. All these philosophers, however, upheld the norms of the feudal order and stressed the need to observe them.

** The Four Books of Confucianism are the *Analects of Confucius, Mencius, Great Learning,* and the *Doctrine of the Mean.*

An incense burner of the Yuan dynasty, a pottery tripod painted in yellow, green and blue with an openwork body and a dragon-phoenix decoration on top

A stone human figure, a Yuan dynasty relic placed in front of the tomb of Yelu Chucai in the Summer Palace

was founded in Dadu for the training of Moslem scholars. The Arab architect Ekhtiar made outstanding contributions to the design and construction of the Yuan capital.

Communication with Africa grew under the Yuan dynasty. According to Marco Polo's *Travels*, Kublai Khan sent an Egyptian official at his court to Fuzhou to teach sugar-refining techniques to the local people. The same book also says that Kublai Khan sent an envoy to Madagascar, who delighted the emperor with an account of the island country upon his return. The well-known Moslem traveller, ibn Batuta (c.1304-c. 1378), who was born in Morocco, gave his impressions of the Yuan capital city in his book, *The Delights of a Traveller in Beautiful Lands*.

The establishment of the Mongol khanates mentioned above opened a new chapter in China's communication with Europe. Beginning with the times of Kublai Khan, Euorpean envoys, missionaries and merchants came to the Yuan empire, while their Chinese counterparts visited Europe. At one time followers of Nestorianism numbered 30,000 in the Yuan capital. In 1278 Sao Ma, a native of the capital city who served as patriarch of the Nestorian church, led a pilgrimage to Jerusalum. He went to Bagdad and arrived in Naples via Constantinople before he was received by King Phillipe IV in France and King Edward I in England. Returning to Rome, he was received by Pope Nicholas IV.

Following Sao Ma's visit Pope Nicholas IV sent Giovanni de Montecorvino to China. He lived in the Yuan capital for 31 years, built three churches there, translated the New Testament into the Mongolian language and, as archibishop of the Catholic church in the city, converted several thousand people to his religion. Catholic priests even went to the imperial palaces for religious ceremonies. After Montecorvino's death Emperor Shundi (Togontemur, r. 1333-68) sent a mission to Rome where it was received by Pope Benedict XII. In 1342 a mission sent by the Pope arrived in Shangdu, the Upper Capital of the Yuan empire, and presented beautiful horse to Emperor Shundi, and his ministers celebrated the occasion by writing their "Odes to the Heavenly Horse." The mission stayed in Dadu for three years before returning to Rome. Otto Ricco, a venetian, visited Yangzhou in East China and traveled to the Yuan capital by the Grand Canal to live there for three years before returning home. In his travel notes he gave a good description of His Majesty's Hill and Celestial Lake in the city. Much better known, of course, is Marco Polo, his fellow Venetian, who came to China with his uncle at the age of 15 after a most arduous journey across the Pamirs and the Gobi Desert. He lived in China for 17 years and became a trusted official at the court of Kublai Khan. In 1291, Kublai Khan decided to marry Princess Cocacin to Arghun, Khan of the I1-Khanate, at the latter's request. Marco Polo escorted the princess to the I1-Khanate in the company of the envoy from that country and then returned to Venice. His *Travels*, written on the basis of his oral accounts, described his experience in the Yuan empire and praised the magnificence and prosperity of its capital city. It was a major contribution to European understanding of China and the city of Beijing.

In spite of its flourishing economy and culture, however, the Yuan capital was the scene of ethnic struggles, political and religious strife, and palace coups. As the years went by, the Yuan regime became corrupt and decadent, and its financial resources exhausted. The country was plagued by natural disasters and epidemics, and the capital city fell into decline. In 1368 Zhu Yuanzhang (1328-98) founded the Ming dynasty after a series of peasant uprisings weakened the Yuan regime. Xu Da, one of Zhu's generals, led his troops toward the Yuan capital, whereupon Emperor Shundi fled to Shangdu with the empress, the imperial consorts, and the crown prince. Xu Da and his men entered the city on the second day of the eighth moon, putting an end to the Yuan dynasty. This turned a new page in the history of Beijing.

which occupied the former territory of Western Liao, the Ogdai Khanate which covered the upper reaches of the Irtysh River and the area east of the Balkhash Lake, and the I1-Khanate which was located south of the Caucasus. While maintaining their independence, the four khanates all recognized the Yuan emperor as the Great Khan. The extension of the Yuan empire to parts of Central and West Asia facilitated the cultural exchange between China and those regions. Many Chinese craftsmen and doctors went there for a long or short visit. Both Taoist leader Qiu Chuji and Qidan statesman Yelu Chucai were once in Central Asia. Chinese gunpowder was introduced into Europe through the Arabs. On the other hand, the medical science and astronomy of the Arabs found their way into the Yuan capital. The Persian astronomer Jamal al-Din brought there the Moslem calendar which was once adopted by Kublai Khan. He developed an armillary sphere and six other astronomical instruments, and was put in charge of the Moslem observatory. A great number of Moslem books were kept in the Imperial Library, mostly Arab works on calendar-making, astronomy and the making of astronomical instruments, medical science and pharmacy. A special department was established under the Royal Institute of Medicine, on the initiative of Aisha from Syria, for the study and practice of Moslem medical science and pharmacy. A Moslem Imperial College

Chapter VI

BEIJING UNDER THE MING AND QING DYNASTIES

The City and the Palaces

The Four City Walls

In 1368 Zhu Yuanzhang, founding emperor of the Ming dynasty, ascended the throne in Yingtian and renamed the city Nanjing, meaning "southern capital." He changed Dadu to Peiping Prefecture, and made his fourth son, Zhu Di, the Prince of Yan, in charge of the prefecture. He died of an illness in 1398 and was succeeded by his grandson, known historically as Emperor Jianwen. The authority of the young emperor was challenged by the Prince of Yan, his uncle, who rose in rebellion at Peiping in 1399, captured Nanjing after four years, and took over the throne. Seeing the strategic importance of Peiping and considering it a place for "the rise of a dragon," he decided to make it his capital so that he could exercise effective control over North China. In 1403 he changed

Peiping to Beijing, meaning "northern capital," and designated the area around the city as Shuntian Prefecture. Thus he was the first emperor of the Han ethnic group in Chinese history to make Beijing the political center for the whole country. For a total of 588 years, the city served as the national capital for the Yuan, Ming and Qing dynasties.

In 1406 Zhu Di issued an imperial decree for the removal of the imperial capital from Nanjing to Beijing. Work started in the fifth moon of the next year to build palaces, temples and altars in the city. He placed his ministers in charge of the mammoth project, which involved the felling of logs, the quarrying of rocks, the making of bricks and tiles, the burning of lime, the acquisition of coloring material, the dredging of the Grand Canal to facilitate transportation and, finally, the recruitment of the workforce for all these jobs. The logs had to conform to rigid specifications. And it was very difficult to get them out of the mountains, as one can see from the folk saying, "only 500 out of every 1,000 logs can be taken out of the valleys." The logs which did reach Beijing were stored at Damucang (big-log warehouses), located along an alley in present-day Beijing which retains the same name. The space of the warehouses was equivalent to 3,600 regular rooms. The logs were in fact oversupplied, with the result that 380,000 of them remained there after the completion of the palaces. The rocks had to be shaped into huge slabs for laying the foundations of palaces and temples and paving the approaches. More than 10,000 slabs, each weighing at least five tons, were used for these purposes. In addition, 20 million bricks were used for the courtyards in the palace complex, where the grounds were paved with three to seven layers of bricks. The tiles, including the black, glazed and gilded ones, had to be made according to detailed lists giving a great variety of sizes and specifications. In particular, it took a long time to produce the glazed tiles by making the biscuits, carving out the patterns, putting on the glaze, and firing the biscuits. To obtain lime, workers had to be sent into the mountains where they quarried limestone and built kilns. Large quantities of coloring material were also needed for the palace walls which were red on the outside and golden-colored on the inside.

Since much of the building material came from South China, the Grand Canal was dredged for speedier transportation.

Construction of Beijing as the Ming capital started in 1417 and was completed in 1420. In 1421 Emperor Yongle moved the capital from Nanjing to Beijing, making the former the secondary capital.

The city of Beijing was built under the Ming dynasty on the basis of Dadu of the Yuan dynasty. The designers adopted the strong points of planning done under previous dynasties and used the layout of Nanjing as a reference. There were four enclosures: the Forbidden City, the Imperial City, the Inner City, and the Outer City.

Known today as the Former Palace or the Palace Museum, the "Purple Forbidden City" was the place where the emperor lived with

Portrait of Zhu Di, known as Emperor Yongle of the Ming dynasty

Turret and wall of the Forbidden City ▷

his family and discharged his duties as head of the state. It was also the center of the city. It differed from its counterpart under the Yuan dynasty in the following respects:

a. A more concentrated layout. Similar to the Changle, Weiyang and Jianzhang Palaces in Chang'an under the Han dynasty, the Yuan palaces were spread relatively far and wide because the three groupings around the Inner Palace, the Palace of Prosperity, and the Palace of the Rising Monarch were cut off from one another by the Celestial Lake even though they all centered around Jade Flower Islet. The Forbidden City under the Ming dynasty enclosed the equivalents of all these palaces, including the offices of the emperor, the bedchambers of the emperor and empress, and the residences of the empress dowager, the imperial consorts and other court ladies, and of the crown prince and his brothers.

b. A more impressive appearance at the front. The two gates in front of the Yuan palaces, called Gate for the Worship of Heaven and Beautiful Main Gate, were quite close to each other. In the Northern Song capital of Bianliang (present-day Kaifeng), however, a long and broad Celestial Avenue led to the palaces. Taking the latter as their model, designers of the Ming Forbidden City pushed the southern walls much farther from the palace complex, forming an axial line between two gates, South-Facing Gate and Meridian Gate, and adding much depth and grandeur to the "Purple Forbbiden City."

c. A hill behind the palaces. There had been no hill in the Imperial Garden of the Yuan dynasty. In the early years of the Ming dynasty, the "Purple Forbidden City" in Nanjing leaned against a hill at its back. The palace zone in Beijing was given a similar feature. The earth excavated from the moat around the Forbidden City was used to build a 49-meter-high hill in the Imperial Garden, which was called His Majesty's Hill under the Ming and changed to Prospect Hill under the Qing. In 1751 five pavilions were erected on the hill under the Qing emperor Qianlong with such fancy names as Everlasting Spring for the middle one, Appreciating the Scenery and Good View All Round for the two left ones, and Gathering Fragrance and Rich Enjoyment for the two right ones.

d. Placing the Ancestral Temple and the Altar of Land and Grain beside the palaces. Under the Yuan dynasty, the Ancestral Temple where the emperor offered sacrifices to his ancestors was located inside the Qihuamen (Gate of Homogeneous Civilization), which has become today's Chaoyangmen (Facing-the-Sun Gate), at the eastern end of the capital city, while the Altar of Land and Grain, where the emperor offered sacrifices to the God of Earth and of the Five Cereals, was placed far away from the palaces — inside today's Fuchengmen (Gate of Great Tranquility). After Beijing became capital of the Ming dynasty, these two important buildings were replaced beside the eastern and western court offices at the Gate for Receiving the Mandate of Heaven which was changed to Tian'anmen (Gate of Heavenly Peace) under the Qing dynasty and retains the same name today. The Ming designers applied the ancient principle of placing the Ancestral Temple to the left of the imperial palaces and the Altar of Land and Grain to their right. The former has become the Working People's Palace of Culture, the latter the Zhongshan Park (Sun Yat-sen Park).

e. Placing the Forbidden City exactly at the center of the city. The palace complex was located at the southwestern corner of the Outer City under the Liao dynasty, somewhat to the west of the center of the Outer City under the Jurchen dynasty, and at the center of the east-west axis of the city but slightly to the south under the Yuan dynasty. The Ming designers placed the Forbidden City exactly at the center of Beijing by moving the northern walls of the Outer City southward.

The Imperial City, which surrounded the Forbidden City, had a periphery of nine kilometers. It has six gates: the Gate of the Great Ming on the south, which was changed to the Gate of the Great Qing under the Qing dynasty, plus the Left and Right Gates of Lasting Peace and the East, West and North Gates of Peace. The last was changed to its present name, the Gate of Earthly Peace. An Imperial Way lay before the Gate for Receiving the Mandate of Heaven (the Gate of Heavenly Peace), flanked by a "Thousand-Step Corridor" on either side to form a vast square. The central government offices handling civil affairs occupied the left side of the square, while those in charge of the armed forces stood on the right. In contrast, the government offices in the Yuan capital had shown a far less symmetrical distribution.

Thus the Imperial City of the Ming dynasty enclosed a number of important institutions — the central government offices in front of the palace complex, the Ancestral Temple of the imperial family on the left and the Altar of Land and Grain on the right, the Chancery and the Imperial Archives to the left of the palaces and the Xiyuan (West Garden, which has become today's Central-South Lake and North Lake or Beihai Park) to their right, as well as the numerous offices providing services for the palaces. The walls of the Imperial City were reinforced with bricks, painted red, and covered with yellow glazed tiles on top. The common people were refused entry into the Imperial City, which was the intermediate zone between the Inner City and the Forbidden City.

Enclosing the Imperial City, the Inner City had a periphery of 22.5 kilometers, protected by walls which were 12 meters high, 18.6 meters thick at the base, and 15 meters wide at the top. The battlements on the walls were 1.8 meters high. There were three gates on the southern side — the South-Facing Gate in the middle, the Gate of Literary Virtue on the east, and the Gate of Military Virtue on the west; two gates on the eastern side — the Straight East Gate in the north and the Facing-the-Sun Gate in the south; two gates on the western side — the Straight West Gate in the north and the Gate of Great Tranquility in the south; and two gates on the northern side — the Gate of Stability on the east and the Gate of Victory on the west. The nine gates served different purposes. Officials went to the imperial court sessions through the South-Facing Gate. Merchants were required to enter or leave the city through the Gate of Literary Virtue where they had to clear with a tax office. Scholars generally used the Gate of Military Virtue where they were accommodated in the premises of the various provincial and county guilds. The armed forces left on expeditions through the auspicious Gate of Victory and returned through the Gate of Stability, an indication that they had brought peace and order to the empire. Vehicles loaded with food grain entered the Facing-the-Sun Gate to arrive at the granaries inside the gate. Those carrying logs brought from South China along the Grand Canal stopped at the storage grounds outside the Straight East Gate. Night-soil carts left by the Gate of Stability to reach the disposal grounds outside the gate. Vehicles for the transportation of coal entered and left by the Gate of Great Tranquility which led to the Mentougou coal mines. Watercarts carrying water from the Jade Spring Hill in the western suburbs entered the city through the Straight West Gate to reach the imperial palaces. There was a strict ban on funeral processions through the South-Facing Gate, the main gate of Beijing. Even after the death of the emperor, the imperial family had to use the Facing-the-Sun Gate for funeral purposes.

In 1439 towers were added to the nine gates of the Inner City. The South-Facing Gate was provided with a main tower and three minor ones. The eight other gates of the city were each given a tower for the main gate and another for the minor gate on the outside. The South-Facing Gate consisted of one main gate and two minor gates on the left and right. In addition to the tower on the main gate in the middle and those on the two minor gates, there was an embrasured watchtower in front. Erected on the high gate, the embrasured watchtower, called "arrow tower," extended into a spacious hall in the rear and had a number of openings on its wall for defense purposes. Protected by the embrasured watchtower, the main tower was placed on an elevated terrace and shined with its red pillars. The roof was built in the *xieshan* palace style and fitted with three layers of eaves, which made the structure all the more impressive. An archway was built outside each of the nine city gates, and a turret erected on each of the four corners of the city wall which was surrounded by a deep and wide moat. A stone bridge was put up outside each city gate and fitted with a sluice gate underneath. The South-Facing Gate, the Gate of Literary Virtue, and the Gate of Military Virtue were further protected by three "water barriers," i.e., three rows of iron railings on the moat. The nine gates and their towers made the city both attractive and easy to defend.

The wall of the Outer City circled round the turrets on the southeastern and southwestern corners of the Inner City. They were not built until 1553 under Emperor Jiajing of the Ming dynasty. In 1550 all the nine gates of the Inner City were closed against the Mongol troops which had advanced to the city wall. After their withdrawal, court ministers recommended the construction of an Outer City for defense. The project was started three years later. The designers proposed a city wall of 60 kilometers to encircle the Inner City on all sides. By 1564, however, only a 14-kilometer section enclosing the southern suburbs of the Inner City had been completed, and the court realized that the project was far too big for its limited financial resources. The unfinished Outer City wall had seven gates, with three on the southern side — the Gate of Everlasting Stability in the middle, the Left Gate of Peace in the east, and the Right Gate of Peace in the west; two on the eastern side — the Wide Channel Gate, plus the East Informal Gate around the east corner of the city walls; and two on the west side — the Gate of Pervasive Tranquility, which was changed to the Gate of Pervasive Peace under the Qing dynasty, plus the West Informal Gate around the west corner of the city wall.

Plan of Beijing During the Ming-Qing Period

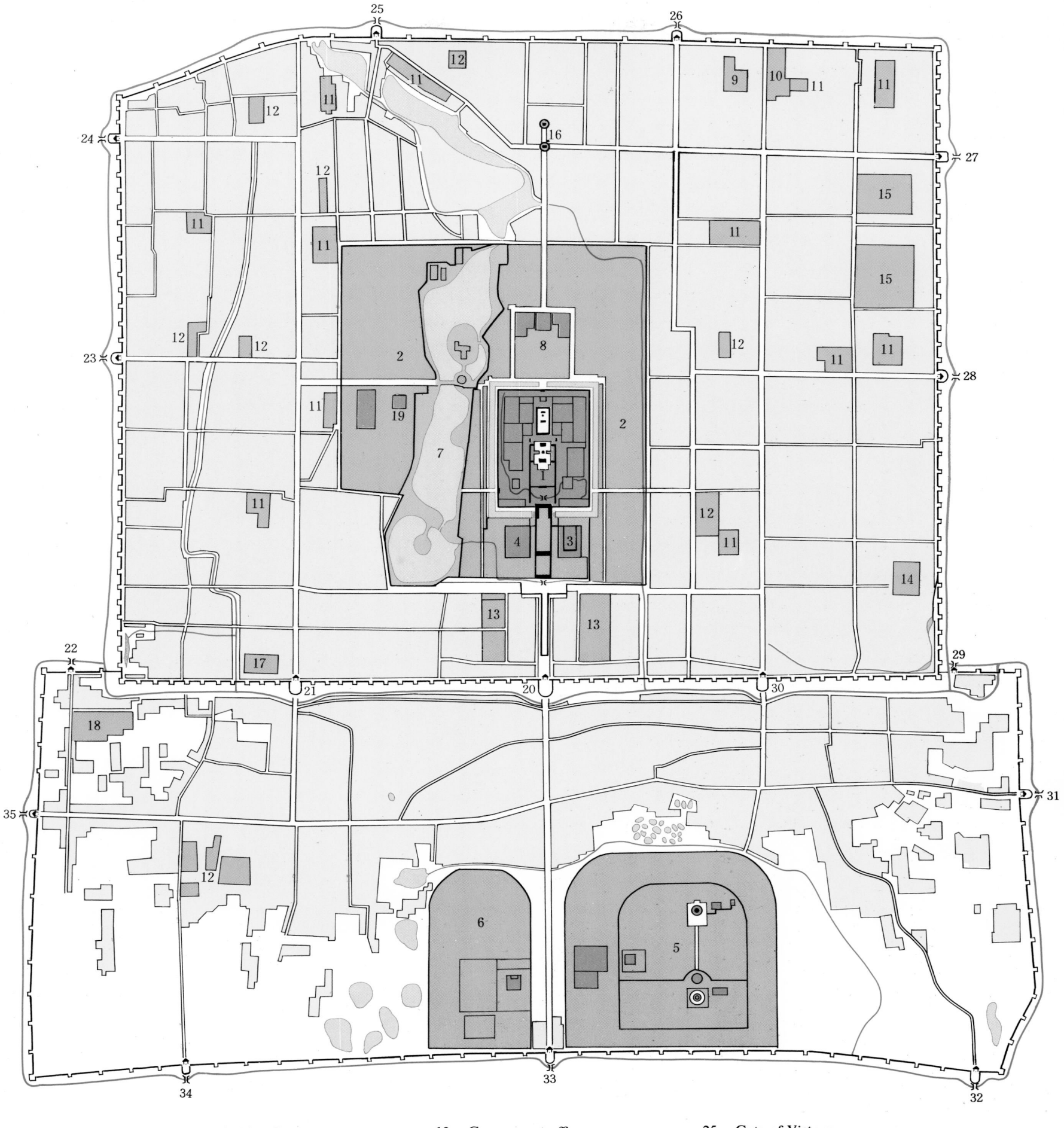

1. Forbidden City
2. Imperial City
3. Ancestral Temple
4. Altar of Land and Grain
5. Temple of Heaven
6. Altar of the God of Agriculture
7. West Garden
8. Prospect Hill
9. Imperial College
10. Lamasery of Harmony and Peace
11. Main mansions of the princes
12. Temples

13. Government offices
14. Metropolitan examination hall
15. Warehouses
16. Bell and Drum Towers
17. Elephant House
18. Barracks
19. Church
20. South-Facing Gate
21. Gate of Military Virtue
22. West Informal Gate
23. Gate of Great Tranquility
24. Straight West Gate

25. Gate of Victory
26. Gate of Stability
27. Straight East Gate
28. Facing-the-Sun Gate
29. East Informal Gate
30. Gate of Literary Virtue
31. Wide Channel Gate
32. Left Gate of Peace
33. Gate of Everlasting Stability
34. Right Gate of Peace
35. Gate of Pervasive Peace

Map of Beijing drawn during the Qianlong reign of the Qing dynasty

Tower on the South-Facing Gate

"Arrow Tower" in front of the South-Facing Gate. It has 52 embrasures at the front and 21 each on the left and right sides.

"Arrow Tower" in front of the Gate of Victory. Built in 1439, the fourth year of the Zhengtong reign of the Ming dynasty, it was an important structure for the defense of Beijing in the Ming and Qing dynasties.

A gateway in Beijing under the Qing dynasty

Turret on the southeastern corner of the Inner City of Beijing. Built in the Ming dynasty, it has a total of 144 embrasures.

Bell Tower and Drum Tower

A moat surrounded the Outer City wall. The two "informal" gates were provided with strong defense works — "water barriers" consisting of iron railings on the moat.

The plan of the city of Beijing looked like the Chinese character " 凸 ", (*tu* meaning "protruding"). An eight-kilometer axis ran through the city from north to south, starting from the Bell Tower and Drum Tower north of the rear gate of the Imperial City and ending at the Gate of Everlasting Stability at the center of the southern side of the Outer City. The Forbidden City, the Imperial City, the Inner City, and the Outer City all fanned out symmetrically from this axis to form a harmonious mosaic of buildings. The completion of the city of Beijing early in the 15th century, with the Forbidden City at the center, demonstrated the strength of a unified empire, its rich resources, the ingenuity of its people, and the attainment of its architects who built the best capital city ever constructed in China.

Designed to ward off enemy attacks, the four enclosures of Beijing also represented the socio-political hierarchy. The Forbidden City comprised the emperor's court chambers and living quarters. Enclosed by the three other cities, it represented the nation's supreme authority and enjoyed the best protection. The Imperial City was dominated by the premises of central government offices and institutions providing services for the palaces, and was inaccessible to the common people. The Inner City was, under the Qing dynasty, inhabited by officers and men of the Eight Banner organization* and their families. People of the Han nationality were allowed to enter the city but not to live there. The Outer City was, also under the Qing dynasty, an area inhabited by the Han people as well as Beijing's business district. Thus the four enclosures divided the population into four sections — the imperial family, the aristocracy, the soldiers, and the plebeians, giving everybody an idea of his place in society. As the main threat to the nation's security came from the north, only two gates were opened in the city wall on the northern side. In time such awareness of the menace from the north evolved into a geomantic concept, giving rise to mystic interpretations of the two north gates. The city walls, gates, embrasured towers, and moats were all designed for the defense of the imperial capital. In fact, there were 20,772 battlements and 12,602 embrasures on the walls of the Inner City and Outer City.

Beyond the four walls lay a colossal wall which safeguarded the political center of the Chinese empire. This was the Great Wall. It was repaired, reinforced and expanded many times under the dynasties or kingdoms of Qin, Han, Northern Wei, Eastern Wei, Northern Qi, Northern Zhou, Sui, Tang, Song, Liao, Jin (Jurchen) and Yuan.

After the Ming forces overthrew the Yuan dynasty, the troops of the feudal nobility of the nomadic Mongols still dominated the Gobi Desert. They constantly sent troops to invade the Central Plains and threaten the capital. Later the Jurchens rose in Northeast China and sent troops to attack the capital. To protect Beijing from invasion by the Mongols and Jurchens, the Ming regime strengthened the defenses in North China and initiated large-scale repairs of the Great Wall. The Great Wall renovation project was unparalleled in history, surpassing those undertaken under all previous dynasties since the reign of the First Emperor of the Qin dynasty (221-206 B.C.) in scale,

*The Eight Banner organization was the form by which the Manchu rulers organized their armed forces on the basis of their tribal *niulu* system. Whenever the Manchus marched on a military expedition or a hunting trip, they grouped every 10 participants as a basic unit called *niulu*. Later the number of people in a *niulu* grew to 300. Five *niulu* or 1,500 persons formed a *jiala*, and 7,500 persons, a banner. Each banner was identified by the flag of a particular color — yellow, red, blue or white, or a flag with one of these four colors along its border.

engineering quality, and strategic value. The reconstruction of the Great Wall, including continuous repairs, reinforcement and expansion, lasted more than 2,000 years and was not completed until the Ming dynasty.

The Great Wall winds its way from Shanhai Pass in the east to Jiayu Pass in the west along a total length of 5,000 kilometers. It remains largely intact to this day. Fortifications were built and troops stationed at strategic points. Juyong Pass, Badaling Pass, Gubeikou Pass and Shanhai Pass were important fortifications for the defense of Beijing.

Located some 50 kilometers northwest of Beijing, Juyong Pass was built in a 20-kilometer-long valley commonly known as Guangou (Pass Gully). Seventy-two scenic spots are said to have existed here. Hence the term "the 72 scenic spots of Guangou Valley." The mountains are covered with emerald forests acknowledged as one of the "Eight Views of Yanjing." Juyong Pass is noted for its beautiful scenery as well as its strategic position. Ming poets described it as a strategic barrier created by nature itself.

Since ancient times, Juyong Pass has been the northwestern gateway to Beijing. The name of the pass is said to have its origin in the workers and slaves recruited for construction of the Great Wall under the First Emperor of the Qin dynasty. During the Ming and Qing dynasties, Juyong Pass became an important fortification for the protection of Beijing. It has two defense points which are also the entrance and exit of the Guangou Valley. The one in the south is called Nankou (South Exit) while the one in the north is the famous Badaling.

Located at a strategic point on the big mountains, and commanding a full view of the area down below, Badaling is considered the most formidable barrier at Juyong Pass. A fortress was built in 1505 or the 18th year of the reign of the Ming emperor Hongzhi. It had an eastern and a western gate. On the lintel over the eastern gate is a plague reading: "Juyong Outer Town." It was inscribed in 1539 or the 18th year of the reign of the Ming emperor Jiajing. The plague on the lintel over the western gate reads: "Key to the Northern Gate." It was inscribed in 1582 or the 10th year of the reign of the Ming emperor Wanli. There are two crenellated platforms on top of the archways of the brick-and-stone gates. The Great Wall extends its way along the two sides of the platform marked "Key to the Northern Gate." The Badaling section of the Great Wall was built along the mountainside at a varying height and width, averaging 7.5 meters in height and 5.5 meters in width. The foundation is built with huge slabs of rocks, and the wall is lined with huge bricks on the outside and filled with earth and pebbles within. The top is paved with square bricks. The ramparts are on the inner side while the battlements are on the outer side. The battlements are filled with lookouts on top and with embrasures below.

There is a great number of platform forts on the Great Wall at the two sides of the Badaling fortress, spreading out at intervals of about 500 meters along the terrain. One type of them, called "wall platforms," are guarded by patrols and sentries. The other type, known as battle platforms, contain two stories — an upper story of lookouts and embrasures and a lower story where the soldiers stayed and stored their weapons. The beacon towers, also called "smoke towers," were intended for the communication of military information. When the enemy attacked, fires were kindled at night and smoke was sent out amid the roaring of cannon during the day. It was decided in 1466, or the 2nd year of the reign of the Ming emperor Chenghua, that an attack by 100 emeny troops or more was to be indicated by one puff of smoke plus one cannon roar, an attack by 500 men or more by two puffs of smoke and two cannon roars, etc., up to five puffs of smoke and five cannon roars in case of an invasion by

Jiayu Pass of the Great Wall. Located in the southwestern corner of today's Jiayuguan City, Gansu Province, it was built as the western terminus of the Great Wall in 1372, the fifth year of the Hongwu reign of the Ming dynasty.

Site of Old Dragon Head in the east of today's Shanhaiguan City, Hebei Province. It is the starting point of the Great Wall.

The Badaling section of the Great Wall

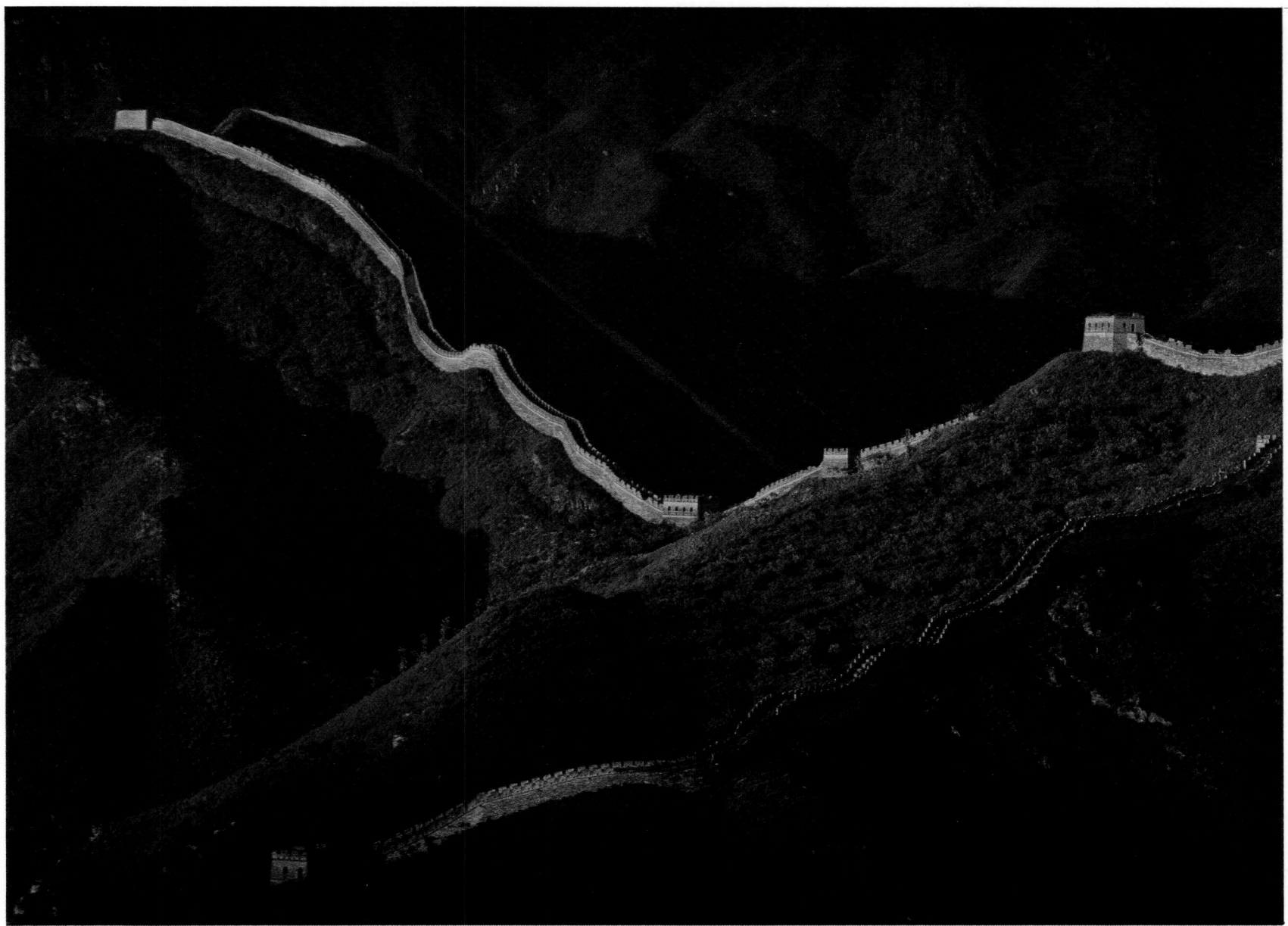

The Huanghuacheng section of the Great Wall

10,000 or more enemy troops. Some of the beacon towers were built on top of the Great Wall while others were built on the mountain peaks.

Gubeikou is a strategic gateway of the Great Wall north of Beijing. In 1214, the second year of the Zhenyou reign of the Jurchen dynasty, the Tiemen(Iron Gate) Pass was built at Gubeikou. In 1378, the 11th year of the Ming emperor Hongwu's reign, a fortress was built at Gubeikou. Two kilometers in circumference, the fortress has a gate on its north, south, and east side. The section of the Great Wall along the two sides of Gubeikou was uniquely built, for part of it crosses the Chao River on which three sluice gates have been erected. Close to Gubeikou are sections of the Great Wall called Huanghuacheng and Mutianyu, which present interesting sights because they are located on top of ridges or span mountain streams.

On the peaks of Badaling, Gubeikou, Huanghuacheng or Mutianyu, one gets a commanding view of the Great Wall. Like a dragon, it extends into the distance across precipitous mountains and through misty clouds.

The Forbidden City: Layout and Philosophy

The name of the Forbidden City or "Purple Forbidden City" comes from a concept of ancient Chinese astronomers, who considered the North Star the center of the cosmos and the abode of the Emperor of Heaven. Since the emperor on earth was believed to be the son of the Emperor of Heaven and purple was the symbolic color of the North Star, the palaces of the temporal sovereign, which the common people were not allowed to enter, acquired the mystic name of "Purple Forbidden City."

Many famous palaces in Chinese history, like the Epang Palace of the Qin dynasty, the Weiyang Palace of the Han dynasty, and the Daming Palace of the Tang dynasty, have all disappeared. Our knowledge about them comes only from historical records and relics. However, the Purple Forbidden City of the Ming and Qing dynasties is kept intact in the city of Beijing as the largest group of wooden structures in China and one of the centuries-old palace complexes seldom seen in the world. From here 14 emperors of the Ming dynasty and 10 emperors of the Qing dynasty ruled China for a total of 491 years, exerting much influence on Chinese and world history.

The wall surrounding the Forbidden City is covered and solidified with a special kind of fine-mud bricks. The brickmakers deposited mud in a pond, obtained the fine substance floating on top, made biscuits from it, and put these in kilns. Each city-wall brick, as it was called, had to be 48 cm. long, 24 cm. wide, 12 cm. thick, and 24 kilograms in weight. The 12,000,000 bricks so produced were polished and laid tightly against one another to form a city wall that was 7.9 meters high, 8.62 meters wide at the base, 6.66 meters wide at the top, and 3,428 meters in circumference. The space enclosed by the city wall was a little over 723,600 square meters. The wall was surrounded by a 52-meter-wide and six-meter-deep moat lined with feldspar which looked both solid and impressive. The top of the wall was crenellated on the outside for defense. A turret stood on each of the four corners of the city wall.

Each turret was a square tower measuring three bays on each side. With three layers of eaves, the roof was supported by vermilion pillars decorated with elegant designs. The upper eaves, constructed in the *xieshan* style, had four upturned corners. The middle eaves were also in the *xieshan* style. The lower eaves formed a multi-angular top. Gilded on top, the roof of the turret showed an ingenious combination of 72 ridges on its three layers of eaves.

The Forbidden City had the East Flower Gate on its east, the West Flower Gate on its west, and the Gate of Divine Might on its north. There were three gates on the south—the Gate for Receiving the Mandate of Heaven (changed to the Gate of Heavenly Peace under the Qing dynasty), the Gate of Correct Demeanor, and the Meridian Gate.

The Gate of Heavenly Peace, the front gate of the Forbidden City, remains almost the same as it was rebuilt under the Qing dynasty in 1651. The gatetower, erected on a 13-meter-high terrace, has five vaulted gateways underneath. It is double-eaved in the *xieshan* style and covered with yellow glazed tiles. On its south side are 10 vermilion columns and 36 rhomboid-latticed windows mounted on a red skirting board. The structure is nine bays wide and five bays deep, and is surrounded by marble balustrades.

The Gold Water River in front of the Gate of Heavenly Peace is spanned by five rainbow-shaped marble bridges called Gold Water Bridges. There is a pair of carved ornamental columns in front of the gate and another pair behind it, each pair guarded by a pair of stone lions. A mythical beast called *hou* carved in stone squats on top of each column. The *hou* on each of the columns in front of the gate gazes toward the sky. In former times it was supposed to watch over the emperor's behavior whenever he was outside his palace. If the emperor was gone for too long, the stone beast would say: "Your

Majesty! Do not spend too much time enjoying yourself outside the palace. Please come back soon to take care of state affairs. We have nearly worn our eyes out longing for your return." Thus the stone beast was given the name of "awaiting the emperor's return." The *hou* squatting on each of the two columns behind the Gate of Heavenly Peace gazes toward the palace. It was supposed to watch over the emperor's behavior inside the palace. If the emperor indulged himself in pleasure for too long in the palace, it would say: "Your Majesty! Do not spend too much time enjoying yourself inside the palace. Please come out to see the people's sufferings. We have nearly worn our eyes out longing for your arrival." This particular stone beast, therefore, acquired the name of "awaiting the emperor's arrival."

The Gate of Heavenly Peace was also the site for the issuance of imperial edicts. The ceremony went on like this: The emperor's edict was first placed in a miniature pavilion decorated with dragons and, guided by someone carrying an imperial staff, taken to the gatetower, where it was read out by an official, first in the Manchu language and then in the Han language. The civil and military officials lined up to the south of the Outer Gold Water River Bridges knelt toward the edict thrice and kowtowed thrice each time they knelt. The official authorized to issue the edict fed it into the mouth of a gilded wooden phoenix and lowered it to a tray held by a kneeling official before it was replaced in the dragon pavilion, sent to the Board of Rites for engraving and printing, and made known to the whole country. The ceremony, called "issuing an imperial edict through a golden phoenix," was symbolic of the supremacy of imperial as well as religious authority.

The Meridian Gate was the main gate of the Forbidden City. It was separated from the Gate of Heavenly Peace by a midway structure called the Gate of Correct Demeanor. The three gates standing from north to south in front of the imperial palaces added depth, solemnity, dignity and holiness to the Forbidden City. Erected on a high terrace, the Meridian Gate looked like the Chinese

The palace complex of the Forbidden City

Wall of the Forbidden City

Turret of the Forbidden City

The moat surrounding the Forbidden City

Plan of the Forbidden City

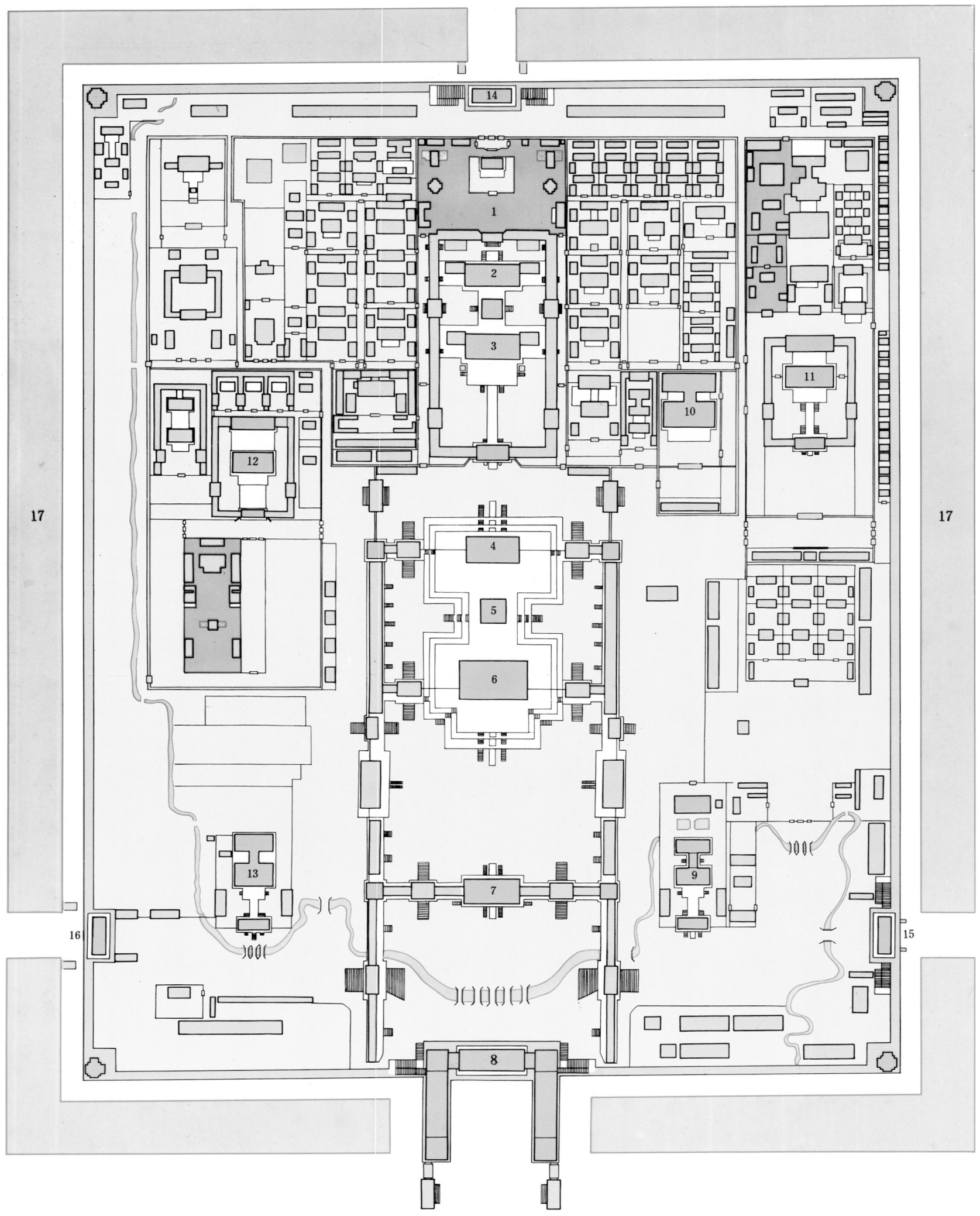

1. Imperial Garden
2. Hall of Terrestrial Tranquility
3. Hall of Celestial Purity
4. Hall of Preserved Harmony
5. Midway Hall of Harmony
6. Hall of Supreme Harmony
7. Gate of Supreme Harmony
8. Meridian Gate
9. Hall of Literary Glory
10. Hall of Ancestral Worship
11. Hall of the Norms of Government
12. Hall for the Consolation of Mothers
13. Hall of Military Prowess
14. Gate of Divine Might
15. East Flower Gate
16. West Flower Gate
17. Tongzi River

character *ao* (凹), meaning "hollow," on its plane figure. The middle tower was nine bays wide and had two layers of eaves. Together with four other towers, two on each side, it formed a five-tower structure known as the Five-Phoenix Tower. There were five gateways. The middle one was for exclusive use by the emperor. The empress had the right to pass through it only once in her life — at the time of her marriage ceremony. The three scholars who came first, second and third in a metropolitan examination had the right to leave the palaces through the middle gateway after they received their laureates from the emperor, but on no other occasion. Officials usually passed through two of the four gateways on the east and west sides. Two of the gateways, one on each side, remained closed unless there was a major court session, for which one on the east side was opened for civil officials, and another on the west side for military officers. During the Qing dynasty the emperor appeared on the tower of the Meridian Gate to attend a ceremony to accept the prisoners of war after a victorious military expedition. His regular court sessions were scheduled for the 5th, 15th and 25th day of each month. If he had moved his court to a place outside Beijing, the princes and officials lined up along the Imperial Way in front of the Meridian Gate were allowed to disperse after they were reviewed by a ritual official.

The Meridian Gate was also the place where the emperor punished his officials by flogging, which took place on the east side of the Imperial Way in front of the gate. Under the Ming dynasty, when court minister Shu Fen and his colleagues advised the emperor, in 1519, to cancel a trip to the south, he and some 130 other officials were flogged, and 11 of them died of the torture. In 1524, middle-and lower-ranking officials gathered and cried at one of the palace gates to drive home their demand for attendance at major ceremonies. Emperor Shizong considered their action outrageous and gave order for the flogging of 134 officials of rank five or under, and 17 of them died. In 1568, High Counsellor Shi Xing suffered flogging after he expressed disagreement with Emperor Muzong in a memorial he wrote to the court. The emperor even came to the Five-Phoenix Tower above the Meridian Gate to watch the flogging. The cruel

Gold Water River running across the square in front of the Gate of Supreme Harmony

Five Phoenix Tower on the Meridian Gate

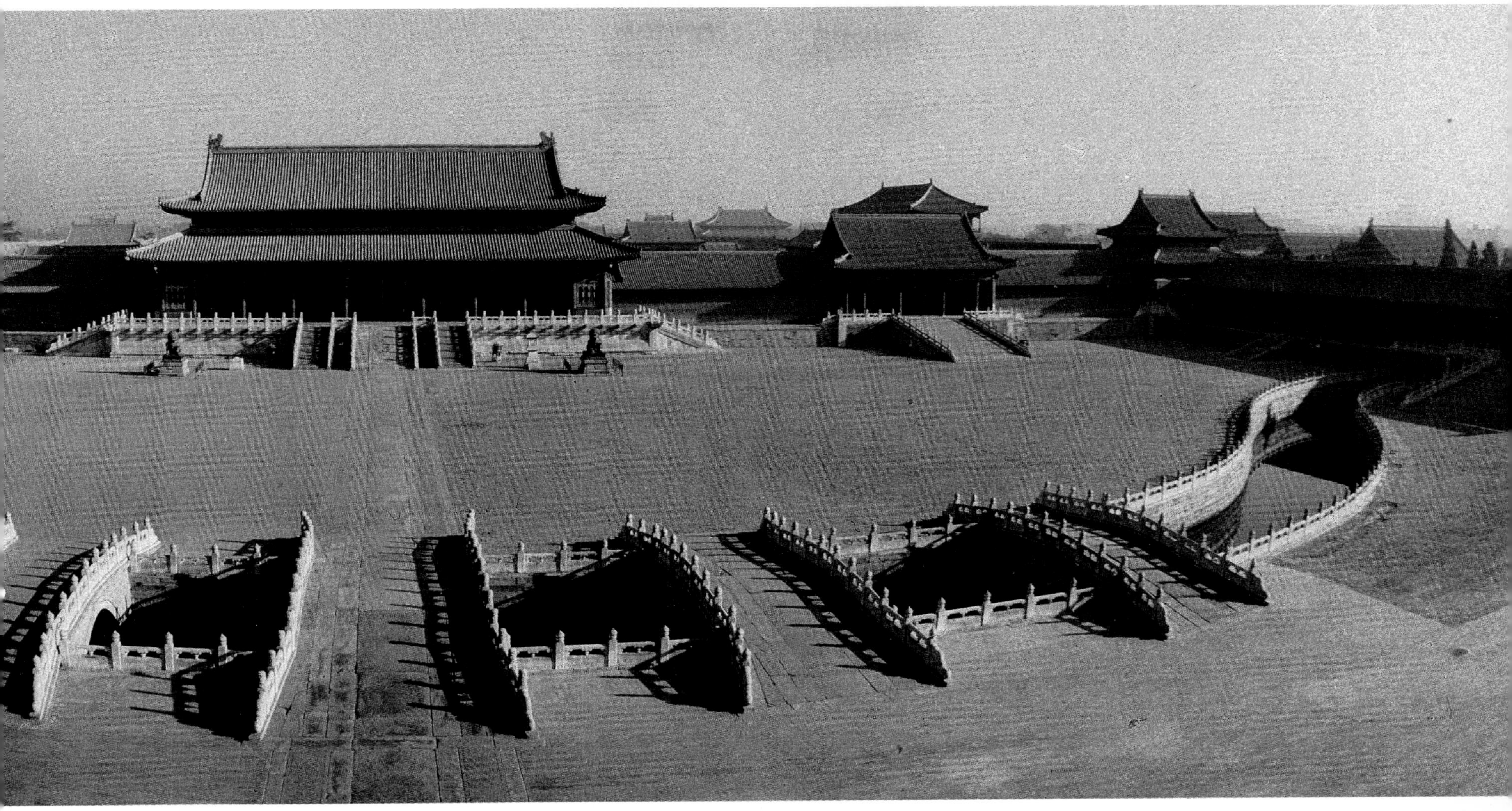

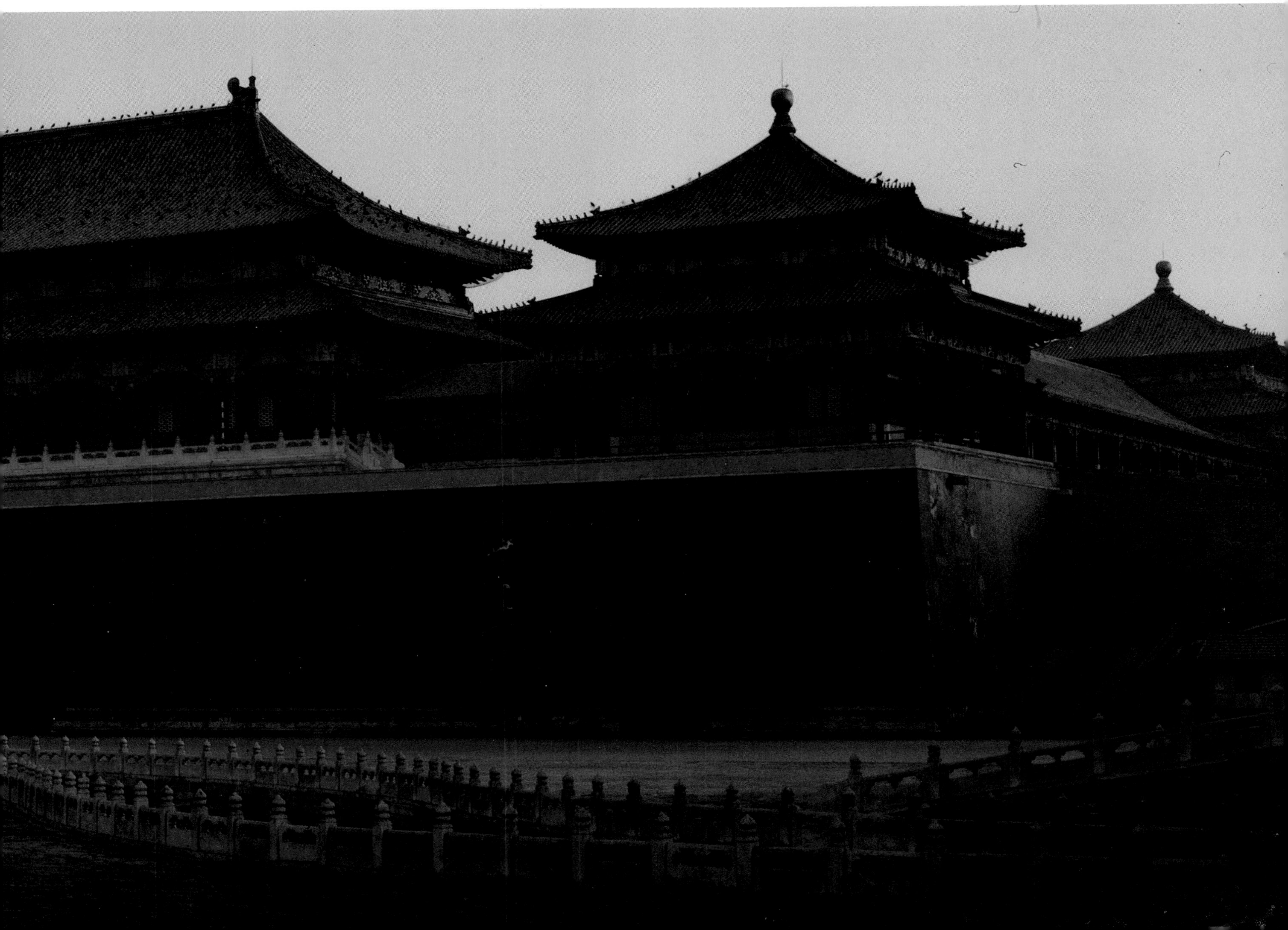

Stone lion in front of the Gate of Heavenly Peace

Plaque inscribed with the name of "Gate of Justice" in Manchu and Han languages

practice, called "court flogging," was not abolished until after the founding of the Qing Dynasty.

After entering the Meridian Gate one comes to the Gate for Paying Tribute to Heaven which leads to the three major halls of the Forbidden City. It was changed to the Gate of the Norms of Government and then to the Gate of Supreme Harmony in the Qing dynasty. Nine bays wide and four bays deep, the gate is the most magnificent one in the Forbidden City. According to a rule formulated in the early years of the Ming dynasty, civil and military officials came here every morning to report to the emperor who handled state affairs in their presence. This practice was known as "governing the state from the imperial gate." But it was given up later because some of the Ming emperors indulged themselves in wine and women and neglected their duties. Drawing a lesson from the fall of the Ming regime, the Qing emperors made a point of performing their duties everyday, a subject we will deal with in a later section. Between the Gate of Supreme Harmony and the Meridian Gate lies a square of 26,000 square meters. The Gold Water River, a clear stream which winds its way from west to east across the square, is spanned by five bridges. The finely-carved marble stone balustrades on both banks create a refreshing atmosphere of solemnity and tranquility. Standing in the square before the Gate of Supreme Harmony, you get the feeling of being in the midst of a gorgeous three-dimensional painting with a blue sky, yellow glazed-tile roofs glistening in the sunlight, and a green river gurgling between snow-white marble balustrades across the greyish brick ground.

The Forbidden City consists of the Outer Court, the Inner Court and the Imperial Garden. In the Outer Court are the three major halls — the Hall of Supreme Harmony, the Midway Hall of Harmony, and the Hall of Preserved Harmony, which are the chief components, supplemented by the Hall of Literary Glory and the Hall of Military Prowess on the two sides. They were the premises where the emperors presided over grand ceremonies and conducted major political activities. The three major halls were first called the Hall for Paying Tribute to Heaven, the Hall of Overwhelming Glory and the Hall of Scrupulous Behavior. Being exceedingly tall and unprotected by lightening arresters, they were burnt by thunder some 100 days after their completion After their reconstruction in 1441, the sixth year of Zhengtong reign of the Ming dynasty, they were again burnt by thunder in 1557, the 36th year of the Jiajing reign. When they were rebuilt a second time in 1562, the 41st year of the Jiajing reign, Emperor Jiajing, whose personal name was Zhu Houzong, ordered the construction of a Temple of the God of Thunder lest the new halls be destroyed again. He also changed the Hall for Paying Tribute to Heaven to the Hall of the Norms of Government, the Hall of Overwhelming Glory to the Hall of the Leading Star, and the Hall of Scrupulous Behavior to the Hall of the

People's. Sovereign. By the beginning of the Qing regime, the Manchu military aristocracy had come to the Central Plains from outside the Great Wall and unified China. The primary concern of the Qing ruling class was peace, harmony and stability, i.e. perpetuating its rule in a multi-national China. As the political center of the Qing regime, the Forbidden City was a typical embodiment of this policy. In 1645, the second year of the Shunzhi reign of the Qing dynasty, the hall of the Norms of Government, the Hall of the Leading Star, and the Hall of the People's Sovereign were rebuilt and renamed the Hall of Supreme Harmony, the Midway Hall of Harmony and the Hall of Preserved Harmony. The word "harmony" was stressed in the three names. In 1651, the eighth year of the Shunzhi reign, the Gate for Receiving the Mandate of Heaven was renovated and renamed the Gate of Heavenly Peace. The next year, the rear gate of the Forbidden City was renamed the Gate of Earthly Peace. The two gates, plus the two original gates of the Forbidden City — the East Gate of Peace and the West Gate of Peace, gave prominence to the idea of "peace." The plaques on the lintels of the entrances of the Forbidden City were inscribed in both Manchu and Han languages, demonstrating the Qing emperors' policy for harmony among nationalities and peace in the country.

The three major halls — the Hall of Supreme Harmony, the Midway Hall of Harmony, and the Hall of Preserved Harmony, cover a total of 85,000 square meters. They are located on an eight-meter-high terrace with three layers in the *sumeru* style and surrounded by white marble balustrades. At the foot of each baluster is a finely-carved dragon head which serves as a spillway. On a rainy day the dragon heads spurting water present a scene more impressive than a fountain, while on a fine day they form a sharp contrast of black and white under sunlight.

As the largest and tallest building in the Forbidden City, the Hall of Supreme Harmony is 60.01 meters wide, 33.33 meters long, and 35.5 meters high and has a floor space of 2,377 square meters, symbolic of the immensity of imperial power. It is the place where grand ceremonies were held for the enthronement of the emperor, the royal wedding, the granting of the title of empress, the appointment of commanders for battles, the celebration of the winter solstice, New Year's Day, and the emperor's birthday. Here the emperor accepted the obeisances of his generals and officials on important occasions. Bronze tortoise and crane sculptures are placed in front of the Hall of Supreme Harmony. Tortoises and cranes are symbols of longevity and of an everlasting reign. A time-telling stone sundial and a standard measure of volume are also there, symbolizing good times and bumper harvests. Inside the hall the gilded and carved throne seat, the six pillars decorated with dragons, the sunk panels with images of dragons sporting with balls above the throne seat, and the paintings in gold and other colors on the ceiling all contribute to the splendor of the building.

All these structures, interior decorations and furnishings serve to emphasize the supremacy of imperial power. Fourteen emperors of the Ming dynasty and 10 of the Qing dynasty ruled China from the throne seat here. Empror Taichang of the Ming dynasty reigned for the shortest time — only one month, while Emperor Kangxi of the Qing dynasty enjoyed the longest reign — 61 years. Emperor Qianlong of the Qing dynasty lived the longest — for 89 years, while the Qing emperor Tongzhi died the youngest — at 19. Emperor Hongxi of the Ming ascended the throne at 49, being the oldest crown prince to do so. The Qing emperor Xuantong or Aisin Gioro Pu Yi was placed on the throne at the earliest age — at only two.

The morning court session at the Hall of Supreme Harmony proceeded like this: When the drums were beaten the first time, civil and military officials gathered outside the Meridian Gate to wait solemnly in neat lines. At the second beating of the drums, the ceremonial officials ushered them into the open square in front of the Hall of Supreme Harmony where they lined up in 18 rows according to the nine official ranks. After taking a short rest in the Midway Hall of Harmony, the emperor entered the Hall of Supreme Harmony at the third drum beating and mounted the throne amidst ceremonial music. He took his seat amid clouds of smoke rising from fragrant incense as the ceremonial guards stood at attention on the two sides, creating a majestic scene. Then whips several meters long were lashed three times to add dignity to the atmosphere. Amid the strains of "Long Live the Emperor" the civil and military officials knelt and kowtowed to the emperor. Only then did the session begin according to set regulations. At the end of the session, the officials shouted "Long live the Emperor" amid ceremonial music. The cheers were so loud that they could be heard in the inner halls of the palace. For a grand ceremony as many as 3,000 guards would be employed and colorful sacrificial vessels displayed in front of the throne. The complicated and solemn ceremonies were designed to show that there was only one sovereign and all the people of the country were his subjects.

Situated behind the Hall of Supreme Harmony, the Midway Hall of Harmony is a square structure with a pyramidal roof and a gilded top. The red pillars of the hall and the gilded window frames are compact in composition and unique in style. In the hall there is a throne seat decorated with carved patterns of dragon in golden color and surrounded by valuable objects. Before a grand ceremony the emperor would receive important officials in this hall before proceeding to the Hall of Supreme Harmony. Behind the hall is a terrace which saw many historical events. In 1629, the second year of the Ming emperor Chongzheng's reign, Huangtaiji, Khan of the Later Jurchen (which later changed its name to Qing), sent an army from Shenyang to besiege Beijing. Yuan Chonghuan, Minister of National Defense and Garrison Commander of Hebei and Liaoning, led a cavalry force to lift the siege of the capital. The cavalrymen arrived at

Carved dragon head serving as a spillway at the foot of a baluster

the Wide Channel Gate after an uninterrupted journey of three days and nights, and dealt a crushing blow to the Jurchen army. Furious at the defeat, Huangtaiji forged the story that Yuan Chonghuan had made a secret deal with the enemy. Emperor Chongzheng, who believed the story, summoned Yuan Chonghuan to the terrace in the Midway Hall of Harmony on the excuse of discussing the question of army provisions with him. As soon as Yuan appeared, he was arrested and sentenced to death by slow torture. To honor the memory of the patriotic general, people built the Temple of Commander-in-Chief Yuan in Longtan Lake Park in Beijing. On two other occasions when Beijing was surrounded by Jurchen troops, the woman general Qin Liangyu led an army from Sichuan which was several thousand kilometers from Beijing to rescue the capital. Attractive and sophisticated, she was a good rider and archer, a capable commander and a talented poet. Emperor Chongzheng received her at the terrace in the Midway Hall of Harmony and presented her with wine and a poem he wrote for her, which reads:

The three major halls of the Forbidden City — Hall of Supreme Harmony, Midway Hall of Harmony and Hall of Preserved Harmony

Inside the Hall of Supreme Harmony. The throne in the middle is exactly on the north–south axis of the city of Beijing.

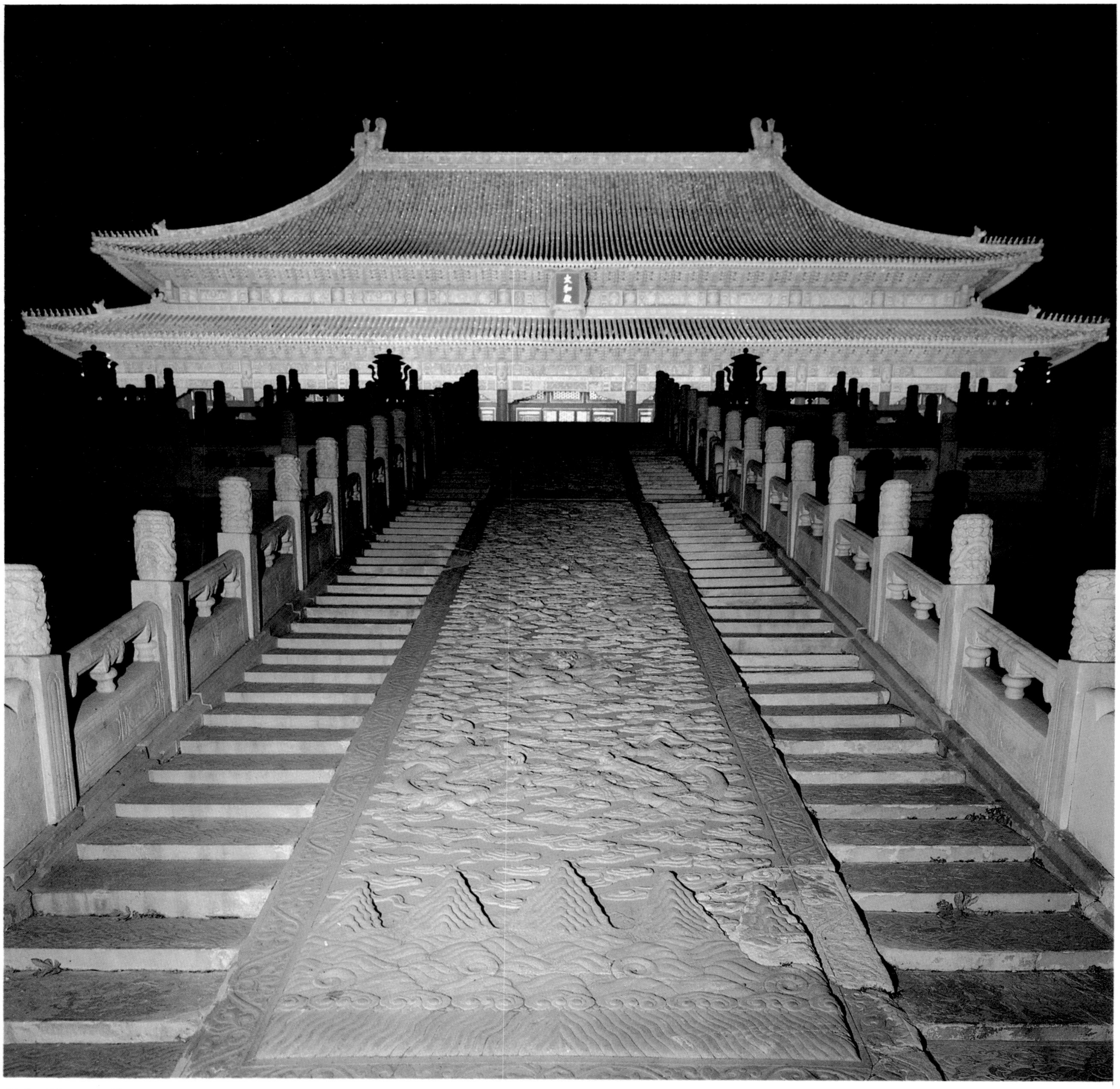
Hall of Supreme Harmony

Stone sundial

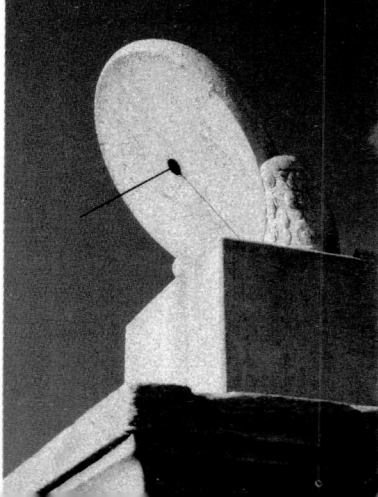

Bronze tortoise

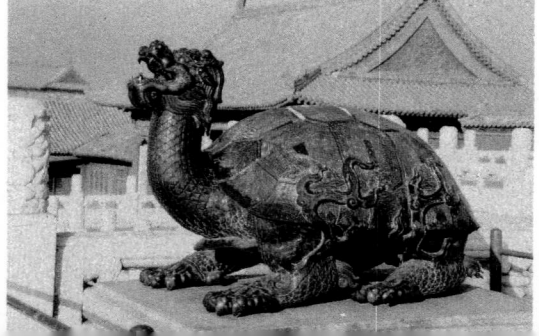

Bronze crane

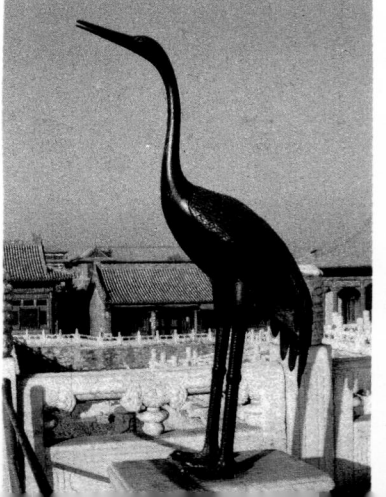

Standard measure of volume

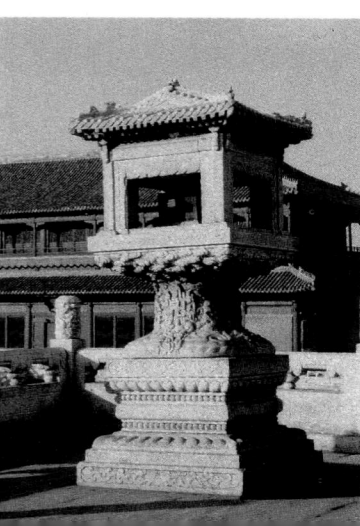

Inside the Midway Hall of Harmony

Inside the Hall of Preserved Harmony

You tailored your own battle robe
From elegant Sichuan brocade;
Mounted on a peach-blossom steed,
You volunteer to tackle the enemy;
Brave men are found everywhere in the country,
But is anyone ready to face the national crisis?
None except a lady from far, far away.

Qing Liangyu returned to Sichuan after recovering lost territory.

Located behind the Midway Hall of Harmony, the Hall of Preserved Harmony is nine bays wide and roofed in a double-eaved *xieshan* style. There is a throne seat in the hall. The huge red pillars, yellow screens, green incense burners and *golden bricks* making up the floor lend the hall a classical brilliance. The term *golden bricks* actually refers to the solidity and fine quality of the bricks which produce a sound as clear as that of golden bells. This is the kind of bricks which form the floors of the Hall of Preserved Harmony and all the other main halls in the Forbidden City. The Hall of Preserved Harmony was the place where the emperor gave banquets for officials and imperial examinations for scholars. In the Qing dynasty, the emperor often gave sumptuous banquets here for Mongolian and other princes on New Year's Eve. On the Lantern Festival which falls on the 15th day of the first lunar month, the emperor feted the aristocrats and generals. Beginning in the mid-Qing period, this hall served as the site of imperial examinations presided over by the emperor himself who listened to the best papers read by the officials before assigning the first, second and third academic titles to their authors. Then the papers of the second and third grades were submitted to the emperor with the authors' names and birthplaces. After the emperors decided on the list of names, it was announced in the square in front of the Hall of Supreme Harmony and then written on posters to be pasted by the Board of Rites on the wall outside the Left Gate of Lasting Peace (the red wall west of the southern end of Nanchizi Street in Beijing today). It was a great honor for scholars to see their names announced on the "Golden Posters." Those who received the title of *jinshi*, meaning a scholar who had passed the imperial examination, had to take another test before they were given official posts.

At the back of the Hall of Preserved Harmony, a huge rock stands midway along the stone stairs leading to the north. The largest in the Forbidden City, the carved rock is of fine quality, greenish in color and well-polished. It is 16.57 meters long, 3.07 meters wide, and 1.7 meters thick, and weighs 250 tons. On the fringes are patterns of curled weeds. On the left and right are motifs of lions and horses. In the middle are nine dragons flying in clouds. At the bottom are images of sea and river waters. The carved rock is noted for its size, fine composition, exquisite workmanship, and artistic charm. But how was it taken to Beijing from Fangshan County in the city's suburbs? In winter time a well was sunk every 500 meters all along a road of more than 50 kilometers from Fangshan to Beijing. Water was lifted from the well to be splashed over the road surface to create ice, and the huge rock was hauled along the frozen path. It took 20,000 laborers 28 days to finish the job at a cost of 110,000 taels of silver. The Forbidden City boasts a countless number of relics, including some of the best rock carvings.

The Hall of Literary Glory is situated left to the three major halls. In front of it is the Gate of Literary Glory and behind it the Main Hall of Worship. Flanked by side halls on left and right, it is an independent palace complex. The Ming emperor Zhengtong had the names of the military and civil officials of the whole country inscribed on the walls of the hall so that he could refer to them when considering their promotion, demotion or dismissal on the basis of their performance. But he did not know how to use the right people. Acting on the bad counsel of Wang Zhen, his favorite eunuch, he left Beijing on a military expedition and was taken prisoner after defeat. On the round screen in the hall is a map of China.

During the Qing period the Hall of Literary Glory became the place where the emperor lectured on the texts of Confucian classics. Before the session the emperor or his representative had to pay respects to the memorial tablet of Confucius in the hall. On the day of the session the emperor would dress himself plainly and take his seat in the hall to receive two instructors, a Manchu and a Han scholar, who knelt twice before him and kowtowed to him six times. After that they presented their interpretation of the classical texts to the emperor, who then spoke on the essence of these texts as the instructors listened to him on their knees. After the session the emperor treated them to tea.

South of the Hall of Literary Glory was the Archives of the Inner Chancery of the Ming and Qing regimes where important files were deposited. Covering 1,295 square meters, it was built with bricks and timber, the former covering the latter. The roof has yellow tiles. The Ming and Qing architectural styles were different, but the premises were used for the same purpose. In the Ming dynasty the building was used mainly to keep records of imperial reigns, memorials to the throne, announcements of official appointments, and chronological books, while in the Qing dynasty books and files of the former capital, known as the old files in the Manchu script, were added to the above categories of papers. Today the building houses over 10 million documents in 74 categories belonging to the central and local governments of the Ming and Qing dynasties over a period of 500 years. A large number of them are in the Manchu script. These are part of the most valuable historical archives preserved in China.

The Hall of Benevolence and Celebrations beside the Hall of Literary Glory was the scene of complicated palace struggles. During the Ming dynasty, Emperor Wanli gave the title of "Prince of Fortune" to Zhu Changxun, son of Lady Zheng, his favorite consort. The prince spent 300,000 taels of silver on his wedding, 280,000 taels of silver on the construction of his mansion in Luoyang, and was

Carved rock with dragon-and-cloud designs at the back of the Hall of Preserved Harmony

granted four million *mu* (over 260,000 hectares) of farmland by imperial order. Lady Zheng planned to secure his nomination as crown prince but failed. Instead, Zhu Changluo was made crown prince. One day, a man with a wooden club in hand beat up the eunuchs at the gate of the Hall of Benevolence and Celebrations, which was the residence of the crown prince, and made his way into the chambers. After he was arrested, he made a confession which implicated Lady Zheng. This gave rise to much indignation in the palace. Frightened, Lady Zheng cried before the emperor and pleaded unguilty, but the emperor told her that she had to ask the crown prince for mercy. After she pleaded with the crown prince, crying on her knees, the court issued an order to give up the case. This is known historically as the "Case of the Man with the Wooden Club." After Emperor Wanli died, the crown prince ascended the throne to become Emperor Taichang. One month after his enthronement, however, he fell ill, and someone presented a kind of red pills to him, claiming that they were elixirs of life. The emperor died after swallowing the pills. Historians call this the "Case of the Red Pills," and it was suspected that Lady Zheng was involved in the case. After Emperor Taichang's death, another emperor was put on the throne. It was rumored that Lady Zheng, supported by Lady Li, another imperial concubine, was plotting to take power and rule the country from the Hall of Celestial Purity. Thus she was forced to move to another hall. This is known as the "Case of Removal to Another Hall." These three cases give some idea of the complexity of palace politics in the late years of the Ming dynasty.

The Chamber of the Source of Literature is located behind the Hall of Literary Glory. Built in 1774, the 39th year of Emperor Qianlong's reign, it was used to store the *Complete Library of the Four Categories of Books.** The two-storied building is six bays wide and has protruding corridors at the front and the back. It is unique in architectural style, and its roof, covered with glazed black tiles which are green along the edges, presents an eye-catching contrast with the vast number of yellow-tiled roofs in the Forbidden City. The ridge of the roof is decorated with sea wave-and-dragon patterns. The Gold Water River running in front of the chamber not only adds beauty to the environment but symbolizes the concept of water overpowering fire or the prevention of fire. In accordance with the ancient Chinese thesis that the five basic elements of the universe balance one another and that black color is symbolic of water which overcomes fire, the roof was covered with glazed black tiles as an auspicious sign that the building would always be protected against fire. An imperial throne is placed at the center of the chamber, and bookshelves line the four walls. *The Complete Library of the Four Categories of Books* kept in the chamber originally comprised 79,337 *juan* bound in 36,304 volumes, which included 3,503 works. Emperor Qianlong brought in

---

* The four categories of books refer to the ancient classics, histories, the works of sages like Confucius, and the collected works of celebrated writers.

famous scholars from all parts of the country in 1772 to take part in the gigantic project, which took 15 years to complete. The scholars copied the treasured works with brush and ink on absorbant *xuan* paper, and finally produced seven copies and a reserve copy. One copy was kept in the Chamber of the Source of Literature in the Forbidden City and another in the Chamber of the Origin of Literature in the Garden of Perfect Splendor. The five other copies were placed in the Chamber of the Beginning of Literature in Shenyang, the Chamber of the Stream of Literature in Chengde, the Chamber of the Collection of Literature in Yangzhou, the Chamber of the Roots of Literature in Zhenjiang and the Chamber of Literary Prosperity in Hangzhou to be read by scholars. The reserve copy was kept in the *Hanlin* Academy in Beijing. As a result of incessant wars, however, only three copies are extant, one in Beijing, another in Gansu Province, and the third copy in Taibei.

The Hall of Military Prowess is located on the right side of the three major halls, with the Gate of Military Prowess at its front and the Hall of Cherished Memory at its back. Flanked by side halls on the east and west, it is a palatial complex symmetrical to the Hall of Literary Glory. It used to be the site for the celebration of the empresses' birthdays. In the last years of the Ming dynasty, Li Zicheng, leader of a peasant insurgent army, captured the capital, overthrew Ming rule and ascended the throne in the Hall of Military Prowess. In the early years of the Qing period, Prince Regent Dorgon led the Qing army into Beijing and placed his headquarters in this hall. During Emperor Qianlong's reign, the hall became the place for the compilation and production of books under the emperor's auspices. The 10,000-*juan* encyclopedia called A *Collection of Books of Ancient and Mordern Times* was compiled and produced here during Emperor Kangxi's reign. Later it was printed by a movable copper type and upwards of 250,000 copper characters were stored in the hall. The copper-type editions of books are appreciated for their excellent quality and popularly known as "palace editions."

Chamber of the Source of Literature

Part of the *Complete Library of the Four Categories of Books*

Behind the Hall of Military Prowess is the Hall of Benevolence and Intelligence commonly referred to as the Hall of the Tiger. It used to be the site where an emperor's coffin was placed prior to the funeral. During the Ming dynasty, the emperor often summoned artists to do paintings here. Once Wu Wei, a landscapist, was called in by Emperor Chenghua to do a painting. Being dead drunk, the artist stumbled into the hall on a pair of worn shoes with dishevelled hair and a dirty face. The sight of him made the emperor bellow with laughter, but he still ordered him to do a piece with pines and a spring. Resting on his knees, Wu Wei made some casual strokes with a brush and finished the painting in an instant, surprising the emperor with his vivid style. He often entered the Forbidden City with a scornful look at the bigwigs. Having offended them, he was sent back to his native place, but he was known as Number One Painter on account of his accomplishments.

South of the Hall of Military Prowess is a three-bay hall called the South Hall of Fragrance. Though small and simple in structure, it is famous for its storage of the portraits of the emperors of China's successive dynasties.

Behind the Hall of Preserved Harmony is the main entrance to the three rear palaces of the Forbidden City—the Gate of Celestial Purity. In a small courtyard in front of it are two gates, one on the east and one on the west—the Gate of National Prosperity and the Gate of the Distinguished Clan. Since they were the immediate entrances to the Inner Court, admission was restricted to ministers on duty and a few people summoned by the emperor. Nobody else was allowed to go in, not even princes or high officials. Ironically, however, peasant insurgents led by Chen Shuang and Chen Wenkui, acting in the name of the "Religion of Heavenly Justice," stormed into the gates with the help of eunuchs inside the palace. This took place on the 15th day of the ninth moon in 1813, or the 18th year of Emperor Jiaqing's reign when the emperor was on his way back from his summer resort in Rehe. On learning the news, Prince Min Ning, who later became Emperor Daoguang, gave orders to have the gates closed. The peasant insurgents piled up firewood to burn the Gate of the Distinguished Clan, but a battalion equipped with fire arms rushed to the scene through the Gate of Divine Might. Overwhelmed in number, the peasant insurgents were defeated. While all this was going on, the whole Forbidden City was thrown into chaos. Some officials got chariots ready for the empress and royal concubines to flee, others hid themselves in cabinets and shivered with fear. One plaque on the lintel of the Gate of the Distinguished Clan still shows some arrow heads reminiscent of the event.

Within the Gate of the Distinguished Clan is a row of one-story buildings, consisting of 12 rooms leaning against the north wall. The rooms on the east side were the premises of the all-powerful Privy Council, first established in 1729, or the seventh year of the reign of Emperor Yongzheng, for the direction of military operations in Northwest China. It was staffed by about five Privy Councilors who assisted the emperor in handling military and civil affairs. They saw the emperor everyday for the handling of important matters. In the Qing government the Privy Council held the highest position among all military and administrative offices and wielded the biggest power, and it was an enlightening innovation to place such an important and highly confidential institution in the shabby rooms at the foot of the walls of the Forbidden City.

The main gate to the Inner Court is the Gate of Celestial Purity. In the early years of Qing rule, the emperor lived in the Hall of Celestial Purity. As the Gate of Celestial Purity was closer to his residence than the Gate of Supreme Harmony, the emperor found it more convenient to conduct state affairs at the former every morning. He came to the gate at eight o'clock in the morning and took his seat on the throne behind a yellow desk at the gate. An official who recorded the proceedings stood to his west, facing the east, while the heads of the various government departments lined up to his east, facing the west, and knelt before him. All other officials knelt in an order arranged by rank. An official reporting to the emperor had to put the text of his report on the emperor's yellow desk and address him on his knees. After the emperor gave his instructions, the Grand Secretaries would write them out in the form of an imperial edict. The Qing emperors were more hard-working than the sovereigns of previous dynasties. For instance, Emperor Kangxi would come to the Gate of Celestial Purity for the daily court session in rain or snow, summer or winter. He presided over court sessions even when he was staying in his temporary palaces away from the Forbidden City.

The Inner Court consists mainly of the Hall of Celestial Purity, the Hall of Union and Peace, and the Hall of Terrestrial Tranquility, which are collectively known as the three rear palaces. They were flanked by the six eastern palaces and the six western palaces. These were the residences of the emperor and members of his family. The three main structures — the Hall of Celestial Purity, the Hall of Union and Peace, and the Hall of Terrestrial Tranquility, are located on the central axis of the Forbidden City. Together with the three major halls in the Outer Court they are called "the three great halls and three great palaces" which make up the core of the Forbidden City. The Inner Court shows a compact layout, strict regional divisions, close links between the halls and pavilions, and magnificence in style and decoration. The Inner Court owes its name to the fact that every courtyard is encircled by corridors and high walls to become a restricted, heavily guarded area.

The names of the Hall of Celestial Purity, the Hall of Union and Peace, and the Hall of Terrestrial Tranquility have a philosophical implication originating in the Confucian classic, the *Book of Changes*, according to which the celestial domain corresponds to the male sex and the earth, to the female sex. This was why the emperor lived in the Hall of Celestial Purity and the empress lived in the Hall of Terrestrial Tranquility. The Hall of Union and Peace located between the above two halls is symbolic of the union of heaven and earth, or the union of the male and female sexes, which results in universal peace and tranquility. The classical meaning of the names made it almost impossible to change them.

In the Ming dynasty and the early Qing period, the Hall of Celestial Purity contained the emperor's bedchamber. The double-eaved building, nine bays wide and five bays deep, is the largest in the Inner Court. It was burnt down and rebuilt several times. Emperor Zhengde of the Ming dynasty was given to luxury and sensual pleasures. He trusted unworthy people and made a mess of court affairs. Every Spring Festival he would have fancy lanterns hung up in his palaces. In 1514, or the ninth year of his reign, Zhu Chenghao, the Prince of Ning, presented to him a uniquely-designed lantern which was hung at a place in the Hall of Celestial Purity where gunpowder was stored in felt tents. This caused a big fire which reduced the hall to a cinder. At the time the emperor was on his way to *baofang* (a room for obscene pleasures). Seeing the hall in the flames, he laughed and said, "That looks better than fireworks." In the same year he gave orders for the recruitment of 100,000 soldiers and laborers to rebuild the hall at a cost of a million taels of silver, which were collected as agricultural tax from all over the country. Since he had no son, his cousin succeeded him after his death to become

Plaque inscribed with the name of "Gate of the Distinguished Clan" in Manchu and Han languages

Emperor Jiajing. A devout Taoist, Emperor Jiajing launched large-scale construction of Taoist temples. He treated so badly the maidens waiting on him that he was almost assassinated by one of them. After this incident, nine warm chambers were set aside on two floors in the Hall of Celestial Purity as the emperor's bedrooms, each with three beds, so he could sleep on any of the 27 beds as a precaution against any attempt on his life.

After Qing rule was established, the Hall of Celestial Purity was renovated and remained the emperor's living quarters. However, due to poor engineering quality the roofs leaked on rainy days. The emperors were forced to live on the Sea Terrace Islet on the Central-South Lake to wait for the completion of the repairs. After the second renovation, although the Hall of Celestial Purity continued to be the emperor's bedchamber, it was used by Emperor Shunzhi and Emperor Kangxi to conduct court sessions, meet officials, hold ceremonies, receive foreign envoys, do reading and writing, and examine memorials to the throne and write instructions on them. It was Emperor Yongzheng who moved his living quarters to the Hall of Mental Cultivation and made the Hall of Celestial Purity the main site for political activities in the imperial palace.

At the center of the Hall of Celestial Purity is the magnificent imperial throne placed against a five-fold screen of quality wood with finely-carved patterns of flying dragons in elegant style. In the center on each fold of the screen is an inscribed motto. One motto reads: "Success is won by determination; extensive achievements depend on hard work." Another says: "Wisdom lies in getting to know people; benevolence means bringing peace to your subjects." The arrangement and decoration in the Hall of Celestial Purity show a domination by the yellow color and by dragon patterns. Actually both are dominant in all the palaces of the Forbidden City, but even more so in the Hall of Supreme Harmony in the Outer Court and the Hall of Celestial Purity in the Inner Court. Of course, different colors are preferred in different countries of the world, and the preference varied from one dynasty to another in China's history. Some countries in the world prefer blue color while others like green, each making its favorite color the noblest one. In China, white was the supreme color of the Shang dynasty (c. 16th-11th centuries B.C.). The Western Zhou dynasty (c. 11th century-771 B.C.) respected red color,

Inside the Hall of Celestial Purity

Brocade-covered box in which the name of the successor to the throne was kept secret

while the Qin dynasty (221-206 B.C.) regarded black as the noblest color. The yellow color won supremacy in later times on the basis of the theory of the five elements formulated in the Confucian classic, the *Book of History*. The five elements refer to five substances — water, fire, wood, metal and earth, among which earth is regarded as the origin of everything else in the universe. Earth has a yellow color, which again is the color of gold, a symbol of wealth and distinction. This was why the emperors preferred to use the yellow color of gold in decorating their palaces. A typical example is the Hall of Celestial Purity where yellow color appears on practically everything — the plaques inscribed with calligraphy, the coiled dragons painted on the beams, the gilded pillars featuring couplets of writings, the screen behind the throne as well as the throne itself, the carpets covering the stairs, the balustrades on the terraces, and the table on which the imperial tripod is placed. As soon as the emperor appeared in a fantastic yellow ,imperial robe embroidered elaborately with gold and silver patterns of dragon, the entire hall would be dominated by a unique aura of dignity.

Speaking of the patterns of dragon used by Chinese emperors, we have to go back to the times when dragon was an object of totem worship in China's primitive tribes. Later on it became a semi-legendary animal with a long body and a beard, as well as horns, scales and feet. It was believed to be capable of walking, diving and flying and gradually recognized as the symbol of the Chinese nation. In feudal times the dragon and the emperor were synonymous with each other. The emperor was the genuine dragon, the son of heaven. Thus patterns of dragon were used extensively in the imperial palaces. In the Hall of Celestial Purity, they are found on the lower fringes of the horizontal boards, on the screen, on the back, arm-rests, bottom and legs of the throne seat, on the carpet, on the balustrades, and on the table on which the incense burners are placed. All these, coupled with an emperor clad in an imperial robe embroidered with patterns of dragons sitting on the throne, would turn the hall into a world of dragons to emphasize the unchallengeable authority of monarchical power.

The zoomorphic figures decorating the ridges of the Hall of Celestial Purity are rich and varied, such as *chiwen* and other dragon decorations. According to the book *Notes on Books in the Imperial Library*, dragons fall into nine categories, each with its distinctive features. The first, *bixi*, looks like a tortoise and can take a heavy burden, and so is used to decorate the base of a stone stele. The second, *chiwen*, is an animal which likes to watch things from a distance, and is therefore placed on top of a roof. The third, *pulao*, is a small, roaring animal and is suited for the handle of a bell. The fourth, *bi'an*, looks like a tiger and usually appears on the gate of a prison. The fifth, *taotie*, has a good appetite and is used on the lid of a food container in the form of a tripod. The sixth, *gongxia* loves to swim and is carved on the balusters of bridges. The seventh, *yaci*, is apt to kill other animals and is often used on the handle of a sword. The eighth, *suanni*, resembles a lion and likes fire and smoke and so is placed on an incense burner. And the ninth, *jiaotu*, is similar to a snail and likes to close itself up, and is used to decorate a door.

Above the throne seat in the Hall of Celestial Purity is a horizontal board inscribed with four Chinese characters, *zheng da guang ming,* meaning "be open and aboveboard." During the Qing dynasty, a box covered with brocade was placed behind the horizontal board which contained the emperor's decision on the successor to the throne. This represented a major reform on the question of succession.

In the Middle Ages, the state systems of various countries fell into two categories. Some of them followed a republican system, such as the Republic of Venice where the state leader was elected by assemblymen to hold a lifelong position. More countries had a monarchy and, in some cases, an elected monarch. For instance, the German King Charles IV issued the Golden Bull in 1356 in which he laid down rules for the election of the German king by seven dukes. China always had a hereditary monarchy. The general rule was succession by the eldest son of the empress. The system helped avoid the fratricide over succession, but it had many defects. For instance, Zhu Yuanzhang, founder of the Ming dynasty and a contemporary of Charles IV of Germany, made his eldest son crown prince, who nevertheless died before he did. So he had to replace him with his eldest grandson Zhu Yunwen. After the latter became emperor, the Prince of Yan, Zhu Di, who was Zhu Yuanzhang's third son, rose in rebellion, captured Nanjing, the national capital, and took over the throne. He became Emperor Yongle and moved the capital to Beijing. The Manchus who founded the Qing dynasty had originally lived in Northeast China beyond the Great Wall and had not followed a system of passing the crown to the eldest son. The Great Khan of the Manchus, Nurhachi, had 16 sons. After his death, a bitter struggle over succession ensued, during which Empress Nala Shi was forced to commit suicide. After Huangtaiji came to the throne, he changed his title from Great Khan to Emperor and founded the Qing regime. He had 11 sons. After he died, all his sons aspired to the throne, resulting in a series of crises. Finally his six-year-old son Fulin was chosen as Emperor Shunzhi. Although Shunzhi had eight sons, three died early. On his deathbed he chose his eight-year-old son Xuanye, who had survived smallpox, as the next emperor. Xuanye, who became Emperor Kangxi, had 35 sons. Trying to prevent fratricide among his sons after his death, and drawing on the lessons of the previous three emperors, he decided to choose one of his sons, not necessarily the eldest one, as crown prince. In 1675 or the 14th year of his reign, he proclaimed his second son, Yunreng, crown prince. To strengthen his position Yunreng built up his own faction, while his brothers did likewise and trumped up charges against Yunreng, each in his attempt to become successor to the throne. The aristocrats, ministers and generals attached themselves to one faction or another to secure their respective positions. The struggle became so fierce that in 1708 or the 47th year of his reign, Emperor Kangxi summoned the officials to the Forbidden City and announced the dismissal of the crown prince. He wept bitterly in front of the officials and lay awake for six days and nights. After this, however, all his sons stepped up their manoeuvres to grab the position. The next summer Yunreng was reinstated as crown prince. But the power struggle in the palace did not stop there. Three years later, Yunreng was deposed as crown prince a second time. The issue remained unsettled even when Emperor Kangxi was incurably ill. Although Emperor Yongzheng inherited the crown, he was suspected of usurping the throne by murdering his father. Taking into account the historical lessons of the previous emperors, he initiated the practice of choosing crown prince without any announcement before his death. It was he who first wrote his decision on a piece of paper, put it in a brocade-covered box, and placed the box behind the horizontal board inscribed with the four Chinese characters, *zheng da guang ming* ("Be open and aboveboard."). After Emperor Yongzheng died, his uncle, Prince Zhuang whose personal name was Yunlu, and others entrusted by the late emperor opened the sealed box and proclaimed the fourth prince, Hongli, successor to the throne, who became Emperor Qianlong. The announcement prevented a struggle over succession. In the late period of the Qing regime, however, the practice was discontinued because Emperors Xianfeng, Tongzhi and Guangxu either had one son only or had no son at all.

The Hall of Celestial Purity is flanked by two smaller halls and encircled by a 40-bay corridor forming an independent sub-area. There are symmetrical gates along the east and west walls. The side hall on the east is the Hall for Publicizing Benevolence which was used to keep authentic copies of books of the Song, Jurchen, Yuan and Ming dynasties as well as Ming replicas of books of the Song dynasty. A horizontal plaque bearing Emperor Qianlong's inscription hangs in the hall. An imperial catalog gives us some idea of the rich collections at the time.

The side hall on the west is called the Hall of Infinite Benevolence, which again has an inscription in Emperor Qianlong's handwriting. It is an essay dedicated to the hall and contains the sentence, "Criticism brings happiness; flattery portends evil."

In the east section of the sub-area is the Hall of Correct Demeanor for keeping the emperor's crown, robes and footwear. To its north is the imperial tea storage, while to its south the imperial pharmacy.

The Hall of Diligence located in the west section of the sub-area used to be the emperor's study. Emperor Kangxi received his education here as a child. In later times the emperors came here every autumn to examine files on convicts punishable by death before deciding on their execution. At the western end of the sub-area is the South Study where members of the Imperial Academy offered advice to the emperor whenever he asked for it. At the eastern end is the Upper Study where the princes did their reading and writing.

The Hall of Union and Peace is located between the Hall of Celestial Purity and the Hall of Terrestrial Tranquility. It is a square, single-eaved building with a gilded spire and four upturned ridges. In the Qing dynasty it served as the place where people offered congratulations to the empress on her birthday, New Year's Day and the winter solstice. On these occasions the emperor's concubines and the wives of princes, aristocrats, and high officials paid respects to the empress by kneeling and kowtowing to her. Starting with the reign of Emperor Qianlong (r. 1735-96), 25 jade seals of the emperor were kept here under the charge of a senior eunuch. None of the seals could be used unless the eunuch had secured the emperor's personal permission through the cabinet ministers. On the east side of the hall is an ancient Chinese clepsydra made of bronze, a device for counting time by drips of water. In 1013, the ninth year of the Tiansheng reign of the Northern Song dynasty, Yansu invented a method called the lotus drip. He drilled holes in the upper part of a clepsydra so that any surplus water would flow out, to keep a constant water level and thus raise the accuracy of the timepiece. Apart from water, mercury or sand was used to register time. In 979, the 4th year of the Taipingxingguo reign of the Northern Song dynasty, Zhang Sixun made a "mercury-drip clock" to replace the "water-drip clock." In the Yuan dynasty, Zhan Xiyuan invented a "five-wheel sand-drip clock." All these were landmarks in the evolution of the clepsydra. The bronze clepsydra in the Hall of Union and Peace is more than five meters high and has three sections. It rests on a platform in a square pavilion with double eaves and a coffered roof. After the appearance of the mechanized chime clock, however, the clepsydra became a museum piece.

The Hall of Terrestrial Tranquility is located behind the Hall of Union and Peace. Together with the Hall of Celestial Purity and the Hall of Union and Peace, it rests on an I-shaped foundation. The double-eaved hall is nine bays wide and five bays deep. It is similar to the Hall of Celestial Purity in style, only smaller in dimensions. It was the principal hall for the empress in the Ming dynasty. It remained so in the Qing dynasty but only in name because the empress no longer lived here. In 1656, the 13th year of the Shunzhi reign of the Qing dynasty, it was changed radically after the style of the Manchu palace in Shengjing, present-day Shenyang, in the following ways:

First, the original Ming windows with rhombic patterns were replaced by windows with straight grids and with the paper pasted on the outside. Before the Manchus conquered the Central Plains, they had lived in Northeast China where the weather was colder than south of the Great Wall. Their houses had windows operated from the outside and the paper was also pasted on the outside. The same custom was adopted for the Hall of Terrestrial Tranquility in the Forbidden City.

Secondly, the hall's central door was moved to a side room in the east wing. Opposite to the door, a stove and a pot were placed by the north window to stew meat for sacrificial ceremonies. This was also done in the style of a similar hall in the Manchu palace in Shengjing.

Thirdly, in a room in the west wing three *kang* (heatable brick beds) were built along the north, south and west walls without any space in between. Seats were placed on the *kang* for princes and court officials to help themselves to some sacrificial meat. First they would attend a sacrificial ceremony according to the shamanist practice of the Manchus. Then they would cook the pork used as sacrifice in a pot and eat it on the *kang* in a room in the west wing.

By the custom of the Manchus in Northeast China, a room had three *kang* along the north, south and west walls. The south bed was most respectable followed by the ones on the west and the north. At night, members of the family, male or female, would sleep on a bed assigned according to his or her status. The same custom was followed in the Hall of Terrestrial Tranquility in the Forbidden City. Sacrificial ceremonies were held in the palace. The Manchus believed

Tiles with dragon designs used for eaves in the Forbidden City

Decorated ridge of the Hall of Celestial Purity

A passageway lined by the Six West Palaces in the Forbidden City

Bronze clepsydra in the Hall of Union and Peace | Stove for cooking sacrificial meat in the Hall of Terrestrial Tranquility

in shamanism, which means sorcery. The primitive religion divides the universe into a paradise, a human world and a hell. A shaman or sorcerer could bring people happiness or cure their sickness by his prayers. When he presided over a sacrificial ceremony, he wore the hat and robe of a god, beat his waist drum and shook his waist bells. Chanting incantations, he moved about in a mysterious way to give the impression that he had become the incarnation of a god or ghost. Later the same kind of ceremony was introduced into the palace, but now the gods to be worshipped included Sakyamuni, General Guan, a famous warrior of the Three Kingdoms period, as well as Mongolian gods, representing a combination of various religious beliefs. Sacrificial ceremonies were held in the Hall of Terrestrial Tranquility in the mornings and evenings, and a major one would be attended by the emperor and empress. Incense was burnt on such occasions and the sacrificial objects included cakes, wine and pork from pigs slaughtered for such occasions. Songs were sung, and poems recited to the accompaniment of music. Four pigs were slaughtered for an ordinary ceremony and as many as 39 sacrificed for a major one in spring or autumn. The slaughtering and stewing were done in the hall , and the cakes were also made there. After a ceremony, the participants ate the meat right in the hall.

Fourth, the room in the east wing of the Hall of Terrestrial Tranquility served as the wedding chamber of the emperor. The room , known as the East Chamber of Warmth, was used for the purpose by Emperors Kangxi, Tongzhi and Guangxu and also by Emperor Xuantong who was dethroned at the time of the 1911 Revolution but was allowed to stay in the Forbidden City in the early period of the republic. The red door of the room was decorated with the gilded Chinese character " 囍 ", meaning double happiness. A red wall inside the door was decorated with the same gilded character, meaning happiness for the emperor and empress right after they entered the door. The dragon-and-phoenix bed was placed against the northern wall of the chamber.

The Six East Palaces and Six West Palaces, which are located on the two sides of the three rear halls, contained the bedchambers of the royal concubines. Every palace forms a courtyard covering an area of about two hectares. It consists of a front chamber for reception purposes, a bedchamber and side chambers. These palaces are linked by roads at both ends of which are the gates and houses for the guards. Every courtyard is neatly laid out. Aside from the front gate , it has a gate on each of the four sides opening out to a path or an alley.

Beginning with the reign of Emperor Yongzheng of the Qing dynasty, the Hall of Mental Cultivation was the emperor's bed-chamber as well as his office. The hall is an I-shaped structure. The front and rear chambers are linked and encircled by covered corridors. The front chamber was the place where the emperor conducted state business, while the rear chamber served as his bedroom. The structure of the building features a compact layout in a tranquil environment. The bedchamber for the Qing emperors had been in the Hall of Celestial Purity. After the death of Emperor Kangxi, Emperor Yongzheng's father, his coffin was placed here before the funeral. Yongzheng, who was rumored to have usurped the throne by murdering his father, chose to live in the Hall of Mental

Cultivation instead of the Hall of Celestial Purity. The former thus became the bedchamber and office for him and the Qing emperors after him.

In the front chamber of the Hall of Mental Cultivation is the throne seat under a painted coffered ceiling. Bookshelves are placed on the left and right of the chamber. This was where the emperor received his ministers and conducted day-to-day affairs. On the two sides are the East and West Chambers of Warmth.

Located to the east of the main hall, the East Chamber of Warmth is tastefully furnished and has a dignified atmosphere. The carpeted floor glimmers under a number of palace lanterns. A partition screen stands in the western corner while a small table is placed in the eastern corner. In the center of the chamber is a throne seat, behind which is a yellow gauze curtain with a black canopy draping to the floor. Another throne seat, placed behind the curtain, was provided for the empress dowager to "conduct state affairs from behind a curtain" i.e., to listen to the report of court ministers and give them instructions without seeing them. She was supposed to act on behalf of a child emperor. The practice, dictated by the feudalistic segregation between men and women, was non-existant in the Ming dynasty. Zhu Yuanzhang, founder of the Ming dynasty, was keenly aware of the historical lesson that disturbances in the palace were often caused by court ladies taking power into their hands. Thus he issued an order to the effect that though the empress was the country's first lady, she must not meddle in politics. As for the royal concubines, they were only supposed to provide pleasant company for the emperor and should do nothing more. Among the 24 emperors of the Ming and Qing dynasties who ruled China from the Forbidden City, four Ming emperors and five Qing emperors were enthroned before they came of age. Emperor Wanli of the Ming, who ascended the throne at the age of 10, was aided by Prime Minister Zhang Juzheng. When Emperor Shunzhi of the Qing came to the throne at only six, he was assisted by two princes regent — Prince Zheng, whose personal name was Ji'erhalang, and Prince Rui, whose personal name was Dorgon. When Emperor Kangxi of the Qing ascended the throne at eight, he was aided by four ministers. Xuantong, the last emperor of the Qing, was enthroned when he was only two. His father, Prince Chun, was appointed Prince Regent. The practice of "conducting state affairs from behind a curtain" was initiated during the reign of Emperor Tongzhi of the Qing. When he became emperor at six, he was aided by eight ministers appointed by the late emperor. But his mother, Imperial Consort Cixi, carried out a coup d'etat in league with Prince Gong, Yixin, killed the regents, and seized power. Thus together with Empress Ci'an, Cixi began to conduct state affairs from behind a curtain. But real power was in the hands of Cixi, who had now become Empress Dowager. After Emperor Tongzhi died at an early age and was succeeded by the four-year-old Guangxu, Cixi continued to dominate the court. Here we will not go into the advantages and disadvantages of the practice. However, the concluding passage in the "Biographies of Empresses and Imperial Consorts" in A Draft History of the Qing Dynasty blamed the fall of a dynasty on the rule by a woman, Cixi. This seems to be an oversimplification of history.

The West Chamber of Warmth, located on the west side of the main hall, has a stately and awe-inspiring atmosphere. The horizontal board hanging in the hall is inscribed with four Chinese characters *qin zheng qin xian* which means "Be diligent at state administration and trust only the virtuous." A wise feudal ruler is indeed distinguished from a worthless one by diligence at his tasks or indulgence in a decadent life and by trusting upright people or endearing the obsequious and sinister ones. At the western end of the chamber is an exquisite and tranquil room where Emperor Qianlong kept three rare models of calligraphy, namely, the *Kuaixue Copybook* by the celebrated ancient calligrapher Wang Xizhi, *Zhongqiu Copybook* by his son Wang Xianzhi, and *Boyuan Copybook* by Wang Xun. Thus he called the place the "Hall of Three Rarities." Later he compiled a collection of 340 calligraphic works by 135 calligraphers from the Wei and Jin dynasties to the end of the Ming dynasty, all of which had been preserved in the Forbidden City, and gave it the title of *Calligraphic Models of the Hall of Three Rarities*. It was acknowledged as a priceless collection of calligraphic works. Emperor Qianlong was extremely fond of the writing brush and was an accomplished calligrapher. Couplets and horizontal inscriptions in his handwriting remain on the walls of the chamber.

The rear section of the Hall of Mental Cultivation served as the emperor's bedchamber. Five bays wide from east to west, it is luxuriously furnished and is said to have had as many as 724 decorative articles during the Tongzhi reign. In the central room of

Inside the Hall of Terrestrial Tranquility

Rear chamber of the Hall of Mental Cultivation serving as the emperor's bedroom

East Chamber of Warmth of the Hall of Mental Cultivation

Hall of Three Rarities. A small room covering an area of eight square meters, it was tastefully furnished and noted for its collection of copybooks of calligraphic models.

the suite are a heatable bed, a desk, and a chair on either side of the desk. In the east inner room and west inner room are the emperor's beds, called the dragon beds. The walls of the east inner room are inlaid with mirrors, while the west inner room is provided with a green gauze screen. At night the curtains of the beds in both rooms would be drawn as a precaution against any attempt on the emperor's life. The Hall of Consolation to the east of the emperor's bedchamber used to be the empress's bedchamber whenever she lived with the emperor in the Hall of Mental Cultivation. The Hall of Swallows' Happiness to the west of the emperor's bedchamber was the bedchamber for the imperial concubines whenever they were summoned to live with the emperor. Usually they lived in the rooms to the east and west of the Hall of Consolation and the Hall of Swallow's Happiness. Remarks by a Qing emperor and his daily activities were recorded in a book called *Records of the Emperor's Daily Activities*. A Department of Records of the Emperor's Life was set up in the Forbidden City, which was staffed by officials specializing in such routine.

Behind the Hall of Mental Cultivation lies the Six West Palaces, which served as living quarters for concubines. The Six West Palaces are the Hall of Immortality, the Hall of Modest Ladies and the Hall of Preserved Elegance from south to north on the east, and the Hall of Lucky Start (later known as the Hall of the Ultimate Origin), the Hall of Eternal Spring and the Hall of Universal Happiness from south to north on the west. Though there was a great number of buildings in the Forbidden City, the premises were still very crowded. In the early years of the reign of Zhu Yuanzhang, the first emperor of the Ming dynasty, it was stipulated that the staff of the imperial palace should be made up by 75 male officials and 18 female ones working in six bureaus and one division. The total number of 93 was 150 less than the palace staff of the Tang dynasty which had 190 male officials and more than 50 female ones, or 240 people working in six bureaus and 24 divisions. But the restriction remained on paper. According to what an old Ming eunuch told Emperor Kangxi, there had been as many as 9,000 palace maids and 100,000 eunuchs in the Forbidden City in the Ming dynasty. The number of people was so big that there was simply not enough food to go round. Everyday a few of them might die of hunger. The figures may be a little exaggerated, but we can be sure that there was a surprisingly big number of palace maids and eunuchs in the Ming dynasty. A eunuch was a male servant employed in the Forbidden City. Most of them had been forced to accept castration because their families were poor. The great majority

of them remained hard laborers all their lives and died miserably. Very few of them won the emperor's favor to become influential courtiers. Most of the palace maids were forced to work in the palace at around 10 years of age to wait on the empress and royal concubines. For instance, under Emperor Jiajing as many as 1,080 palace maids were chosen on four occasions. Some of them were taken to the palace at a very early age, including a few of them who later became concubines. For example, Wan, concubine of Emperor Chenghua, had come to the Forbidden City at the age of four. Zhang Yu, concubine of Emperor Tianqi, had been recruited at seven, while Lizhuang, concubine of Emperor Taichang, had been in the palace since she was 10. The palace maids led an extremely miserable life. They would be reprimanded, flogged or even beaten to death once the emperor, empress or royal concubines were displeased with them. Unable to stand the misery, some of them committed suicide. Emperor Jiajing of the Ming had over 200 palace maids beaten to death. A maid might also win the emperor's favor and become a concubine. Shang, a maid for Emperor Jiajing, happened to be liked by him when she was 13. She received the title of "Shang the Beauty" and enjoyed the noblest status. However, the majority of the maids were condemned to a lonely life in the palace where they wasted their youthful years. *The Lyrics of the Palace* written by Chen Li reads:

Ten thousand beauties are locked in the Six Palaces,
Spending their youthful years in low spirits;
Wild parties go on under brightly-lit lanterns deep into the
   night,
And the emperor finds no time to see the attractive maidens.

Even if they were made royal concubines, some of the palace maids came to a miserable end. After Zhang Yu, concubine of Emperor Tianqi, became pregnant, she was envied and hated by the emperor's wet nurse and Wei Zhongxian, a powerful and sinister eunuch. She was locked up in an isolated palace and was not given food or drinking water for more than 10 days. One rainy day she crawled out of the door to drink the water running down from the eaves and died on the spot. Some of the royal concubines became sacrificial objects for a dead emperor. After the death of Zhu Yuanzhang, the first Ming emperor, 14 concubines were forced to die and were buried with him. Emperor Hongxi of the Ming who had been on the throne for only one year, was buried with four of his concubines. Another Ming emperor, Xuande, reigned 10 years and was buried with 10 concubines. The most cruel and astonishing case

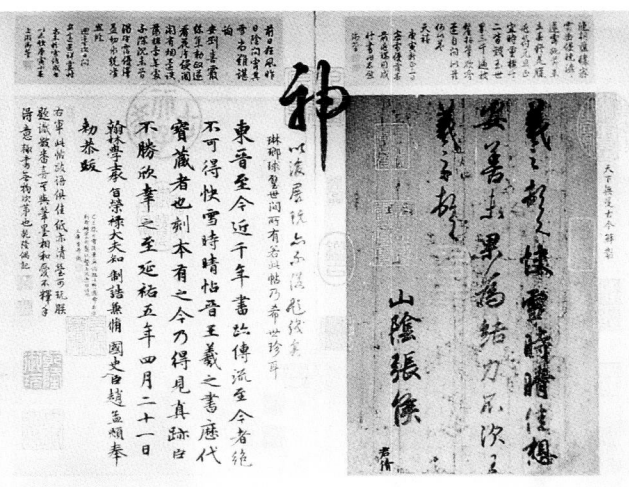

The Kuaixue Copybook by Wang Xizhi

The "dragon bed" in the rear chamber of the Hall of Mental Cultivation

Ornaments worn by the emperor

The book *Records of Emperor Yongzheng's Daily Activities*

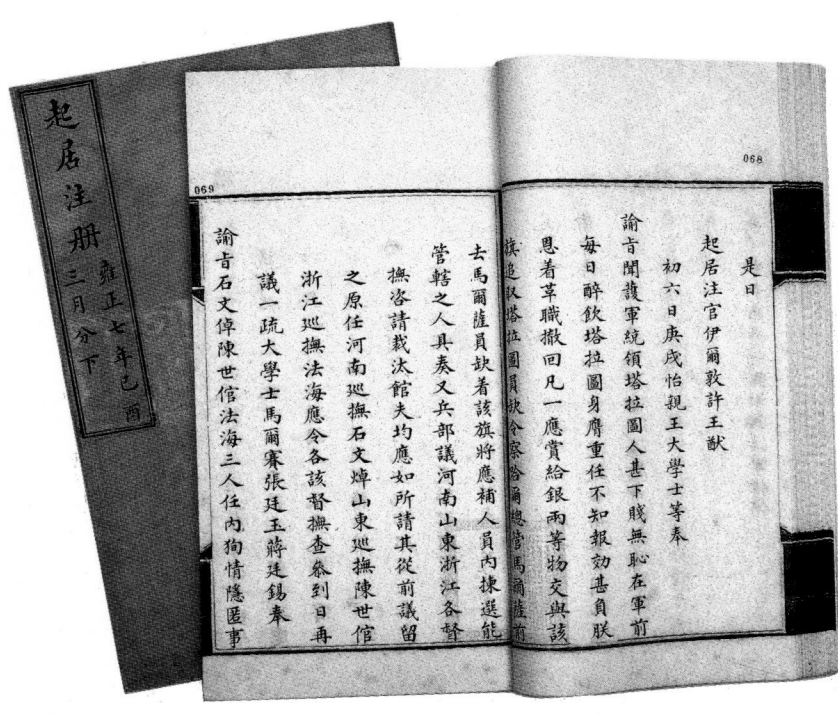

of making royal concubines funeral objects happened after the death of Emperor Yongle of the Ming. *Records of the Yi Dynasty* (1392-1910), a Korean book of history, contains the passage:

> After the emperor died, more than 30 people in the imperial palace were buried with him. On the day of the burial, they were first treated with food and wine in a hall. When they were led to the deathbed hall, they burst into a deafening wave of crying. A small bed was provided for each of them, over which a noosed rope hung from the ceiling. They were ordered to place their necks in the nooses before the beds were removed from under them. Before Lady Han was hanged, she turned to Jinhei, who had been her wet nurse, and said, "Mother, I'm leaving." Before she could finish these words, an official removed the bed she was standing on. Thus she died together with Cui, another court lady.

This is a most tragic picture of making people burial objects. The inhuman practice was followed for four of the five emperors in the early period of the Ming dynasty. The second emperor, Jianwen, was overthrown by his uncle, Emperor Yongle, in 1402 and disappeared without a trace when the troops of the latter broke into his palace. It was not until the reign of the sixth Ming emperor Yingzong that the practice was abolished. The situation under the Qing dynasty was different and will be dealt with in a later section.

The Hall of Immortality is the southernmost one on the east side of the Six West Palaces. This hall was the scene of a bitter power struggle among the court ladies. One of them, Wan, was brought into the palace at the age of four. After she grew up she waited on the crown prince Zhu Jianshen and was liked by him. When the crown prince ascended the throne to become Emperor Chenghua at the age of 16, Wan was already 35, but she remained as clever and attractive as ever and continued to enjoy the emperor's favor. Empress Wu, who had found out about Wan's intimacy with the emperor in his adolescent days, punished her by flogging. This angered the emperor, who deposed the empress and replaced her with another lady, Wang. He liked Wan even more and summoned hardly any other woman to stay with him, and she always accompanied the emperor on his pleasure trips. The second year after his enthronement she gave birth to a boy, the emperor's first son. Delighted, the emperor gave her the title of Imperial Consort.

But the boy died when he was less than a year old. Wan was never pregnant again, but she became increasingly arrogant and imperious toward the other ladies in the palace. In order not to lose the emperor's favor, she would force any pregnant concubine to induce an abortion by taking medicine.

Among the ladies forced by Wan to have an abortion was Ji, another royal concubine. Daughter of an ethnic minority official in Hexian County, Guangxi, Lady Ji was taken prisoner by Emperor Chenghua in a battle in Southwest China. Since she was knowledgeable and good-looking, she was appointed an official in charge of the storehouses in the palace. As soon as she was discovered by the emperor, she was summoned to stay with him and soon became pregnant. When Imperial Consort Wan got wind of this, she ordered a maid to take the fetus out of Ji's body with a hook. Considering this an atrocious crime, the maid did not carry out the order, but reported to Wan that she had only seen a tumor. Ji was banished to the Hall of Peaceful Pleasure for "recuperation."

But Ji did give birth to a boy. Afraid of persecution by Wan, however, she asked the doorkeeper, a eunuch by the name of Zhang Min, to drown the baby. Zhang Min refused, saying, "This is the first time the emperor has got a son. How could we abandon the prince?" He fed the baby with a mixture of porridge and honey. After Lady Wu, the deposed empress, learnt about this, she too helped raise the child.

One day when Emperor Chenghua called in Zhang Min to comb his hair, he looked into the mirror and sighed, "I am getting old, but I still have no son." Going down on his knees, Zhang Min reported: "Your Majesty, you do have a son." Astonished, the emperor demanded to know the whole story. Zhang Min said, "We have been looking after the prince secretly inside one of West Palaces. He is six years old now. We didn't dare report to Your Majesty." When the emperor had the boy brought to him, he saw his hair draping to the floor. The prince threw himself into his father's embrace. The emperor made the boy, Zhu Youtang, crown prince and proclaimed the decision to the whole country. Lady Ji was given the title of Imperial Consort and placed in the Hall of Immortality.

Palace lantern in the Hall of Eternal Spring

Dressing table in the Hall of Eternal Spring

Enamel hand mirror in the Hall of Preserved Elegance. Made in Britain in the 18th century, the frame of the mirror is inlaid with diamonds and the handle with a watch.

On learning the news, Imperial Consort Wan cried day and night, cursing, "The bastards cheated me!" But she did not give in. Imperial Consort Ji died all of a sudden soon afterward. Historians believe that she was murdered by Wan, who even tried to eliminate the crown prince. When she invited him to a meal, his grandmother, Empress Dowager Zhou, told him, "My grandchild, go there but don't eat anything." Anytime when Wan gave him something to eat, he would say, "Thank you, I'm full." When she gave him a bowl of soup, he would say, "I suspect there is poison in it." All of her attempts failed, and she died in despair.

Being the northernmost one among the Six West Palaces, the Hall of Preserved Elegance is known worldwide as Empress Dowager Cixi's residence. Surnamed Yehe Nala, she was given the title of Empress Dowager Cixi by her son when he ascended the throne. As she lived in the Hall of Preserved Elegance, one of the Six West Palaces, she was also referred to as the West Empress Dowager while Empress Dowager Ci'an, who once lived in the Hall of Quintessence, one of the Six East Palaces, was called the East Empress Dowager. Cixi was born in 1835, the 15th year of Emperor Daoguang's reign. Her father, Hui Zheng, was a middle-ranking official in a prefectural government. In 1851, the first year of Emperor Xianfeng's reign, she was brought into the Forbidden City at the age of 17 and given the title of Noble Lady, a royal concubine of the lowest rank. Later she was promoted to a higher rank, but remained unhappy because she had hardly any contact with the emperor. Finally, when she was singing in the Imperial Garden one day, she attracted the emperor and was summoned to stay with him. In 1856, the sixth year of Emperor Xianfeng's reign, she gave birth to the emperor's only son, Zai Chun, and so got a further promotion. The next year she became Imperial Consort.

When Emperor Xianfeng died in his mountain resort in Rehe in 1861 after a reign of 10 years, Zai Chun succeeded to the throne to become Emperor Tongzhi. Both the empress, Ci'an, and the new emperor's mother, Cixi, were given the title of Empress Dowager. The 27-year-old Cixi managed to take power through a coup d'etat in 1861 and, together with the other Empress Dowager, started to "conduct state affairs from behind a curtain." Everyday they would

Portrait of Empress Dowager Cixi

Inside the Hall of Preserved Elegance

Bronze dragon in front of the Hall of Preserved Elegance

receive the high officials, civil and military, listen to their reports, read memorials to the court, and examine and approve the imperial edicts drafted by cabinet ministers, which would then be proclaimed to the whole country and to foreign envoys. After the two empresses dowager ruled China "from behind a curtain" for 12 years, they returned power, though only nominally, to Emperor Tongzhi, but he died a year later. Then the four-year-old Zai Tian, Tongzhi's cousin and Cixi's nephew, succeeded to the throne to become Emperor Guangxu, and the two empresses dowager resumed the practice of ruling the country "from behind a curtain." Empress Dowager Ci'an died in 1881, the seventh year of Emperor Guangxu's reign, and Empress Dowager Cixi became the sole ruler. She ruled China for 47 years, from 1861, the first year of the Tongzhi reign, to 1908, the 34th year of the Guangxu reign. In 1911, three years after her death in 1908, a bourgeois revolution broke out, the feudal rule of the Qing dynasty was overthrown, and the Republic of China was inaugurated. During Empress Dowager Cixi's rule of half a century, China went through the darkest period in its 5,000-year history. In treaties signed with foreign powers, the Qing regime ceded much territory and paid heavy indemnities to them, bringing disgrace to the nation. At home it suppressed, exploited and tyranized the people and committed massacres. In fact, many important personages and events that produced an impact on the progress of modern Chinese history had something to do with the Hall of Preserved Elegance and Empress Dowager Cixi.

In 1884, the 10th year of the Guangxu reign, Empress Dowager Cixi spent over 600,000 taels of silver to have the Hall of Preserved Elegance renovated for celebration of her 50th birthday. The existing hall remains the way it was when she lived there. A large, quiet courtyard lies in front of the hall. A pair of bronze spotted deer and a pair of bronze dragons, each grasping a ball, are placed in front of the terrace. Since the dragon was symbolic of imperial authority, the arrangement was an expression of the court ministers' submission to the power of the Empress Dowager.

The Hall of Preserved Elegance standing on the terrace is a single-eaved, five bay structure in the *xieshan* style. At the back of the

Clocks and porcelain vase in the Hall of Preserved Elegance

124

main chamber is an exquisitely carved panelled wall of *nanmu* wood with a glass frame symbolizing happiness and longevity. On a platform in front of the wall is a carved padauk screen inlaid with a mirror with the Chinese character for "longevity." In front of the screen is the seat for the Empress Dowager, who used to sit there to accept the obeisances of court officials. On the east side of the chamber is a wood-and-glass cupboard covered with green gauze which divides the chamber from the chamber on the east side. The east side chamber and the east inner chamber are also divided by a finely carved wooden partition screen. The furniture is made of padauk or inlaid with shells. Ivory carvings of dragon, boats and pagodas enhanced the splendor of these chambers. The chamber is divided from the west side chamber by a wood-and-glass cupboard decorated with carvings of orchid and covered with a gauze curtain. Two heatable brick beds lie below the windows on the north and south in keeping with the Manchu custom. Empress Dowager often took a rest here. The west inner chamber used to be her bedroom. The partition structure consists of a large elaborately carved wooden frame enclosing large pieces of glass and a door in the middle. From the bedroom (the west inner chamber), the Empress Dowager could see what was going on in the west side chamber. The two chambers are thus separated from and yet linked with each other. On the northern side of the bedroom is the Empress Dowager's bed. In front of the bed is a wooden canopy carved with the Chinese character for "longevity" and patterns of gourds symbolizing an endless line of descendants. It is a most valuable piece of wood carving of the Qing dynasty. Inside the wooden canopy is the bedstead covered by two blue silk curtains embroidered with patterns of Chinese wisteria. Cotton quilts with silk and brocade covers embroidered with dragons, pheonixes and flowers are stacked on the bed. The bedroom may be considered an art gallery. For instance, the padauk structure is carved with patterns of strings of grapes growing on the vines. The vivid design and matchless handicraftsmanship make it a masterpiece of traditional wood carving. The hall has a rich collection of works of art. In addition to wood carving, it exhibits some of China's best lacquerware carvings, ivory carvings, embroideries, jade carvings, palace lanterns, carpets, porcelain, antiques, cloisonné, gilded articles inlaid with precious stones, etc.

To the west of the Six West Palaces is an architectural complex made up of three halls — the Hall for the Consolation of Mothers, the Hall of Longevity and Good Health, and the Hall of Peaceful Old Age. They were the residences of the empress dowager and imperial concubines of her generation, who would move here from the Six East Palaces and the Six West Palaces after the emperor's demise. The concubines of a deceased emperor were not supposed to meet the new emperor until they were more than 50 years of age. Even the empress dowager did not see her son, the new emperor, except on such important occasions as New Year's Day, the winter solstice, the emperor's birthday, and her own birthday, when the emperor would come to her residence to pay respects to her. The empress dowager and the concubines of the late emperor usually led a secluded and lonely life year after year. This group of palaces was called "the widows world."

First built in the Ming dynasty, the Hall of the Consolation of Mothers was once the residence of Imperial Consort Zheng, a favorite of Emperor Wanli, who moved there after his death. It was renovated on a large scale and changed into a double-eaved structure in the *xieshan* style in the early Qing period. Lined with covered corridors in the front and at the back, it acquired a total space of seven bays. Empress Dowager Xiaozhuang was its first occupant in the Qing dynasty. She was a concubine of the first Qing Emperor, Huangtaiji. Xiaozhuang was her posthumous title. A Mongol surnamed Bo'erjijite, she came from an aristocratic family. Her father, Zaisang, was appointed lord of the Horqin tribe. She was chosen by Huangtaiji at the age of 14. At 27 she gave birth to Fulin, who later became Emperor Shunzhi. But then Huangtaiji died unexpectedly, having left no will on the question of succession. A fierce struggle broke out between his eldest son Haoge, who was not a child by Bo'erjijite, and his 13th younger brother Dorgon, both in their prime and each in control of a strong army. Bo'erjijite, now 33, maneuvred cleverly and pursuaded both contestants to give up their claim to the throne. Finally she succeeded in making her six-year-old son, Fulin, Emperor Shunzhi. She was rumored to have married Dorgon in secret and promised to make him Prince Regent in exchange for his support for Fulin's enthronement. All this means she killed three birds with one stone — marrying the younger brother of her husband, installing her son as emperor, and making herself empress dowager. Later she punished Dorgon for having once tried to usurp the throne and took power into her own hands. After Emperor Shunzhi died, the eight-year-old Xuanye ascended the throne to become Emperor Kangxi. As empress dowager of the generation of the emperor's grandfather, she helped Kangxi get rid of Aobai, a powerful and truculent minister, and personally administered state affairs. After attending a court session, Emperor Kangxi would pay respects to the Empress Dowager, report important matters to her, and ask for her instructions. She died in 1687, the 26th year of Kangxi's reign, at the age of 75. Bo'erjijite made important contributions to China's unification, stability and prosperity at the time and is regarded as an outstanding political leader of the Qing period.

The Hall of Longevity and Good Health lies to the west of the Hall for the Consolation of Mothers while the Hall of Peaceful Old Age is located to the north of the latter. Both of them are secluded quarters for empresses dowager and imperial concubines of the same generation. The Hall of Peaceful Old Age was rebuilt by Emperor Qianlong in 1751, or the 16th year of his reign, for the 60th birthday of his mother Niugulu. She had come to the mansion of Prince Yong at the age of 13. After she grew up, she gave birth to Hongli, who later became Emperor Qianlong, and was promoted Imperial Consort. After Qianlong's enthronement, she moved to the Hall for the Consolation of Mothers. She made three tours of South China, three tours of east China, and one tour of Central China and paid three visits to Mt. Wutai. Grand celebrations were held for her 60th, 70th and 80th birthdays. For her 60th birthday, all the roads and streets from the West Flower Gate to the Garden of Clear Ripples (today's Summer Palace) were decked out with colorful lanterns. An opera stage was put up for a great variety of performances at an interval of a few dozen metres along the road. Birthday presents on display included small artificial hills of silk and pagodas composed of feathers from peacocks' tails.

Emperor Qianlong had a golden pagoda built to store the hair his mother had combed off in her lifetime. Some 3,000 taels of gold were used on the golden pagoda which is 147.2 cm. high and 70.4 cm. wide at the base. Decorated with pendants of precious stones, it is considered a masterpiece for its perfect composition, elegant style, and superb workmanship.

However, very few empresses dowager and concubines of deceased emperors were as lucky as the mothers of Emperors Shunzhi and Qianlong who lived in times of peace and prosperity, enjoyed respect and luxury, and even ruled the country. The majority of palace widows led an austere, lonesome life, wasting their years away even though many of them were still young or in their prime.

In the widows' world there were many private halls for the worship of Buddha. The Hall of Flowers north of the Hall of Peaceful Old Age was used by empresses dowager for this purpose during the Ming dynasty, and so was it under the Qing. The two-storied northern section of the Hall for the Consolation of Mothers was rebuilt into a spacious hall for Buddha worship with a tall, beautifully carved statue of Trikala Buddhas in a gilded lacquer niche. Similar halls are found in the Hall of Longevity and Good Health and the Hall for the Consolation of Mothers. Even the towers and pavilions in the peaceful and secluded garden of the Hall for the Consolation of Mothers were changed into premises for Buddhist practice detached from the rest of the imperial palace. Among these were the main structure in the garden called the Hall of Ever-Present Luck as well as the Tower of Buddha's Image to the east, the Tower of Auspicious Clouds to the west, the Tower of Maternal Blessings at the back and the Mid-Lake Pavilion in the center of the garden. Here incense was burnt and sutras read all year round to create a Buddhist atmosphere. Outside the halls the chiming of bells accompanying the sutra recitals were heard in a desolate environment of withering grass and thinning groves. Enduring their widowhood, the retired court ladies spent their remaining years seeking consolation in a spiritual world and praying for happiness in their next lives.

The Hall of Ancestral Worship and the Six East Palaces are located to the left of the three rear halls. Located in front of the Six East Palaces, the Hall of Ancestral Worship is symmetrical to the Hall of Mental Cultivation. It has an independent courtyard and two seven-bay halls. It was built in the early period of the Qing dynasty for the emperors to offer sacrifices to their ancestors. They sent officials for sacrificial ceremonies here on the first and 15th days of each month, on New Year's Day, and other festivals, on sending out an army or its triumphant return and for the granting of titles to members of the royal family and the nobility.

Behind the Hall of Ancestral Worship lies the Six East Palaces where the empress and imperial concubines used to live. The Six East Palaces are the Hall to Usher in Happiness, the Hall of Eternal Harmony and the Hall of Justice from south to north on the east side, and the Hall of Benevolence, the Hall for Receiving Celestial Favor, and the Hall of Quintessence from south to north on the west side.

Golden Pagoda for the Storage of Hair

The names of the Six East Palaces, like those of the Six West Palaces, have been changed several times, and we need not go into the details. Under the regulations of the Qing dynasty, one empress was supposed to live in the central hall while two imperial consorts, four second-rank concubines, six third-rank concubines and an unspecified number of concubines of still lower ranks — "noble ladies," "always-present ladies," "ready-to-respond ladies" and so on were assigned to the 12 halls of the Six East Palaces and the Six West Palaces. But there were frequent departures from these regulations. Emperor Kangxi had in his harem 31 women with the title of empress or imperial consort or concubine plus eight "noble ladies" and a greater number of women of lower ranks. In the late years of the Qing dynasty, Emperor Tongzhi had only three concubines in addition to the empress, while Emperor Guangxu had only an empress and two consorts. Xuantong, the last emperor, was placed on the throne at the age of two and was overthrown three years later. He was allowed to stay in the Inner Court of the Forbidden City after his abdication in 1912. Nominally he had an empress and a consort.

The Hall of Benevolence is the southernmost building on the west side of the Six East Palaces. The front gate, the Gate of Benevolence, faces south. The structure consists of a front hall and a rear hall in a two-courtyard complex. Once it was the residence of Tongjia, concubine of Emperor Shunzhi of the Qing. On March 18, 1654, or the 11th year of Shunzhi's reign, she gave birth to Xuanye who later became Emperor Kangxi. Emperors Qianlong and Daoguang both lived here in their crown prince days. Emperor Guangxu's favorite consort, Zhen, also lived here. In 1900, the 26th year of Guangxu's reign, when the eight-power allied forces invaded

Beijing, she was drowned in a well by a eunuch acting on the orders of Empress Dowager Cixi, who had just left for Xi'an with Emperor Guangxu.

The Hall of Quintessence is the northernmost building on the west side of the Six East Palaces. In the Ming dynasty it was the crown prince's residence. The front hall is called the Hall of the Rising Dragon and the rear one the Hall of the Sages, and a small hall further behind is called the Hall of the Dragon's Virtue. Two of the names have to do with the fact that every Chinese feudal monarch called himself the genuine dragon son of heaven, and so the crown prince was the offspring of a dragon. No wonder that the concept of a dragon was incorporated in the name of the residence of the crown prince. In the Qing dynasty when the crown princes moved to the Hall for the Sound Growth of the Successor south of the Six East Palaces, the Hall of Quintessence became the residence of imperial concubines for some time. Emperor Daoguang's empress surnamed Niugulu and her son Yining, who later became Emperor Xianfeng, also lived here. Emperor Xianfeng composed a poem with the title "In Memory of the Old Times," in which he recalled the days he spent with his mother in this hall. The lines read:

I lived in that hall till I was seventeen;
When I came to the throne,
Alas, I was bereft of my dear mother;
How she had nursed me
When I fell critically ill at nine!
Tears run down my cheeks
The moment I think of the bygone days.

Well where Consort Zhen was drowned

Carved coiled dragon on the Nine-Dragon Wall

The Nine-Dragon Wall

When Xianfeng was 10 his mother died at the age of 33. Later his empress, also surnamed Niugulu, lived in the same hall. As mentioned earlier in this chapter, Empress Niugulu, referred to as the East Empress Dowager after the death of her husband because she lived in one of the East Palaces, ruled China "from behind a curtain" jointly with Cixi, the West Empress Dowager.

Further east to the Six East Palaces is an architectural complex called the Palace of Peace and Longevity. It was built by Emperor Qianlong as his residence after retirement. His grandfather Emperor Kangxi, had ascended the throne at the age of eight and died at 69 after a reign of 61 years. Qianlong became emperor at 25. He declared that he wouldn't dare enjoy a longer reign than his grandfather did and that he would retire after a maximum of 60 years. And sure enough, when he was 85, he handed over the throne to the crown prince, who took over as Emperor Jiaqing. Previously, when Qianlong was just over 60, he had launched a large project on the basis of the old buildings in the northeastern corner of the Forbidden City. Rectangular in shape and enclosed by walls on four sides, and accessible through six gates, the new palace covers over 46,000 square meters. It has more than 1,000 divisions cleverly designed for different purposes. The structure presents a variety of sights in a unique layout. The front section consists mainly of the Hall of Norms of Government and the Hall of Peace and Longevity. The rear section is divided along three routes — the central route featuring mainly the Hall of Character Cultivation and the Hall of Delightful Longevity, behind which are the Hall of Harmony and the Pavilion of Prospective Happiness; the eastern route along the Pavilion for Reading and the Pavilion of Cheerful Melodies behind which is the four-storied Hall of Birthday Celebrations, and the Pavilion of Buddha's Light and the Pavilion of Flowers of the West Heavens to the northeast; and the western route along the Garden of the Palace of Peace and Longevity, also known as Emperor Qianlong's Garden. The whole complex is an epitome of the Outer and Inner Courts and the Imperial Garden in the Forbidden City.

The Nine-Dragon Wall is a glazed-tile screen wall in front of the Palace of Peace and Longevity. It rests on a *sumeru* base of white stone and is covered with a yellow-tiled roof in palace style. The nine huge dragons in bas-relief are playing with balls against a backdrop of sea waves. They look vigorous and come to life. The surface of the screen wall is composed of 247 glazed tiles in seven colors, adding up to 29.4 meters in width and 3.5 meters in height. In comparison with two other Nine-Dragon Walls, one in Datong, Shanxi Province,and the other in Beihai Park in Beijing, the one in the Forbidden City shows a higher level of skill and a better color effect. Looking southward from the Hall of the Norms of Government, one finds that the head of the dragon in the center of the screen wall faces the throne seat in the hall.

The Hall of Character Cultivation lies at the center of the rear section of the Palace of Peace and Longevity. It was built as the residence for the Emperor Emeritus. At its back is the Hall of Delightful Longevity, a palace building in the *xieshan* style with tilted eaves. A huge structure, it has a spacious front hall flanked by long corridors, each accessible through a door. It is the most imposing building in the Palace of Peace and Longevity. The partitions and the two stories inside the hall are built with quality wood like *nanmu* and padauk. The beautiful carvings and ornaments inlaid with gold and jade are considered priceless. Though it was built by Emperor Qianlong for his retired life, he never lived there. Instead it was later taken over by Empress Dowager Cixi as her bedchamber around the time of her 60th birthday. She spent more than 10 million taels of silver on the grand celebrations of her 60th birthday in the Hall of Delightful Longevity. The Hall of Harmony at the back has two long corridors with stone carvings on the walls. Along the paths are man-made hills, flowers and artificial ponds. A corridor behind the Pavilion of Harmony leads to the Pavilion of Prospective Happiness, by the side of which is the well where Lady Zhen, Emperor Guangxu's favorite consort, was drowned by an eunuch on Empress Dowager Cixi's order.

Along the front section of the eastern route is the opera theatre at the Pavilion of Cheerful Melodies which will be described later in this book. Passing through the Pavilion for Reading one arrives at the Hall of Birthday Celebrations, which features the traditional style of a courtyard in South China, looking unique among the magnificent palaces for its compact layout and tranquility. It has four stories with a main chamber and two side chambers encircled by a corridor on each floor. The ceilings and beams are painted in the typical style of Suzhou in Southeast China against a backdrop of polished brick walls in white wash. Behind the Hall of Birthday Celebrations is the Hall of Prospective Fortune which has a large grotesque rock known as the Peak of Beauty in the center of its courtyard. Placed on a

Murals and enamel pagoda in the Pavilion of the Flowers of the West Heavens

marble *sumeru* terrace encircled by bronze balustrades, the rock is 4.5 meters high and fascinates visitors with its unusual shape and clearly discernible cracks and holes. Emperor Qianlong composed an "Ode to the Peak of Beauty," in which he wrote, "The huge rock has countless small holes, an intriguing gift of nature in the Forbidden City." A rock like this is a priceless means of decoration in the art of Chinese gardening. It brightens up the courtyard in every direction.

The Pavilion of Buddha's Light and the Pavilion of the Flowers of the West Heavens are located north of the Hall of Prospective Fortune. Leaning against the palace walls, the two buildings have courtyards and share a staircase and a covered corridor between their second floors. The stairs lead up to the Pavilion of the Flowers of the West Heavens on the east and the Pavilion of Buddha's Light on the west. The latter is a small two-story building and has three small courtyards arranged in a row from north to south. The Pavilion of the Flowers of the West Heavens, also a small two-story building, is seven bays wide and has a protruding corridor at the front. Its roof is covered with yellow glazed tiles. These two structures are distinguished not so much by their architectural flamboyance as by their beauty of simplicity. Because of their remote location, they were spared from the looting and arson committed by the eight-power allied forces which invaded Beijing in 1900. Even today they are valued for their rich collections of Buddha statues and pagodas found in rooms on one floor above another. For instance, the inside walls of the second floor of the Pavilion of the Flowers of the West Heavens are full of niches with a statue of Buddha in each. The placid-looking images of Buddha are each different from another in facial expression and posture. A statue of Tsong-Kha-pa (1357-1419), founder of the Yellow Hat Order of Lamaism, looks solemn and lifelike. The floor is dominated by the statues of all the main Buddhas of Lamaism, supplemented by 10,900 mini-statues of Buddha. The entire hall shines with the gilded sculptures. On the ground floor are six tall Buddhist pagodas with an enamel surface. The complicated techniques and excellent workmanship make them masterpieces of Buddhist art.

Imperial Gardens

Gardens Within the Forbidden City

The main palace gardens laid out during the Ming and Qing dynasties were the Imperial Garden behind the Hall of Terrestrial Tranquility at the center and the gardens in the Palace of Peace and Longevity and the Hall for the Consolation of Mothers on the two sides. The countless pavilions in the gardens were designed for the emperor, empress and imperial concubines to relax and enjoy the scenery, while the great number of halls were intended for worshipping the gods, holding Buddhist ceremonies, keeping rare copies of books or rest and convalescence. These features distinguish palace gardens from ordinary ones.

Situated behind the Hall of Terrestrial Tranquility, the Imperial Garden was once called the Rear Garden. It was built in 1417, the 15th year of the Yongle reign of the Ming dynasty. It has been renovated many times but retains its original layout even today. Many of the halls and pavilions, trees and rockeries are 15th-century relics of the Ming dynasty. The graden is 90 meters long from north to south and about 140 meters wide form east to west, covering an area of over 12,000 square meters. The main structure in the garden is the Hall of Imperial Peace located at the northernmost point of the central axis of the Forbidden City. Five bays wide and three bays deep, the hall faces south and has a double-eaved roof covered with yellow glazed tiles and decorated with a gilded spire. Resting on a marble *sumeru* terrace, it has a protruding platform in front and pillars and boards all round. It is characterized by a unique design and delicate stone carvings of dragon patterns. The surrounding walls form an independent courtyard in the garden. There are two symmetrical buildings behind the Hall of Imperial Peace — the Pavilion to Usher in Light in the northwest and the Imperial Pavilion for Viewing the Scenery in the Northeast. The Pavilion to Usher in Light leans against the walls of the Forbidden City. Poetic lines were written to praise the scenery:

> The tall pavilion stands by the red palace walls;
> From here one enjoys a fascinating scene
> Of the snow-capped West Hills on a bright day.

Inside the Hall of Imperial Peace. The hall is for the worship of the Supreme Master of the Heavens, the honorary title for Lao Tse, the founder of Taoism. Every year at the beginning of spring, summer, autumn and winter, or the lst, 7th, 13th and 19th solar terms, the emperor would come here to burn incense and make obeisances to the Taoist God. Taoist ceremonies would also be held here on the Chinese New Year's Day and other festivals.

Imperial Pavilion for Viewing the Scenery

the surface of the water. The Pavilion of Ten Thousand Springs and the Pavilion of One Thousand Autumns, which form the third pair, were built in 1533, the 12th year of Emperor Jiajing's reign. Both are double-eaved, capped with an umbrella-shaped roof, and placed on a square base. Shaded by pine trees, they look tall and attractive. Finally, there are two more symmetrical pavilions in the southern part of the garden. These square and four-pillared structures look delicate under glazed-tile roofs and within balustrades. The trees, flower beds and ponds are all distributed proportionately, enhancing the charm and tranquility of the garden.

Built in an area measuring 160 meters from north to south and 37 meters from east to west, which means a total space of 5,920 square meters, the garden of the Palace of Peace and Longevity is at once compact and spacious, open and secluded, and is innovative in many ways. It has four courtyards within the Gate of Lasting Happiness. The main structure in the first courtyard is the Pavilion of Ancient Glory. The man-made hills, rocks and pavilions in the courtyard show the superb taste of the designer. Inside the Pavilion for Bestowing Wine is a stream where the emperor and his scholar friends gathered to drink wine and improvise poems. The practice was initiated during the two Jin dynasties (A.D. 265-316 and 317-420), when people gathered by a stream on the third day of the third lunar month and drifted cups of wine downstream. When a cup stopped in front of someone, he would pick it up and drink it. The same custom was later introduced into the palace. In the southeastern corner is a small courtyard separated form the rest of the garden by the Corridor of the Carpenter's Square representing a departure from the rigid square-shaped garden and adding variety to the scenery. In the northwestern corner of the garden is the Pavilion of Morning Glow built on a man-made hill and connected with the Pavilion for Bestowing Wine down below by a corridor along the hillside called Hill-Climbing Corridor, a straight one which contrasts the zigzag one called the Corridor of the Carpenter's Square. The main structure in the second courtyard is the Hall of Nostalgia. The lake and the rocks in the courtyard give it a quiet, classical flavor. The third courtyard is dominated by man-made hills featuring peaks, cliffs, caves and grotesque rocks. To the north of the hills is the Pavilion of Excellent Views and to the west is the Pavilion of Delight. On one of the hilltops is the Pavilion of Paramount Elegance which has corridors leading to the rest of the garden. At the southern foot of the hills is the Pavilion of Three Friends. The "three friends" refer to pines, bamboos and plum blossoms which maintain their beauty and charm against the winter cold. The pavilion is provided with a heatable earthern bed where the emperor could take a rest while touring the garden in winter. It has a moon-shaped door and a floor covered with bamboo mats. The padauk carvings of plum blossoms and the jade carvings of plum blossoms and bamboo leaves look fresh and harmonious. The main structure in the fourth and last courtyard is the Tower of Elusive Dreams situated in its northern part. It is also called the Labyrinth Tower because it is built as an intriguing system of divisions which people can appreciate fully only by taking at least 20 different positions. Visitors often lose their way while walking through the doors. The corridors and low halls around the tower divide the courtyard into sub-areas each with a different scenery. There is a hill consisting of a pile of rocks in front of the tower, on top

Opposite to the Pavilion to Usher in Light is the Hill of Accumulated Elegance, a man-made hill built in undulating lines to create a labyrinth of dark shades and bright spots. A zigzag path along the hillside leads through intriguing caves up to the Imperial Pavilion for Viewing the Scenery on top of the hill. The pavilion is a square one with four pillars and a glazed-tile roof. It has a partition door on each of the four sides and a throne seat in the center. Each year the emperor and empress would climb up to the pavilion on the Double Ninth Festival, i.e., the ninth day of the ninth lunar month. From the pavilion they could get a clear view of Prospect Hill Park in the north and the neat rows of cypresses and pines in the palace gardens in the south.

In addition to this pavilion, there are eight more pavilions in the garden positioned symmetically to the east and west of the central axis. Surrounded by hills and brooks, flowers and trees, they enhance the beauty and dignity of the environment. First, there are the Pavilion of Emerald Jade and the Pavilion of Gathered Fragrance in the northeast and southwest corners of the garden. Both were built in 1536, the 15th year of Emperor Jiajing's reign. They are square structures each with four pillars and a peaked roof covered with yellow, blue and green glazed tiles arranged in a chessboard pattern. Next are the Pavilion of Floating Greenery and the Pavilion of Deposited Jade built in 1583, the 11th year of the Wanli reign of the Ming dynasty. Open on all sides, each of them stands on a bridge and has a protruding terrace. Under each bridge is a rectangular pond in which goldfish show their beautiful scales whenever they appear on

Cobblestone path in the Imperial Garden

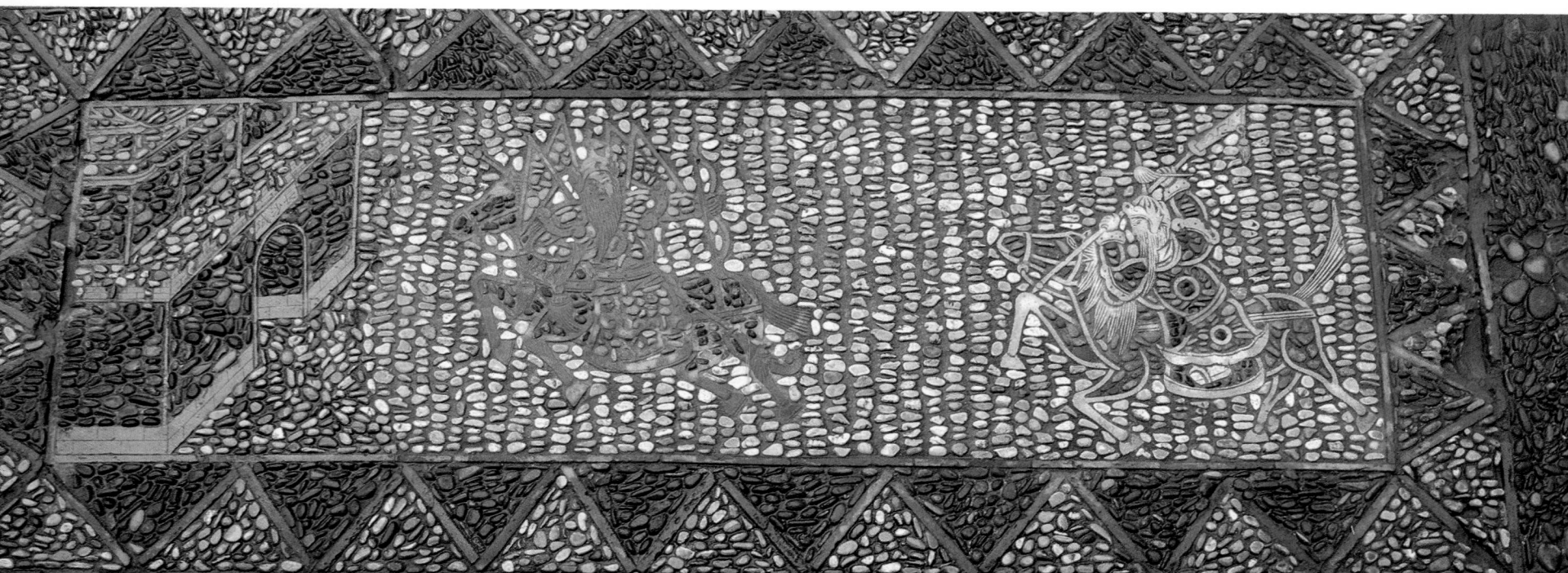

The "drifting-the-cup stream" in the Pavilion for Bestowing Wine

Green Shell Pavilion in the garden of the Palace of Peace and Longevity

133

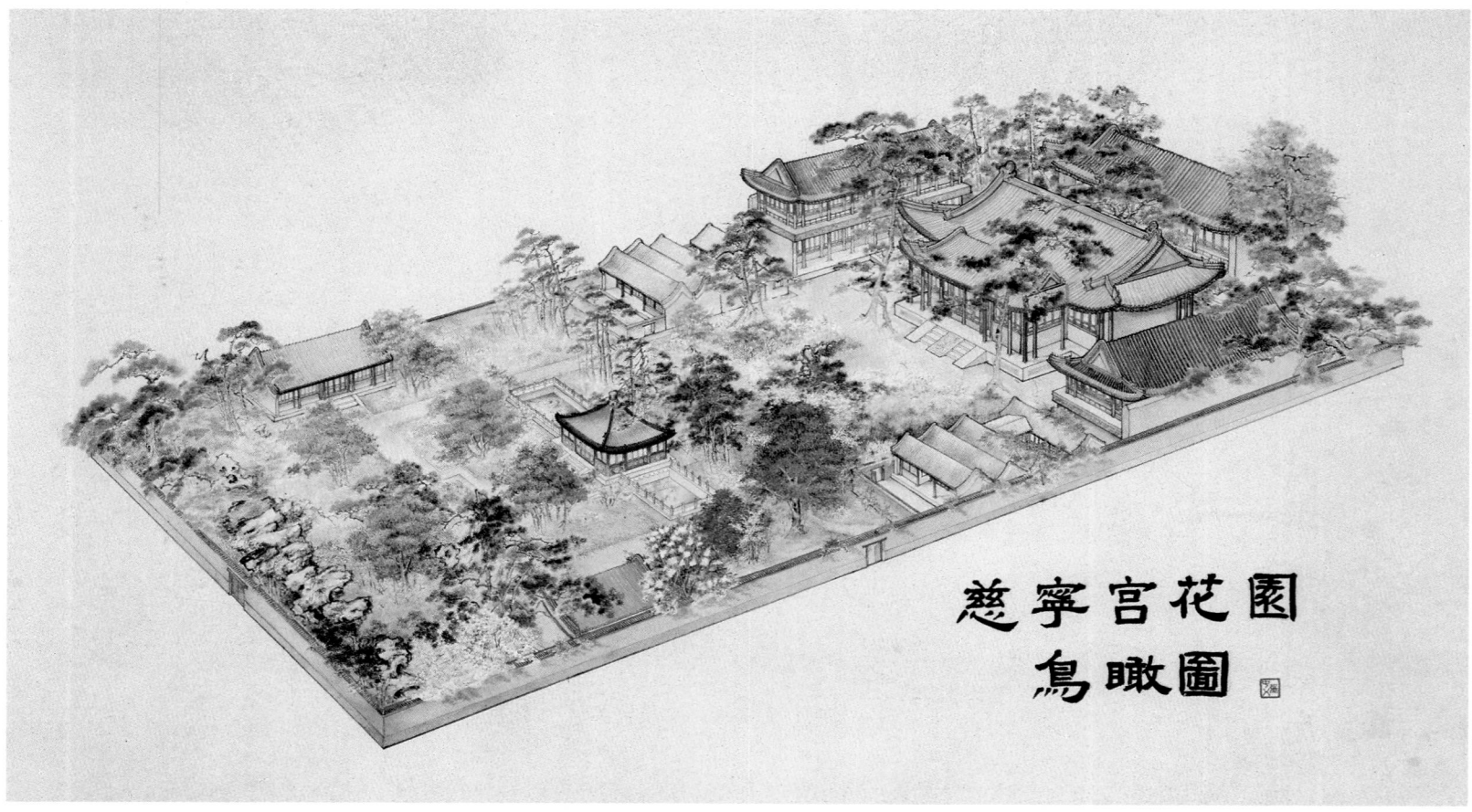

Bird's-eye view of the garden of the Hall for the Consolation of Mothers

of which is the Green Shell Pavilion decorated with patterns of plum blossoms. It is placed on a *sumeru* terrace in the shape of five petals. The round fence boards are carved with plum branches on both sides, and plum blossoms are painted on the eaves and beams. The five ridges on the roof symbolize the five petals of a plum blossom. This small pavilion, which has five pillars and five ridges, looks like a large basket of plum blossoms and is therefore referred to as the Plum Blossom Pavilion.

Covering an area of 6,800 square meters, the garden of the Hall for the Consolation of Mothers is slightly larger than the garden of the Palace of Peace and Longevity. The garden has 11 towers and pavilions, most of which are private chambers for the worship of Buddha. The scenery is mostly found in the southern part of the garden where the land is flat and spacious, the lanes straight and the hills, rockeries, and winding paths kept to a minimum. This was intended to make things easier for the empress dowager and imperial concubines of her generation in view of their advanced age, fragile health and disillusionment. The artificial hills, ponds and scattered buildings remind one of a mountain valley. The cypresses and lilacs create a simple and yet elegant environment.

The gardens in the Forbidden City show characteristics which vary with their purposes. The Imperial Garden was the place for the emperor to take a rest. It is symmetrically laid out with a broad vision and a classical taste. The garden in the Palace of Peace and Longevity used to be frequented by Emperor Qianlong after his retirement. Its unique layout lies in the ever-changing scenery, the refined crafts-manship, and the fabulous decorations. The garden of the Hall for the Consolation of Mothers served the empress dowagers and imperial concubines in their annoying widowhood. It is spacious and dotted with premises for the worship of Buddha. The design is simple and plain; the atmosphere is quiet and solemn. The gardens in the Forbidden City are among the treasures of China's traditional art of gardening.

Other Imperial Gardens and Parks

In addition to the Imperial Garden, the garden of the Palace of Peace and Longevity and the garden of the Hall for the Consolation of Mothers, Beijing also boasts several other imperial gardens and parks. Among them are the Prospect Hill, the West Garden, the Zoo and the South Sea Garden.

North of the Forbidden City stands a hill known as His Majesty's Hill in the Ming dynasty. It is also known as the Coal Hill because coal was stored there for use in the palaces. It was renamed Prospect Hill in 1655, the 12th year of the Shunzhi reign of the Qing dynasty. Along the hillside is a thick forest and a grassland teeming with deer and cranes. The site was used as a hunting ground in the Ming dynasty. The Hall for Observing Military Virtue was the place from where the emperor watched archery contests. Emperor Chongzhen, the last Ming ruler, received his ministers in the hall. Along the north hillside is an orchard known as the Northern Orchard or as the Garden of One Hundred Fruits for its great variety of fruit trees. Shaded by the fruit trees is the Hall of Imperial Longevity built after the style of a Taoist temple. In 1749, the 14th year of the Qianlong reign of the Qing dynasty, it was rebuilt at another site to face the central peak of Prospect Hill. In keeping with the Taoist tradition, it has a nine-bay main hall flanked by two halls on the left and right in addition to a kitchen, a storehouse, a pavilion housing stone steles, a pavilion provided with a well, and stone lions. The Qing emperors worshipped the images of their ancestors in this hall. The west hillside is planted with pines and cypresses and flowers.

The Prospect Hill was built with earth. On the Double Ninth Festival the emperor would ascend the hill to enjoy the view of the imperial palaces and the scenery of the entire capital city.

The last emperor of the Ming dynasty, Chongzhen was a self-conceited man who liked flattery and turned a deaf ear to criticism. On March 18, 1644, the 17th year of his reign, a peasant insurgent army under Li Zicheng stormed into the capital. Chongzhen fled the Forbidddn City and ascended His Majesty's Hill, from where he saw the capital in flames. Returning to the imperial palace, he drank more than 10 cups of wine in desparation. Then he ordered Empress Zhou to commit suicide and stabbed Princess Changping with his sword. saying, "Why should you have been born in my family?" He went on to stab Princess Zhaoren and several of his concubines. Li Zicheng's army occupied Beijing's Inner City during the night. On learning the news in the morning, Chongzhen tolled the palace bell to summon his officials, but nobody came. Deprived of all support and in utter despair, he stumbled to a Chinese scholar tree at the east side of His Majesty's Hill, threw away his crown, and hanged himself on the tree.

To the west of the Forbidden City is the West Garden, also nown as the Celestial Lake, which consists of the South Lake, the Central Lake and the North Lake. These were the most important parks within the boundaries of the Imperial City in the Ming and Qing dynasties.

The South Lake, so named because it was in the south of the Celestial Lake extended from north of the Moon Tower (today's New China Gate) to the south of the Centipede Bridge. Moon Tower was built in 1758, the 23rd year of the Qianlong reign. It had two stories, each seven bays wide, red pillars and a yellow glazed-tiled roof. It is believed that Emperor Qianlong had it built for his favorite Frangrant Consort, or Consort Rong, who came from a noble family of the Uygur nationality. Her uncles and brothers won merits during a battle fought by the Qing army in southern Xinjiang, received the titles of dukes, and settled in Beijing. The Fragrant Consort acquired her name by the fact that she emitted a delightful aroma wherever she went. A virtuous and charming woman, she was also skilled in horsemanship and archery, and so was very much liked by the emperor. Having spent several years in the palace, she became homesick. Since most of the Uygur people were Moslems, the emperor gave orders for houses to be built after the Moslem style and created a Moslem settlement. A mosque was also put up. The Moon Tower was constructed for the Fragrant Consort to look in the direction of her native place whenever she was homesick. In a poem on the Moon Tower, Emperor Qianlong wrote:

In the winter I gaze at the icy lake;
To the south is the residence of the charming lady;
Rows of houses form a Moslem settlement;
I direct my thoughts to the western frontiers,
And pray for peace and order along the borders.

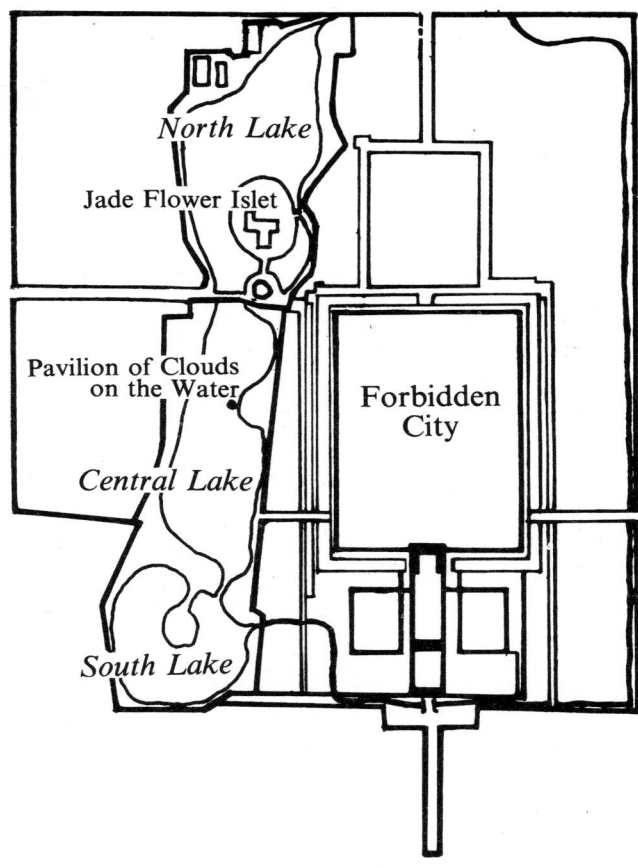

Plan of the South Lake, the Central Lake, and the North Lake

Prospect Hill

Bird's-eye view of the South Lake, the Central Lake, and the North Lake

Moon Tower by the South Lake

The poem reveals the political intentions of Qianlong, who built the Moon Tower with the stability of the western frontiers in mind.

Not far to the north of the Moon Tower is a clear lake with an islet at the center. In the early years of the Ming dynasty, a terrace was built on the islet. Since it was located to the south of Celestial Lake, it was called the South Terrace. On the north side of the terrace was the Kiosk of Emerald Waves where the Ming emperors boarded their dragon boats to cruise on the lake. On the Double Fifth Festival (the fifth day of the fifth lunar month) in 1625, the fifth year of the Tianqi reign, Emperor Tianqi went on the lake with three eunuchs in a small dragon boat. A strong wind upturned the boat. Two eunuchs were drowned, but the emperor was saved by the third eunuch. A passage in the "Lyrics of the Tianqi Hall" reads:

Thunderous cheers swept across the lake
When a real dragon was lifted from under the water.

In the early years of the Qing dynasty the South Terrace was renovated into a palace structure on the water. It was called the Sea Terrace Islet reminding one of a fairyland on the sea in ancient Chinese legend. In summer the site was adorned with emerald waves and green willows. The air was enlivened by the singing of cicadas and

Sea Terrace Islet

136

sweetened by the fragrance of lotus flowers. Painted boats plied the clear water, while fish were visibly swimming at the bottom. In winter the lake became icebound, and was surrounded by pines laden with snow. Towers and pavilions and man-made hills, trees and flower beds enhanced the charm of the islet. The main structure on the Sea Terrace Islet was the Hanyuan Hall. In 1898, the 24th year of the Guangxu reign, Kang Youwei and other bourgeois reformists launched a movement to change the old system for "national rejuvenation with the support of Emperor Guangxu. The reforms lasted 100 days before they were crushed by the diehards under Empress Dowager Cixi who, through a coup d'état, arrested and killed the reformists. Emperor Guangxu was put under house arrest in this hall on the Sea Terrace Islet and died there after 10 years.

The Central Lake covers the area starting in the north of the Centipede Bridge and terminating in the south of the Golden Turtle and Jade Rainbow Bridge (today's Beihai Bridge). It is called the Central Lake because it is the central section of the Celestial Lake. The scenery is divided into three areas — the south bank, the west bank, and the east bank.

Located on the south bank within the Gate of the West Garden, the Hall of Diligent Government faces the Sea Terrace Islet across the lake. It used to be Emperor Kangxi's temporary office in summer or when construction projects were going on in the Inner Court premises. A small riverlet runs by the west side of the Hall for the irrigation of paddy fields about half an acre in area. Known as Garden of Abundant Water, this is the patch of land where Emperor Kangxi experimented with new rice strains. He also invited his ministers here for visits or banquets. Another tastefully furnished hall in the garden, later named the Hall of Health and Longevity, was the place chosen by Emperor Qianlong for imperial banquets. There is also the Studio of Spring Lotus Roots surrounded by man-made hills and ponds, towers and pavilions, and shady woods. To the north of the studio is a two-story Hall of Countrywide Peace in Western style, which was used by Empress Dowager Cixi to entertain women guests.

The main building along the western bank is the Tower of Violet Light. It was originally a terrace in the Ming dynasty where a shelter was built for the emperor to watch horsemanship and archery contests and dragon boat races. The terrace was changed into a tower in the Qing dynasty, where the emperor gave examinations to candidates for prestigious military degrees in addition to watching horsemanship and archery performances. Emperor Qianlong had the protraits of meritorious generals painted on the tower, just as Emperor Xuandi (r. 74-49 B. C.) had done on the Unicorn Tower during the Western Han dynasty. Here he also feted Mongol princes and Moslem leaders, entertaining them with performances on ice and songs and dances. A poem reads:

The guests marvel at a thousand acrobats
Performing on ice;
And the emperor presents his poem to them
Amid melodious strains of music.

The Tower of Violet Light used to be the place for the emperor to receive foreign envoys. In 1874, the 13th year of the Tongzhi reign, Emperor Tongzhi received here envoys from Japan, Russia, the United States of America, France, the Netherlands and Britain, who presented their credentials to him. This was the first time a Qing emperor formally accepted the credentials of foreign envoys. The railway of the Tower of Violet Light deserves special mention. In 1864, the 3rd year of the Tongzhi reign, a British engineer built the first railway in Beijing which extended over half a kilometer outside the Gate of Military Virtue. The next year it was put into trial operation but was soon abandoned. In 1888, the 14th year of the Guangxu reign, the Tower of Violet Light railway was built within the area of the three lakes. About 1.5 kilometers long, it started from outside the Gate of Oceanic Charm along the Central Lake in the south, ran along the banks of the Central and North Lakes, and terminated at the Tranquil Heart Studio. For some time, Empress Dowager Cixi and Emperor Guangxu came to the Hall of Diligent Government to conduct state affairs by a small train. After they finished the routine, they would go to the Tranquil Heart Studio for lunch by the same train. Since the Empress Dowager worried that the whistling of the train would affect the geomantic balance of the Forbidden City, the small train was pulled along by eunuchs with ropes. Not far from the Tower of Violet Light and within the west gate of the Central Lake was the Hall of the Empress's Dignity used by Empress Dowager as her bedchamber. It was burnt down during the invasion by the allied forces of the eight powers in 1900 and renamed the Hall for Cherishing Benevolence after reconstruction.

The Hall of Boundless Blessings is the main structure along the east bank. It faces the Tower of Violet Light across the Celestial Lake.

A group of Buddhist structures is found here. In the early years of the Qing dynasty, eunuchs were ordered to act as monks in these temples and perform Buddhist duties. On the *Zhongyuan* Festival which falls on the 15th day of the seventh lunar month, Buddhist ceremonies were held here during the Ming and Qing dynasties. According to Buddhist legend, Maudgalyayana, one of Sakyamuni's disciples, discovered that his deceased mother was being surrounded by hungry ghosts in the nether world, and asked Buddha to save her. Sakyamuni told him if he could prepare one hundred kinds of food and offer them to monks near and far on the *Zhongyuan* Festival, his mother would be salvaged from hell. The festival is also called the Ullambana Festival. On every *Zhongyuan* Festival, a ceremony would be held in front of the Hall of Boundless Blessings, sheds for ghosts would be put up, scriptures recited, fireworks set off, and lanterns lit on the lake. Eunuchs holding lanterns shaped like lotus leaves lined the banks to light up the Celestial Lake, which would look like a sky dotted with twinkling stars. To the west of the hall is the Pavilion of Clouds on the Water housing a large stone stele inscribed with words in Emperor Qianlong's calligraphy, "Autumn Breeze on the Celestial Lake," which makes the site one of the Eight Views of Yanjing.

The North Lake is so named because it is situated in the northern section of the Celestial Lake. Today it is called Beihai (North Sea) Park. Southwest of the front entrance to the park is an enclosure known as the Round City, originally an islet south of Jade Flower Islet. It is said that Emperor Zhangzone of the Jurchen dynasty once came here with his favorite concubine and wrote the line, "Two persons sit on a mound." The lady wrote in response, "A moon shines by the sun." In the Yuan dynasty a hall with a cone-shaped roof was built and a brick wall was added in the Ming dynasty. The wall is five meters high and 276 meters in perimeter, covering an area of 4,500 square meters.

Tower of Violet Light

Pavilion of Clouds on the Water

In the Round City is the Hall for Receiving the Light, a square hall with a *Xieshan* roof and a corridor protruding from each of the four sides. The roof is covered with yellow glazed tiles and trimmed with green ones. The upturned roof corners give it an imposing air. In the hall there is the statue of a graceful seated Buddha carved from an entire piece of jade. Well-polished and glistening with white color, the statue is 1.6 meters high and is inlaid with precious stones. The Buddha statue was contributed by Ming Kuan, a monk from Beijing, in 1898 or the 24th year of the Guangxu reign. He had acquired it in Burma with the funds he raised there. The jade statue was first presented to Empress Dowager Cixi and then moved to the Round City. The pavilions, rockeries and trees outside the hall are well laid out. To the east of the hall is an ancient pine with a large top. Looking sturdy and fresh, it is said to be 800 years old.

Jade Flower Islet is the center of the Beihai Park. In the Yuan dynasty, a Hall of Pervasive Cold was built on the islet, but it had become totally dilapidated by the middle period of the Ming dynasty. In 1651, the 8th year of the reign of the Qing emperor Shunzhi, the White Dagoba was built on the hill of the Jade Flower Islet. The spire, placed at a height of 112 meters, was the highest point in the whole city. (The dagoba itself was 35.9 meters high.) The White Dagoba is a brick-and-wood structure. Inside is a 28.8-meter-high pillar, on top of which is a gilded box containing Buddha relics. The White Dagoba consists of three parts — the base, the body and the top. The folded *sumeru* base is built with bricks and stone to support a body shaped like an inverted alms-bowl. The three lower layers of the body are

Wall of the Round City

Jade Flower Islet in the Beihai Park

round platforms under a protruding belly. The upper part of the body consists of the wheel signs, and further up are two bronze umbrella-like covers carrying 14 copper bells. The top of the dagoba is a gilded spire. Standing on Jade Flower Islet, the dagoba enhances the charm of Beijing. The Qing emperors built the White Dagoba to emphasize the policy of upholding Lamaism. South of the White Dagoba four halls were built along the central axis — the Hall of Karma, the Hall of Universal Peace, the Hall of Enlightenment and the Hall of the Dharma Wheel — as sites for Lamas to carry on their religious practice. They also served as places for Buddhist practice in general.On the 25th day of the 10th lunar month, the Lamas would open the entrance gates, burn incense and recite scriptures. Lanterns would be put up from the foot of the hill on Jade Flower Islet to the top of the White Dagoba. The Lamaist dagoba also served a military purpose. There used to be signal poles on the dagoba and signal cannons were mounted on the hill. In an emergency flags would be hoisted on the poles in daytime and lanterns lit at night, and the cannons would be fired to alert people.

To the east of the White Dagoba is a semi-circular brick citadel called the Crescent Moon City. In the east part of the city is a decorated archway. The main attraction of the east hillside lies not in the temples or halls but in the towering ancient trees. In summer the east hillside on Jade Flower Islet would be covered by the shades of trees which cannot be penetrated by sunlight. Thus a stone stele was inscribed with the words in Emperor Qianlong's calligraphy, "Jade Islet in Shady Springtime." This is also one of the Eight Views of Yanjing. To the west of the White Dagoba are the Hall of Mental Delight, where the Qing emperors received ministers, and the Tower of Evening Celebrations overlooking the lake. Along the hillsides on Jade Flower Islet and by the side of Celestial Lake are the 25-bay Extended Pavilion in a crescent moon shape called the Pavilion for Inspecting Old Scripts. The walls of the pavilion are inlaid with 495 pieces of stone carvings of famous Chinese calligraphy known as "Calligraphy from the Hall of Three Rarities." Emperor Qianlong wrote in a poem:

> Why is the Extended Pavilion so famous?
> Because it is the home of excellent calligraphy
> From the Hall of Three Rarities.

This is why the Extended Pavilion is also called the Pavilion for Inspecting Old Scripts. It has the most complete collection of stone carvings of Chinese calligraphy discovered so far. To the north of the White Dagoba sheer cliffs, winding stairs, zigzag corridors, and kiosks are found everywhere. Towers and pavilions were built on top of the rocky hills, and caves were dug underneath. One can get to the

Jade statue of Buddha in the Round City

White Dagoba on the Jade Flower Islet

lakeside by climbing over the hills and going through the caves. The main buildings by the lakeside are the Hall of Ripples on the east and the Studio of Peaceful Journey on the west. Beyond these are the Pavilion of Light on the Water on the east and the Pavilion of Distant Voyage on the west. The four structures and the adjacent 60-bay Extended Pavilion form a crescent moon shape along the shady side of the hill. A 300-meter-long corridor with white marble balustrades lines the Extended Pavilion. At the two ends of the corridor stand two small fort-like structures — the Tower Beside the Waters at the eastern end and the Pavilion for Sharing the Coolness at the western end, both of which face the Five Dragon Pavilions across the Celestial Lake.

With the White Dagoba as the center of the axis, the Jade Flower Islet is laid out circularly in the shape of an umbrella. The halls, towers and kiosks were constructed and the rockeries, trees and flowers furnished on this principle to provide a brilliant example of the Chinese art of gardening.

A circular covered corridor skirts the lake at the northern foot of the hill on Jade Flower Islet. It is 300 meters long and lined with white marble balustrades. There used to be two docks on the east bank of Celestial Lake northeast of Jade Flower Islet. They were known as "halls on the water" —one for docking dragon-shaped boats and the other for docking phoenix-shaped boats. The dragon boat, 33.89 meters long and 9.17 meters wide, had a tower which was gilded and painted in bright colors. Along the banks are bamboo groves and two kiosks surrounded by all kinds of flowers. By the east side of the docks stand the Pavilion for Quiet Meditation and the Painted Boat Studio. The former is a three-bay structure facing water on three sides and hills on all four sides. A carved stone bridge with nine twists spans a pond to present a poetic scene. North of the bridge is a stone archway. Beyond the bridge a corridor leads up to the hill. Like the Pavilion for Quiet Meditation, the Painted Boat Studio north of it was built in 1757, the 22nd year of the Qianlong reign. Built on water, the picturesque studio looks like a floating boat, which accounts for its name. It almost emerge with the water to produce a fairyland-like effect. A poem reads:

Anyone who dines here wonders if he is in heaven;
Leaning on the balustrade by the pond,
One feels as if he were in a mirror.

Crescent Moon City in the Beihai Park

Bas-reliefs on the stele called "Jade Islet in Shady Springtime"

Stele inscribed with characters meaning "Jade Islet in Shady Springtime"

A complex of structures, including the Painted Boat Studio, centers around a lotus pond. In addition to the studio in the north, there is the Hall of Spring Rain, Forest and Pond in the south where one can enjoy a broad view of the vast lake and winding banks.In the east is the Pavilion of Fragrance in the Mirror where one can enjoy the beauty and aroma of lotus flowers. In the west is the Pavilions for Enjoying the Scenery. Surrounded by corridors,this group of structures forms a tranquil, secluded environment. Two small courtyards are found in the northeast and southwest corners. A zigzag corridor in the northwest leads to a small room called the "Small Treasure," a delicately furnished retreat with grotesque rocks at the back. The bamboos rustling in the breeze give a poetic flavor to the surroundings.

To the northwest of Jade Flower Islet and along the northwest bank of Celestial Lake are five pavilions—the Pavilion of the Dragon's Benevolence in the center and four others in the east and west. Together they are called the Five Dragon Pavilions. They are linked by bridge in a S-shape and lined with balustrades. The five pavilions feature both symmetry and variety. They were used by the emperor and empress to enjoy the moon, avoid summer heat, watch the fish in the lake and look at the display of lanterns.

To the northwest of the Five Dragon Pavilions is the Tower of Ten Thousand Buddhas built by Emperor Qianlong for the 80th birthday of his mother in 1770, the 35th year of his reign. The largest gold statue of Buddha weighed 588 taels and a small one weighed 58 taels. The 10,000 gold Buddha statues were placed on three decks for worship in the Tower of Ten Thousand Buddhas. During the invasion by the allied forces of eight powers in 1900, all the gold statues of Buddha were taken away, and the tower itself was destroyed. To the east of the tower is the Hall of Heavenly Kings, an exquisite Buddhist hall with a glazed-tiled archway in front and a glazed-tiled wall at the back. To the west of the Hall of Heavenly Kings is the Nine-Dragon Wall, and to the east is the Tranquil Heart Studio.

The Tranquil Heart Studio is considered the cream of the art of gardening as manifest in Beihai Park. With hills to the east and a temple to the west, leaning against a wall in the north and facing the vast lake in the south, it is a park within a park encircled by a white wall. The site is ingeniously laid out. In the front courtyard stands the

Pavilion for Inspecting Old Scripts in the Beihai Park

Extended Pavilion in the Beihai Park

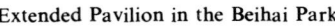

141

Tranquil Heart Studio

studio with an open corridor in front and a pavilion at the back. Corridors stretching out from its two sides encircle a square pond which dominates the courtyard and which is provided with carved stone balustrades on the north and south. Narrow paths extending from the two sides of the building lead to another courtyard which again is centered around a large pond behind which the Corridor of Murmuring Spring and the nearby pavilions look only secondary. The man-made hills present an ever-changing scene. At the highest point northwest of the hill is the Tower of Emerald Ripples. The Tea Roasting Room is linked with the Corridor of Murmuring Spring by yet another corridor even though the two are separated by a pond. The zigzag paths and undulating terrain reminds one of a fairyland. The towers and pavilions, rockeries and ponds, flower beds and trees are properly laid out with much originality. The philosophy of the whole design seems to give prominence to the ponds, man-made hills and rockeries while assigning a supplementary role to the buildings and using them as partitions, with the result that there are hills beyond hills, buildings beyond buildings, and one courtyard beyond another. The German philosopher G.W.F. Hegel regarded the Chinese art of gardening as "an all-out effort to copy the free Nature." The Tranquil Heart Studio is a successful effort to achieve the purpose.

To the northwest of the Forbidden City are the zoos for enjoyment by the imperial family. In the Ming dynasty, the Tigers' City and the Leopards' House northwest of Celestial Lake were the largest and best-known palace zoos. Emperor Zhengde liked to watch tigers. One poem says:

The court ladies love the songs and dances from West China.
And the Emperor has just come back from the Tigers' City.

The Leopards' House was located northwest of the Tigers' City. North of the Tigers' City was a zoo where rhinoceros, elephants, seals and lynx were kept. By the side of the Tower of Violet Light was the House of One Hundred Birds where rare birds like peacocks, multi-colored parrots and white cranes were raised in addition to martens, lynx and seals. In the Ming dynasty tigers, leopards, rhinoceros and elephants were given official ranks. A tiger was fed on the basis of the allowance for an army general and an elephant was financially treated as a high-ranking military commander.

The zoos were abandoned in the early years of the Qing dynasty. Emperor Kangxi had a new Tigers' City built to the west of the west section of the Enjoying-the-Spring Garden in Beijing's western suburbs. Encircled by a brick and stone wall, the zoo was covered with a grid reinforced with iron wires, and a tower was built on the side from where people could watch the tigers. Cubs were raised here and would be sent to the hunting ground after they grew up. Like other carnivorous animals, the tigers were fed with a certain amount of meat every day. The large ones were given 2.5 kilograms, the medium-sized ones, two kilograms, and the small ones, 1.5 kilograms. The cubs each received one kilogram. During Emperor Qianlong's reign, a convicted monk was going to be put to death in the capital. The original penalty was the dismemberment of his body. But the monk claimed that he could conjure up wind and rain and subdue dragons and tigers. He was thus put into the tigers' lair by order of the emperor as a test of his magic powers. As the guards watched from the tower, a tiger roared and swooped down on the monk, who fought the tiger bare-handed. The fight lasted a whole day. By the evening both were utterly exhausted and fell on the ground. They were injured, but neither of them died. During Emperor Jiajing's reign, a tiger ran out of the zoo because of careless

Nine-Dragon Wall in the Beihai Park

Five Dragon Pavilions in the Beihai Park

Site of the Garden of Good Deeds (Garden of Ten Thousand Animals)

management. It broke into a village where it killed one person and wounded another and ate one pig and two dogs. Several hundred soldiers were called out to look for the tiger, but it was not until several days later that they found and killed it. The families of the victimized villagers were compensated, some officials were punished for neglect of duty, and the Tigers' City was rebuilt.

By the late period of the Qing dynasty, the Tigers' City had become a stretch of wasteland and the animals were nowhere to be found. In 1906, the 32nd year of the Guangxu reign, another zoo called the Garden of Ten Thousand Animals was built at the old site of the Garden of Good Deeds outside the Straight West Gate of Beijing. The next year 57 animals were purchased from Germany, including Indian elephants capable of performing acrobatic feats, white deer, wild deer, African deer, American deer, zebras, wild oxen, lions, Australian ostriches and egrets in addition to 52 birds. Then rare animals and birds were sent in from various localities in the country. Among them were grey cranes and mandarin ducks from Haizhou, pheasants from Zhejiang, wild boars and egrets from Sichuan, flying tigers from Guangxi, emerald-featherd birds, flying snakes, and parrots from Guangdong, yaks from Shaanxi, thrushes and white swallows from Fujian, and pheasants from Fengtian in Northeast China. The German consul in Sichuan presented the zoo with two bears raised by him and a scholar from the United States contributed three Tibetan dogs. Pavilions, towers and kiosks were built and cages were provided. A big zoo gradually took shape. In 1908, the 34th year of Emperor Guangxu's reign, the imperial zoo received the first group of foreign visitors. After touring the zoo, the Nepalese envoy said that in Beijing "There is a Garden of Ten Thousand Animals with big towers and pavilions and a great variety of animals. It is one of the wonders of the world."

South Garden, also known as South Sea, was 10 kilometers outside Gate of Everlasting Stability to the south of the Forbidden City. It was the biggest natural hunting ground in Beijing during the Yuan dynasty. As a nomadic people, the Mongols loved horsemanship and archery. After Kublai Khan made Beijing his capital, he converted much of the farmland in the suburbs into pastures. Later he accepted the advice of officials of the Han nationality and changed the pastures back into farmland. But he preserved the South Garden and often went hunting there. Emperor Yongle of the Ming dynasty was fond of martial arts and hunting. He expanded South Garden into a hunting area 60 kilometers in perimeter and surrounded it

with a wall which had four gates. As the emperors of the Ming later preferred literary studies to martial arts or even indulged themselves in wine and women, South Garden declined, but it regained its prosperity under the Qing because the Manchus, too, were good horsemen and archers who loved hunting and the practice of military skills. South Garden became a famous nine-gate hunting enclosure with 94 springs, two rivers—the Liangshui River and Tuanhe River, plus lush woods and a great variety of game including deer, pheasants, wild rabbits and river deer. There were two hunting seasons every year, spring and winter, when the game was driven into the garden and mounted men hunted the animals down with arrows. The killing of a tiger, considered the king of animal world, would offer the greatest satisfaction to the hunter and prove his courage and wisdom. Ambitious emperors of the Qing dynasty such as Emperors Kangxi and Qianlong enjoyed hunting down a tiger. The Qing government organized a battalion of 600 tiger killers who accompanied the emperor on his hunting trip in South Garden in spring. An office for the direction of hunting operations was established on a platform by a river and several lakes with a total of 72 ferries. The platform was 19.2 meters high and 38.4 meters in perimeter. A "Grand Review" was conducted by the emperor from the platform. The emperor would ascend the platform with the soldiers of the Eight Banners standing on both sides. Led by ministers and generals, the soldiers would march forward while shouting and blowing horns. After the parade, the emperor would go back to a tent, take off his armor, distribute rewards and give a banquet. As many as 1,000 tables were laid for the ministers, generals and soldiers. Emperor Qianlong once received envoys in the midst of a display of fireworks. In the early years of the Qing dynasty, a Grand Review was held every three years in South Garden. Later the Grand Reviews took place at irregular intervals, and not necessarily in South Garden either. Beginning with the middle period of the Kangxi reign, another hunting ground was laid out and the Mountain Manor for Avoiding Summer Heat was built, and the emperor seldom came to South Garden. However, in 1777, the 42th year of the Qianlong reign, the Tuanhe River was dredged, and the Tuanhe River Resort was built three kilometers inside the entrance of Huangcun Village at the southwest gate of South Garden. The site remains to this day.

Decorations on the stone bridge to the Tranquil Heart Studio

Retreat for Revealing One's Mind in the Fragrant Hills

Temple of Clarity in the Fragrant Hills

Archway of glazed tiles at the Temple of Clarity

The Three Scenic Hills and Five Gardens

In an area extending from Haidian to the West Hills in Beijing's western suburbs, the natural scenery of mountains and rivers facilitates the creation of beautiful gardens. As early as the beginning of the 10th century, the state of Yan under Liu Shouguang built a number of luxurious mansions here. Early in the 11th century, imperial resorts were established in this area by the rulers of the Liao dynasty. Toward the end of the 12th century, Emperor Zhangzong of the Jurchen dynasty launched projects to develop the scenic area of the Fragrant Hills. Thus the West Hills gradually became a resort for the imperial family and the nobility. Emperor Zhengde of the Ming dynasty had gardens built at the old site of the Temple of Perfect Tranquility at Jug Mountain (today's Longevity Hill) and called it the Garden of Excellent Hills. During the Qing dynasty gardens far surpassing those of the Liao, Jurchen, Yuan and Ming dynasties appeared because the Qing emperors loved hunting and pleasure trips. Apart from South Garden and the three lakes described earlier in this chapter, the Qing dynasty contributed to the art of gardening mainly by developing the "three hills and five gardens" in the western suburbs. They are: the Garden of Congenial Tranquility in the Fragrant Hills, the Garden of Light and Tranquility in the Jade Spring Hill, and the Garden of Clear Ripples (later known as the Summer Palace) in the area of the Longevity Hill, the Enjoying-the-Spring Garden, and the Garden of Perfect Splendor.

The Fragrant Hills, the best-known among the West Hills, are liked for their green solpes and clear waters. An ancient poem reads:

Once you come out of the city,
You are greeted by a transparent river;
From the top of the tower,
You capture a full view of the mountain greenery.

The Fragrant Hills look pretty all year round because of the colorful blossoms in spring, the shady trees in summer, the crystal clear sky and the mountainsides tinged red by smoke trees in autumn, and the snow-clad hills in winter. "The Snow-clad West Hills on a Clear Day" is one of the Eight Views of Yanjing.

Emperor Kangxi of the Qing dynasty had resorts built in the Fragrant Hills and embellished the scenic spots there. One of his favorite creations was the Pavilion of Greenery from where he could both see his capital city in the distance and enjoy the scenery nearby. As a result of large-scale construction under Emperor Qianlong, 20 scenic spots appeared within the boundary wall of the Fragrant Hills. They are the Hall of Diligent Government, the Fine View Tower, the Green Cloud Boat, the Studio for Modest Studies, the Pendant Hill, the Emerald Kiosk, the Boundless Greenery, the Deer-Taming Slope, the Toad Peak, the Dwelling-in-Clouds Tower, the Musical Brook, the Temple of the Fragrant Hills, the Pines Rustling in the Breeze, the Pavilion of Greenery, the Cranes Crying at Night, the Tea Sampling Room, the Rainbow Path, the Jade Milk Spring, the Red-Colored Forest in Autumn and the Pavilion of Fragrant Rain. Outside the boundary wall of the Fragrant Hills are eight more scenic spots: the Site for Admiring the Sun, the Hibiscus Lawn, the Fragrant Dew Cave, the Dwelling-in-the-Moon Cliff, the Jade Chain Cliff, the Double Agate Hill, the Forest of Jade Tablets and the Bell Separated from the Clouds.

The 28 sights include halls, pavilions, kiosks, towers, temples, studies, boat-shaped structures as well as natural scenic spots. The Deer-Taming Slope is a large expanse of hillside land where groups of deer are raised. The tamed deer with big horns ran in the thick forests and across lush grass, enhancing the charm of the mountain forests. At the Toad Peak a huge rock looks like a semi-recumbent toad with a protruding belly, opening its mouth and raising its head toward the west. The Cranes Crying at Night is a hexagonal kiosk where cranes cried loudly under the moon in a frosty night. The Red-Colored Forest in Autumn refers to the large expanses of smoke trees on the southern and northern slopes which turn red in late autumn, a scenery which defies the painter's brush. Even the resorts are full of natural charm. The Retreat for Revealing One's Mind was built under Emperor Jiajing of the Ming dynasty at the foot of a hill and on the bank of a river. It has a semi-circular lotus pond and a pavilion at its side encircled by a corridor. Surrounded by cypresses and pines and rocks, it shows a unique architectural style in a quiet atmosphere. The Double Clear Springs are two refreshening springs near the Temple of the Fragrant Hills with the name written in Emperor Qianlong's handwriting. A villa was built at the foot of the hills with a pond, a kiosk, and a bamboo grove in its garden. The site is enjoyable

Partial View of the Garden of Perfect Splendor

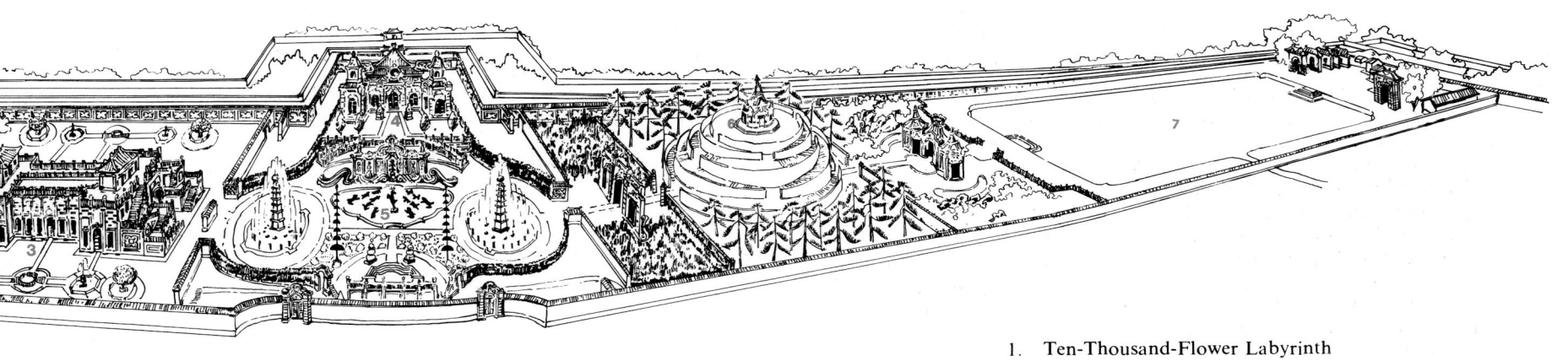

1. Ten-Thousand-Flower Labyrinth
2. Sharing the Delights
3. Hall of Universal Peace
4. Tower for Looking Afar
5. Fountain
6. Hill Beside the Square River
7. Square Sea

Site of the Gate of the Temple of Buddha's Blessings in the Enjoying-the-Spring Garden

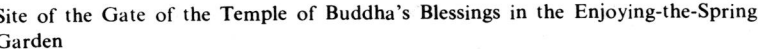

The light boat takes me downstream,
Crossing the Kunming Lake in no time;
On the bank I change to a chariot,
And arrive in Front Garden after a few zigzags.

The Front Garden was another name for the Enjoying-the-Spring Garden which was located to the south of the Garden of Perfect Splendor. The former was overshadowed by the construction of the latter. Today the structures in the Enjoying-the-Spring Garden are nowhere to be found, except for the ruins of the gates of two temples, the Temple of Buddha's Protection and the Temple of Buddha's Blessings, which can be seen outside the west gate of Beijing University.

The Garden of Perfect Splendor is located north of the Enjoying-the-Spring Garden and east of the Summer Palace. It was built in 1709, the 48th year of Emperor Kangxi's reign, and started as a small residential garden belonging to Prince Yong. After Prince Yong succeeded to the throne, he rebuilt the garden on a colossal scale. Besides improving the original hills, pools and pavilions, he added many new structures in the style of imperial offices. After Emperor Qianlong ascended the throne he made six tours of areas south of the Yangtze River and gave orders to remodel the garden after the style of famous gardens in South China. While expanding the garden northward, he built the Garden of Eternal Spring to its east. To the south of both gardens he combined several residential gardens into one and called it the Garden of Blossoming Spring which was later changed to the Garden of Ten Thousand Spring Seasons. The three were collectively known as the Three Gardens of Perfect Splendor, or simply as one garden bearing the same name. The total area was 346 hectares. The building space equalled that of the whole Forbidden City. The water surface was as large as the Kunming Lake. With advantages of a unified state, political stability, abundant material and financial resources, the Qing regime recruited skilled workers from all over the country to build the garden. Construction went on for some 150 years through the reigns of Emperors Kangxi, Yongzheng and Qianlong before the masterpiece of Chinese gardening was finally produced. The Garden of Perfect Splendor was the largest of the three. It had 18 gates and 40 scenic spots, each being a miniature complex of towers and pavilions. Water surfaces were interlocked with land areas, hills and rockeries contrasted flowers and trees. Each zone offered a fresh view. The front part served as the imperial court, in which the Open-and-

Site of the Western-Style Buildings in the Garden of Perfect Splendor

167

Aboveboard Hall was the main structure. A plaque inscribed with the words "be open and aboveboard" in Emperor Yongzheng's calligraphy hung in the middle of the hall. In 1793. Emperor Qianlong received George Macartney, envoy from England, in this hall. There was a lake at the back of the hall called the Front Lake. On the north bank of the lake was the Hall of Nationwide Peace and Order which faced the Open-and-Aboveboard Hall across the lake. Emperors Yongzheng and Daoguang both died in the Hall of Nationwide Peace and Order. There were two more halls in this complex: "Spring for Heaven and Earth" on the east and "Happiness in Harmony" on the west. The two halls were the living quarters of Emperor Qianlong. Further back was the Tower of Clear Light with a panoramic drawing of the garden on the inside wall.

The Hall of Universal Peace and Harmony, one of the 40 scenic spots, was located on a terrace on the lake with water all round. Built in the shape of 卍 , it was well designed and beautifully laid out. The High Mountain and Long River Hall was a two-story building skirted by a stream in front, which bordered on a spacious ground. On the Lantern Festival Emperor Qianlong would take his empress and concubines to the upper floor of the hall to watch a display of lanterns. No fewer than 5,000 people would participate in the performance. The entire hall and the nearby pavilions were lit up, and the lanterns formed a succession of patterns. Then fireworks were sent up to the sky amidst singing and dancing. Other scenic spots included Carving the Moon and Parting the Clouds, A Natural Scroll of Painting, the Studio of Parasol Trees, and The Water Blends with the Sky. While the buildings in the front area of the garden were stately and gorgeous, those in the rear were delicate and graceful. In the east part of the Garden of Perfect Splendor was a huge lake called the Sea of Good Fortune or the East Lake. The vast, clear lake was surrounded by ten islets, including three named after fairylands in Chinese legend at the center.

The Garden of Eternal Spring was named after the Hall of the Immortal of Eternal Spring where Emperor Qianlong lived before he came to the throne. Based on water scenery, the layout included scenic wonders modelled after those in North and South China as well as buildings in Western style. The main structure was the Chunhua Studio named after a collection of famous calligraphy of the Song dynasty toward the end of 10th century which had been reprinted on the orders of Emperor Qianlong. The Lion Forest in the northeastern corner of the garden was copied after a famous garden of the same name in Suzhou, southeast China. Sixteen sights in the garden created a garaceful scenery typical of South China. In the northern part of the garden were buildings and fountains in the style of the Renaissance period in Italy, bearing such names as Sharing the Delights, Birdcage, Hall of Universal Peace, Water-Tower, Ten-thousand-Flower Labyrinth, etc. These buildings were designed mainly by the Giuseppe Castiglione and other Jesuits and constructed by Chinese workers. A water-tower was built by a fountain furnished with sculptures of the 12 animals representing the 12 Earthly Branches — mouse, ox, tiger, rabbit, dragon, snake, horse, sheep, monkey, cock, dog and pig, used to symbolize the years in which people were born. Every two hours water would gush out of the mouth of one of the animals and the cycle went on round the clock. The Ten-Thousand-Flower Labyrinth was an imitation of the maze found in a European garden at the time. The emperor would order the eunuchs to play hide-and-seek along the intricate paths and watch the game from a high place. A Square River was created and a model of Venice placed in the middle, and man-made hill was built on the bank. Sitting on the hill, the emperor enjoyed the view of "the city of Venice."

The Garden of Blossoming Spring (the Garden of Ten Thousand Spring Seasons), built in the middle of Emperor Qianlong's reign period, was a combination of several small gardens. The water scenery was created out of many small pools, and the land area was a combination of that of several residential gardens. As an integration of natural scenery and architectural complexes, it had 30 scenic spots. The designers borrowed from the strong points of the original well-known gardens but improved the old sites by giving them an overall layout, a sophisticated combination of land and water, architectural perfection and poetic flavor. The garden was rebuilt during Emperor Tongzhi's reign after its destruction and renamed the Garden of Ten Thousand Spring Seasons.

The three gardens forming the Garden of Perfect Splendor had a periphery of 10 kilometers. There were 108 scenic spots in the three gardens — 40 in the Garden of Perfect Splendor itself, which was later increased to 48, 30 in the Garden of Eternal Spring, and 30 more in the Garden of Ten Thousand Spring Seasons. In addition to the beautiful scenery and elegant buildings, there were thousands of precious flower beds and trees, priceless paintings and calligraphy by celebrities of various historical periods, rare or even only copies of classical books, clocks, bells, bronze tripods, pottery and porcelain antiques, pearls and jewels, gold and silver articles, and other invaluable cultural relics representing the best in traditional Chinese culture.

However, the garden was plundered and burnt by foreign invaders twice, first in 1860 and then in 1900. The relics were all gone, and the garden lay in ruins.

The Life of Emperors and Empresses

Ascending the Throne

The Ming (1368-1644) and Qing (1644-1911) dynasties had 26 emperors who reigned for a total of 543 years. Zhu Yuanzhang, founding emperor of the Ming, established his capital at Yingtian (present-day Nanjing). When he was succeeded by Emperor Jianwen, Zhu Di, the Prince of Yan, revolted and took over the throne. Nineteen years later, in 1421, Zhu Di moved his capital to Beijing. Among the 16 emperors of the Ming, three (Hongwu, Jianwen and Yongle) were enthroned in Nanjing, the other 13 in Beijing. It may be interesting to note that of the 13 emperors crowned in Beijing's Forbidden City, eight were enthroned when they were less than 18 years of age: Emperors Chenghua and Hongzhi at 17, Emperor Chongzhen at 16, Emperor Tianqi at 15, Emperors Zhengde and Jiajing at 14, Emperor Wanli at nine, and Emperor Zhengtong at eight.

As the previous Chinese dynasties, the Ming dynasty followed a system of monarchy, under which the title of Crown Prince was conferred on the eldest son of the emperor as a regular practice. It was given to the second son, and sometimes to the eldest son of the Crown Prince, in case the eldest son died before the emperor, or to the third son in case both the eldest and the second sons died before the emperor. But there were exceptions among the 13 Ming emperors crowned in Beijing. One of them was Emperor Zhengtong. Young and ambitious, he embarked on a military expedition at the instigation of the eunuch Wang Zhen, but was defeated and taken captive. In the crisis the Empress Dowager entrusted state affairs to the emperor's younger brother, who became Emperor Jingtai shortly afterward. The second exception was Emperor Zhengde. He had two daughters but no son, and so was succeeded by his cousin, who became Emperor Jiajing. A third case was Emperor Tianqi who was succeeded by his half-brother, Emperor Chongzhen, because all his three sons had died young.

Toward the end of the Ming dynasty, bitter and intricate struggles broke out in the royal house over succession to the throne. Lady Wang, mother of Emperor Tianqi, was insulted and beaten to death by Lady Li of the West Chamber when the emperor was only a five-year-old crown prince. Lady Li put the prospective emperor in the custody of her cronies in the hope of taking power into her hands someday. Lady Liu, mother of Emperor Chongzhen, fell into disfavor after giving birth to Chongzhen and finally died in despair. Chongzhen was raised first by Lady Li of the West Chamber and then by Lady Li of the East Chamber. As Chongzhen was only five when his mother died, he could remember nothing of her. When he heard that one of the maids of honor looked like his mother, he ordered a court artist to do a portrait of her, which was then enshrined for worship. Even more tragic was the fate of Lady Zhao, who was ordered to commit suicide by a forged imperial decree after she had offended Wei Zhongxian, a powerful eunuch. After burning incense before the image of a Buddha, she wept bitterly and hanged herself in sorrow.

The House of Qing had a line of 12 emperors, or 10 if reckoned from the time the Qing army marched through a Great Wall pass and entered Beijing. Five of the emperors were under eight when they

acceded to the throne: Emperor Kangxi at seven, Emperors Shunzhi and Tongzhi at five, Emperor Guangxu at three, and Emperor Xuantong at two—an average of 4.4 years of age. Thanks to a different system of succession to the throne, the internal strife in the Qing palace was not as fierce as that in the Ming period. The 12 emperors of the Qing can roughly be divided into three categories according to the method by which they chose their successors The first included the four emperors in the early Qing period, when nobody was granted the title of Crown Prince. Emperor Kangxi did name a Crown Prince, but he abolished the title afterward. The heir to the crown was chosen by consultation among Manchu nobles or by decision of the dying emperor. For example, when Emperor Shunzhi passed away at 24, five of his eight sons had died. Which of the

Imperial robe of the Qing dynasty

Portrait of Emperor Qianlong

In 1908, when Emperor Guangxu's nephew, Aisin-gioro Pu Yi, was only two, Empress Dowager Cixi decided to make him heir to the throne as both she and the emperor were terminally ill. Her decree to this effect threw the mansion of Prince Chun, Pu Yi's father, into confusion. Pu Yi cried and hit the eunuch who tried to take him to the palace. The Prince Regent, the Grand Councillor and the eunuchs all felt helpless until Pu Yi's wet nurse came and stopped his crying by giving him the breast. Everybody agreed that the emperor designate should be taken to the palace by his wet nurse.

On seeing Cixi, Pu Yi screamed and cried even louder. She ordered someone to give him a string of candied haws, but the baby emperor threw it on the floor. Displeased, Cixi told a eunuch to take him away.

The emperor and the empress dowager died on the second and third days after Pu Yi was taken to the palace. Shortly afterward, the ceremony of enthronement was held in the Hall of Supreme Harmony, at which Pu Yi was given the title of Emperor Xuantong. After the performance of many long and tiresome formalities before the ceremony, the two-year-old emperor was carried up to the enormous throne, but he could not stand the ordeal any longer. The emperor's father, the Prince Regent, was kneeling in front of the throne and supporting his son with both hands. He told him not to fidget, but the emperor struggled and cried, "I don't like it here. I want to go home." As the desperate Prince Regent was sweating all over amid the kowtowing of the officials, the emperor cried louder and louder. His father tried to calm him down by saying, "Don't cry, ... It'll soon be finished, it'll soon be finished."

When the ceremony was over, the court officials looked dejected because they regarded the emperor's cries and his father's words, "it'll soon be finished," as a bad omen. Sure enough, a revolution took place three years later, which overthrew the Qing dynasty and ended China's 2,000-year-old feudal monarchy.

remaining three should be the heir? After careful deliberation, the court picked the third son, Xuanye, as Emperor Kangxi because he had survived smallpox, a fatal disease in those days. In the second category were four emperors in the mid-Qing period. To ease the rivalry over the crown, Emperor Yongzheng initiated a system of keeping the name of the heir in secret until after his death. The name was contained in a sealed casket placed behind a plaque inscribed with four characters meaning "be open and aboveboard" hanging in the Hall of Celestial Purity of the Forbidden City. The next three emperors — Qianlong, Jiaqing and Daoguang — all followed the practice. The four emperors in the late Qing period belonged to the third category. Owing to one reason or another, no Crown Prince was designated secretly in this period. Emperor Xianfeng had only one son after the early death of his other son. Neither Emperor Tongzhi nor Emperor Guangxu had a son. Finally, Xuantong, the last emperor, was overthrown in the 1911 Revolution.

The enthronement of an emperor is supposed to be a grand and elaborate ceremony anywhere in the world. However, it turned out to be a relatively simple affair in the Forbidden City because it usually took place during the state funeral for the deceased emperor. The ceremony generally began with an official offering sacrifices to heaven and earth, the ancestors of the royal family, and the God of the Five Cereals, after which the new emperor, in mourning dress, knelt and kowtowed before the memorial tablet for the late emperor. After changing into a ceremonial robe, he knelt and kowtowed before the Empress Dowager. Finally, he received the obeisances of the ministers of the inner court in the Midway Hall of Harmony and of the leading civil and military officials in the Hall of Supreme Harmony. As the country was in mourning, no music was played and no banquet given. When the ceremony was over, the emperor went on observing mourning.

However, everything has its exceptions. Emperor Zhengde of the Ming dynasty was succeeded by his cousin, who became Emperor Jiajing. He had previously been made Prince of Anlu by the father of the deceased emperor. On arriving in the capital, Emperor Jiajing first stayed at his temporary palace outside the Gate of Military Virtue, where he was offered congratulations by civil and military officials. Only after that did his enthronement take place. Emperor Qianlong of the Qing abdicated at the age of 86 after a reign of 60 years, and a ceremony was held at which he handed over the reins of government to his son, Emperor Jiaqing. The enthronement of Emperor Xuantong, the last sovereign of the Qing dynasty, proceeded in difficulty and commotion, as described below.

The Royal Wedding

An emperor's wedding was called the "Grand Nuptials." Of the 14 Ming emperors ruling the country from Beijing, including Emperor Yongle who first had his capital in Nanjing, 10 married before they came to the throne. Thus they married as a crown prince or a prince. Only the weddings of the other four who married after enthronement qualified as "Grand Nuptials." The emperors differed vastly from one another in their married life.

Emperor Zhengtong of the Ming ascended the throne at nine. At 16 he married Qian, who became empress by an imperial edict. After the emperor was taken prisoner during a war, the empress cried and prayed day and night till she lost her sight in one eye. The emperor was eventually repatriated, but by then he had been dethroned. The emperor and empress were unhappy for the rest of their lives, but Lady Qian was always good to her husband and tried her best to soothe him.

Emperor Zhengde married Xia after he came to the throne. But he did not like her and chose to live in baofang, a room set aside for obscene pleasures. Disguised as an ordinary citizen, he toured the country and ruined his health by leading a dissipated life. He died young, a victim of sexual obsession.

Emperor Jiajing had three empresses. The first, née Chen, was an extremely jealous woman. One day the emperor had tea with her and one of his consorts. When the consort handed him a cup of tea, he fondly looked at her hand. This displeased the empress, who stood up and threw her cup on the floor. The emperor flew into a rage, which so terrified the empress that she fell ill and died soon afterward. The second empress, also née Chen, was deposed after she lost the emperor's favor and died in loneliness. By then the emperor still had no son. Zhang Fujing, Grand Secretary of the Inner Chancery, said to him, "In ancient times, to have a vast number of descendants, an emperor had not only his empress, but also three consorts, nine concubines, 27 shifu (female court officials in name) and 81 yuqi (female court officials who ranked below shifu), and he placed them in six palaces." The emperor accepted his advice and married Fang, who became his third empress. However, the emperor was attracted by the beauty of Consort Cao, who thus became a thorn in Fang's side. One night, when the emperor was sound asleep, Yang Jinying, a maid of honor, tried to strangle him. When Empress Fang discovered this and untied the rope around his neck, the emperor spat blood and could not speak. The empress forged an imperial decree which charged Consort Cao with failure to report the attempt at murder and sentenced her to *lingchi,** thus getting rid of her.

Emperor Wanli acceded to the throne at 10. At 16 he married Wang, who remained his only empress throughout a reign of 48 years. A kind and magnanimous lady, Empress Wang was tolerant toward Zheng, the emperor's favorite consort, and the two got on well with each other. The empress died a natural death after holding the highest female rank for 42 years. By contrast, another concubine of the emperor, Consort Wang, led a miserable life. Mother of the crown prince who later became Emperor Taichang, she was ordered to live in seclusion after affending Consort Zheng. When she was seriously ill, the crown prince was unable to see her until after he got special permission from the emperor. The crown prince had to pry open the lock on the gate of the palace where his mother was interned. Now a blind, decrepit old lady, she clutched her son's clothes and cried bitterly before she died.

In the Qing dynasty, five emperors married before enthronement and four after it. The last emperor, Xuantong, who was enthroned at two, did not marry till long after his abdication at five.

Prior to an emperor's "Grand Nuptials," he sent an envoy to present betrothal gifts to the bride's family; this was called *nacai*. The envoy then presented clothes to the bride's parents; this was called *dazheng*. The day before the wedding ceremony, the emperor, seated in the Hall of Supreme Harmony, ordered an envoy to inform the bride's family of the wedding date and grant the bride the title of Empress. The bride knelt and kowtowed before accepting the title. On the wedding day, while the emperor sat in the Hall of Supreme Harmony, the envoy went to escort the empress to the palace. Accompanied by an impressive entourage, the empress would arrive

---

* A capital punishment by which the executioner put the accused to death by first cutting off his limbs and then piercing his throat.

in an imperial carriage through the Meridian Gate amid drumbeats and strains of music. After that a banquet would be given by the emperor in the Hall of Supreme Harmony in honor of his father-in-law and other male relatives, and another banquet by the empress dowager in the Hall of Preserved Harmony in honor of the mother of the empress and other female relatives. Finally, the emperor and empress drank the nuptial cup in the Hall of Terrestrial Tranquility before they retired to the bridal chamber, the Eastern Chamber of Warmth, for the wedding night.

The Eastern Chamber of Warmth, a side-room in the Hall of Terrestrial Tranquility, was used as a bridal chamber by three emperors during the Qing dynasty—Kangxi, Tongxhi and Guangxu—and by Xuantong, the last emperor, who was allowed to stay in the Forbidden City after the 1911 Revolution. It was decorated for the "Grand Nuptials" with the big golden character *Xi* (囍), meaning "double happiness," pasted on the crimson palace gate. Immediately inside the gate was a screen wall inscribed with the same character in red against a golden background. The richly furnished bridal chamber was ablaze with red candles. Against the north wall was a nuptial bed covered with a crimson satin dragon-and-phoenix sheet. A stack of dragon-and-phoenix quilts glittered under a colorful "100-Son Canopy."

Embroidered on the "100-Son Canopy" are figures of children enjoying themselves in different ways: cooling under a tree, angling, pushing or riding in a cart, crossing a bridge or playing nearby, performing or watching a performance. The emperor and empress spent only three nights on the nuptial bed under the "100-Son Canopy" before they moved to the palace designated as their regular living quarters.

However, not all the empresses who married according to the rites of the "Grand Nuptials" turned out to be lucky. Emperor Shunzhi's wife was a Mongol, a cousin of his. Their marriage was

Royal Wedding of Emperor Guangxu (Painting)

100-Son Canopy

Portrait of Emperor Yongzheng's consort

arranged by Dorgon, the Prince Regent, who wanted to strengthen his own position through the marriage. The empress was pretty, but the emperor did not like her. He said, "From the day she became my empress, we have differed in our views, and the result is an inharmonious royal family." He insisted on deposing the Mongolian empress although his officials tearfully pleaded for her. After parting with her, Emperor Shunzhi had another empress, but he did not like her either. He bestowed all his affections on Consort Dong'e, who nevertheless died when he was only 24. Deeply grieved, the emperor did not hold court for five days and died of sorrow a few months later. It is also said that the emperor did not die but, dressed in *kasaya,* left the palace and went to Mt. Wutai where he became a monk. This may not be true, but it indicates the emperor's devotion to Consort Dong'e.

Emperor Shunzhi was succeeded by his son Emperor Kangxi who, unlike his father, loved his empress. The emperor was overwhelmed with grief when his empress died in 1689, the 28th year of his reign. According to a French Jesuit who witnessed the event, the emperor wept at the empress's coffin twice and kept vigil there for several hours. After the coffin was placed temporarily in one of the outskirts of Beijing, the emperor went there on horseback everyday after concluding his court session.

In the case of Emperors Guangxu and Tongzhi, whose marriages were arranged by Empress Dowager Cixi, there was no love to speak of between husband and wife. As Emperor Guangxu found a like-minded companion in Consort Zhen, she was hated by Cixi, who finally had her drowned in a well which is still preserved in Beijing's Palace Museum. For Emperor Guangxu, his reign of 34 years was an experience of sorrow and indignation in both political and family life.

172

A distinctive feature of the Manchu royal family was that none of the empresses came from the Han people, the main nationality of China. This was probably due to the Qing court's peculiar system of choosing beauties once in every three years. By an imperial decree, girls between the ages of 13 and 17 who were "banner-persons"*must register with the Board of Revenue each year. At a designated time girls in this age group from the provinces and the capital were gathered inside the Gate of Divine Might in the Forbidden City. Lining up according to age, they were led by a eunuch to the front of the Hall of Terrestrial Tranquility for the emperor to make his choice. Only those who were not chosen by the emperor could marry other people. If any of the girls recruited by the royal house married another person, she and her family would suffer severe punishment. Shuddering at the prospect of a secluded life in the palace, the girls cried as they waited in the line, in which case the eunuchs threatened to flog them. The brave ones protested by saying, "We bid farewell to our parents and came here to be chosen by the emperor. If we are chosen, we will be confined in the palace and separated from our parents forever. Every human being has human sentiments. How could we help crying at such a fatal moment? We are not even afraid of death. Flog us if you want to." But none of their protests could alter an inhuman system under a feudal dynasty.

---

* Every Manchu was called a "banner-person," a term derived from "Eight Banners," the military-administrative organization of the Manchus in the Qing dynasty.

Administration of the Empire

After Beijing was made capital of the Ming dynasty, it became the political center of the country with administrative, judicial, supervisory, educational and military agencies at the central level as well as an army of more than 400,000 men. From here the emperor issued administrative and military decrees to all parts of the country to exercise his highly centralized power.

In the early Ming, the Offices of the Left and Right Prime Ministers were abolished, and all power was concentrated in the hands of the emperor. Though an Inner Chancery was installed later, it was responsible only for clerical work, such as writing comments on memorials to the throne and issuing edicts on the emperor's instructions. The emperor administered the country by conducting court sessions, receiving high officials, appointing or removing civil and military officials, giving instructions on memorials to the throne, etc. In addition to regular court meetings, the emperor presided over "grand court sessions" on important occasions such as New Year's Day, the winter solstice and his birthday, not to handle any particular state affair but to show the immensity of imperial power.

In the Han dynasty, the emperor held court every five days. During the Tang, the court session took place everyday. In the early Ming, it was held every morning, then every noon, and finally on dates containing numerals 3,6 and 9. Eventually the court sessions were discontinued altogether, and civil and military officials never saw the "son of heaven" except when he gave an audience or attended a lecture. In the 26 years from 1471 to 1497, or from the seventh year of the reign of Emperor Chenghua to the 10th year of the reign of Emperor Hongzhi, officials saw neither of the two emperors.

Emperor Jiajing estranged himself from his officials only three years after his enthronement. He granted only one audience to them during his 45-year reign. Unable to communicate with the emperor, the officials knelt before the Forbidden City as an indication of their complaint. On one occasion 229 officials headed by Minister of the Chancery Jin Xianmin knelt before the Left Gate of Smoothness of the Forbidden City, and they refused to leave even after a eunuch sent by the emperor ordered them to disperse. They knelt for six hours and cried and pounded at the gate, making a noise which could be heard deep in the palace. The incident ended in the arrest and punishment of the officials.

Imperial seal. Made of gold, jade or wood, imperial seals are decorated with carvings. It was stipulated in a decree issued by Emperor Qianlong that an emperor should have 25 seals to be kept in the Hall of Union and Peace.

Imperial sedan chair

Emperor Daoguang's instructions,written in red, on memorials to the throne

Crowned at 10, Emperor Wanli reigned for 48 years. But he led a secluded life and showed no interest in state affairs even after he was 17. He did not conduct one court session or grant a single audience in 29 years. Under his rule, the Inner Chancery existed only in name, and the secretaries of the Chancery discharged their duties in a perfunctory manner. When they had a meeting, they greeted one another, wrote inscriptions and passed them around, and then left without having discussed any question. Frustrated by the lack of response to his memorial to the throne and his request for an audience with the emperor, a high official tendered his resignation and left his post without waiting for approval. Finally, only one secretary remained in the Inner Chancery, who stayed behind closed doors for three whole months. Of the ministers of the Six Boards,* only one was working, while the other five had left. In the Censorate, the post of Grand Censor was vacant for eight years. When the situation along the frontiers became critical, Minister Zhao Huan and other officials knelt at the Gate of Literary Glory and petitioned the emperor to attend to state affairs. The emperor was nowhere to be seen. When dusk came, the officials were ordered to disperse. Zhao Huan said in a memorial to the throne: "If the palace comes under enemy attack one day, could Your Majesty still plead illness and refuse to leave your bedchamber?" Again, there was no response.

Eight rulers of the Ming dynasty from Emperor Chenghua to Emperor Tianqi were far removed from their officials during a reign of 167 years. State power fell into the hands of treacherous eunuchs, and the court was torn by internal strife. Plagued by internal and external troubles, the Ming dynasty finally collapsed.

When the Qing dynasty replaced the Ming, it inherited most of the government institutions of the latter but, drawing lessons from its mistakes, resumed the system of "governing the state from the imperial gate"** that was instituted in the early Ming but given up later. To strengthen its rule, the Qing court established a Privy Council. Besides handling memorials to the throne, the emperor presided over regular court discussions and gave an audience or a banquet to high officials from time to time. Some of the Qing emperors were the most hard-working rulers in China's more than 2,000 years of feudal history.

---

* This refers to the Board of Civil Service, of Revenue, of Rites, of War, of Justice and of Works.

** In the Qing dynasty, a throne was placed at the Gate of Celestial Purity where the emperor heard reports from high officials and issued orders.

Emperor Kangxi, the second Qing emperor, started to rule with full power at the age of 14. He followed the system of "governing the state from the imperial gate" with only some technical changes. In sweltering heat or bitter cold, he arrived at the imperial gate at eight o'clock in the morning for a serious discussion of state affairs with civil and military officials.

The Privy Council was established during the reign of Emperor Yongzheng, son of Emperor Kangxi. There were about five ministers in the Privy Council who were granted an audience by the emperor every day for deliberations on important administrative and military affairs, after which they issued orders to officials at central and local levels on the emperor's instructions.

Emperors of the Qing often received high officials to listen to their reports or remonstrances. When Jin Fu, Governor-General of Waterways, differed from Governor Yu Chenglong on ways to harness the Yellow River, Emperor Kangxi ordered them to come to Beijing for a debate in his presence. He also sent officials to the Yellow River valley to solicit the opinions of local authorities and old people on the different plans of Jin and Yu. Before making the final decision, the emperor himself inspected the river, consulted relevant literature, and convened court sessions to discuss the matter.

Emperor Kangxi sometimes invited high officials to have dinner with him, to enjoy the flowers in his garden, or to drink wine and exchange poems with him. It was customary for Qing emperors to give banquets for the leaders of ethnic minorities, including the Mongols, the Tibetans and the Uygurs. Emperor Qianlong, who was proficient in several languages, spoke to Manchu princes, Han officials, envoys from Mongolia and the Uygurs in Xinjiang, and Panchen Lama VI from Tibet in their respective tongues. In this way he publicized the Qing dynasty's basic policy of unity and harmony among the Manchu, Han, Mongolian, Hui, Tibetan and other nationalities in China. To keep abreast of developments at the grassroots, the Qing emperors authorized officials to send sealed, confidential memorials to the throne, which, folded in accordion form, could cover everything from important state affairs and the behavior of officials to weather conditions, food prices, and summer and autumn harvests.

The measures adopted by the Qing regime to strengthen its centralized feudal administration and raise efficiency formed a sharp contrast with conditions in the Ming dynasty.

The Worship of Gods

In a feudal country, the worship of gods and the defense of the nation by armed force are the two major responsibilities of the monarch. In medieval China, as in medieval Europe, both monarchical authority and religious authority were regarded as supreme. But while Pope Leo III crowned Charlemagne on the Christmas of 800 in St. Peter's Basilica in Rome, religious leaders in China had nothing to do with the enthronement of an emperor. However, the emperor was required to offer sacrifices to gods at the time of his enthronement. Monarchical authority and religious authority relied on each other for support, and it is difficult to say which was the subject and which the object. From the standpoint of ancient Chinese philosophy, religious authority should be the subject and monarchical authority the object; thus the emperor was called the "son of heaven." But in reality the order was reversed. For instance, some emperors dared to suppress Buddhism and destroy its scriptures. In China, monarchical authority was monistic and religious authority pluralistic, as indicated in the saying, "A god indwells everything created by Heaven."

The practice of offering sacrifices to gods was handed down from dynasty to dynasty with an ever-increasing number of gods.

In the Ming and Qing dynasties, an amazing number of gods were worshipped by the emperor. They were classified as follows:

Gods of Heaven: God of the Sun, of the Moon, of Stars, of Winds, of Clouds, of Thunder, of Rain.

Gods of Earth: Gods of the Five Mountains, of the Five Principal Mountains, of the Remote Mountains.

Gods of Water: Gods of Rivers, of Lakes, of Seas, of Pools, of Springs.

Gods of Agriculture: God of Farming, of Silkworms, of the Five Cereals, of Locusts, of Drought.

Gods of War: God of the Flag, of Horses, of Warships, of Cannon, of Blunderbusses, of Crossbows.

Gods of Society: God of the Emperor, of Meritorious Officials, of Able Generals.

Gods of Religion: Gods of the Buddhist Temples, of the Taoist Temples.

Gods of Culture: Confucius and the God of Scholarly Honors.

Gods of Everyday Life: God of Doors, of the Kitchen, of Wells.

There were hundreds of gods to whom sacrifices had to be made. Like human beings, the gods were divided into classes, and the sacrifices offered to them were also graded. A "major sacrifice" conducted by the emperor in person was presented to the God of Heaven, of Earth, of the Ancestral Temple, of Land, and of Grain and to Confucius; an "intermediate sacrifice," conducted by either the emperor or by an official on his behalf, was presented to the God of the Sun, of the Moon, of Farming and of Silkworms; and a "group

Location of the Temple of Heaven, Temple of Earth, Altar of the Sun and Altar of the Moon

1. Temple of Heaven   2. Temple of Earth   3. Altar of the Sun
4. Altar of the Moon

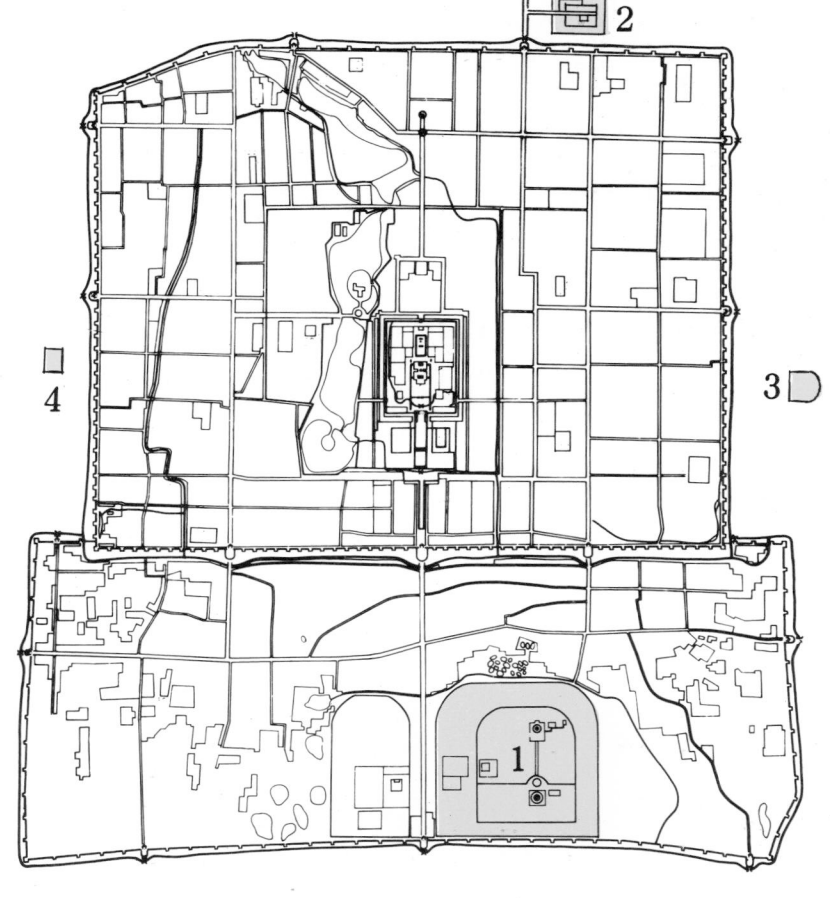

Altar of Heaven

Top platform of the Altar of Heaven

Imperial Vault of Heaven

Tablet of "Supreme Ruler of the Universe" in the Imperial Vault of Heaven

sacrifice," conducted by an emperor's official, was presented to the God of Medicine, of Fire, of Towns and of Jade Springs. A god might be upgraded under certain circumstances. For instance, Emperor Qianlong upgraded the God of Drought and offered a "major sacrifice" to him when he prayed for rain during a dry spell which had lasted many years.

The altars and temples in Beijing are symmetrically arranged, with the Temple of Heaven in the south, the Temple of Earth in the north, the Altar of the Sun in the east and the Altar of the Moon in the west. The Temple of Heaven is the most majestic of the four.

Occupying an area of 2,700,000 square meters, which is quadruple the area of the Forbidden City, the Temple of Heaven is the largest extant group of buildings ever erected for sacrificial purposes in China. As the site for the Ming and Qing emperors to offer sacrifices to Heaven and pray for good harvests, the temple is enclosed by a double wall, of which the northern half is circular, representing heaven, and the southern half is square, representing earth. A 2.5-meter-high and 360-meter-long causeway known as the Bridge of Cinnabar Stairway or Sacred Way connects the temple's three main buildings — the Altar of Heaven, the Imperial Vault of Heaven and the Hall of Prayer for Good Harvest.

Located at the southern end of the causeway, the Altar of Heaven was the place where the emperors offered sacrifices to heaven. It was first built in 1530, the 9th year of the reign of the Ming emperor Jiajing, when glazed blue bricks were used for both the surface of the platform and the balustrades. When it was rebuilt in 1747, the 12th year of the reign of the Qing emperor Qianlong, the bricks were replaced by green marble on the surface of the platform and by white marble on the balustrades. The altar is a circular three-tiered structure, the top platform being 23 meters in diameter and five meters above ground level. Each staircase has nine steps, and the railings along each tier are made up of stone slabs in multiples of nine because nine is the numerical epitome of *Yang* which signifies heaven and the emperor. In the center of the platform is a circular stone surrounded by nine rings of fan-shaped stone slabs. There are nine slabs on the first ring, 18 on the second, and 27 on the third, leading up to 81 on the ninth and outermost ring. The stone slabs are responsive to sound. When a person speaks at the center of the platform, he hears an echo, louder and fuller than his voice, coming from underground. This is because the sound waves are amplified when they come back from the white marble balustrades to the center stone and then to the ears of the speaker. The altar has four gates, one on each side, which is composed of three doors and four marble pillars. To the southwest of the altar is the Signal Lantern Platform with a lantern made from a single tree trunk which is 20-odd meters high. In the old times a 2.55-meter-long "heavenly lantern," with a 1.28-meter candle burning inside, was hung on the post.

Drum and bells on which the *Music of Harmonious Reconciliation* was played

The Echo Wall

The Temple of Heaven was also a site for the emperor to pray for rain. Emperor Kangxi did so in the summer of 1678, the 17th year of his reign, during a long drought in the Beijing area. On September 2, 1679, when an earthquake of magnitude eight hit Beijing, the spacious courtyards in the temple became a sanctuary for the emperor and the nobility who stayed in tents there.

Located to the north of the Altar of Heaven, the circular Imperial Vault of Heaven contained a tablet of "Supreme Ruler of the Universe" written in both Chinese and Manchu. Incense was burned in front of the tablet the day before the emperor offered sacrifices to heaven. The tablet was carried in a sedan chair to a tent at the Altar of Heaven on the day of the sacrificial ceremony and moved back to the circular vault as soon as the ceremony was over. Sacrifices were offered to heaven amid strains of the *Music of Harmonious Reconciliation* played on bells and inverted bells, flutes and vertical flutes, a drum, a zither-like plucked instrument called *qin*, a big bell called *bo* and a wind instrument called *chi*. Thirty-two bells were arranged in two rows, 16 in each, and they produced a musical range because their walls varied in thickness.

The Imperial Vault of Heaven was first built in 1530 under Emperor Jiajing of the Ming and then rebuilt in 1752, the 17th year of the reign of Emperor Qianlong of the Qing. Single-roofed and covered with deep-blue glazed tiles, it looks like a sapphire umbrella when viewed at a distance. The structure is 19.5 meters high and 15,06 meters in diameter. Its dome is supported by eight pillars arranged in a circle with a *zaojing** ceiling. Surrounding the vault is a circular "Echo Wall" composed of polished bricks. A whisper at one end of the wall can be heard clearly at the other end.

There is also a "Three Echo Stone" — the third stone in the walkway leading from the southern entrance to the vault. A shout or hand-clap over this stone, which lies at the center of the circular wall, produces three echoes because the sound travels by equal distance to any point of the wall and moves back and forth three times before it is absorbed by the wall and the air. A display of acoustic oddity like this is rare among the relics of ancient architecture.

Situated in the north of the Temple of Heaven is the Hall of Prayer for Good Harvest. Agriculture was the foundation of the economy of the Chinese empire, and food was the first essential for its people. Farm produce had much to do with the people's living standard as well as state revenue. Both the Yuan and Ming dynasties were overthrown by peasants who rose in rebellion after successive years of famine. As the Ming emperors took warning from the fall of the Yuan and the Qing emperors from the fall of the Ming, it became customary for the Ming and Qing emperors to come to the hall and pray for good harvests, the requisite of the country's peace and prosperity, in the first month of the lunar year.

* *Zaojing* refers to an elaborate coffer in three tiers. Round at the top and square at the bottom, it has a bright jewel decoration in the center.

Hall of Prayer for Good Harvest ▷

Zaojing ceiling in the Hall of Prayer for Good Harvest

Bell Tower in the Altar of the Moon

Altar of the Sun

Temple of Earth

The Hall of Prayer for Good Harvest was originally known as the Hall of Great Sacrifice, a rectangular structure built at the same time as the Forbidden City under Emperor Yongle of the Ming dynasty. In 1545, the 24th year of the reign of Emperor Jiajing, the hall was changed to a circular structure as it remains today according to the old notion of a round-shaped heaven. It was provided with a conical three-tiered roof of glazed tiles crowned with a gilded ball. The tiles on the first, second and third tiers were colored blue, yellow and green respectively. The building got its present name, Hall of Prayer for Good Harvest, in 1751, the 16th year of the reign of Emperor Qianlong of the Qing dynasty. In 1752 deep-blue glazed tiles were used for all three tiers of the roof to blend with the color of the sky.

The circular hall, 38 meters high and 30 meters in diameter, stands on a three-tiered terrace. Each tier is paved with fine stone slabs and surrounded by an ornately carved white marble balustrade.

The hall displays the unique features of traditional Chinese architecture. It is a purely wooden structure supported by pillars and brackets with mortise and tenon joints and not a single nail. Of its 28 red-lacquered *nanmu* (a fine hardwood) pillars, the four central ones are the thickest and are painted with golden coiled dragons, symbolizing the four seasons of the year. Surrounding them are an inner circle of 12 pillars representing the 12 months on the lunar calendar and an outer circle of 12 more pillars representing the 12 two-hour periods into which the cycle of day and night was traditionally divided in China. The hall has a *zaojing* ceiling carved in beautiful designs. In the center are a throne, a screen, and the tablets for the gods of heaven and earth.

The Temple of Heaven has been attracting visitors with its unique shape, imposing layout, gorgeous colors and splendid architecture.

The Temple of Earth, also called Square Pool Temple, was where the Ming and Qing emperors offered sacrifices to the God of Earth. Located to the east of the Gate of Stability, it was first built in 1530, the 9th year of the reign of the Ming emperor Jiajing, and was rebuilt many times during the Qing. The altar in the temple is square — the shape of earth as conceived by ancient Chinese. It consists of two tiers of white marble with glazed surfaces, the upper tier being 20 square meters and the lower tier about 35 square meters, and is enclosed by a low wall. There are carvings of the Five Sacred Mountains and the Four Great Rivers* on the lower tier. The altar faces the north, with three white stone gates on the north and one each on the east, west and south. Each gate has two pillars.

To the south of the altar is the House of the God of Earth, where the tablet for the god is placed for worship.

The sacrifice to the God of Earth was conducted at sunrise on the day of the summer solstice every year.

A circular Temple of Heaven in the south faces a square Temple of Earth in the north — a symmetrical embodiment of the ancient Chinese notion about heaven and earth.

The Altar of the Sun, as the name suggests, was the site of imperial sacrifice to the God of the Sun. Known also as Altar of the Rising Sun, it is located in the eastern suburbs outside the Facing-the-Sun Gate. It was built in the same year as the Temple of Earth and, like the latter, was renovated time and again during the Qing.

The altar is a square white marble platform with a glazed red surface symbolizing the sun. Surrounded by a low wall, it faces the west, with three white stone gates on the west and one each on the east, north and south. Each gate has two pillars.

The sacrifice to the God of the Sun was conducted at sunrise on the day of the spring equinox every year.

The Altar of the Moon is situated in the western suburbs outside the Gate of Great Tranquility. The Ming and Qing emperors offered sacrifices here on the evening of the autumn equinox every year.

This altar was also built in 1530 and was rebuilt a number of times under the Qing. It is a square white marble platform with a glazed white surface symbolizing the moon. Facing the east, the altar is enclosed by a low wall and has three white stone gates on the east and one each on the north, south and west. Each gate has two pillars.

The two altars described above, one in the east and the other in the west, express the old-time belief that the sun and the moon, facing each other, shine forever in the boundless sky.

---

* The Five Sacred Mountains refer to Taishan in Shandong Province in the east, Huashan in Shaanxi Province in the west, Hengshan in Shanxi Province in the north, Hengshan in Hunan Province in the south, and Songshan in Henan Province at the center. The Four Great Rivers refer to the Yellow River, the Yangtze River, the Huai River and the Ji River.

The Emperor's Studies

Emperor Kangxi once said, "Read a book and you gain by a book; read a day and you gain by what you read that day." This is a wise maxim.

Apart from administering state affairs and conducting sacrifice to gods, reading was an important part of the life of the Ming and Qing emperors. An emperor had generally received good education before acceding to the throne. While crown prince, he underwent rigorous training under a tutor employed by the emperor. Since the emperors of the Qing were Manchus, one of China's ethnic minorities, they had to study even harder in order to be equal to the task of ruling the country after their conquest of the Central Plains.

Emperor Kangxi started teaching his son Yunreng, the crown prince, to read and write when the boy was only four. The emperor assigned two Grand Secretaries as his tutors when he was six, and sent him to a school with both Manchu and Han teachers when he was 14. The following passages from *A Record of the Daily Life of Emperor Kangxi* describe the strict programme the emperor designed for his sons:

Emperor Kangxi Reads a Book (painting)

Emperor Kangxi's desk for doing exercises in mathematics. Made of *nanmu* (a fine hardwood), it is 96 cm. long, 64 cm. wide and 32 cm. high. The desk is covered with a silver board inscribed with several mathematical tables. The desk has drawers of different sizes for storing measuring and drawing instruments.

Gilded celestial globe. Made during the reign of Emperor Qianlong, it has an enamel base, a gold stem shaped like a dragon head, and a gold bracket with dragon patterns. The globe itself is coated with gold and inlaid with 100-odd jewels symbolizing stars.

Imperial ink sticks of the Qing dynasty

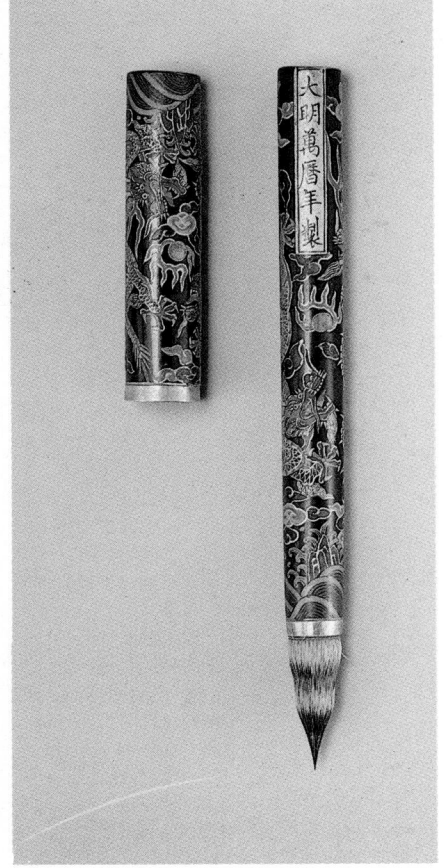

Imperial writing brush of the Qing dynasty

From 5 to 7 a.m.: The Crown Prince went to school, bowed to his teachers, and started reciting the *Book of Rites,* a Confucian classic. The emperor's order for him was to "recite the book 120 times." When the Crown Prince had recited a paragraph several times, he made a mark and went to the teachers, who checked whether he had memorized it accurately. Only then did he go on to the next paragraph.

From 7 to 9 a.m.: After hearing reports from his ministers at his court session, Emperor Kangxi came to the school. With the *Book of Rites* in hand, he listened to his son's recitation until he was satisfied.

From 9 to 11 a.m.: The Crown Prince copied several hundred Chinese characters and a chapter of a text in Manchu.

From 11 a.m. to 1 p.m.: The Crown Prince had his lunch and granted a lunch to his teachers. There was no break after lunch. Sitting in a proper manner, the Crown Prince started to recite again.

From 1 to 3 p.m.: The Crown Prince practiced archery in the courtyard, a course in both martial arts and physical training.

From 3 to 5 p.m.: Emperor Kangxi came to the school again to check the recitation and comprehension by his several sons.

From 5 to 7 p.m.: Emperor Kangxi ordered his sons to have an archery contest in the courtyard. He set an example by hitting the target each time.

Dusk came and the classes were over. The Crown Prince kept up his studies without interruption, whether in the hottest days of summer or in the coldest days of winter.

Among the rulers of the Qing, Emperor Kangxi was the most avid reader. He began his studies at the age of five and ascended the throne at eight. Reading Confucian classics daily, he committed almost every word to memory. In his late teens he once spat blood because he was studying too hard. When he was 24, he set aside a room in the inner court as his study, calling it the South Studio, and chose two Han scholars to discuss the classics with him. The emperor continued his studies even during his summer vacation on the Sea Terrace Islet.

During the eight-year Revolt of the Three Princes,* when military reports kept pouring into the court day and night and both soldiers and civilians in Beijing felt uneasy about the critical situation, the Imperial Academy petitioned Emperor Kangxi to cut

his daily study sessions to one in every two days, but he rejected the idea, saying, "Let the sessions go on every day; I want to quench my thirst for knowledge!"

Emperor Kangxi made his first inspection tour of south China at the age of 31. Arriving in Nanjing, he had his boat moored at Yanziji on the south bank of the Yangtze and read books far into the night.

The emperor often discussed philosophical questions with scholar-officials till midnight. He was also a good calligrapher, having copied numerous samples of outstanding calligraphy. He wrote inscriptions on a thousand or so plaques for temples. Once he did several dozen pieces of calligraphy outside a palace gate in front of officials and asked them for comments.

From boyhood to old age, Emperor Kangxi studied sedulously in order to be able to run the country well. He said, "I loved reading at an early age. Though I am old, I still keep a book in hand. The country's affairs are highly complicated. How can a monarch confined in the Forbidden City know them all? To avoid mistakes, I must learn from the ancients by reading their books."

The readings of a feudal emperor usually included Confucian classics, histories, and books on literature and art. Emperor Kangxi had two studies, the Yuanjian (Mirror of Literature) Studio and the Peiwen (Scholarly Honor) Studio, in Changchunyuan (Enjoying-the-Spring Garden). Named after the two studios were three voluminous books compiled under his sponsorship: the 450-*juan Yuanjian Classified Encyclopedia,* the 444-*juan Peiwen Book of Rhymes and Phrases* and the 100-*juan Peiwen Manual of Calligraphy and Painting.* The emperor's interest ranged from mathematics, astronomy and geography to optics, medicine and anatomy. He was surrounded by a number of scientists, Chinese and foreign, among whom were some well-known Jesuits.

As early as 1516, the 11th year of the reign of the Ming Emperor Zhengde, a Portuguese by the name of Rafaal Perestrello came to China by boat, completing the first sea voyage from Europe to China. He was followed by Matteo Ricci, an Italian, who presented his *Atlas of the World* to the Ming court and translated Euclid's *Elements of Geometry* into Chinese jointly with Xu Guanqi, a court official. They were followed by other Jesuits.

* In the early Qing, Wu Sangui, Geng Jimao and Shang Kexi, Commanders of the Ming army, were made Princes of Pingxi, Jingnan and Pingnan respectively after their surrender to the Qing court. They gradually built up separatist regimes antagonistic to the central authorities. When Emperor Kangxi decided to take back their domains, they started a revolt known in history as the "Revolt of the Three Princes."

In 1645, the second year of the reign of Emperor Shunzhi of the Qing dynasty, the German Jesuit Johann Adam Schall von Bell designed a new calendar for the court. It was named "Shixian Calendar" and adopted for use throughout the country. Schall von Bell was made Imperial Astronomer. Jesuits who served at the Qing court under Emperor Kangxi came from many countries—Italy, France, Germany, Austria, Portugal, Spain, Holland, Belgium, Switzerland, Poland and Mexico. As an enlightened monarch, Emperor Kangxi employed, trusted and respected Jesuits with scientific training and picked up from them knowledge of natural sciences developed in the West.

Emperor Kangxi took a special interest in mathematics. Every day or every other day, he studied geometry, algebra and trigonometry with the French Jesuits Joachim Bouvet and Jean-Francois Gerbillon and the Portuguese Jesuit Thomas Pereira, who taught him in Manchu in the Forbidden City's Hall of Mental Cultivation. The instructors also accompanied the emperor to the Sea Terrace Islet and the Enjoying-the-Spring Garden. The emperor memorized the theorems and did the exercises after each lesson.

Emperor Kangxi also attached importance to astronomy. He appointed the Belgian Jesuit Ferdinand Verbiest as Imperial Astronomer, who modified the old instruments in the astronomical observatory. A few decades later, under Emperor Qianlong, many new instruments were added, including a quadrant, a celestial globe, an altazimuth, an equatorial theodolite, a zodiac theodolite, and an armilla called *ji*.

Emperor Kangxi never missed a chance to see a solar eclipse. He watched heavenly bodies in the astronomical observatory in Nanjing during an inspection tour. Two important works were compiled under his auspices — the *Essence of Mathematics and Physics* and the *Manual of Music*, which contain information on Western mathematics and musical notation and which exerted a profound influence on astronomy, mathematics and music in China.

The emperor enjoyed making experiments. By putting up a small flag in his courtyard, he observed the direction and speed of wind. He ordered the establishment of wind observatories in various places and asked for weather reports from the provinces. From the data obtained he drew the conclusion that "wind does not have the same force beyond a thousand *li*; rain does not mean the same amount of precipitation beyond a hundred *li*." He also dabbled at anatomy and personally dissected a hibernant bear.

At 58 Emperor Kangxi made a survey of the Yongding River and did such field work as driving the piles, installing the instruments, and making the records. *The Complete Atlas of the Empire* was compiled over a period of 30 years under his direction. Based on surveys of all regions in China, the atlas contained the maps of the provinces drawn according to the principles of modern cartography. Half a century later, in 1780 or the 15th year of the reign of Emperor Qianlong, a "Map of Beijing Under Emperor Qianlong" appeared as a marvel in the history of cartography. Drawn on a large scale, it was probably the best map of a capital city found anywhere in the world at the time.

Emperor Kangxi followed the developments in science and technology in the West. To promote cultural exchange, he sent Joachim Bouvet back to France in 1693, the 32nd year of his reign, to present a large number of Chinese books to King Louis XIV. He also extended his goodwill to Peter I of Russia. However, he was limited in his knowledge about the West and was not aware of the rise of the Western powers. Being a feudal monarch, he could not possibly transform the Qing empire in spite of the cultural nourishment he derived from Western capitalism.

Drawing instruments used in the Qing court

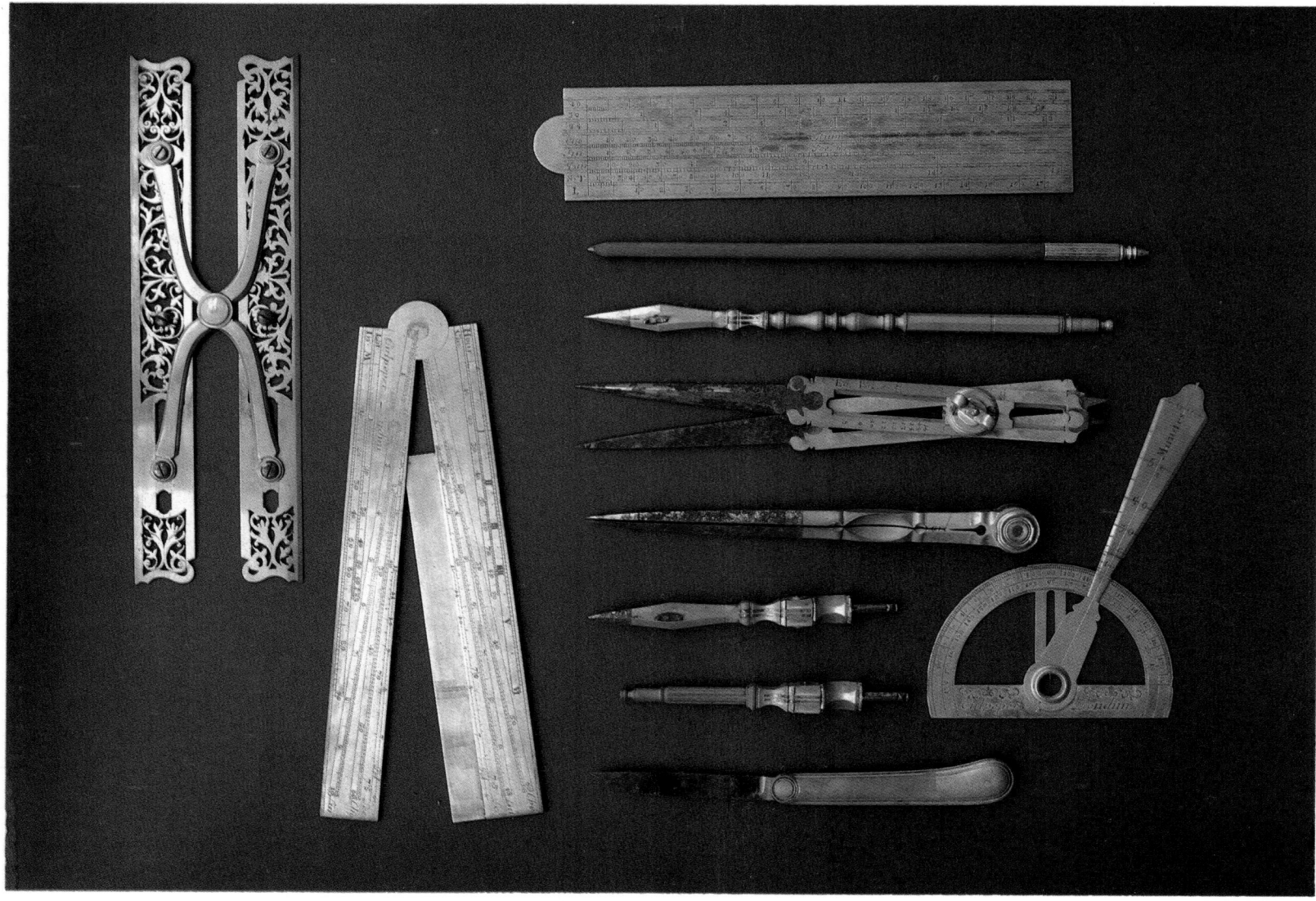

Life Style

Emperors were men, not gods. Though they were busy with the handling of state affairs, they found time for their hobbies and personal pursuits. An emperor's interest and temperament, philosophy and sentiments, endowments and idiosyncrasies, ideas and deeds had an important bearing on the shaping of state policies, the choice of officials, the people's life, and the prosperity or decline of his empire.

Emperor Yongle was the first of a line of Ming emperors who lived in the Forbidden City. Before he became emperor, he had been the Prince of Yan. A story about his usurpation of the throne goes as follows:

Taking advantage of the weakness of Emperor Jianwen's new regime, the Prince of Yan plotted a rebellion. Suspicious of his intentions, the emperor issued an edict condemning him. To hoodwink the emperor, the prince feigned madness. He raved in the market, snatched food and wine from pedestrians, or even slept in the streets. The emperor sent an official to his mansion to inquire about his health. On a hot day in summer, the prince wore a ragged fur coat and walked around with a stick in his mansion. With dishevelled hair and a dirty face, he came to a stove, shivered all over, and kept saying, "How cold! How cold!" Convinced of his madness, the official reported back to Emperor Jianwen. Meanwhile, the prince secretly gathered his forces and led troops southward to attack Nanjing, capital of Emperor Jianwen. After four years of fighting, he seized the throne and moved the capital to Beijing.

Emperor Yongle had courage, wisdom and high aims, and treated prople with sincerity. Under his rule, the Ming dynasty became strong and prosperous. He led seven military expeditions against Mongolia. On his order, the eunuch Zheng He and his fleet crossed the Indian Ocean and reached as far as the east coast of Africa. The history of Beijing and of the Ming dynasty would have been rewritten had it not been for Emperor Yongle's talent, vision and use of the right people.

Emperor Zhengde was hedonistic and licentious. He ascended the throne at 14. Two years later, he ordered the building of palaces in the West Garden where he set aside a chamber called *baofang* (the "Leopard's House") for obscene pleasures. From morning to night he stayed there with beautiful women, musicians and eunuchs. Once a sycophantic official brought to him 12 girls of the Hui nationality, who sang and danced for him till daybreak, but then he wanted the show to continue.

Things grew from bad to worse when the emperor started to leave the palace and visit other parts of the country incognito. Wherever he went, his guards seized large numbers of girls and brought them back in dozens of carriages. Because of this, unmarried women and widows hurried to get married before the emperor came. In one place all the widowers got new wives during a single night.

Emperor Zhengde took a number of carriages with him during one of his pleasure trips. Each vehicle carried 10 to 20 monks, with women sitting among them and balls hanging overhead. As the carriages sped off, the balls struck the shaven heads of the monks, who collided with the women with whom they were not supposed to have any contact. The emperor bellowed with laughter at the sight of this.

During another pleasure trip Emperor Zhengde took a fancy to Liu, a woman married to a musician, and brought her back to *baofang* where they lived together and became inseparable. He gave her the title of Beauty Liu and took her on a trip to South China. When they arrived at Tongzhou, only 10 kilometers from Beijing, the emperor told her to stay there till someone came to fetch her. As they said goodbye to each other, Beauty Liu gave him her hairpin, declaring that she wouldn't go with anyone who didn't produce the souvenir. But the emperor lost it on the way. After arriving at Linqing, about 500 kilometers from Beijing, the emperor sent for her. But she told the messenger, "I dare not go without seeing the souvenir." The emperor took a boat and hurried back to Tongzhou day and night to bring her.

Shu Fen and 106 other court officials had advised against the emperor's trip to the south. Infuriated, he punished them by ordering them to kneel at the Meridian Gate 12 hours a day for five successive days and had them flogged afterward.

Emperor Zhengde fell into a pond when the small boat he was using for fishing there capsized. After he was brought ashore, he spat blood and soon died. He had regarded military expeditions and political affairs as mere games and treated his officials and his people as dirt, and finally died a ludicrous death.

Emperor Jiajing was a Taoist devotee, though the state religion

Emperor Yongzheng on a Pleasure Trip (painting)

185

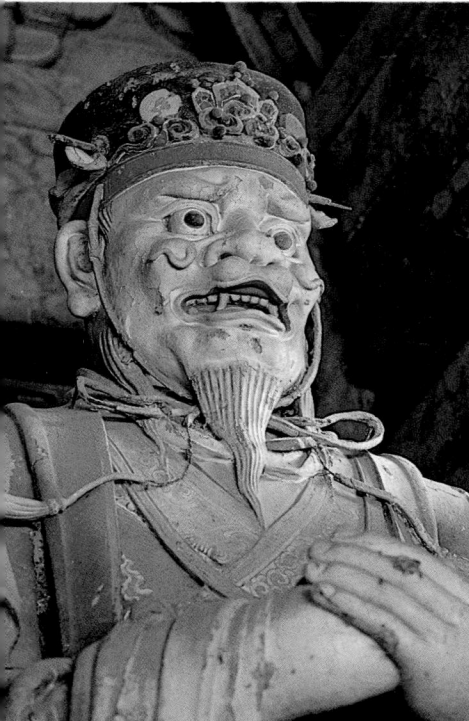

Clay sculptures of Buddha in the Temple of Great Wisdom. Situated in today's Haidian District, Beijing, the temple was built in 1513, the eighth year of the Zhengde reign of the Ming dynasty. It houses 28 clay sculptures of Buddha.

of the Ming was Buddhism, not Taoism. Zhu Yuanzhang, the founding emperor of the Ming, had been a Buddhist monk. Upon his ascension to the throne, he appointed a distinguished monk as advisor to each of the princes in his empire. Monk Daoyan, advisor to the Prince of Yan (later Emperor Yongle), was a policy maker who helped the prince plan his revolt. It was a common practice under the Ming to accord privileges to Buddhist monks and nuns, build Buddhist temples, make Buddhist sculptures, and carve Buddhist scriptures. In Beijing, one can find many treasures of Buddhist art handed down from the Ming, such as the bronze bell in the Temple of Awakening, the murals of Buddha and of gods in the Temple of the Sea of Dharma, the wooden statues of Buddha in the Temple of Wisdom Attained, and the clay sculptures of Buddha in the Temple of Great Wisdom. However, the Ming dynasty started to decline as it entered its middle period. Buddhism, which preaches happiness in one's next life, could not free the emperors from their current worries. While enjoying all the glory and wealth men could expect, they were now anxious to become immortals. It was under these circumstances that Emperor Jiajing turned to Taoism.

The emperor ordered the building of tall and spacious Taoist temples with gilded Taoist statues. He spent much of his time making elixirs of life and was so devoted to Taoism that he virtually put aside government affairs for more than 20 years. This led to the monopoly of state power by Yan Song and his son. Later, when the Yans were discredited and their property confiscated, it was found that they had stored 3,983 gold ornaments and utensils plus 32,969 taels of bullion. People used a pun to satirize Emperor Jiajing, written in Chinese as 嘉靖: "*Jia*(家 instead of the original character 嘉) means family and *jing* (尽 instead of the original character 靖) means exhaustion." In other words, no family led a decent life under Emperor Jiajing.

Emperor Tianqi liked carpentry. When he ascended the throne at 16, the Ming regime had deteriorated further and was approaching its doom. Externally it faced the threat posed by the Later Jurchen. Internally the struggle among the various factions intensified, the financial resources were being exhausted, and the people were boiling with discontent. All this, however, escaped the attention of the emperor, who continued to be preoccupied with carpentry.

Emperor Tianqi had a wet nurse, née Ke, who had a close relationship with the eunuch Wei Zhongxian, and both were liked by the emperor. Originally a rascal in the countryside, Wei castrated himself to become a eunuch after he lost money by gambling. Though he was an illiterate, he knew how to flatter the emperor and usurped power in collaboration with Ke.

Emperor Tianqi was a good carpenter but not a wise sovereign. He liked building houses, using the axe, the saw, the plane and the chisel with even greater skill than professionals did. Assisted by his attendants, he kept working day and night throughout the year. When he had finished building a house, he was delighted, but then he pulled it down and started building a new one. He took off his imperial robe when working, looking just like an ordinary carpenter. No officials, except Wei Zhongxian and a few others, were allowed to come close to him at such moments. A crafty eunuch, Wei knew how to get the emperor's approval on important matters at the right moment. Busy with his carpentry, the emperor would tell him impatiently, "Do it anyway you see fit." This was how Wei gradually took power into his hands. The Ming dynasty became rotten to the core and was finally replaced by the Qing.

The second ruler since the Qing army's conquest of the Central Plains, Emperor Kangxi enjoyed hunting as well as reading. He encouraged horsemanship and marksmanship out of the need to defend the country. He went hunting during his inpection tours. Three times he galloped on the plains and boated on the Songhua River in Northeast China, where he checked over frontier defence and paid tribute to ancestral tombs. Six times he traveled west of Beijing to see the military strongholds in Shanxi and nearby areas, and shot down a tiger during one of his return trips. To strengthen his rule over Mongolia, he led troops into the Gobi Desert three times. To inspect the Yellow River valley and acquaint himself with local conditions, he went south six times and left his footprints in six of China's southern provinces. A scroll painting, *Emperor Kangxi's Historic Tour of the South*, depicts the event.

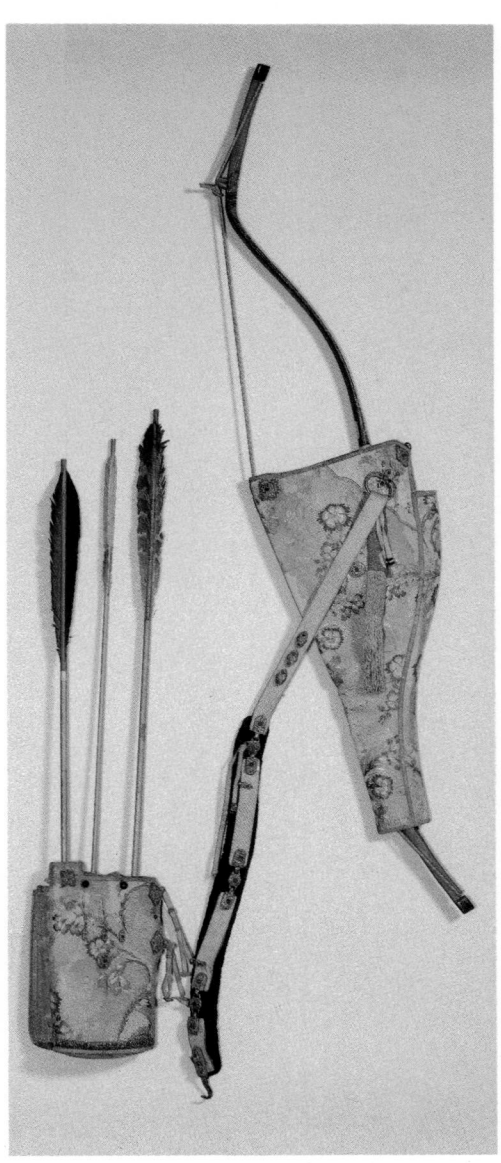

Bow, arrows and quiver

A Hunting Trip (painting of the Qing dynasty)

187

In 1703, the 42nd year of Emperor Kangxi's reign, a summer resort was established in Chengde 250 kilometers northeast of Beijing. The emperor named it Mountain Manor for Avoiding Summer Heat. Construction of the palaces there was not completed until the time of his grandson, Emperor Qianlong. Kangxi spent five or six months at the resort every year for a total of 20 years up to the time of his death in 1722.

The summer resort is also referred to as the Imperial Palace at Chengde or the Imperial Resort at Rehe (former name of Chengde). High mountains, thick forests and a pleasantly cool climate make it an ideal place for the emperor to take a rest while attending to the most important affairs in summer. By the time of Emperor Qianlong 72 scenic spots had been created within a periphery of 10 kilometers.

Round Citadel. Located in today's Haidian District, Beijing, it was built in the early years of the reign of Emperor Qianlong. A circular wall surrounds two buildings. Outside the wall are halls and chambers, in front of which is a platform for reviewing troops. There used to be barracks for Eight-Banner soldiers and pillboxes around the citadel.

Armor used in parades in the Qing dynasty. It is different from the armor used in a battle. Instead of metal plates, the coat of mail is made of yellow satin embroidered horizontally with gold threads. The helmet is made of patent leather and inscribed with gold-colored words in Sanskrit.

Show of Horsemanship (painting of the Qing dynasty)

Temple of Universal Tranquility in the Mountain Manor for Avoiding Summer Heat

Hall of Refreshening Mist and Ripples in the Mountain Manor for Avoiding Summer Heat

Tower of Mist and Rain in the Mountain Manor for Avoiding Summer Heat

While the lakes and pavilions possess the charm of a South China landscape, the hills and woods are typical of the wilderness in the north. In the Garden of Ten Thousand Trees there, Emperor Qianlong feted Mongol princes and other ethnic minority leaders in addition to reviewing his troops. The Qing artist Qian Weicheng (1720 - 1772) did a painting of the summer resort in its best years.

The emperor's bedchamber at the resort is called the Hall of Refreshening Mist and Ripples. It was built in 1710, the 49th year of the reign of Emperor Kangxi. Northeast of the Good Luck Island, the largest island in the lake area, is the Green Lotus Islet on which stands the Tower of Mist and Rain. In late summer or early autumn, when hills and lakes are shrouded in mist and rain, the tower and the surroundings look just like a painting by Mi Fei (1051 - 1107), a famous landscapist of the Northern Song dynasty.

Outside the walls of the Mountain Manor for Avoiding Summer Heat are two groups of temples collectively known as the Eight Temples Beyond the Great Wall, which were built as a symbol of the Qing court's policy of strengthening its ties with the Mongols, Tibetans, Uygurs and other nationalities.

The Temple of Universal Tranquility, which stands at the northern end of the eastern group of temples, was built in 1755, the 20th year of Emperor Qianlong's reign. Covering an area of 23,000 square meters, it houses a wooden statue of Buddha which has a height of 22.23 meters and a weight of 110 tons. Carved out of five kinds of wood — pine, cypress, elm, fir and linden, it is the largest wooden statue of Buddha found in China so far.

In 1681, the 20th year of Emperor Kangxi's reign, the Mulan* Hunting Grounds were established some 100 kilometers north of the city of Chengde for hunting and military training. They covered an area of more than 10,000 square kilometers. Emperor Kangxi went there 48 times. Being an excellent hunter, he captured 135 tigers, 20 bears, 25 leopards, 10 macaques, 14 David's deer, 96 wolves, 132 boars and several hundred deer even though he was in his later years.

Emperor Qianlong liked prose and poetry as well as painting and calligraphy. He was thoroughly conversant with Han culture although he was a Manchu who spoke his native tongue, wrote his native script, followed the custom of his people and, like many other Manchus, was a good horseman and archer. He received training in Han art and literature when he was a child prince. Enthroned at 25, he kept writing essays and poems wherever he was — in the Forbidden City or at a temporary lodge, during a hunting trip or an inspection tour. He said, "I dabbled in painting and calligraphy in my boyhood. Since I became emperor, I have always found time to wield the writing brush, finishing one volume after another without my knowing it."

The emperor was particularly fond of calligraphy. This can be seen from the great numbers of his inscriptions on paintings and the calligraphic works handed down from the Qing dynasty, and from the stone tablets and plaques bearing his handwriting at historic sites. He copied the works of masters of calligraphy and collected his handwriting in *The Copybook of the Jingsheng Studio*. His postscript to *The Copybook of the Hall of Three Rarities* shows his excellent grasp of Chinese calligraphy. He once said that he had copied over a hundred times the masterpieces in *The Kuaixue Copybook* by Wang Xizhi, the great calligrapher of the Jin dynasty.

---

* In the Manchu language *mulan* means hunting deer by imitating their cries.

Ice-skating Performance (painting of the Qing dynasty)

Emperor Qianlong died at the age of 89. He left behind 1,067 essays and 43,830 poems which were published in 586 volumes. He was by far the most prolific writer and poet among the monarchs in Chinese history.

Emperor Jiaqing, the 15th son of Emperor Qianlong, was chosen by his father as successor to the throne. In the early years of his reign the secret White Lotus Society staged armed uprisings in five provinces on the Central Plains, and the government suppressed them in nine years at a cost of 200 million taels of silver. This weakened the Qing regime, which went downhill politically and economically.

Emperor Jiaqing was a mediocre monarch. He went to the Mountain Manor for Avoiding Summer Heat and the Mulan Hunting Grounds every year. He also liked to watch ice-skating performances. According to historians, ice-skating performances were given in the China's imperial palaces in the 11th century, if not earlier. In the Ming dynasty skating performances were given in the West Garden in winter. But skating had long been popular among the Manchus in the Northeast, and became even more so after the Qing army entered Beijing. A "skating battalion" was formed in the army. In preparation for ice-skating performances for the emperor, well over a thousand good skaters were selected for training in the palace in winter every year.

For a performance to be enjoyed by the emperor, the skating rink at the Celestial Lake was decorated with colorful lanterns, and tents and flags were put up all around. The 1,600 performers were divided into eight banners of 200 persons each according to the eight-banner military system of the Qing. Three decorated gateways were set up on the rink. As Emperor Jiaqing and his top officials watched from a platform, the performers in colorful costumes glided through two gates in two lines and formed two impressive circles on the glittering rink. The performance included speed skating, figure skating and ice hockey. Sometimes the emperor joined the fun by sitting on an "ice bed" pulled along by eunuchs.

Empress Dowager Cixi was an opera fan. Watching opera performances had always been a major entertainment for the Qing emperors and empresses. Performances would be presented on a festival or the birthday of the emperor or empress. There was a Royal Theatrical Troupe which, as time went by, put on Peking Opera performances in the main. Peking Opera, then a new theatrical form combining singing, recitation, acting and acrobatics, had evolved from several types of local opera being staged in Beijing around 1790, the 55th year of the reign of Emperor Qianlong.

Four stages were built for the royal family to watch opera

Theater of Harmonious Virtue in the Summer Palace

performances: the Tower of Melodious Voice in the Forbidden City, the Theater of Fun for Everybody in the Garden of Perfect Splendor, the Tower of Clear Voice in the Mountain Manor for Avoiding Summer Heat, and the Theater of Harmonious Virtue in the Summer Palace. Like the Tower of Melodious Voice, the Theater of Harmonious Virtue had a three-storied stage with trap doors for angels to descend from heaven and devils to emerge from underground. The largest theater in the Qing dynasty, it is a triple-eaved, 21-meter-high structure built in 1895, the 21st year of the reign of Emperor Guangxu.

When Empress Dowager Cixi attended an opera performance in the Summer Palace, she took a seat in the Hall of Health and Happiness facing the stage. The Royal Theatrical Troupe started performing for Cixi the first day after her arrival in the Summer Palace. When her birthday came, they would perform for nine successive days. The troupe spent 110,000 taels of silver on costumes used in performances for Cixi's 50th birthday, and the stage itself had been built at a cost of 710,000 taels of silver. There is a photo of Cixi in a theatrical robe, an indication of her love of opera.

Empress Dowager Cixi was a gourmet. She had four meals a day with 99 dishes for the main meal and 50 for each of the other three. She was fastidious about clothing. In the Summer Palace alone, she had over 3,000 trunks of jewels and clothes. Every time she changed her dress she ordered the attendants to bring her dozens of suits for her to make the choice. But as Cixi lived during the twilight of the Qing dynasty, she could not afford to be as extravagant as her predecessors in the Ming dynasty, when there were 370,000 utensils and 8,000 cooks in the imperial kitchen, and when 630,000 kilograms of fruits and delicacies were supplied to the imperial palace each year. Nevertheless, Cixi ruined the Chinese nation by squandering large sums of money designated for national defence.

Imperial Mausoleums

Beijing first became the political center of China in the Yuan dynasty (1271 - 1368). But the Yuan rulers left us no tombs because they had no specific funeral rituals. As a rule, the coffin for a Yuan emperor was made of a *nanmu* trunk cut in two pieces and hollowed to the size of the body of the deceased. The body was placed in between the two pieces of wood, which were bound together and buried in the wilderness. Horses were sent to the burial ground to trample over it, which became untraceable once it was overgrown with grass.

The Ming dynasty followed an entirely different practice. The emperor gave orders for the construction of his mausoleum right after his enthronement. The founding emperor, Hongwu, died in

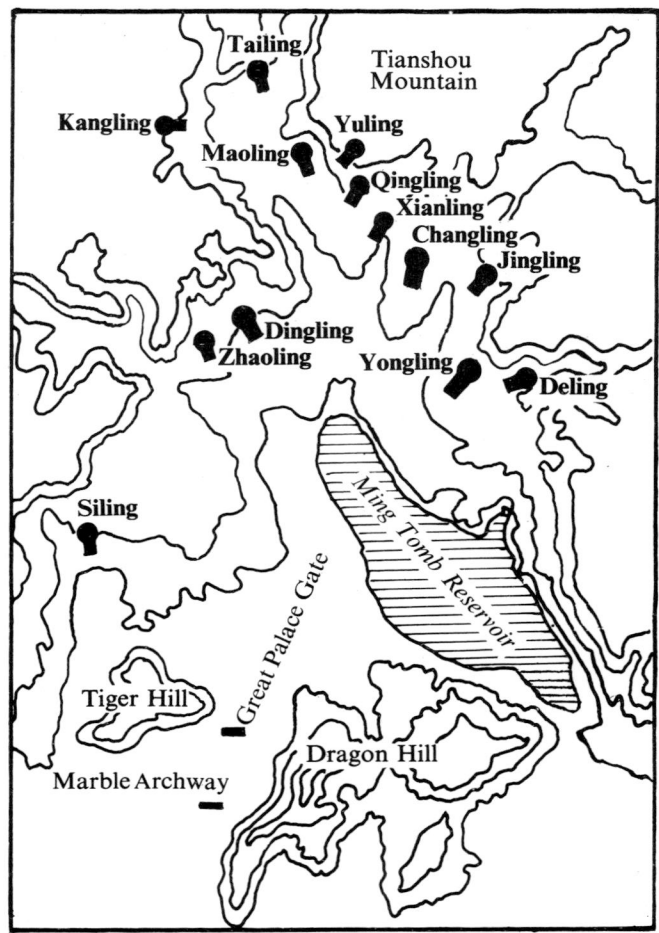

Sketch Map of the Ming Tombs

Marble archway at the Ming Tombs

![Great Palace Gate at the Ming Tombs]

Great Palace Gate at the Ming Tombs

Stone lion along the Sacred Way

Nanjing and was buried in the Ming Tomb there. His successor, Emperor Jianwen, was overthrown by his uncle and disappeared without a trace. Emperor Jingtai was dethroned by his half-brother in a palace coup. When he died, he was buried as a prince in the western suburbs of Beijing. The other 13 Ming emperors and empresses were all buried at the foot of Tianshou Mountain in Changping County some 50 kilometers northwest of Beijing. The mortuary complex, enclosed by a 40-kilometer wall, is known as Thirteen Tombs of the Ming Dynasty or as the Ming Tombs for brevity. Construction of this complex continued for more than 200 years from 1409, the seventh year of the reign of Emperor Yongle, to 1644, the 17th year of the reign of Emperor Chongzhen.

Each of the 13 tombs is located at the foot of a hill and has a separate layout. Each is linked with the others by a road called the Sacred Way. The largest mortuary complex in China, the tombs show a classic elegance and splendor that is overwhelming. The design manifests a clear order of importance and precedence.

The outermost point of the mortuary complex is a huge marble archway supported by six pillars. Built in 1540, the 19th year of the reign of Emperor Jiajing, it is 14 meters high and 28.86 meters wide and provided with five arches and 11 tower-like decorations. It is the largest extant archway in China. In feudal China, archways were used to advocate the feudal code of ethics, symbolize power, or promote philanthropy.

To the north of the archway is the Great Palace Gate, the entrance to the mortuary complex. It is the starting point of the Sacred Way. An avenue extends from here to the Dragon and Phoenix Gate, a road lined with 24 stone animals and 12 stone human figures. The stone statues, carved in 1435 or the 10th year of the reign of Emperor Xuande, include four each of six types of animals: lion, griffin, camel, elephant, unicorn and horse, with two standing and two kneeling down; and four each of three categories of officials: military, civil and meritorious officials. In Chinese such stone human

Sacred Way at the Ming Tombs ▷

193

Changling's Chamber of Divine Favor (interior view)

Changling's Chamber of Divine Favor (exterior view)

figures are called *wengzhong*, a name attributed to General Ruan Wengzhong of the Qin dynasty, garrison commander at a frontier town credited with many military exploits. After he died, the first emperor of the Qin had his statue carved in memory of his meritorious service. Thus stone human figures planted in front of imperial mausoleums came to be known as *wengzhong*. The statues at the Ming Tombs, characterized by simplicity and vigor, are each carved out of a single piece of white marble, the biggest measuring 30 cubic meters.

Each of the 13 Ming tombs has its special features, but a standard layout is common to all. To reach the tomb, one first crosses a stone bridge spanning a river. Beyond the bridge are the entrance gate, the stone stele pavilion, the Gate of Divine Favor, the Chamber of Divine Favor, the stele tower and a circular wall surrounding the burial mound called "City of Treasures." Of the 13 tombs, Changling (tomb of Emperor Yongle) is best-known for its magnificent architecture and Dingling (tomb of Emperor Wanli) for its underground palace.

Lying at the foot of the central peak of the Tianshou Mountain, Changling contains the remains of Emperor Yongle and Empress Xu. The first and largest of the 13 tombs, it was built in 18 years. In front of the burial mound is an imposing Chamber of Divine Favor where sacrifices were offered to the deceased emperor. The hall has a double roof and is 66.75 meters wide and 29.31 meters deep. It is also called Nanmu Hall because its ceiling is supported by 32 gilded *nanmu* (a fine hardwood) pillars and the beams, purlins and rafters all consist of the same material. Each of the four largest pillars, 14.3 meters high and 1.17 meters in diameter, was shaped out of a single *nanmu* trunk.

Dingling is the tomb of Emperor Wanli and his two empresses. It was built in six years at a cost of 8,000,000 taels of silver. The highlight of this tomb is its underground palace. Occupying an area of 1,195 square meters, the underground palace consists of the antechamber, the central chamber, the rear chamber, and left and right annexes. All are vaulted stone structures built without a single beam or column. In the central chamber are three white marble throne seats for the emperor and his two empresses, and before each seat is a set of five objects — an incense burner, two candlesticks and two vases, all of yellow glazed pottery, plus an "eternal lamp," a bronze bowl with a floating wick. More than 3,000 objects have been unearthed from the underground palace, among which are such treasures as Emperor Wanli's gold filigree crown decorated with two dragons playing with a pearl and the empresses' phoenix crowns.

The tombs of the first two Qing emperors, Nurhachi and Huangtaiji, who died before the Qing army conquered the Central Plains, are located in Shenyang, Northeast China. The tomb of Nurhachi and his empress is called Fuling, and that of Huangtaiji and his empress, Zhaoling. Pu Yi, the last emperor of the Qing, died in 1967 as a citizen of the People's Republic and was not buried in an

Stele Tower of Dingling. As the sign of the tomb, the tower contains a stele bearing the characters meaning "Tomb of Emperor Wanli of the Ming Dynasty."

Wengzhong (stone human figure) along the Sacred Way

197

The central chamber of Dingling's underground palace

The rear chamber of Dingling's underground palace. The coffin of Emperor Wanli is placed in the center, flanked by the coffins of his two empresses.

Emperor Wanli's gold filigree crown

The empress' phoenix crown

Dingdongling in the Eastern Tombs of the Qing. In the picture, the tomb of Empress Ci'an is on the right and that of Empress Dowager Cixi is on the left.

imperial tomb. The nine other Qing emperors were buried at two sites known as the Eastern Tombs and Western Tombs of the Qing Dynasty.

Located at the foot of the Changrui Mountains some 100 kilometers northeast of Beijing, the Eastern Tombs contain the remains of five Qing emperors and their 15 empresses and 136 concubines. The mortuary complex was divided into an inner, middle and outer circle marked off with red, white and blue posts along the border. The outer circle had a periphery of more than 200 kilometers within which the gathering of firewood and the grazing of herds were forbidden.

At the center of the mortuary complex is Xiaoling, the tomb of Emperor Shunzhi, the first Qing ruler to govern China from Beijing. He chose the site during a hunting trip there. Attracted by the beauty of the environment, he took a *peishe** off his finger and threw it into the distance, declaring he would be buried wherever it fell. Thus he determined the location of Xiaoling.

After Emperor Shunzhi died, his coffin was kept in the Hall of the Emperors' Longevity in today's Prospect Hill Park. Civil and military officials confined themselves to vegetarian food for 27 days, official documents bore blue instead of red stamps for 100 days, soldiers and civilians were forbidden to slaughter animals for 49 days, and weddings and music performances were suspended for a month. Where the bier passed, officials in mourning dress knelt on both sides of the road along a distance of 100 kilometers.

To the east of Xiaoling are Jingling, tomb of Emperor Kangxi, and Huiling, tomb of Emperor Tongzhi, both of which are simple and plain.

The tomb of Emperor Qianlong is called Yuling, which lies to the west of Xiaoling. The underground palace of Yuling has been excavated and is open to the public. The path leading to the tomb is lined with finely carved Buddha statues. The doors and walls of the arched chambers are inlaid with Buddha statues in bas-relief and inscribed with Buddhist scriptures in 30,000 characters. The coffin of Emperor Qianlong, flanked by those of his two empresses and three consorts, is placed on a stone platform in the central chamber.

To the west of Yuling is Dingling, tomb of Emperor Xianfeng. Xianfeng's empress Ci'an and consort Cixi (later known as Empress Dowager Cixi) were not buried with him in the same tomb but in another one called Dingdongling located east of Dingling. As Cixi was a powerful and despotic ruler during her lifetime, her tomb is the most conspicuous of the tombs of all Qing empresses and consorts.

_____
* A plectrum-like ivory device used by an archer.

The Western Tombs of the Qing lie at the foot of the Yongning Mountains in Yi County, Hebei Province, about 120 kilometers southwest of Beijing. The mausoleum area is surrounded by peaks rising one above another. Tailing, tomb of Emperor Yongzheng, is the central one in the mortuary complex. Historians tend to speculate on the reason why Yongzheng chose a burial site away from the Eastern Tombs which included one for his father, Emperor Kangxi. One interpretation is that he was ashamed to see his father in the other world because of his usurpation of the throne.

Emperor Yongzheng disciplined his officials, punished the corrupt ones, and banned the erection of stone statues in front of tombs. No more statues appeared at the tombs of the Qing emperors thereafter.

Muling in the Western Tombs of the Qing

Changling, tomb of Emperor Jiaqing, lies west of Tailing, and Muling, tomb of Emperor Daoguang, lies further west. Muling had originally been built as one of the Eastern Tombs. After its completion, however, the underground palace was flooded. Emperor Daoguang punished the officials in charge of the project and had the tomb dismantled and another one built among the Western Tombs.

To the east of Tailing is Chongling, tomb of Emperor Guangxu. Construction of the tomb did not start until after the death of the emperor. Several million taels of silver were allocated for the project, but the money was embezzled by the official in charge for the building of his own mansion. Three years later the last Qing emperor Xuantong abdicated. Completed in the early years of the Republican period, the tomb for Emperor Guangxu was simply furnished.

With a periphery of more than 100 kilometers and a 21-kilometer wall, the Western Tombs of the Qing contain chambers totalling 1,000 bays in space and 100-odd stone structures. The total floor space of the buildings in this mortuary complex is more than 500,000 square meters.

The Eastern and Western Tombs of the Qing are the last two mortuary complexes for China's feudal rulers, comparable in scale and magnificence to the Thirteen Tombs of the Ming dynasty.

Buddha statues in the underground palace of Yuling

Culture and Art

Education

Beijing was China's educational center during the Ming and Qing dynasties. After the Ming government moved its capital from Nanjing to Beijing, it founded the Imperial College, the highest institution of learning. There were two imperial colleges in the Ming period—one in Nanjing known as the Southern College and another in Beijing called the Northern College. Since the Imperial College was supposed to train high-level officials for the emperor, the street where it was located acquired the name of Foster-the-Virtuous Street.

The Confucian Temple adjacent to the Imperial College stands on the northern side of the street. In fact it connects with the college through a sidegate. The four memorial archways in the Confucian Temple command the respect of China's elite.

Students from countries like Korea, Siam (Thailand) and Annam (Viet Nam) joined Chinese students in classical studies at the Imperial College which had an enrollment of about 10,000 during the Yongle reign of the Ming. The Ming government stipulated that the metropolitan examination and the palace examination be held once every three years. Thousands of candidates flocked to the capital from all parts of the country in an examination year. A total of 22,649 successful candidates received the title of *jinshi* (Advanced Scholar) through 77 examinations during the period from 1415, the 13th year of the Yongle reign in which the first metropolitan examination was given in Beijing, to 1643, one year before the fall of the Ming dynasty.

The Ming government also ran various courses in the Imperial Medical Institute, the Board of Astronomy, and the Translation Bureau to train people in medicine, astronomy, calendar making and linguistics. The Translation Bureau had eight departments where the students learned foreign languages like Burmese and Sanskrit as well as the languages of China's ethnic minorities, such as Mongolian, Tibetan and Uygur.

After the Qing government made Beijing its capital, it closed down the Imperial College in Nanjing while keeping the one in Beijing as the country's highest institution of learning. The students included Confucian scholars from the Han nationality, Manchus and Mongols, as well as students from Japan, Korea, the Ryukyu Islands and Russia. Separate schools were established for members of the royal family, members of the royal clan, and Banner People (Manchus) in addition to the Metropolitan schools and the Jintai College for the Hans and other ethnic groups. During the Qing dynasty most of those who had passed examinations in the provinces, referred to as *juren* or "Recommended Men," came to Beijing to take part in the metropolitan examination once every three years. In 1883, the ninth year of the reign of Emperor Guangxu, more than 16,000 candidates from 16 to 103 years of age came to the capital from all over the country to sit for the metropolitan examination. During the Qing dynasty 26,840 people received the *jinshi* degree as a result of 114 metropolitan examinations.

The imperial examination system initiated for the selection of civil officials in the Tang dynasty was followed by successive generations for more than 1,000 years. Whoever received the *jinshi* degree by passing the metropolitan examination won honor for his family and his ancestors. In a broader sense, anyone who earned any civil examination degree would be regarded with high esteem.

As the old saying goes:

> For 10 long years a scholar studies hard
> In front of a cold window
> Without receiving public attention;
> He becomes famous overnight
> Once he passes the metropolitan examination.

When a person passed a civil examination, his name would be inscribed on a stone stele as an honor granted by the court. The stone steles in the Confucian Temple shows the names of all those who passed the triennial examinations in about 600 years beginning with 1312, the first year of the Huangqing reign of the Yuan dynasty. The steles are known as the name-list steles for *jinshi* or those who passed the metropolitan examinations. In the Ming dynasty many of the names inscribed in the Yuan period were effaced and replaced by those of the Ming period. That is why few steles of the Yuan dynasty are found in the Confucian Temple. Today 198 stone steles with the name-lists of the Yuan, Ming and Qing periods are preserved in the temple, complete with the native places of 51,624 successful candidates and their respective places in the competitions. The steles are considered priceless relics.

Archway on Foster-the-Virtuous Street

道洽大同

興天地參

聖協時中

有生民來

聖集大成

安悟備道發中和得其門治時期由昌

肇家治國平天下信致堂

Inside the Hall of Great Attainments in the Confucian Temple. As the main hall in the temple, it was the place where the emperors of the Yuan, Ming and Qing dynasties offered sacrifices to Confucius.

The famous Biyong (Jade Disc) Hall, where the emperors discussed classics with advanced scholars, was the central building in the Imperial College during the Ming-Qing period. Built in 1784, the 49th year of the reign of Emperor Qianlong, the square hall has double eaves, pointed corners and roofs covered with yellow glazed tiles. Standing at the center of a circular pool, the hall is surrounded by white stone balustrades, while the pool is spanned by four marble bridges. This constitutes an architectural pattern known as "a square hall at the center of a circular pool." When the Qing emperors lectured at the Imperial College, they did so from a rostrum in the hall. They visited the college for the express purpose of showing their respect for Confucius as well as their intention to train scholar-officials who were talented by Confucian standards.

Radical changes took place in the educational system in the late period of the Qing dynasty. In 1862, the first year of the reign of Emperor Tongzhi, the College of Languages was founded to train people in five foreign languages—English, French, Russian, German and Japanese. Then the Academy of Mathematics was initiated for children of the Eight Banners, i.e., of the Manchus, to study foreign languages and natural sciences. In 1898, the 24th year of the reign of Emperor Guangxu, the University of the National Capital was established as the predecessor of the present Beijing University. It had a department for the training of teachers, which became the predecessor of the present Beijing Normal University. In 1909, the first year of the reign of Emperor Xuantong, the Office for Sending Students to the United States was founded as the prototype of the Qinghua University. Finally several missionary schools were established, such as the Yuying Middle School, Peking Academy and Bridgman Middle School.

Biyong (Jade Disc) Hall in the Imperial College. Located to the west of the Confucian Temple, the hall has a rostrum from which the emperor gave lectures.

Science and Technology

Several outstanding scientists rose to prominence during the later period of the Ming dynasty, including Li Shizhen, Xu Xiake, Song Yingxing and Xu Guangqi. Li Shizhen (1518-93), who had worked in the Imperial Medical Department, compiled the *Compendium of Materia Medica*, a definitive work on Chinese pharmacology. Xu Xiake (1586-1641), who visited Beijing, was well-known for his *Travels*, a book on Chinese geography. Song Yingxing (1587-c.1660), who came to Beijing twice to sit for the metropolitan examination, wrote *Expositions of the Works of Nature*, an encyclopedia on Chinese agriculture and handicrafts. Xu Guangqi (1562-1633), who served as Minister of the Board of Rites and concurrently Grand Secretary of the Inner Chancery in the capital for a long time, made great contributions to the development of science and technology in his time. Setting great store by traditional Chinese production techniques, he wrote *A Complete Treatise on Agriculture* which deals with all aspects of farming. He also studied natural sciences of the West and introduced them to China.

In 1516, the 11th year of the Zhengde reign of the Ming dynasty, a Portuguese named Rafaal Perestrello came to China by boat, marking the arrival of the first European ship along the China coast. In 1601, the 29th year of the Wanli reign of the Ming, the Italian missionary Matteo Ricci brought several Western scientific and technical books to Beijing. One of these was the *Atlas of the World*. Based on a Western atlas of the five continents, it was marked out with longitudes and latitudes and provided with Chinese annotations. The atlas did much to open the eyes of Chinese scholars to the outside world.

While preaching the Jesuit religion, Matteo Ricci propagated the natural sciences of the West. Xu Guangqi learned Western sciences from him and together they translated into Chinese Euclid's *Elements of Geometry* as the first book of Western science translated since the arrival of missionaries in China. Matteo Ricci also worked together with a Ming official named Li Zhizao to translate and compile the *Rudiments of Arithmetic* which had considerable influence on the development of Chinese mathematics. After his death Matteo Ricci was buried at Chegongzhuang outside the Gate of Great Tranquility in Beijing. *An Illustrated Book of Miraculous Western Appliances*, co-translated by Jean Terrenz, a Swiss, and Wang Cheng, is the earliest book on mechanics rendered into Chinese.

In the early years of the Qing dynasty Chinese scholars, in collaboration with Jesuits, translated and compiled *A New Book of Western Calendar*, first entitled *Chongzhen Calendar*. Based on a Danish astronomer's cosmic system, the book explains European astronomy systematically. Using authentic astronomical data and

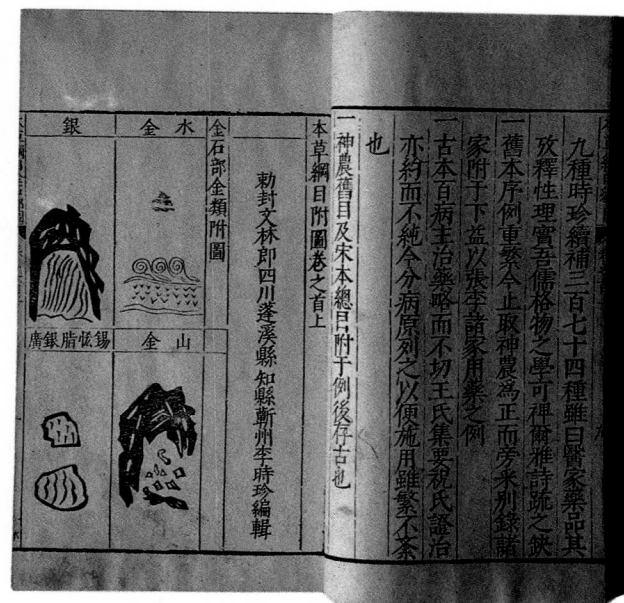

Block-printed edition of *Compendium of Materia Medica*. The blocks were engraved by Zhang Dingsi in 1604, the 31st year of the Wanli reign of the Ming dynasty.

scientific ways of calculation, it ensures a high degree of accuracy in calendar-making. This was a branch of learning new to Chinese scholars at the time.

After Emperor Chongzhen hanged himself and the Qing forces crossed the Great Wall, the Jesuits revised the calendar and presented it to the Qing Emperor Shunzhi. The calendar, published under a new title, proved to be of much help to the accurate observation of heavenly bodies.

An observatory built in 1442, the seventh year of the reign of Emperor Zhengtong of the Ming dynasty, stands on the west side of the site of the former Building-the-Country Gate in Beijing's East City District. It was a 14-meter-high brick platform where a whole range of large bronze astronomical instruments were placed. Supplementary to the platform were two auxiliary buildings, the Hall of Celestial Abstruseness and the Sundial Hall.

Matteo Ricci and Xu Guangqi

Tomb of Matteo Ricci

Celestial globe made during the Kangxi reign of the Qing dynasty

Armilla made during the Qianlong reign of the Qing dynasty

Quadrant made during the reign of Emperor Kangxi

◁ Astronomical observatory built in the Ming dynasty

208

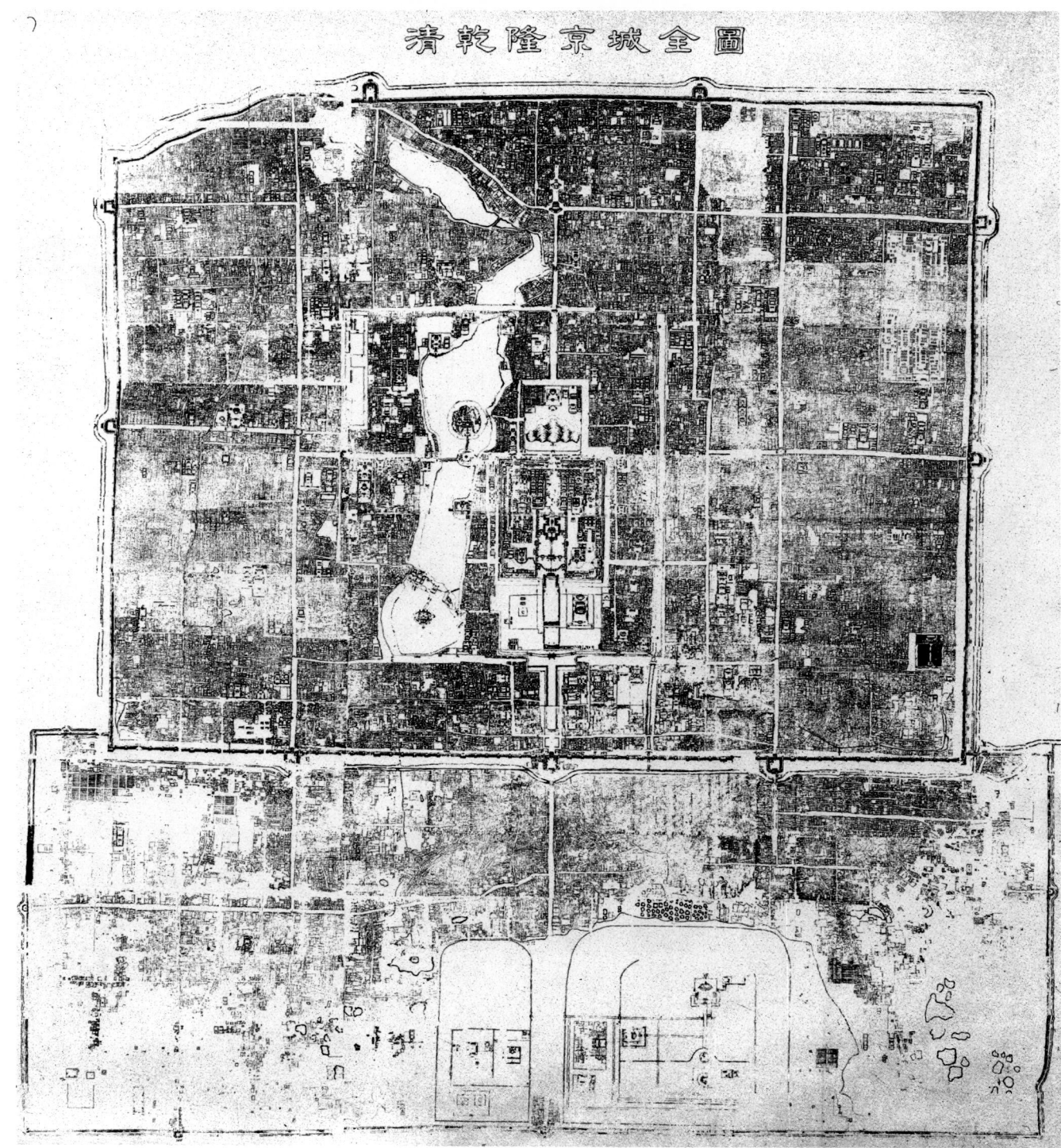

Map of Beijing Under Emperor Qianlong

The observatory of the Qing dynasty, based on that of the Ming, showed further progress due to achievements in astronomy and mathematics in the Kangxi-Qianlong period as well as introduction of scientific methods from the West. Some new astronomical instruments were developed, such as the quadrant, the celestial globe, the altazimuth, the equatorial armilla, the new armilla and the sextant. In addition, the *Essence of Mathematics and Physics* was compiled as an encyclopedia on Western mathematics. The book had an important influence on the development of astronomy and mathematics in China. All these achievements rejuvenated Chinese astronomy after years of decline.

A nationwide geographical survey was conducted during the Kangxi period, resulting in the compilation of *The Complete Atlas of the Empire* based on scientific methods. After revision and substantiation during the reigns of Emperors Yongzheng and Qianlong, *Qianlong's Complete Atlas of the Empire* was produced as an important work of Chinese cartography. In particular, *Map of Beijing Under Emperor Qianlong,* the first map of the capital city drawn by modern methods on a large scale in 1750, the 15th year of the Qianlong reign, was the best map of any capital city in the world at the time and a breakthrough in the history of world cartography.

An outstanding work in the history of Chinese mathematics, *Quick Methods for Determining Segment Areas,* was produced in 1763, the 28th year of the Qianlong reign, by Ming Antu (?-1765), a celebrated versatile scientist of the Mongolian nationality who had been a scientific advisor to Emperor Kangxi and who was in charge of

the Imperial Institute of Astronomy and Calendrical Calculations. The book was a result of his 30-odd years of study and was later completed by his son and his students.

Important contributions were made to the development of science and technology by the noted mathematician Li Shanlan (1810-82) and the famous engineer Zhan Tianyou (1861-1919) in the late period of the Qing dynasty. Li became interested in mathematics as a child and attained a high academic level in 30 years. In 1868, the 7th year of the Tongzhi reign, he came to Beijing and was appointed President of the College of Languages and of the College of Mathematics. After painstaking studies he arrived independently at the same fundamental concept of calculus as developed by Leibniz and Newton in the West and subsequently completed the transition from elementary to advanced mathematics. The Chinese mathematic terms coined by him, such as *daishu* for algebra, *weifen* for differential calculus, and *jifen* for integral calculus, have been passed down to the present time in China and Japan. Li Shanlan was also the first scholar to introduce Newton's three cardinal principles of mechanics to China. The results of his research in mathematics were incorporated in a book entitled *Mathematics from the Zeguxi Studio*.

Zhan Tianyou, who eventually became a famous engineer, was enrolled at Yale University in the United States as a major in railway engineering in 1878, the fourth year of the Guangxu reign. By his diligence he achieved an excellent academic record and came first in his class during the graduation examinations. Returning to China, he was assigned to build a railway from Beijing to Zhangjiakou

Bronze statue of Zhan Tianyou

(Kalgan). The line, surveyed, designed and built entirely by Chinese engineers, was noted for its low cost, high quality and great speed of construction. When European and American railway engineers came to China to see the line, they expressed admiration for the engineering feat. A bronze statue was erected to commemorate Zhan Tianyou at the Qinglongqiao (Black Dragon Bridge) station where an inscription praised his outstanding merit in avoiding a tunnel in the construction of the line.

Literature

Popular literature achieved progress during the Ming period, when the *zhanghui* type of novels, i.e., those divided into standardized chapters, became the main trend. Each chapter is headed by a couplet giving the gist of what follows. The serialized story is written in neat paragraphs to present an intriguing plot. The four well-known *zhanghui* novels in the Ming period are *The Romance of the Three Kingdoms, Outlaws of the Marsh, Journey to the West,* and *Flowering Plum in a Golden Vase.* They marked the zenith of classical Chinese fiction and produced a tremendous social impact.

The Romance of the Three Kingdoms is China's first historical novel and one of the longest works in the history of Chiness literature. Through its sharp portrayal of some 400 characters, including Cao Cao, Guan Yu and Zhuge Liang, it presents a vivid panorama of the complicated political and military struggles during the period of the Three Kingdoms. The novel has been recognized almost universally for its miraculous characterization of the wicked and crafty Cao Cao, the loyal and faithful Guan Yu, and the wise and invincible Zhuge Liang, who, as a personification of political-military genius, directed the spectacular Battle of Red Cliff.

Outlaws of the Marsh is a masterful account in praise of peasant uprisings. Based upon true historical events taking place in the Liangshan Marsh during the last years of the Northern Song dynasty, it focuses on the theme, "the government compels the people to rise in arms," and successfully creates a host of characters each with a distinct personality. It exposes and condemns the crimes and corruption of the landlord class in power. With its increasing popularity, *Outlaws of the Marsh* became a source of inspiration for literary works of later times.

Journey to the West describes how the Tang dynasty monk Xuan Zang (Hsuan Tsang or Tripitaka) makes his way to the Western Heavens (India) to procure Buddhist scriptures. He is escorted by his three disciples — Sun Wu Kong (the Monkey King), Zhu Ba Jie (Pigsy) and the Monk from Sandy River (Sandy). On the way the party defeats all the deities and demons and overcomes unbelievable hardships before it reaches the Western Heavens and obtains the Buddhist scriptures.

Wu Cheng'en, author of this novel, is described as a "keen and intelligent man who was extremely well-read." Though he never did well in official examinations, he showed a stubborn character. He refused to be pitied by others, and remained aloof and unconventional. As a child he was fond of folk legend, and developed a love for popular stories as he grew up. Later, on the basis of *pinghua* (professional storytelling) and *zaju* (poetic drama set to music), he took great pains to finish his great mythical romance.

In the novel Sun Wu Kong, the Monkey King, is daring, resourceful and alert. He manages to master the mystical feats known as the 72 transformations and overcomes 81 ordeals, defeating all the demons and evil spirits and removing all the obstacles to the party's advance. One famous episode is "the Monkey King Creates Havoc in Heaven.' Hoisting his banner in the Palace of Heaven, he declares, "People take turns to be emperor; my turn comes next year." Afraid of his prowess, the heavenly army, a hundred thousand strong, flees in panic at the mere sight of him, and the whole Palace of Heaven is plunged into chaos. The episode became a favorite subject for drama, storytelling, painting and puppet shows.

Flowering Plum in a Golden Vase, a novel of considerable length, evolved from an episode in *Outlaws of the Marsh*, in which the hero Wu Song kills the wife of his elder brother, an adulteress guilty of murdering her husband in collusion with the adulterer. Unfortunately, the real name of the author is unknown. In the novel the author portrays the evil deeds of the aforementioned adulterer named Ximen Qing and his corrupt life. Focussing on the relationship between the adulterer and the adulteress, the author describes the mentality of people of every description, from court officials to ordinary merchants. Thus he presents a vivid picture of the corruption and loose morals of a section of society in his time.

Famous novels produced during the Qing dynasty in the *zhanghui* style include *Strange Tales from a Lonely Studio*, *The Scholars*, *A Dream of Red Mansions* and *Flowers in the Mirror*. Among the authors of these novels Cao Xueqin, author of *A Dream of Red Mansions*, lived for a long time in Beijing and Li Ruzhen, author of the *Flowers in the Mirror* was a native of the city.

Cao Xueqin, author of *A Dream of Red Mansions*, was born into an aristocratic family. His great-grandfather, grandfather, father and uncle held the hereditary post of Textile Commissioner for Jiangning Prefecture (present-day Nanjing and adjacent counties), an official in charge of the manufacture of silk fabrics for the imperial household. The Qing Emperor Kangxi made five inspection tours to South China, and four times he stayed in the house of the Caos. Cao Yin, the author's grandfather, had been responsible for printing the *Complete Poems of the Tang Dynasty*. As a good poet and playwright he produced many works, one of which was the *Poems of the Lian Pavilion*. As a boy Cao Xueqin lived the life of a member of an aristocratic family, which nevertheless declined because his father got involved in factional conflicts among the ruling class and was dismissed from office. After the confiscation of its property the family had to move to Beijing. Reduced to poverty, Cao Xueqin lived in the western outskirts of the capital. He was so poor that his family often survived on thin gruel and he had to buy wine on credit. It was during these bitter years that he wrote his great novel, *A Dream of Red Mansions*.

The theme of the novel is the tragic love between the girl Lin Daiyu and Jia Baoyu, darling son of an aristocratic family. In the process of describing the tragedy of love and marriage among the main characters, the author portrays feudal China in the mid-18th century. The novel touches upon so many aspects of society that in a way it is an encyclopedia of Chinese life in the author's time. Furthermore, the Grand View Garden described in the novel has become a model of classical Chinese garden designing. With its numerous incidents, a great number of characters of different types, a close-knit plot, a clear and logical way of presentation, and a rich language, the novel is regarded as the greatest of China's classical novels.

Flowers in the Mirror is a noted satirical novel which describes imaginary foreign lands toured by Tang Ao, a poor scholar, and a group of merchants. In the Kingdom of Gentlemen the prime minister is modest, amiable and easy to talk to while the townsfolk are polite, kind-hearted and square in buying and selling. The Kingdom is the author's utopia.

In the novel Li Ruzhen, the author, also narrates the stories of 100 gifted women in the Kingdom of Maidens who are noted for their courage, insight, talent in literature, or skill in martial arts. Overshadowed by them, the men show a sense of inferiority. The author not only depicts men and women as equals, but goes on to stress female supremacy. Thus the novel is admired for its democratic idea of advocating a higher status for women in feudal China.

Drama

Drama flourished in Beijing during the Ming and Qing dynasties.

Zaju, which gained popularity under the Yuan dynasty, made further advances in the Ming period. The repertoire included some 1,000 items. In 1583, the 11th year of the Wanli reign, the outstanding dramatist Tang Xianzu came to Beijing from Linchuan, Jiangxi Province, to take the imperial examination. He earned the degree of *jinshi* and was made a low-ranking official. Frustrated by the uncertainties of official life, he resigned and went back home to do his writing.

Peony Pavilion is the best known of his works. It is the story of a young woman, Du Liniang, who sees the man she loves, Liu Mengmei, in a dream. But as soon as she wakes up, he disappears. Being lovesick, she falls ill and eventually dies. As her soul enters her body again, she comes back to life. A successful romanticist, the playwright sings the praises of the young people's struggle for the emancipation of the individual and the freedom to love the person of their own choice. By the time *Peony Pavilion* was published, the *kunqu* and *yiyang* operas from south China had become popular in Beijing, and theatrical troupes had started giving performances in public theaters in downtown areas. The staging of *Peony Pavilion* created a sensation among theater-goers in the capital.

The prosperity of theatrical art in Beijing culminated in the birth of two masterpieces in early Qing dynasty. These were the *Palace of Eternal Youth* and the *Peach Blossom Fan*. Hong Sheng, author of the *Palace of Eternal Youth*, had been studying at the Imperial College for more than 20 years without ever passing the imperial examination. Though poverty-stricken, he remained proud and unconventional. He spent ten years writing the *Palace of Eternal Youth* which describes the tragic love between the Tang dynasty Emperor Minghuang (Emperor Xuanzong, r. 712-756) and his favorite concubine Yang Yuhuan. When the script was finished, it was eagerly copied by many. The performance of the opera made a furor However, in 1689, the 28th year of the Kangxi reign, Hong Sheng was dismissed from the Imperial College because the opera had been performed during the mourning period for Lady Tong, empress of Kangxi. The playwright returned to his native town and was drowned after getting drunk.

Kong Shangren, author of the *Peach Blossom Fan*, had been a scholar of the Imperial College in Beijing. In 1699, the 38th year of the Kangxi reign, he completed the opera which describes the love between Li Xiangjun, a famous courtesan, and Hou Fangyu, a well-known man of letters. When the *Peach Blossom Fan* was performed at a teahouse outside the South-Facing Gate, it attracted capacity audiences for months.

After the mid-Qing period Peking opera, a new form of stage art, gradually took shape. In the early years of the Qing dynasty Yangzhou in Jiangsu Province, a hub of land and river traffic, became a flourishing town with a growing population and rich merchants profiting from the salt trade. Theatrical troupes giving different types of performance, such as *kunqu* opera, Shaanxi opera, and *bangzi* opera, flocked to the river port. When Emperor Qianlong toured South China, local officials and merchants brought together a number of troupes to perform for him. Returning to the capital, Qianlong brought back with him quite a few famous actors specializing in different operatic forms. In 1790, the 55th year of the Qianlong reign, a top-level opera troupe from Anhui Province, the *Sanqingbang*, came to Beijing to offer performances for the emperor's 80th birthday. The troupe presented a challenge to the popularity of other troupes which had arrived in Beijing at earlier times to perform the *bangzi* opera from Shanxi, the *han* opera from Hubei, and the *kunqu* opera from Jiangsu. The Anhui opera troupe absorbed the best in the other operatic forms, innovated its repertoire, singing, acting and costumes, adopted some of the vernacular language of Beijing, and suited its performance to local custom. Peking opera emerged in the process.

The basic elements of Peking opera are singing, recitation, acting and acrobatics, all of which have to follow a strict convention and demanding rules. The musical accompaniment, language, costumes, properties and make-up in Peking opera are highly refined. The pattern of facial make-up varies with the age, status, disposition and socio-political position of the character.

Peking opera has four main types of characters: *sheng, dan, jing* and *chou*, or the male lead, the female lead, the painted face and the clown. *Sheng* characters are divided into *lao sheng* (middle-aged or elderly men), *xiao sheng* (young men), and *wu sheng* (warriors). *Dan* characters include *qing yi* (females of the demure type), *hua dan* (females of the coquettish type), and *lao dan* (older women). *Jing* or

Peking Opera Performance (painting of the Qing dynasty)

painted-face characters are divided into *zheng jing* (the principal civilian parts), *fu jing* (the subordinate civilian parts), and *wu jing* (the military parts). *Chou* or clowns include *wen chou* (civilian clowns), *wu chou* (warrior clowns), and *chou po* (clownish older women).

These divisions are made to suit the plot, the characterization, and the artistic treatment.

The Peking opera theaters were first identical with the larger teahouses where customers paid only for the tea but not for the show. It was only later that tickets for the performance were sold. The teahouses were then mostly located at Dazhalan (Great Fence) Street in the Outer City because they were forbidden to operate with their uproarious noises in the Inner City close to the palace.

Residents in the capital were particularly fond of Peking opera. As it was winning popularity, famous actors emerged to rival with one another with their different styles. The repertoire increased steadily with the rise of outstanding actors. As many as 3,800 operas were being presented for a time.

In addition to the Peking opera troupes performing for the public, a special troupe served the imperial court. It was called the Times of Peace Troupe which presented mostly operas about immortals coming down from heaven to join in celebrations in the palace or programs eulogizing the good times for enjoyment by the emperor and empress.

Compilation of Books

Shortly after Emperor Yongle of the Ming dynasty ascended the throne he moved the capital from Nanjing to Beijing, after which he instructed Grand Secretary Xie Jin and other officials to compile the *Yongle Encyclopedia*. Over 3,000 scholars were brought together to take part in the work. After five years of painstaking efforts, the *Yongle Encyclopedia* was completed as a classified book unprecedented in Chinese history. The 22,937-*juan* edition includes 7,000-8,000 important pre-Ming titles. Divided into 11,095 thread-bound volumes, it is written in more than 370 million characters. It was so voluminous that only one original copy could be made by hand without ever going to the printer.

In 1567, the first year of the Longqing reign, a duplicate copy of the *Yongle Encyclopedia* was made and stored in the Imperial Historical Archives. The main hall of the archives, built in 1534 or the 13th year of the Jiajing period, is located at today's Nanchizi Street. The building is an arched, pillarless structure constructed exclusively with stone and bricks. Roofed with yellow glazed tiles, it is surrounded with white marble balustrades. The hall served as the premises of the archives during the Ming-Qing period. Inside is a large stone *sumeru* base on which were placed 152 gilded, copper-coated, camphorated cabinets with carved cloud-and-dragon designs. They were used to keep important documents of the Ming and Qing dynasties.

The original copy of the *Yongle Encyclopedia* stored in Nanjing was destroyed at the time of the collapse of the Ming government. The duplicate copy in Beijing was mostly burnt or taken away by the Anglo-French allied forces and the allied forces of the eight powers. Only a small part of this outstanding book is extant.

Handwritten imperial copy of the *Yongle Encyclopedia*, produced during the Jiajing reign of the Ming dynasty

Main hall of the Imperial Historical Archives

Inside the Imperial Historical Archives

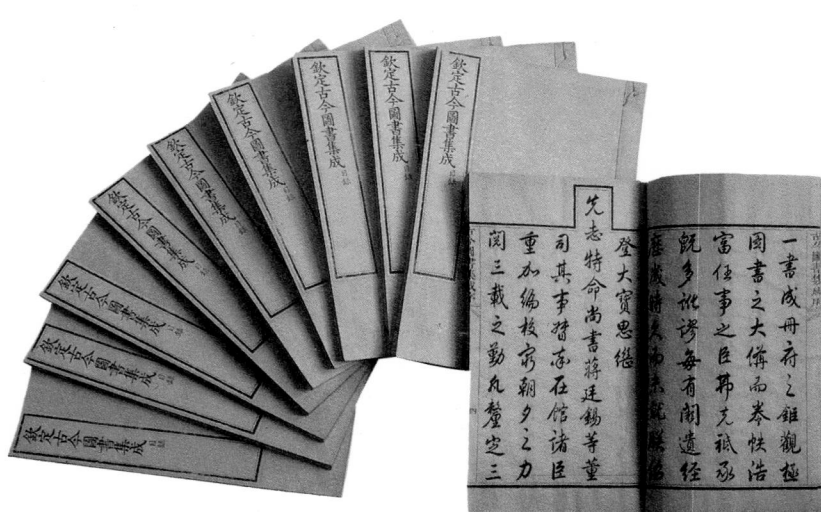

A Collection of Books of Ancient and Modern Times printed by movable type of copper during the Yongzheng reign of the Qing dynasty

Another massive book stored in the Imperial Historical Archives was the *Veritable Records of the Ming Dynasty*. It was stipulated by the Ming government that whenever a new emperor ascended the throne he should appoint officials to compile a veritable record of the previous reign by sorting out historical data in chronological order. After a record was completed, two copies would be made. The original one was kept in the Imperial Historical Archives and the duplicate in the Inner Chancery. The *Veritable Records of the Ming Dynasty, 3,045 juan* in all, is a historical work of great value. In addition, two books about Beijing were compiled, namely, the *Yongle Gazetteer of Shuntian Prefecture* and the *Wanli Gazetteer of Shuntian Prefecture,* both of which provide important data on Beijing.

Compilation of books in the Qing dynasty assumed an even larger scale. Emperors Kangxi and Qianlong brought all famous scholars to the capital to sort out and compile books totalling more than 100 titles in 100,000 *juan*. Among these books were *Peiwen Book of Rhymes and Phrases,* a dictionary compiled according to Chinese rhymes in 444 *juan;* the *Gazetteer of the Qing Empire* totalling 500 *juan;* the *Complete Poems of the Tang Dynasty* in 900 *juan;* and the *Complete Prose Writings of the Tang Dynasty* in 1,000 *juan*. In 1700, the 39th year of the Kangxi period, scholars started the compilation of a new encyclopedia of 10,000 *juan* in 5,000 volumes. Entitled *A Collection of Books of Ancient and Modern Times,* the book was completed in 1725 after 25 years of laborious efforts. It covers six major fields — astronomy, geography, ethics, botany and zoology, Neo-Confucianism and economics. Under the six categories are 32 divisions and 6,109 sub-divisions.

A Collection of Books of Ancient and Modern Times is the greatest Chinese encyclopedia preserved in China to this day. It was printed by movable type of copper. The printed characters are clear and elegant, the paper is spotlessly clean, the ink dark and shiny, and the binding exquisite.

Another literary undertaking, entitled the *Complete Library of the Four Categories of Books,* was also compiled in the Qing period as the largest collection of books in China's history.

Following the system of the Ming dynasty, Qing emperors also ordered officials to compile veritable records of the current dynasty. The *Veritable Records of the Qing Dynasty* consists of 12 parts in 4,363 *juan.* According to the regulations of the Qing dynasty, each record must be written in five copies and each copy in three languages — Manchu, Mongolian and Han. The covers were decorated with red or yellow damask. There were two formats, the larger and the smaller. Upon completion, the records were kept in the Hall of Celestial Purity, the Imperial Historical Archives, the Inner Chancery and the Chongmo Tower in Shengjing, Northeast China. Two copies of the records were deposited in the library of the Inner Chancery, one for the emperor's perusal. In 1773, the 38th year of the Qianlong reign, the emperor decided to compile *A Collection of the Local Literature of Beijing* which includes practically all the historical documents on the capital. Two other valuable books about Beijing produced in the Qing period are the *Kangxi Gazetteer of the Shuntian Prefecture* and the *Guangxu Gazetteer of the Shuntian Prefecture,* both of which are noted for their rich source material.

After the completion of the manuscripts, wood blocks would be engraved for printing. Both public and private printing shops were fairly developed in the Qing dynasty. Of these the imperial press at the Hall of Military Prowess in the palace was the most remarkable. The books printed there were done elaborately and provided with elegant silk covers and red, yellow or black jackets. The thread-bound volumes were usually wrapped with brocade at the corners for protection. The deluxe editions were totally wrapped in brocade.

At the imperial press, books were produced by engraved wood blocks, movable type, or the multi-printing plate. Books printed from engraved wood blocks were usually valued for their clear format, excellent paper, quality ink, careful proofreading, and elegant style. Wood-block printing was used mostly for classics and Buddhist scriptures. When the movable type was used, the printer had to set type by picking individual characters. The type could be either copper or wood. *A Collection of Books of Ancient and Modern Times* is the largest book ever printed by copper movable type in China. Unfortunately, the copper characters and plates were later melted for the minting of copper coins. The *Rare Book Series* printed by the imperial press, covering 138 titles, is the greatest work done by wooden movable type. Unfortunately, the wood characters were later used as firewood by the palace guards.

The multi-printing plate might be a two-colored, four-colored or five-colored plate. The remarkable printing techniques used in the Qing dynasty can be seen from Emperor Kangxi's *Poems at the Mountain Manor* printed by a red-and-black plate, the *Collected Poems of the Tang and Song Dynasties* printed by a four-colored plate; *A Collection of Ancient Prose* printed by a five-colored plate, the *Ode to Shengjing* in the seal script printed by engraved wood blocks in 1743, the eighth year of Emperor Qianlong's reign; the *Complete Atlas of the Empire* printed by a copper plate in 1760, the 25th year of the Qianlong period; the *Tripitaka in Manchu Script* printed in red color during the Qianlong reign; and, last but not least, the military maps drawn by the Jesuits and plated in Europe.

Painting

The Ming dynasty is an important period in the history of Chinese painting, noted especially for the paintings done by scholars. As men of letters and artists of the empire gathered in Beijing, many painters came to the fore. An Imperial Painting Academy was set up in Beijing. Yu Shenxing of the Ming dynasty states in his *Writings Produced at the Mountain House in Gucheng:*

> Emperor Huizong of the Song dynasty established the Academy of Calligraphy and the Academy of Painting. The members of the Academy of Calligraphy were, in fact, incumbent secretaries in the Hall of Literary Glory. The members of the Academy of Painting were the junior secretaries serving in the Hall of Military Prowess.

The Ming emperors Xuande (Zhu Zhanji), Jingtai (Zhu Qiyu), Chenghua (Zhu Jianshen) and Jiajing (Zhu Youtang) were all art lovers and painters of landscapes, flowers and birds, human figures, grass and insects. It is said that they often tried to compete with Emperor Huizong (Zhao Ji) of the Song dynasty, a well-known painter and a great connoisseur of brushwork. Under the Ming dynasty famous painters were often summoned to the Imperial Painting Academy by the emperor.

During the Yongle reign of the early Ming period, Bian Wenjin, a noted painter of flowers and birds in the meticulous style, and two other famous painters of the time, Jiang Zicheng and Zhao Lian, were made royal painters working in the palace. They were known as the "three matchless artists in the Forbidden City."

Dai Jin of Qiantang (present-day Hangzhou), who started as a silversmith in the palace, was later placed in the Imperial Painting Academy. Once he was ordered to do a painting entitled *Fishing on the Autumn River.* The fisherman in the picture was clothed in a red robe usually worn by a high official, for which Dai was charged with a malicious attempt to confuse court officials with the common folk. This angered the emperor, who gave the order to have him executed. To escape punishment, Dai and his disciple went into hiding in a monastery. After getting a priest drunk, Dai stole his Buddhist certificate. Then he had his disciple shave his head, disguised himself as a monk, and fled to his native town.

Dai Jin's landscapes are noted for their ink-and-wash techniques and bold, vigorous strokes. He was reputed as a master landscapist.

Dai was the precursor of the "four great painters of the Ming dynasty" —Tang Yin, Shen Zhou, Wen Zhengming and Qiu Ying. Tang Yin, whose courtesy name was Bohu, had been to Beijing to sit for the metropolitan examination. But he was degraded for involvement in the "case of examination hall." *

He called himself a "gifted scholar leading an unconventional life." After making extensive tours of China's mountains and rivers, he settled down to earn a living by selling his paintings. Tang wrote a poem on his philosophy:

> I do not sell elixirs of life as the Taoists do,
> Nor do I meditate like a Buddhist;
> As soon as I get up,
> I do a painting of the green mountains for sale,
> Never using any ill-gotten money in my life.

Tang Yin was a remrkable painter of landscapes and human figures. One of his paintings, *Going Home on a Donkey,* presents a poor scholar in a shabby robe riding home on a donkey along a mountain stream in the autumn wind. It is strongly reminiscent of life. Tang's works are noted for an imposing scene, elegant brushstrokes and a skilful use of ink-and-wash techniques. The courtesy name of the painter, Tang Bohu, is widely known because it is the name of the hero of a popular novel entitled *The Maiden's Three Disarming Smiles* which was adapted for professional storytelling.

Dong Qichang, a famous painter in the late Ming period, passed the metropolitan examination in Beijing and earned the degree of *jinsji* in 1589, the 17th year of the Wanli reign. Later he became Minister of the Board of Rites. Dong did not have a good reputation as an official, but he achieved enduring fame as a painter and calligrapher. His paintings of mountains, streams, trees and rocks are admired for the meticulous brushwork, skilful use of ink, and elegant style.

Among the Ming dynasty murals in Beijing, those at the Fahaisi or Temple of the Sea of Dharma are most remarkable for their

---

* When Tang Yin took part in a metropolitan examination in Beijing, dishonest practices by some candidates were discovered and reported to the imperial court. The court authorities punished a large number of candidates. Tang Yin, like many others, was arrested and imprisoned.

Pines Rustling over a Mountain Path (painting by Tang Yin)

Pavilion on Fairy Mountain (painting by Qiu Ying)

Visiting Ancient Sites at Fengjing (painting by Dong Qichang)

Mt. Lushan (painting by Shen Zhou)

Murals in the Temple of the Sea of Dharma ▷

Murals in the Temple of the Sea of Dharma

Eight Horses (painting by Lang Shining)

magnificence and fine presentation. The temple is located at the southern foot of the Cuiwei Mountain in today's Shijingshan District. Built in 1439, the fourth year of the Zhengtong reign, the halls of the temple stand on the mountainside one above the other. The walls inside the entrance are decorated with colored paintings. The main hall facing the entrance is roofed with yellow glazed tiles. On the northern wall of the main hall behind the platform is a picture about the Heavenly Emperor and other celestial beings. All of the figures have distinctively individual characteristics, such as the dignity and solemnity of the Sakra-davanam-Indra, the mighty power of the Heavenly Emperor, and the kindness of the Heavenly Empress. The portraits of the three principal Bodhisattvas are especially well done. They are graceful, lifelike and spirited. The frescos at the Temple of the Sea of Dharma are rare treasures of art which can rival the murals of the Song and Yuan dynasties at the Dunhuang grottos.

In the Qing dynasty the court paintings surpassed those of the Ming period and the paintings by artists outside the court also showed phenomenal progress. In fact, it was a period when all kinds of paintings flourished—landscapes, flowers and birds, human figures and genre. In addition, a new type of art appeared—Gao Peiqi's finger painting. As the capital of the Qing dynasty, Beijing was the center of art boasting many famous painters.

Following the practice of the Ming dynasty, the Qing court also set up an Imperial Academy of Painting. The Pavilion of Pleasure south of the Hall of Good Omens in the Forbidden City was the imperial studio where the court painters did their work when they were summoned to do so by the emperor.

Emperors Shunzhi, Kangxi and Qianlong of the Qing were not only art lovers but good painters themselves. That explains why the court painters in the Qing period were more active than those in the Ming period. One special feature of the Qing court paintings lies in the prominence of works hailing military exploits.

Emperor Kangxi made six tours of the South. In 1689, the 28th year of his reign, a painting of the royal excursion to the south was done on his order in memory of his second visit. Song Junye, Senior President of the Censorate, was appointed the organizer and superviser. Song invited his teacher Wang Hui to Beijing at a high salary. Accepting the invitation, Wang came with his disciple Yang Jin. Before the painting was started, Wang dispatched Yang to visit all the places covered by Kangxi during his tour and made detailed sketches authentic to the scenes. Wang Hui did not make the draft until he had all the source materials in hand. The draft was divided into four sections totalling 12 rolls. It was only after Emperor Kangxi looked over the draft and gave his approval that the painting was started. The whole picture, done with color on silk, was completed in three years. There are more than 20,000 people in the picture. The official title is *Emperor Kangxi's Historic Tour of the South*. On the occasion of his 60th birthday, Emperor Kangxi put Wang Yuanqi in charge of doing another painting entitled *Longevity*. These were the two most important events for court painters in early Qing dynasty. During this period a few other paintings also won royal appreciation. They were *Farming and Weaving* by Jiao Bingzhen, *The Dawn of a Spring Day in a Han Palace* by Leng Mei, and *Thirty-Six Scenes at the Mountain Manor* by Shen Yu.

The court painters were even more active during the Qianlong reign. While following strict rules, they innovated the techniques. Emperor Qianlong ordered court painters to do pictures on his royal excursions and military conquests. He was accompanied by them on all his tours.

One of the products, *The Grand Royal Excursion to the South*, is noted for an imposing atmosphere, a tight composition, and a magnificent panorama done in delicate lines. The draft was revised several times on Qianlong's personal instructions before the wood blocks were cut for printing. Most of the paintings on war themes done on the orders of Qianlong praise his military accomplishments. Dignified and lively, they manifest a high level of technique.

The court painting *Watching Horsemanship at the Garden of Ten Thousand Trees*, also known as *Banquet at the Garden of Ten Thousand Trees*, records a historical event in 1754, the 19th year of the Qianlong reign. In the fifth month of the year the emperor, while staying at the Mountain Manor, gave a banquet in honor of three Jungar tribal chiefs and conferred noble titles on them in the interest of strengthening Qing government rule in the Xinjiang region. The

picture shows Emperor Qianlong watching horsemanship performances in the company of his court officials, the three Jungar nobles, and their retinue in the Garden of Ten Thousand Trees at the Mountain Manor. The painting is remarkable for a spectacular scene and a multitude of people. The important officials are presented in a way that tells their distinctive personalities. Although the painter signed himself as Lang Shining, it is actually a joint creation by Chinese and foreign artists serving at the court.

Lang Shining was the Chinese name of Giuseppe Castiglione, an Italian artist born in Milan in 1688. He came to China in 1715, the 54th year of the Kangxi reign, at the age of 27. Later he was summoned by Emperor Yongzheng to the court to do a painting in Western style entitled *Seeking Good Luck,* which won the praise of the emperor.

Apart from drawing portraits of Emperor Qianlong, Lang Shining did many paintings on his military achievements. He was also good at flowers and horses. *Eight Horses* is one of his famous paintings. He took part in designing and supervising the construction of Xiyanglou or Western-Style Buildings in the Garden of Perfect Splendor. He died in Beijing in 1766, the 31st year of the Qianlong reign, and was given the posthumous title of *shilang,* or Vice-Minister of one of the Six Boards. Other foreign painters, known in Chinese as Ai Qimeng and Wang Jicheng, also left behind some very good paintings.

Western-style painting differs from traditional Chinese painting in the treatment of the perspective and light-and-shade. Zhou Yigui, a court painter of the Qing dynasty, once said:

> In western-style painting the treatment of light-and-shade and distances are so precise that the errors are reduced to a minimum. The human figures, houses and trees all have shades. The use of color in Western-style painting is also completely different from that in Chinese painting. To create the shade, the painter narrows it down by drawing a triangle. The palace buildings they draw on the walls look so real that people are almost ready to go in.

It is interesting to note that Lang Shining and other foreign painters successfully incorporated some good points of Chinese painting into their Western-style productions. On the other hand, Chinese court painters like Jiao Bingzhen and Leng Mei also assimilated the merits of Western-style painting and exhibited them in their works, such as the concentration of the focus, the use of perspectives for houses, and the creation of light-and-shade for pillars. Although Western painting had been introduced into China in the late Ming period, no interflow was effected between Chinese and Western painters until the Qing dynasty. However, the absorption of the good qualities of Western painting did not change the independent course of development of traditional Chinese painting.

As for the painters working outside the court, the chief representatives were the "Four Monks" in the early Qing period — Hong Ren, Kun Can, Zhu Da and Dao Jiwai; and the "Eight Eccentrics of Yangzhou" in the mid-Qing period —Wang Shishen, Huang Shen, Jin Nong, Gao Xiang, Luo Pin, Li Fangying, Li Shan and Zheng Xie. The eight earned the name because they lived in Yangzhou for a long time and had a common style of painting. Among them Li Shan had served in the Inner Court and Zheng Xie had received the academic degree of *jinshi* by passing the metropolitan examination in Beijing.

Zheng Xie, whose courtesy name was Banqiao, had been dismissed from office before he settled in Yangzhou where he earned a living by selling his paintings. He was also versed in poetry and calligraphy. As a painter he excelled in orchids and bamboos. Here is a famous passage from Zheng Xie's writings describing his experience in painting bamboos:

> Living in my house on the river, I got up very early in autumn and watched the bamboos. The mist, sunlight and shadows as well as the dews seemed floating amid the dense bamboo leaves and sparse stems. After watching the scene for some time I felt inspired, ready to use the brush. By then the bamboos in my mind were no longer the bamboos in sight. Presently I began to grind the inkstick, spread out the paper, and started to paint. All of a sudden another transformation took place: the bamboos I was painting with my hand were no longer those in my mind.

It can be seen from this passage that, to portray bamboos, Zheng Xie first made observations, then refined the materials obtained from such observations, and finally expressed his feelings in free, bold strokes. Zheng's paintings are noted for their elegance, rhythm and vitality.

In the late Qing period there were two outstanding painters— Ren Bonian or Ren Yi and Wu Changshuo or Wu Jun. Wu Changshuo's favorites are human figures, landscapes and flowers. He stressed resemblance in spirit, not in appearance. In his paintings he created an effect of rugged power and strength. He also excelled in the use of color. Despite the fact that both Wu Changshuo and Ren Bonian lived in Shanghai for long years, they profoundly influenced the artists of modern China, particularly painters in Beijing.

As the capital of the Ming and Qing dynasties, Beijing had the largest collection of rare paintings. Since superb paintings in history embody the essence of civilization, they have always been treasured by the people. The old Chinese saying that "a foot of good painting sells for an inch of gold" shows how highly people value the works of art. After Beijing became the capital of the Jurchen dynasty, large-scale collection of rare paintings started. It is recorded in books of history that Emperor Huizong of the Northern Song dynasty had made an unprecedented collection of famous paintings from the Wei dynasty (220-265) down to his time, totalling 6,396 pieces. When the Jurchen troops took prisoner of him they moved a large number of the priceless paintings from the Song capital Bianjing (present-day Kaifeng, Henan Province) to the Jurchen's Middle Capital (present-day Beijing). After the Yuan government conquered Jurchen and Southern Song (1127-1279), its capital Dadu became the site for the largest collection of paintings. After the overthrow of the Yuan, most of its paintings were taken over by the Ming court. After the Qing government conquered the Ming, the Forbidden City became the treasure house of famous Chinese paintings of all periods. The palace halls in the Forbidden City boast the finest collection of Chinese paintings and calligraphy.

Calligraphy

Calligraphy enjoyed its heyday in the Ming dynasty. Famous calligraphers of many schools gathered in Beijing.

In the early Ming period Shen Du was the exponent of calligraphic art. By an edict issued by Emperor Yongle, outstanding calligraphers could be admitted to the *Hanlin* Academy. Shen Du entered the academy on account of his excellent handwriting. He specialized in the regular script. His works are natural, graceful and well-poised. Emperor Yongle praised him as "Wang Xizhi of the Ming dynasty." Serving in a side-hall of the palace, he was responsible for writing all the imperial decrees and documents. Neat, even, steady and solid, Shen's handwriting was the very kind needed by the court and the Inner Chancery. Thus he became the representative of the official-document style of the Inner Chancery. His handscript of *Admonitions for Respecting Superiors* is still kept in the Palace Museum.

In the mid-Ming period Wen Zhengming was the representative of calligraphers in Beijing. Wen worked in the *Hanlin* Academy for a time. Then he resigned and went back to his native town of Changzhou (present-day Suzhou). As mentioned earlier, Wen Zhengming was a great painter. Here we are discussing him as a remarkable calligrapher. His big characters are perfectly executed. His *lishu* or clerical script has a unique style. His handscripts of *First Visit to the Red Cliff* by the Song dynasty writer Su Shi and *Second Visit to the Red Cliff* by the same author are kept in the Palace Museum. Of the two the second one, written in small characters, is especially valued for the neat, even, steady and vigorous strokes. He wrote it in his 80s.

Yu Qian was another master calligrapher of the mid-Ming period. He was a little older than Wen Zhengming. Yu passed the metropolitan examination in 1421, the 19th year of the Yongle reign, and was assigned to an official post in Beijing. In 1449, the 14th year of the Zhengtong reign, Mongolian cavalrymen under Esen invaded Beijing and took prisoner of Emperor Zhengtong. At this critical hour Yu Qian, as Deputy Minister of War, assumed the responsibility of defending Beijing and prepared carefully for the confrontation. He was promoted to Minister of War. Under his command the Ming defenders defeated Esen. In 1457, the first year of the Tianshun reign, Emperor Zhengtong was reinstated. But Yu Qian was persecuted and imprisoned on a trumped-up charge and died a victim of injustice. A person of great integrity, he was versed in literature and calligraphy. His prose has a free, casual style and

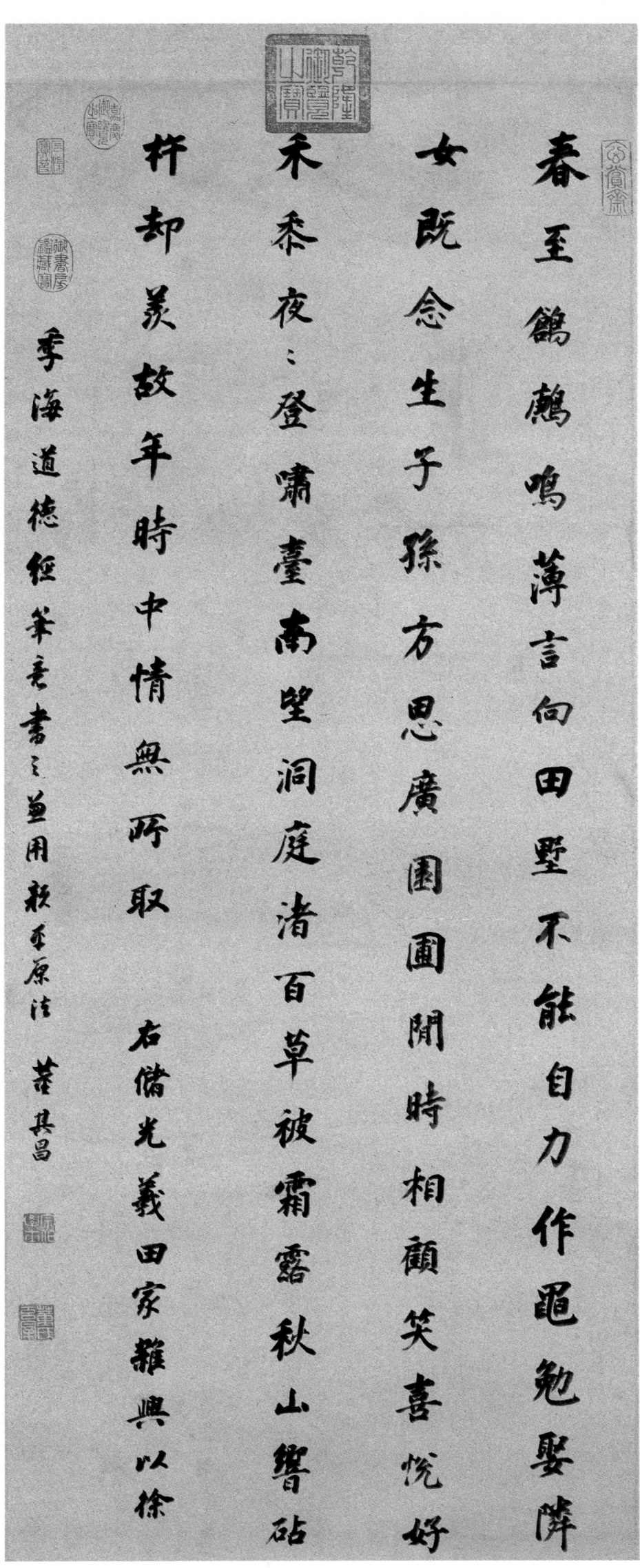

Calligraphy by Dong Qichang

Calligraphy by Wang Duo

carries a torrential force, while his poems are lucid and unaffected. His calligraphy is at once vigorous and graceful. His handscript *An Inscription on the Painting of the Gongzhong Pagoda,* is kept in the Palace Museum.

In the late period of the Ming dynasty Mi Wanzhong was the representative. At the time the two best-known calligraphers were "Dong of the south and Mi of the north". The former refers to Dong Qichang and the latter to Mi Wanzhong. Dong Qichang's painting, as mentioned above, has a style of its own. His calligraphy, commended posthumously by Emperor Kangxi of the Qing, became fashionable for a time and had wide influence. Mi was a native of Wanping, Shuntian Prefecture (present-day Beijing). As a young man he was already famous for his writings and calligraphy. In 1595, the 23rd year of the Wanli reign, he passed the metropolitan examination and became *jinshi.* He served as provincial judge in Jiangxi. Admiring his beautiful handwriting, some of the palace eunuchs asked Mi to write letters for them, but he turned them down. The eunuchs levelled a false charge against him, and he was dismissed from office. As a calligrapher Mi is noted for his perfect execution and free, vigorous style. Since he was fond of strange-shaped rocks, he was known as a "friend of rocks." His prose and poems were published and widely circulated in his time.

By the early Qing dynasty Wang Duo had become the leading calligrapher in Beijing. He had served as Grand Secretary under the Southern Ming dynasty. After his surrender to the Qing government he was appointed Minister of the Board of Rites. Specializing in the cursive script, he was known for his neatness in complexity and bold, vigorous strokes. In his native town of Mengjin, Henan Province, many tablets are inscribed with his handwritings. *The Mountain Garden Copybook* is a collection of stone rubbings of his calligraphy sought after by connoisseurs and beginners.

Calligraphic art reached a climax in Beijing in the mid-Qing period. Emperor Qianlong loved the master calligraphers and eventually became one of them. Steles and horizontal boards inscribed with his handwritings are still found everywhere. Based on collections of the works of various dynasties in the palace, he compiled the *Calligraphy from the Hall of Three Rarities.* The 495 steles from which the rubbings were made cover the handscripts of 135 famous calligraphers from the Wei and Jin dynasties down to the end of the Ming period. The walls of the Hall for Inspecting Old Scripts in the Beihai Park are inlaid with the works of these masters, which are still in perfect condition.

During the Qianlong reign, because of the emperor's love of calligraphy, the examination papers, imperial decrees and other historical documents of the court were all written in the best style. The characters had to be black and shiny, neat and standard. As a result, a "court style" appeared to rival the official-document style of the Ming dynasty.

Zhang Zhao, one of Qianlong's favorite calligraphers, could imitate the emperor's handwritings in addition to maintaining his own style. Writing on behalf of the emperor, he made it almost impossible for people to tell any difference from the emperor's work.

Weng Fanggang was the leading calligrapher in Beijing in the middle and late periods of the Qing dynasty. A native of Daxing in Shuntian Prefecture, he passed the metropolitan examination in 1752, the 17th year of the Qianlong reign, and was appointed Councillor of the Inner Chancery. He devoted himself to the study of classics and was thoroughly conversant with ancient inscriptions on bronzes and stone steles. His research broadened the horizon of the scholars of his time and led to innovations in the style of calligraphy. Under his influence some calligraphers began to shift from a graceful and elegant style to simple and unaffected strokes. Taking the ancient calligraphers as his model, Weng Fanggang made his writing plain and vigorous. He had many of his works published before he died at 86.

Special Handicrafts

Special handicrafts thrived in Beijing during the Ming-Qing period. This had to do with the extravagant life of the imperial family, the aristocracy, the gentry, and other rich people. It was also an offshoot of the growing commodity economy and the economic interflow with foreign countries.

Lacquer box made in the Qing dynasty

The Great Yu Tames the Flood (jade carving of the Qing)

Carved Lacquerware

Lacquer carving is believed to have been introduced into Beijing from Jiaxing Prefecture in Zhejiang Province during the Yongle reign of the Ming dynasty. The roughcast is made of gold, silver, copper or tin. Coats of lacquer are applied to the outside. In some cases several dozen layers are applied while in others hundreds of them are required. Before the lacquer has dried completely, it is carved with decorative designs. Lacquerwares are beautiful decorations as well as durable utensils. Beijing's lacquered products include bowls, plates, boxes, cases, etc. Many of the couches, screens and caskets in the imperial palace were carved lacquer. Beijing's carved lacquerwares are simple and unsophisticated, done in bright colors, and exquisite in design and composition. They also exhibit a rich folk flavor.

Cloisonné

Cloisonné is a kind of enamelware made by applying colored enamels to designs outlined in copper wire on a bronze object. The products of the Jintai reign period of the Ming dynasty (1450-1456) were superb in quality. "Jingtai Blue" is the name for the dazzling color of a frequently used enamel introduced at the time, but has since become the name for Chinese cloisonné enamels in general. Production of cloisonné begins with the casting of bronze to which flat bronze wires are affixed in decorative patterns. Enamels of different colors are applied to fill the *cloisons* or hollows. Then each piece of cloisonné is fired three times, each time with a fresh coat of enamel. Finally the pieces are polished and gilded.

Dignified and elegant, graceful and gorgeous, cloisonné wares were used as decorative articles in the imperial palace and sacrificial vessels in the temples. During the Qianlong reign of the Qing dynasty an enamel pagoda was made and placed in the Room of the Buddhist Pagoda in the Pavilion of the Flowers of the West Heavens. The walls of the room are decorated with Buddhist paintings of mythical tales. Surrounded by the beautiful paintings against the background of an azure sky and white clouds, the pagoda looks attractive with its delicate carvings.

The cloisonné pagoda has a square base in three tiers different in color and design. The pagoda itself has three stories. The first story looks like a square pavilion with painted balustrades at the bottom and double eaves and connected roofs at the top. In the middle of this

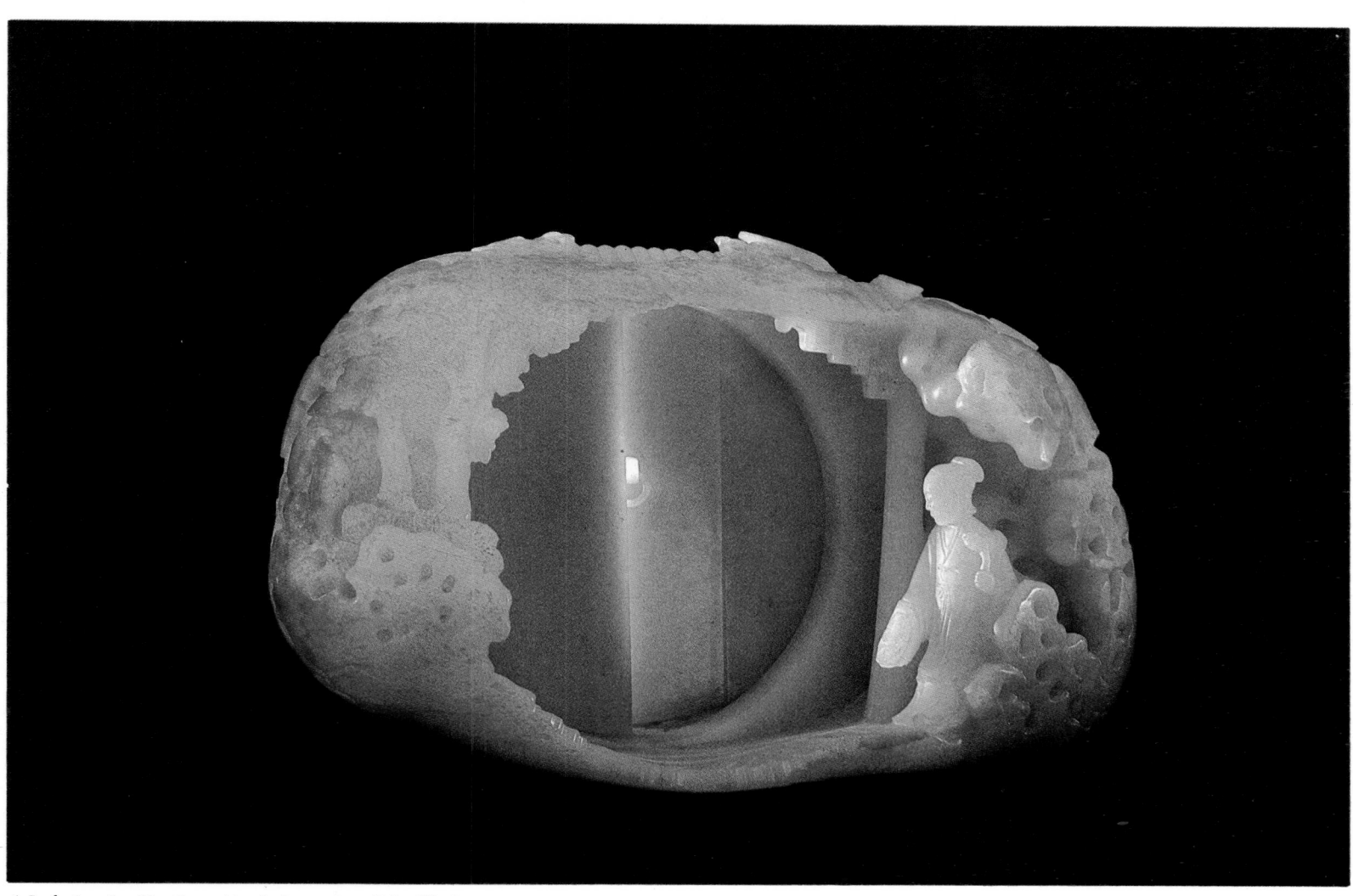

A Lady Leaving Her Door Ajar (jade carving of the Qing)

Plate with design of squirrel and grapes (ivory carving of the Qing)

story is a niche with a statue of Buddha. The second story resembles an octagonal pavilion resting on a base decorated with sky-blue patterns at the four corners, designed to create the feeling that the pagoda towers into the sky. Surrounded with gold-flower beams and pillars and fitted with a double-eaved arc at the top, this story also has a niche with a statue of Buddha. The third story, also in the shape of a pavilion, again has a niche, but the Buddha statue in it has long been lost. Three tiers of eaves are used as ornamental bands around the top of this story, and the elaborate patterns vary from one tier to another.

In the Qing dynasty cloisonné wares were first produced only in the workshops of the court. Later they were also made by artisans working outside the palace. Beijing's cloisonné articles began to be exported during the Daoguang reign. In 1904, the 30th year of the Guangxu reign, cloisonné products from Beijing were exhibited at the Chicago International Fair and won a first-class prize.

Jadeware

Jade carving has a long history in Beijing. As early as the Liao and Jurchen periods many skilled jade carvers came to work in Beijing. The large jade wine-container mentioned earlier in this book is a priceless treasure of the Yuan capital of Dadu. From the Ming dynasty onwards Beijing became a well-known center for the production of jade articles. Because jade is extremely hard, it usually takes several years to finish a finely carved piece.

An experienced craftsman must be skilful in exploiting the natural color and veins of a piece of jade while creating an impressive design. *The Great Yu Tames the Flood,* a product of the Qing dynasty, is a huge block of jade about two meters high and five tons in weight. It took eight years to do this piece of jade carving rarely seen in the world. It is about the legendary hero, the Great Yu, a leader of ancient tribal groups who led his people in dredging waterways and cutting canals to direct flood waters into proper courses. He was also credited with the construction of irrigation canals beneficial to farm production.

Ivory Carving

Special workshops were set up in the Ming and Qing dynasties to produce ivory articles for the court. Beijing's artisans have long been specializing in traditional figurines, flowers, and themes from Chinese history and legend. Ivory was also used to make articles for practical use by the royal family, such as matting and fans. An outstanding work is the album of jade carvings called *Strolling in the Moonlight* totalling 18 sheets, which gives a vivid picture of how people enjoyed themselves in an evening — playing chess, swinging, watching flowers, sampling tea, boating, and looking at paintings.

Porcelain Carving

Carved porcelain refers to vessels decorated with engravings of poems, calligraphy or paintings. Initiated in the Song dynasty, it reached a high level in the Ming period and showed fresh advances under the Qing. The artist first engraved designs of landscapes. flowers, figures or insects on porcelain and then filled in the hollows with glaze. The products are delicately carved and brightly painted.

Silk Flowers

Silk flowers are flowers made of tough silk. Legend has it that Yang Yuhuan, favorite consort of the Tang dynasty emperor Xuanzong, had a scar on her left temple. To have it covered, she asked her maids to pick a fresh flower for her to wear on her hair every morning. In winter, when fresh flowers were not so easy to get, she ordered them to make silk ones as a substitute. The use of silk flowers by the imperial consort made it popular. By the Ming-Qing period silk flowers had undergone much improvement and became known as Beijing flowers. China's silk flowers were first exported to foreign lands in late Qing dynasty.

Bronze Casting

Small bronze articles like basins and bowls and large ones like bells and tripods were made with exquisite workmanship in Beijing in the Ming dynasty. The Yongle Bell, known as the Great Bell or the King of Bells, is an example. It was named after the Yongle reign (1403-1424) during which it was cast. Originally called the Avatamsaka Bell, it was first placed in the printing house for publishing Buddhist sutras in the Han script and was moved to the Temple of Awakening in the western suburbs in 1733, the 11th year of the Yongzheng reign of the Qing dynasty. And this is why the temple is commonly referred to as the Great Bell Temple.

The bell is 6.94 meters high and weighs 46.5 tons. The lip measures 18.5 cm. in thickness and the outer rim is 3.3 meters in diameter. Inscribed on the inner and outer surfaces are 17 sutras totalling 227,000 characters in a boldly executed regular script. The bell tolls in clear and deep tones when it is struck lightly, and sounds vigorous and penetrating when it is struck harder. A passage in *A Visitor's Notebook on Chang'an* says: "Struck day or night, it is heard several dozen *li* away. Its harmonious tone rises and falls in a way that distinguishes it from other bells."

Behind the Temple of Righteous Awakening, also known as the Temple of Five Pagodas, stands an octagonal iron pagoda called the Gilded Pagoda of Many Treasures. It has 152 Buddhist statues.

Apart from the special handicrafts mentioned above, Beijing is also known for its flower lanterns, fireworks and velvet flowers.

The Yongle Bell

Gilded Pagoda of Many Treasures

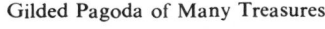

229

Porcelain

China's porcelain became better than ever in the Ming-Qing period. The substance was fine, the glaze lustrous, the colors bright and varied, and the decorations tasteful.

In addition to private kilns, an Imperial Porcelain Manufactory was established at Jingdezhen, the porcelain town in Jiangxi Province, in the Ming dynasty. Eunuchs were sent there to supervise production. The number of government-run kilns reached 58. The products included bowls, dishes, plates, containers, bells, bottles, vases, chessboards, screens, and jars with dragon designs. Huge quantities of procelain wares were produced by the government kilns for use by the imperial household. In 1433, the eighth year of the Xuande reign, 443,500 pieces with dragon-and-phoenix designs were ordered at one time. In 1441, the sixth year of the Zhengtong reign, upon completion of the three main halls in the Forbidden City — the present Hall of Supreme Harmony, Midway Hall of Harmony, and Hall of Preserved Harmony, the court placed orders for large numbers of dinner sets with nine-dragon and nine-phoenix decorations, large jars decorated with blue dragons against a white background, and white porcelain pots decorated with golden dragons and phoenixes. In 1547, the 26th year of the Jiajing reign, 120,260 pieces of porcelain were produced for the palace. It is estimated that during the 45 years of the Jiajing reign the government kilns turned out about one million pieces for the court. In 1591, the 19th year of the Wanli reign, the court ordered 159,000 pieces and then 80,000 more. Officials of the Board of Works petitioned the emperor to suspend or reduce the manufacture of porcelain in view of the poverty of the people caused by the poor soil and successive calamities in the Jingdezhen area. The request was turned down.

The main products of the Imperial Porcelain Manufactory at Jingdezhen were blue-and-white wares, in which the Ming dynasty surpassed the Yuan dynasty by a thin body of fine texture, a lustrous glaze in gorgeous colors, exquisite designs and a rich variety of forms. Blue-and-white porcelain occupies a high place in the history of Chinese ceramics.

During the Ming period a new product, painted porcelain, appeared in red yellow, green, blue, black and purple colors. This represented a new technique of combining the blue underglaze with the overglaze in various colors. Early Ming porcelain was either blue and white or overglazed in red. During the Chenghua reign the five-colored wares made their first appearance. Later large quantities of blue-and-white wares with a five-colored glaze were sent to the court as a new type of ornaments.

In the Ming dynasty large quantities of chinaware were transported to remote border areas inhabited by ethnic minorities. It is recorded in the *Casual Notes on the Wanli Reign* by Shen Defu that the Mongolian and Jurchen envoys used to carry home dozens of carloads of porcelain. The method of packing was described as follows:

> After the wares are purchased, a little soil and a few beans or grains of wheat are dropped into them. One piece is placed above another. Several scores of stacks are bound into block. Then the block is placed in a damp place and sprinkled with water. As time passes, the beans and wheat seeds begin to sprout and stems twine round the stacks and fasten them. Then the block is thrown on hard ground as a test of its sturdiness. If it is not damaged, it is ready to be loaded onto a cart.

The above shows an excellent method of packing in preparation for land transportation.

Ming dynasty porcelain was exported in large quantities. In 1604, the 32nd year of the Wanli reign, the Dutch once attacked a Spanish ship and seized about 60 tons of chinaware. The cargo was shipped to Amsterdam to be sold by auction. Henri IV, the King of France, bought a dinner set. It is recorded in *The Dutch Indian Company and Chinaware* that in 1612, the 40th year of the Wanli reign, 38,641 pieces of porcelain were shipped to the Netherlands. The number reached 69,057 in 1614, the 42nd year of the Wanli reign; 259,380 in 1636, the 9th year of the Chongzhen reign; and 366,000 in 1639, the 12th year of the Chongzhen reign. It can be seen from these figures that Chinese porcelain was quite popular and in great demand in the West during the Ming period.

Five-colored porcelain cup with grape designs made during the Chenghua reign of the Ming dynasty

Five-colored porcelain wine container with egret and lotus designs made during the
Kangxi reign of the Qing dynasty

Polychromatic porcelain vase with peony designs made during the Qing dynasty

to his wedding ceremony. Because of this, aristocrats of the West began to show keen interest in Chinese porcelain. In 1780, the 45th year of the Qianlong reign, Britain placed an order for 800,000 pieces with the Qing government. Chinese porcelain became an important link between the East and the West.

In the Qing dynasty, as in the Ming period, an Imperial Porcelain Manufactory operated at Jingdezhen to supervise the production of porcelain wares for use by the imperial household.

China's porcelain industry experienced a golden era during the reigns of Emperors Kangxi, Yongzheng and Qianlong. The five-colored wares produced in the Kangxi period, commonly known as the Kangxi Five-Colors, are noted for their dignified shapes, variety of decorations, bright colors, and transparent glaze, which represent the fresh advances made under the Qing dynasty.

A famous brand is known as *famille rose*. On the basis of the techniques of the Kangxi Five-Colors, part of the design was first painted in the enamel colour of *famille rose* on a coating of fine white glass powder before firing. *Famille rose* wares produced in the Yongzheng reign are known as the Yongzheng *famille rose* and look even more gorgeous and elegant than the Kangxi Five-Colors. Many of the Yongzheng *famille rose* products are as transparent as a mirror and as thin as paper, described as "thin enough to be blown away by wind and delicate enough to melt under the sun."

Enamel painting was another new technique developed in the Qing period. Colored glazes were used for the painting on the body of the porcelain before it was fired. Most of the vessels were painted and fired in the Manufacturing Department of the Imperial Household. Among the products were bowls, cups, containers, kettles and vases which were made specially for appreciation by the emperor, the empress, and the imperial concubines or for use at sacrificial ceremonies. During the Yongzheng reign the enamel paintings on porcelain presented landscapes, flowers and birds, bamboos and rocks as well as figurines, all accompanied by poems in excellent calligraphy. This initiated the combination of porcelain art with poetry, calligraphy and painting. Under Emperor Qianlong some vessels were decorated with Western-style paintings and had an unusual appeal.

Qing dynasty porcelain wares were very popular abroad. They were exported to Europe in addition to neighboring countries like Japan, Korea and Viet Nam. It is said that once the king of Prussia gave 600 cavalrymen from Saxony to the emperor of a neighboring country in exchange for a quantity of chinaware to add magnificence

Array of Eight Banner Soldiers (painting of the Qing dynasty)

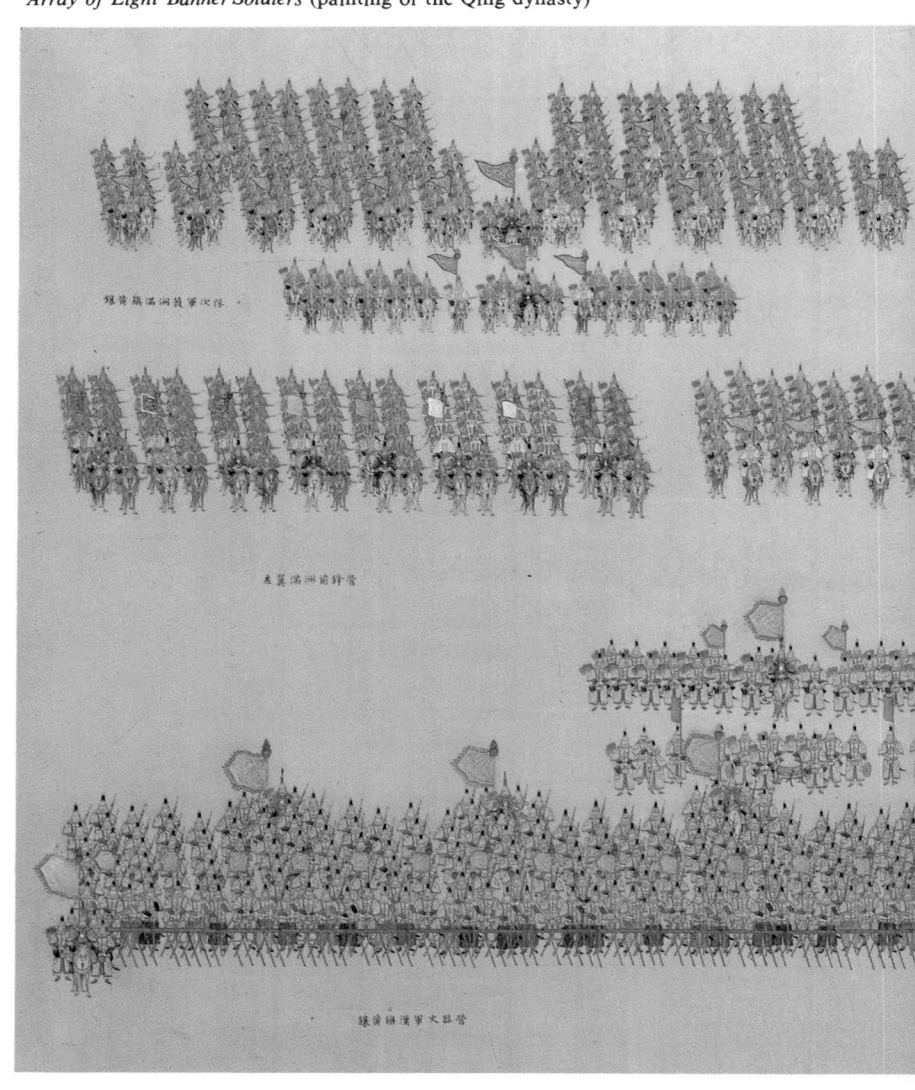

The "Square Courtyards"

The Separate Communities

After the Qing government made Beijing its capital in 1644, the first year of the Shunzhi reign, it placed the Banner People (Manchus) and people of other ethnic groups in different parts of the city. This was something which had never been done in previous dynasties and was never repeated after the Qing.

The military and administrative system of the Eight Banners had been instituted long before the Qing army crossed the Great Wall. Each of the eight banners was identified by the color of its flag, which could be yellow, white, red, blue, yellow-bordered, white-bordered, red-bordered or blue-bordered. There were a total of 24 banners, including the Manchu Eight Banners, the Mongolian Eight Banners, and the Han Eight Banners. But these were generally known as the Eight Banners. Each banner had about 7,000 people, including

officers and men and their families. Thus in early Qing dynasty it was an economic and clan organization as well as a military and political institution. After the officers and men of the Eight Banners entered Beijing, the Qing government seized and enclosed the houses in the Inner City to accommodate the Banner People. The Hans, Huis and people of other ethnic groups living there were forced to move to the Outer City. The houses thus evacuated in the Inner City were either pulled down for reconstruction or sold to the Banner People. Hence the four divisions of the city of Beijing were strictly distinguished from one another.

The emperor lived in the Forbidden City. The imperial gardens and government offices were located in the Imperial City. The Banner People lived in the Inner City, while the Hans and people of other

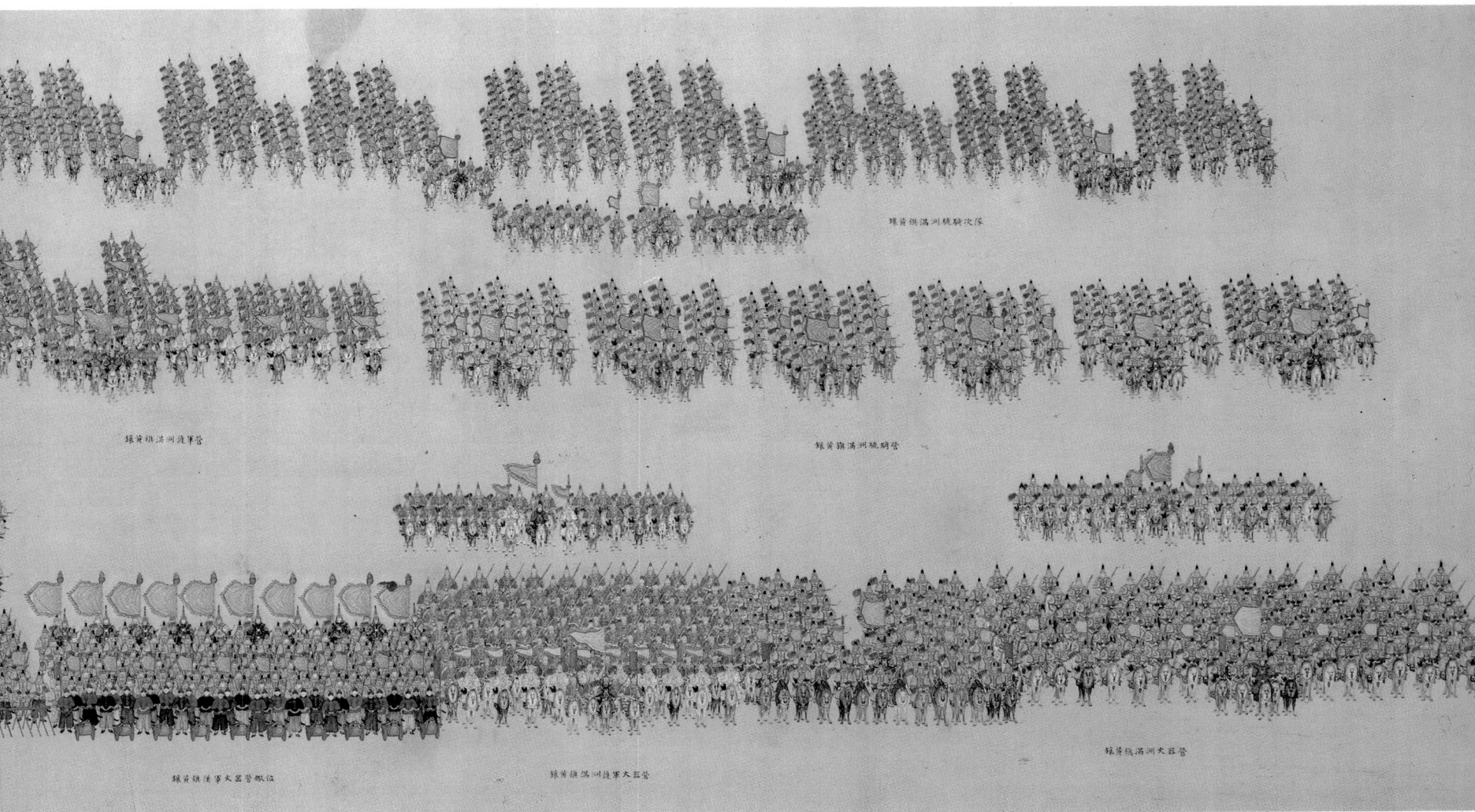

nationalities lived in the Outer City. Each city was surrounded by a brick wall and no transgression was permitted.

In the Inner City the Banner People lived in districts assigned to their respective banners. The Yellow and Yellow-bordered Banner People lived in the northern district. The former lived inside the Gate of Victory while the latter lived inside the Gate of Stability. The White and White-bordered Banner People lived in the eastern district of the city. The former lived inside the Straight East Gate and the latter lived inside the Facing-the-Sun Gate. The Blue and Blue-bordered Banner People lived in the southern district. The former lived inside the Gate of Literary Virtue while the latter lived inside the

Gate of Military Virtue. The Red and Red-bordered Banner People lived in the western district. The former lived inside the Straight West Gate while the latter lived inside the Gate of Great Tranquility. When the Hans or people of other ethnic groups went to the Inner City to call on friends and relatives or burn incense in temples they had to return the same day because they were not permitted to spend the night there. Throughout the city of Beijing 1,755 barriers were erected at both ends of streets and alleys, which were patrolled day and night.

The separation of the Banner People from other residents of the city, however, promoted the development of the business district outside the area of the South-Facing Gate.

Qiandetang Drugstore (painting of the Qing dynasty)

The Business District Outside the Three Front Gates

Early in the Yuan dynasty the national capital, Dadu, was planned according to the architectural conception of "The Artisans' Trades," a section of the *Rites of Zhou,* which calls for placing the royal court in the front and the market at the back. Hence the market area spread from the Pool of Accumulated Waters to the Bell and Drum Towers. By the Ming dynasty the conception had gradually changed to reverse the order, i.e., to place the market in the front and the royal court at the back. In the Qing period business became prosperous outside the area of the South-Facing Gate. The main reasons were:

First, in the Yuan dynasty the terminal wharf for the transport of tribute rice to Dadu by the Grand Canal was at the Pool of Accumulated Waters where ships were crowded and cargoes piled up like hills. Thus the area between the pool and the Bell and Drum Towers became a commercial center. But in late Yuan period the pool

Dazhalan Street outside the South-Facing Gate

Site of the Zhangjiawan Wharf of the Grand Canal. Located in today's Tongxian County, Beijing, it was an important wharf along the Tonghui section of the Grand Canal during the Ming and Qing dynasties.

234

was silted up and became unusable. The business district around the pool gradually declined.

Second, by the Ming dynasty the terminus of rice transport was moved to a point on the east outside the South-Facing Gate. Every year more than 10,000 ships carried some five million piculs of rice from Hangzhou in Zhejiang Province to Beijing along the 3,000-*li* Grand Canal. Apart form rice, other goods were also shipped to and from the capital by these rice boats, which were loaded and unloaded in this area. Thus the commercial center in Beijing moved south.

Third, as mentioned above, in the Qing dynasty the Banner People lived away from the Hans and other ethnic groups. Living in the Inner City, they were interested mainly in horsemanship and archery and did no business. They had to do shopping in the Outer City which was inhabited by other ethnic groups. And since theaters and other centers for amusement were forbidden in the Inner City, the Banner People had to get entertainment in the Outer City.

Fourth, east of the South-Facing Gate was the custom-house at the Gate of Literary Virtue, inside of which, on the west, was the Translation Bureau responsible for receiving envoys and business people from the ethnic minorities. The latter did their business on the market outside the South-Facing Gate. To the west of the same gate was the Gate of Military Virtue, outside of which were the premises of a number of provincial guilds. Most of the scholars coming to Beijing for the metropolitan examination stayed in the inns operated by the guilds. They often visited the shops along the Antiques Street to look for rare old books, calligraphy, paintings and curios. The street thus became a well-known cultural center and a favorite haunt for scholars, painters and calligraphers. The area outside the Three Front Gates of Beijing — the South-Facing Gate, the Gate of Literary Virtue and the Gate of Military Virtue — became a densely populated area where business thrived.

Fifth, after the Hui people (Moslems) moved out of the Inner City, most of them settled in the area along Ox Street to form the largest Moslem community in Beijing. Though most of them did business with a small capital, their commercial activities contributed to the prosperity of the Outer City.

All this made the area outside the Three Front Gates, especially the strip extending from the South-Facing Gate to the Dazhalan Street, a bustling business area with rows of stalls and goods of every description. Many famous shops were located in this district, and some of them are still there. Among them were the Liubiju Sauce and Pickle Shop, the Tongrentang Drugstore, the Duyichu Restaurant, the Neiliansheng Shoemakers' Shop, and the Ruifuxiang Satin, Silk and Fur Shop. The shops and stalls sold almost everything from daily necessities, tea and porcelain to silk fabrics and jewels. Crowded with shoppers from morning till evening, the area was the main business district in Beijing under the Qing dynasty.

The Mansions of Princes

Among Beijing's square courtyards the largest ones were the mansions of princes. Princes of the Ming dynasty would be granted vassalages scattered around the country as soon as they grew up. They were given high ranks but had no population under their control. They received an emolument but were not allowed to interfere with civil administration. Nevertheless, the Ming vassals possessed land and had their own armed forces. Time and again they rebelled against the central government. The Prince of Yan, Zhu Di, rebelled and finally seized the throne.

In the Qing dynasty, when the princes came of age, they were granted a rank and an emolument and moved from the imperial palace to mansions built for them in Beijing. The Qing princes were thus vassals only in name because they had neither land nor a population under their rule, nor any administrative or military power. The mansions of the Ming princes were scattered around the country while those of the Qing princes were concentrated in Beijing.

The mansions of Qing princes were located mainly in the Inner City. There were about 60 important mansions of princes, each

Winding corridor in Prince Gong's Mansion

having a magnificent complex of buildings, spacious courtyards and large gardens. The mansions were built according to official specifications which no one could depart from without imperial approval. It was stipulated that the mansion for each royal prince was to have a five-bay-wide main gate, a seven-bay main hall, a five-bay rear hall, a number of seven-bay bedrooms, and side halls to the east and west. With these buildings the mansion would consist of several courtyards. Many of the mansions had gardens. Most of the mansions have become dilapidated through long years of neglect. So far the best preserved one is Prince Gong's Mansion at 17 Qianhaixi Street on the east bank of Shisha Lake.

Yi Xin, Prince Gong, was the sixth son of Emperor Daoguang. He became a powerful Prince Regent after helping Empress Dowager Cixi stage a coup d'etat. Prince Gong's Mansion is composed of two parts — the buildings and the garden. The total area is 5.7 hectares.

The mansion consists of three complexes of buildings — central, eastern and western. The main entrance is five-bays wide with a pair of stone lions squatting in front. A short distance inside the main entrance is the second gate, again five bays wide. Further inside is the main hall on a raised platform with screens at the back. The hall is roofed with green glazed tiles. Still further inside is the two-storied rear hall which measures 160 meters from east to west and has a total space of 40 bays.

The eastern and western complexes each have three coutyards which are surrounded by chambers and halls.

The garden at the back of the mansion has winding corridors, pavilions, artificial hills and ponds. There are some 20 sights among the exotic flowers and trees and stone paths lined with bamboos. A crenellated ancient wall provided with a gate resembles the Shanhaiguan Pass. Legend has it that the owner of the mansion used to stand on the wall to look in the direction of his native town in Northeast China as a way of easing his homesickness. Some scholars think Prince Gong's mansion and its garden strongly resemble the Rongguo Mansion and Grand View Garden in Cao Xueqin's famous novel, *A Dream of Red Mansions*. Though there is still much controversy over the question, a visit to the mansion helps one appreciate some of the scenes described in the novel.

Prince Yong's mansion had been the residence of Emperor Yongzheng before he ascended the throne. After he moved to the palace, he changed it to a temporary palace used for a short stay and named it Palace of Harmony and Peace. When Emperor Yongzheng died in 1735, his coffin was kept there before burial. His successor, Emperor Qianlong, formally converted it into a lamasery in 1744, calling it the Lamasery of Harmony and Peace.

In the Qing dynasty the Mongols and Tibetans were both followers of Lamaism, and religion was integrated with politics in their case. Making use of this largest lamasery in Beijing, Emperor Qianlong strengthened his ties with the upper strata of the Mongols and Tibetans as well as his rule over the northwest, west and southwest frontier regions. This is clear from the inscription on a stele in the Pavilion of the Imperial Writing-Brush in the lamasery, which explains the origin and significance of Lamaism in Han, Manchu, Mongolian and Tibetan scripts.

The Lamasery of Harmony and Peace has three beautiful archways and five main halls plus many side halls. Laid out in a triangle, the three archways are known as the East, West and North Archways. The building complex is imposing and well-balanced, exhibiting the architectural styles of the Manchu, Mongolian, Han and Tibetan nationalities. Inside the lamasery are many images of Buddha, murals, and works of Buddhist art. Among the most

Gate of the Lamasery of Harmony and Peace

Carved wooden niche for a statue of Buddha in the Lamasery of Harmony and Peace

Archways at the Lamasery of Harmony and Peace

intriguing creations are the Mountain of Five Hundred Arhats, a sculptured wooden niche, and a huge statue of Maitreya, which are praised as the three wonders of the lamasery.

The Mountain of Five Hundred Arhats stands behind the Hall of the Dharmacackra. On the altar is a 5.5-meter-high bronze statue of Tsong-kha-pa (1357-1419), founder of the Yellow Hat Order of Lamaism. The Mountain of Five Hundred Arhats itself is carved out of red sandlewood while the 500 arhats are cast in five metals — gold, silver, bronze, iron and tin.

The tallest building in the lamasery is the three-storied Tower of Infinite Happiness, also known as Tower of the Great Buddha. Inside the tower stands the statue of Maitreya which is 26 meters in height, 18 meters above ground and eight meters below ground. The statue is carved from a single trunk of white sandalwood, a gift sent to Emperor Qianlong by the seventh Dalai Lama who had purchased it from Gurkha (Gorkha) in present-day Nepal. It took three years to transport the huge sandalwood trunk to Beijing. It is said that when the statue was being carved, a hole was dug in the ground to hold the trunk in position. Because of the unusual height of the sculpture, it had to be finished before work could start on the hall that was going to house it.

Murals in the Lamasery of Harmony and Peace. Sakyamuni is seated in the middle, flanked by his disciple Mahabkya on the left and another disciple, Ananda, on the right.

Beijing's Residential Courtyards

The square courtyard is a traditional architectural form in China. It is also the most common type of housing for Beijing's ordinary residents. It is so named because there is a row of one-storied rooms on each of the four sides of a courtyard. The square courtyard has a long history. The pattern appeared when the Yuan dynasty built its capital Dadu. Basing on the architectural theory that a capital city should be a square or rectangular one, the streets of the city were connected with the city gates and were laid out in a chessboard pattern.

Similarly, in the Ming and Qing dynasties Beijing's main thoroughfares ran from north to south while its narrower streets and alleys lay parallel to each other to the east and west of the thoroughfares. The courtyards of the residents lined the north and south sides of the narrower streets and alleys. In each courtyard the rooms were mostly placed on the northern side with the windows facing south. In winter a house like this would provide shelter from the cold northwest wind and be warmed by the sun. In summer it would provide good ventilation and plenty of light.

While differing in size and taste, Beijing's square courtyards are generally built along a north-south axis and symmetrically laid out. The front courtyard has a gate, a screen wall facing the gate, and a screen door between the outer and inner courtyards. There are no windows on the wall along the street. The screen wall stands between the gate and the inner courtyard, which serves as an architectural decoration and gives more depth to the courtyard, creating a feeling of leisure, privacy and quietude.

Further inside is the second gate with a wooden board carved with flower designs hanging above it. Inside the gate is the inner courtyard with the main rooms on the north and the side rooms on the east and west. Traditionally parents of a family live in the main halls facing south which are warm in winter. The rooms along the east and west sides are for the sons and daughters. The main rooms are usually connected with the side-rooms by corridors.

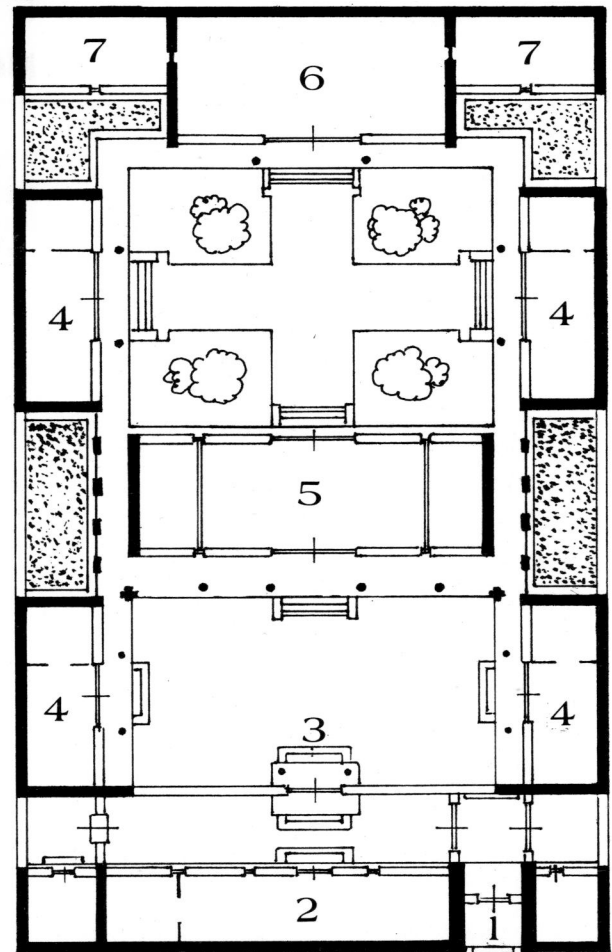

Plan of a Compound with Two Square Courtyards:

1. Main entrance
2. Rooms facing the rear
3. "Hanging-flower" gate
4. East and west side rooms
5. Inner vestibule
6. Main building
7. Small side rooms

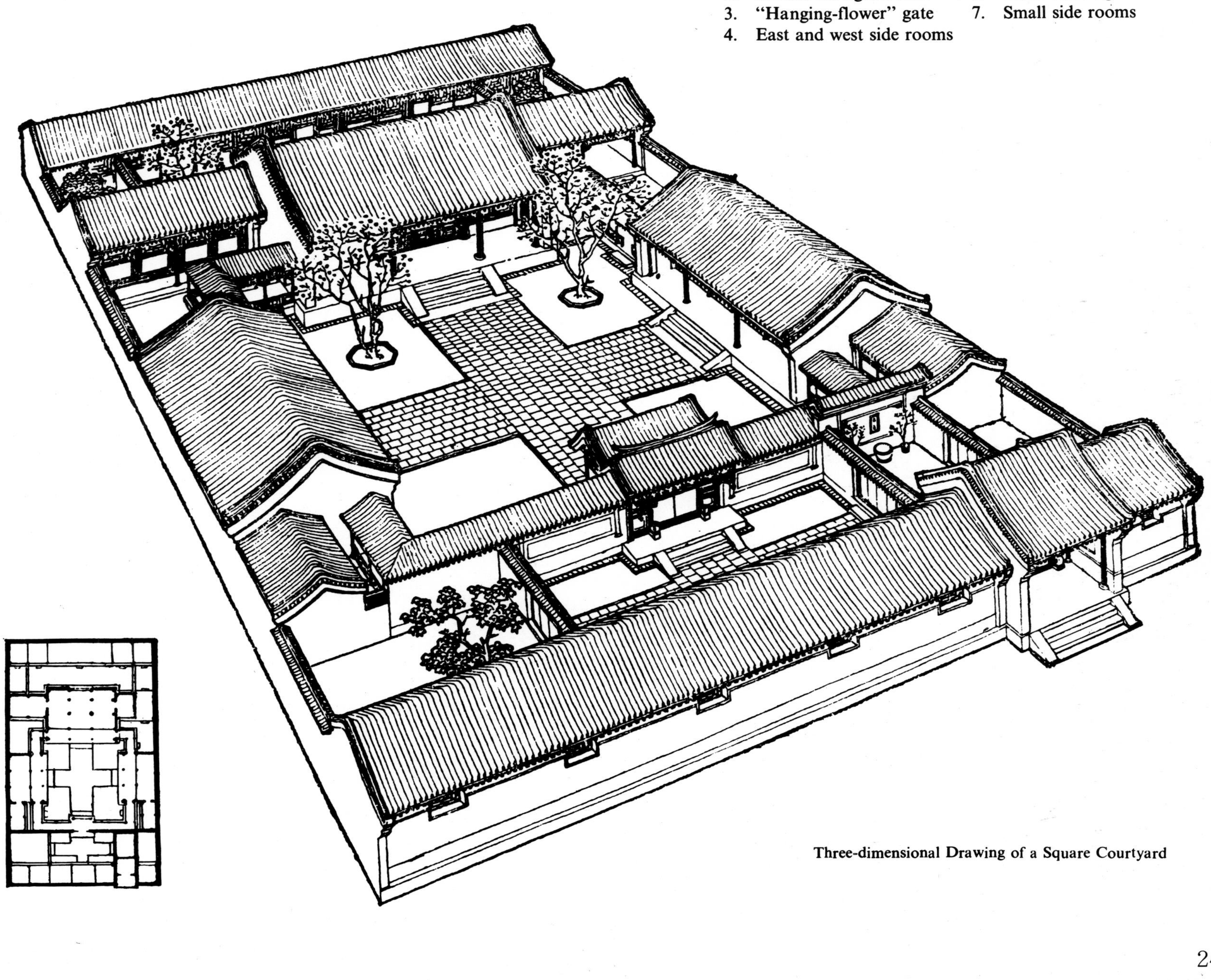

Three-dimensional Drawing of a Square Courtyard

245

"Hanging-flower" gate of a square courtyard — a gate with a wooden board carved with flower designs hanging above it

A yard in a square courtyard

A small courtyard means a single courtyard. A medium-sized one has two or three courtyards. A large one has additional yards on the east and west. In some cases the main rooms and side rooms have covered corridors in the front and at the back. In others there are rockeries, trees and flowers in the yards. On a fine day or moonlit night a yard adorned with trees and flowers presents an atmosphere of charming quietude. In some houses the main rooms in the backyard are flanked by side-rooms at both ends with side-doors opening into smaller yards. In each yard there is a well. The backyard is usually surrounded by a wall with a moongate leading to the rear garden.

A family is the epitome of a country or a cell of a particular society. China's feudal society, dominated by an autocratic monarch, was rigidly stratified. The socio-economic base was a natural economy, and much stress was laid on feudal ethics. The family was

Front gate of a small square courtyard

Main room in a small square courtyard

Side room in a square courtyard

Eaves in a square courtyard

A roof in a square courtyard

Carved brick on a roof in a square courtyard

248

Screen wall in a square courtyard

Stone drum as an ornament at the gate of a square courtyard

Door rings of a square courtyard

A family living in a square courtyard in the Qing dynasty

bound together by economic ties and blood relationships, which again were reinforced by the feudal code of ethics. The code consists mainly in the "Three Cardinal Guides" (ruler guides subject, father guides son, and husband guides wife) and the "Five Constant Virtues" (benevolence, righteousness, propriety, wisdom and fidelity). Even architectural designs and the distribution of rooms had to follow these ethical principles. In fact, the pattern of palaces and of the mansions of princes developed on the basis of the square courtyard. The main hall in a courtyard was placed in the front while the bedrooms were located at the back. In ordinary times the main hall was used to receive guests while on New Year's Day and other festivals it was the place for offering sacrifices to gods and ancestors. The bedrooms at the back facing south were occupied by the parents, and those on the east and west sides were assigned to sons and daughters. In the case of a large family with many children, the youngsters lived in a rear courtyard or in courtyards on the two sides, and the rooms in the courtyard near the gate were used by servants.

In a large feudal family the sons usually married at an early age and continued to live with their parents. It was customary to have several generations living under the same roof. The parents made the decisions on family affairs, including the handling of family assets, the distribution of income and coverage of expenses, and the marriages of the children. By written regulations or by custom the parents' words were the law. Disputes among family members were arbitrated by the head of the family. The buildings surrounding the courtyard served as walls which could ensure safety for the family and separate it from the outside world. The door rings of a square courtyard were made of copper or iron in a shape and design corresponding to the socio-political rank of the head of the family. A feudal family was thus secluded in a yard or a number of yards where the head of the family was the monarch or dictator of a small world.

The Life and Customs of Beijing's Residents

The people living in the tens of thousands of courtyards in Beijing differed widely in ethnic status, profession, culture and education as well as religious belief. In spite of the differences, they had much in common.

As far as clothing is concerned, the Hans mostly wore ample, wide clothes with long sleeves in the Ming dynasty. In hair style the men grew a long hair while the women wore a bun. In the Qing dynasty a Manchu man shaved part of his head and kept a queue. He dressed himself in a mandarin jacket worn over a long gown. The ends of his sleeves, long at the front and short in the rear, looked like hoofs. A Manchu man also had a belt around his waist.

Unlike Han women, Manchu women preferred natural, unbound feet. They wore long gowns fitted with tight sleeves which later became known as *qipao,* meaning a gown worn by a woman belonging to the Eight Banners. After the Qing army occupied Beijing, the Qing government forced every Han man to shave part of his head and wear a queue in the style of the Manchus and change into their clothes. Adoption or rejection of the Manchu style was regarded as an indication of surrender to or resistance against the Qing rulers. It might seem to be only a matter of custom, but the Hans considered it a gross insult hurting their national sentiments. This is evident from a popular saying of the patriotic Hans at the time: "We would rather have our heads cut off than submit to a shaving." As time went on, however, the Hans gradually gave in. Nonetheless, Han women continued to keep their feet bound while Manchu women always had natural, unbound feet.

The festivals celebrated at Beijing's temples were an old form of market fairs. Buddhist followers, men and women, went to the temples to burn incense before the statues of Buddha and do shopping at the same time. With the passing of time the fairs became regular. As the temples were located in different parts of the city, the fairs became regular markets for the local communities. The best known fairs were those held at the Temple of the God of Mount Tai, the Great Bell Temple, the Temple of Prosperity, and the Temple for Protecting the Nation.

Banner women of the Qing dynasty

Bridal sedan chair

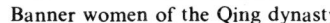

New Year's Temple Fair at Changdian (painting of the Qing dynasty)

A wide variety of goods were on sale at the temple fairs, ranging from delicacies of local flavor and articles of daily use to handicrafts like jadeware, lacquerware, ivory carvings, *ruyi* (an S-shaped ornament made of jade as a symbol of good luck), velvet birds, silk flowers, porcelains, palace lanterns, carpets and cloisonné. There were also stalls selling paintings, calligraphy and antiques.

The entertainment offered at the market fairs included storytelling and acrobatics. Regular theatrical performances were presented at big fairs. Thus the temple festivals were also held to let people relax and have some recreation.

In the Ming dynasty the fair at the Temple of the City God was the largest one. It was held for three successive days every month. At its climax the stalls stretched over five kilometers, and the place teemed with visitors and their horses and carriages.

Beijing is a city with a rich culture and a long history. After the Jurchen dynasty made the city its Middle Capital early in the 12th century, it became the center of scholars and artists of North China. In the Yuan dynasty it developed into the cultural center of the whole country. The residents were lucky enough to enjoy the *zaju* operas written and directed by the great playwright Guan Hanqing. In the Ming period teahouses and wine shops multiplied where customers could enjoy folk art performances like ballad singing, storytelling, comic dialogues and clapper talks. To see Peking opera ordinary residents went to theaters outside the South-Facing Gate while princes and aristocrats invited the opera troupes to perform in their mansions. For the majority of the population, however, it was the temple fairs which provided them with a rich variety of recreation, such as lion dance, land boating, walking on stilts and other folk performances. Scholars who took little interest in such enjoyment would go to the Antiques Street where they looked for paintings, calligraphy, and historical relics.

Beijing's residents subscribed to different religious beliefs. The Manchus believed in shamanisms. They offered sacrifices to heaven by erecting a pole in the southeastern corner of their courtyard and fastening to its top a box containing rice for crows. It is said that Nurchachi, Emperor Taizu of the Qing dynasty, once ran into trouble in his early years and was saved by crows. Thus the Qing rulers wanted to express their gratitude to crows. Actually this was a manifestation of totemism among primitive tribes.

The Mongols and Tibetans, followers of Lamaism, went to the lamaseries to offer sacrifices and pray for happiness. Outside the Gate of Stability was the West Yellow Temple. In 1780, the 45th year of the Qianlong reign, the Sixth Panchan Lama of Tibet came to Beijing for the emperor's birthday but soon passed away in the capital. To honor his memory, Emperor Qianlong built an octagonal Lamaist pagoda in the West Yellow Temple where Panchan had stayed, and named it the Pagoda of the City of Complete Purification, which is generally referred to as the Panchan Pagoda.

The Hui people or Moslems of Beijing went to the mosques for their religious service. Apart from the above-mentioned Ox Street Mosque, the oldest and largest in Beijing which was built in the 10th century, there was another large and old mosque, i.e., the Dongsi Mosque built in the 14th century. In addition to its splendid house, the Mosque has stone steles with inscriptions in Arabic and a handwritten copy of the *Koran*. Apart from the two large mosques, there were dozens of smaller ones along the streets and alleys inhabited by Moslems. In the Qing dynasty Emperors Kangxi and Qianlong issued imperial edicts urging officials and citizens to respect the religious belief and customs of the Hui people.

There were also many Catholic followers in Beijing. In the late Ming period Matteo Ricci came to Beijing and built a preaching hall inside the Gate of Military Virtue. In early Qing dynasty Jean Adam

Main hall of the Dongsi Mosque

Handwritten copy of *Koran* in Arabic. Produced in the Yuan dynasty, it is now stored in the Dongsi Mosque.

Schall von Bell built a cathedral at the site of the hall. Since it was located in the southern district of the city, it was known as the Southern Cathedral. Inside the church a large portrait of the Virgin Mary hung on the wall. The Southern Cathedral was the center of Catholic activities in Beijing. Thousands of Manchu and Han residents were baptized there. In addition, French missionaries built a cathedral at Xishiku, which was known as the Northern Cathedral because of its location. It was the largest cathedral in Beijing.

The Han people accounted for the largest portion of Beijing's population. Most of them believed in Buddhism. There were many temples in the Inner City, such as the Temple of Great Charity, Cypress Grove Temple, etc. On the northern side of the Changhe River outside the Straight West Gate is the Temple of True Awakening built in 1473, the 9th year of the Chenghua reign of the Ming dynasty. The temple is also known as the Five-Pagoda Temple because it has five small pagodas, called Diamond Throne Pagodas, standing on a large square foundation. The bodies of the pagodas as well as the four walls of the foundation are engraved with Buddhist images, floral designs and Sanskrit letters. On the body of the central pagoda, i.e. the Tathagata Pagoda, is a rock known as the Rock of the Buddha's Foot. It is said that when Sykamuni was entering a state of nirvana he stood on this rock and gave his last words to his disciple Ananda, saying, "At the last moment I leave my footprints here; soon I'll pass away." Hence the name of the rock.

To the north of the Shimen Village, Haidian District, was the Auspicious Cloud Convent. Built in the Ming dynasty, it is now in ruins. On the east side of the entrance to the convent is a huge rock on which stands a 20-meter-high, seven-storied brick pagoda known as the Auspicious Cloud Convent Pagoda.

About 20 kilometers west of the city, in the present-day Shijingshan District, are eight temples known as the Eight Great Sites of the Western Hills, of which the fourth one, the Temple of Great Compassion, was built in the Yuan dynasty. Originally called the Temple of Seclusion, it acquired its present name in the Qing dynasty. The statues of the arhats in the temple are said to have been carved by the famous Yuan dynasty sculptor Liu Yuan. At the back of the hall are two 800-year-old gingko trees.

The second one of the eight old temples was built in the Tang dynasty. At first it was named the Dragon Spring Temple. Later it was rebuilt and renamed the Temple of the Awakening Mountain in the Jurchen dynasty. In 1478, the 14th year of the Chenghua reign of the Ming dynasty, it was rebuilt again and changed to the present name—Temple of Divine Light. In the temple there used to be a large octagonal pagoda of carved bricks built in 1071, the 7th year of the Xianyong reign of the Liao period. It was called the Pagoda for Inviting Immortals. At present only the bas-reliefs on the foundation of the pagoda are discernible.

Southern Cathedral (interior view)

Southern Cathedral (exterior view)

The eighth day of the fourth lunar month is the Festival for Bathing the Buddha. On this day all the temples inside and outside the city left their gates open and the priests recited the sutras. Buddhist devotees flocked to the temples to take part in the festivities.

Quite a few of Beijing's residents also believed in Taoism. The White Cloud Temple is the largest Taoist monastery in Beijing. On the 19th day of the first lunar month, a Taoist festival, pilgrims came from far away to pay respects to the statues in the temple.

The largest Taoist temple fair, however, took place at the Temple of the God of Mount Tai on the Divine Peak Mountain about 70 kilometers west of Beijing. As the temple stood on a solitary peak, the pilgrims had to experience a fairly difficult climb.

The fair lasted from the first to the 15th day of the fourth lunar month, when several hundred thousand pilgrims and visitors scaled the heights to pay tribute to the deities. The endless stream continued day and night. When night fell lamps would be lit to look like a myriad of stars. Inside the halls the incense sticks and candles burnt 24 hours a day.

Temple of Great Compassion

Statue of an arhat in the Temple of Great Compassion

Statue of an arhat in the Temple of Great Compassion

Bas-relief on the base of the Pagoda for Inviting Immortals

Statue of an arhat in the Temple of Great Compassion

◁ Pagoda in the Auspicious Cloud Convent

Diamond Throne Pagodas in the Temple of True Awakening

Rock of the Buddha's Foot on the Tathagata Pagoda

Beijing's traditional festivals were much the same as those celebrated in other parts of the country.

Lunar New Year's Day

This is the first day of the first lunar month. On New Year's Eve incense sticks would be burnt and candles lit to usher in the deities. Firecrackers would be exploded throughout the night in the streets and alleys. When the deities were supposed to have arrived, the princes and high officials went to the palace to offer New Year's greetings to the emperor. In an ordinary family the young would make obeisances to the elders to wish them good luck. Later they would go out to pay New Year calls to close relatives and friends. New Year cards were often sent to distant ones. The streets and alleys were thronged with people and the whole city was permeated with a festive atmosphere. Most residents, rich or poor, would have dumplings with meat and vegetable stuffing for their New Year dinner. There was also the custom by which something special was wrapped in one of the dumplings and the person who happened to get it was supposed to have good luck for the whole year. A tiny piece of gold, silver or precious stone would be put into the dumpling in a rich household. A copper coin would serve the purpose in a poor family.

The Lantern Festival

The Lantern Festival falls on the 15th day of the first lunar month. It is also called the *Yuanxiao* Festival because *yuanxiao* (sweet dumplings made of glutinous rice flour) is eaten in the evening of that day. Sumptuous feasts were given and fireworks released in the Inner Court on the same night. Outside the court most homes and shops displayed colorful lanterns, and theatrical performances were presented for the public. The main street outside the South-Facing Gate was decorated with lanterns along both sides and lit up by a rich variety of fireworks. Merrymakers, some riding in carriages, passed by amid music and songs.

The Lantern Market located at the present-day Lantern Market Street, which appeared during the Ming dynasty, offered a great variety of decorative lanterns to customers along with a wide range of other commodities. On the night of the festival married young women dressed in their best went to the South-Facing Gate to touch the rings on the gate of the central tunnel, believing that the auspicious touches would bring them good luck and, in particular, a chubby boy to be born soon.

The Pure Brightness Festival

When spring comes, the environment begins to look fresh and young. The festival, which marks the beginning of spring, usually falls around April 5 on the Gregorian calendar. In the Qing dynasty many of Beijing's residents poured out of the city on this day to pay respects to their ancestors by sweeping their graveyards. Some flew kites over the graveyard when the ceremony was over. People enjoyed seeing kites of many shapes and colors floating in the sky. In the Qing period the streams outside the Straight West Gate were lined with willows, and people went there for a spring outing in a fine weather.

Dragon-Boat Festival

The fifth of the fifth lunar month is the traditional Dragon-Boat Festival all over China. On that day both the royal family and the ordinary people ate *zongzi* (dumplings made of glutinous rice wrapped in bamboo or reed leaves). Legend has it that, out of love for his country and people, the great ancient poet Qu Yuan (340-278 B.C.) drowned himself in the Milo River in Hunan Province in grief and indignation. To pay respects to the poet, people threw *zongzi* into the river as offerings to him. On this day a dragon-boat race was also held in the Tonghui Canal. The day was also called Daughters' Day because married young women returned to their parents' homes for a reunion.

A Brief Chronology of Chinese History

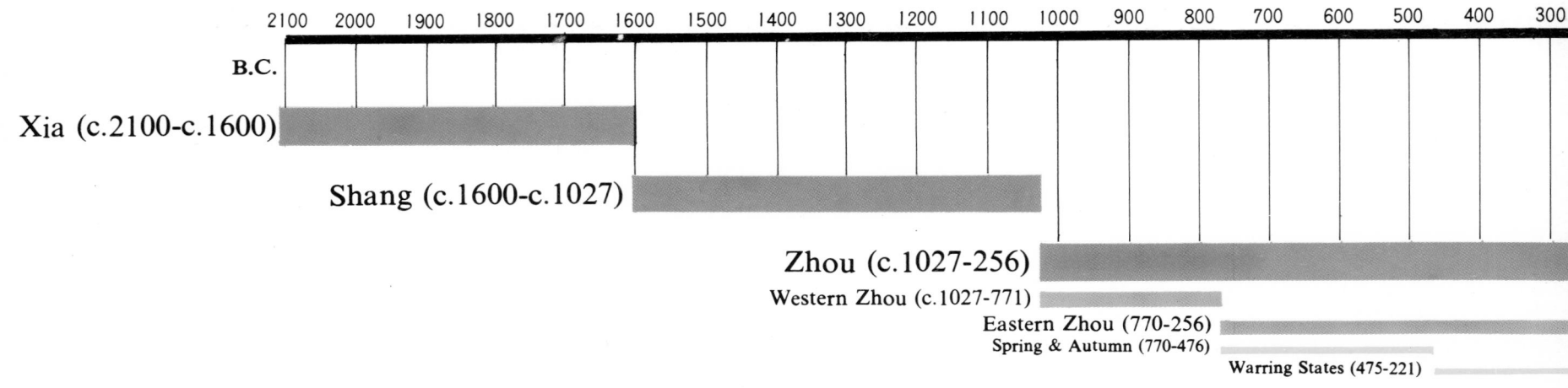

| 2100 | 2000 | 1900 | 1800 | 1700 | 1600 | 1500 | 1400 | 1300 | 1200 | 1100 | 1000 | 900 | 800 | 700 | 600 | 500 | 400 | 300 |

B.C.

Xia (c.2100-c.1600)

Shang (c.1600-c.1027)

Zhou (c.1027-256)

Western Zhou (c.1027-771)

Eastern Zhou (770-256)

Spring & Autumn (770-476)

Warring States (475-221)

Qin (221-20

Han (206 B.C.-220 A.D

Western Han (206 B.C.-8 A.

Northern

Posthumous Title	Name	Reign Title	Period
Yuan Dynasty (1271 — 1368)			
Shizu	Kublai	Zhiyuan	1271-1294
Chengzong	Timur	Yuanzhen	1295-1296
		Dade	1297-1307
Wuzong	Khaissan	Zhida	1308-1311
Renzong	Ayurbadrabal	Huangqing	1312-1313
		Yanyou	1314-1320
Yingzong	Shoodbal	Zhizhi	1321-1323
Taidingdi	Yesuntemur	Taiding	1324-1327
		Zhihe	1328
Tianshundi	Asugbal	Tianshun	1328
Mingzong	Hooshal	Tianli	1329
Wenzong	Tugtemur	Tianli	1328-1329
		Zhishun	1330-1332
Ningzong	Renqinbar	Zhishun	1332-1333
Shundi	Togontemur	Zhishun	1333
		Yuantong	1333-1335
		Zhiyuan	1335-1340
		Zhizheng	1341-1368
Ming Dynasty (1368-1644)			
Taizu	Zhu Yuanzhang	Hongwu	1368-1398
Huidi	Zhu Yunwen	Jianwen	1399-1402
Chengzu	Zhu Di	Yongle	1403-1424
Renzong	Zhu Gaochi	Hongxi	1425
Xuanzong	Zhu Zhanji	Xuande	1426-1435
Yingzong	Zhu Qizhen	Zhengtong	1436-1449
Daizong	Zhu Qiyu	Jingtai	1450-1456
Yingzong	Zhu Qizhen	Tianshun	1457-1464
Xianzong	Zhu Jianshen	Chenghua	1465-1487
Xiaozong	Zhu Youcheng	Hongzhi	1488-1505
Wuzong	Zhu Houzhao	Zhengde	1506-1521
Shizong	Zhu Houcong	Jiajing	1522-1566
Muzong	Zhu Zaihou	Longqing	1567-1572
Shenzong	Zhu Yijun	Wanli	1573-1620
Guangzong	Zhu Changluo	Taichang	1620
Xizong	Zhu Youxiao	Tianqi	1621-1627
Sizong	Zhu Youjian	Chongzhen	1628-1644
Qing Dynasty (1636-1911)			
Taizu	Aisin-Gioro Nurhachi	Tianming	1616-1626 (Later Jurchen)
Taizong	Aisin-gioro Huangtaiji	Tiancong	1627-1636 (Later Jurchen)
Taizong	Aisin-Gioro Huangtaiji	Chongde	1636-1643
Shizu	Aisin-Gioto Fulin	Shunzhi	1644-1661
Shengzu	Aisin-Gioro Xuanye	Kangxi	1662-1722
Shizong	Aisin-Gioro Yinzhen	Yongzheng	1723-1735
Gaozong	Aisin-Gioro Hongli	Qianlong	1736-1795
Renzong	Asin-Gioro Yongyan	Jiaqing	1796-1820
Xuanzong	Aisin-Gioro Minning	Daoguang	1821-1850
Wenzong	Aisin-Gioso Yizhu	Xianfeng	1851-1861
Muzong	Aisin-Gioro Zaichun	Tongzhi	1862-1874
Dezong	Aisin-Gioro Zaitian	Guangxu	1875-1908
	Aisin-Gioro Puyi	Xuantong	1909-1911

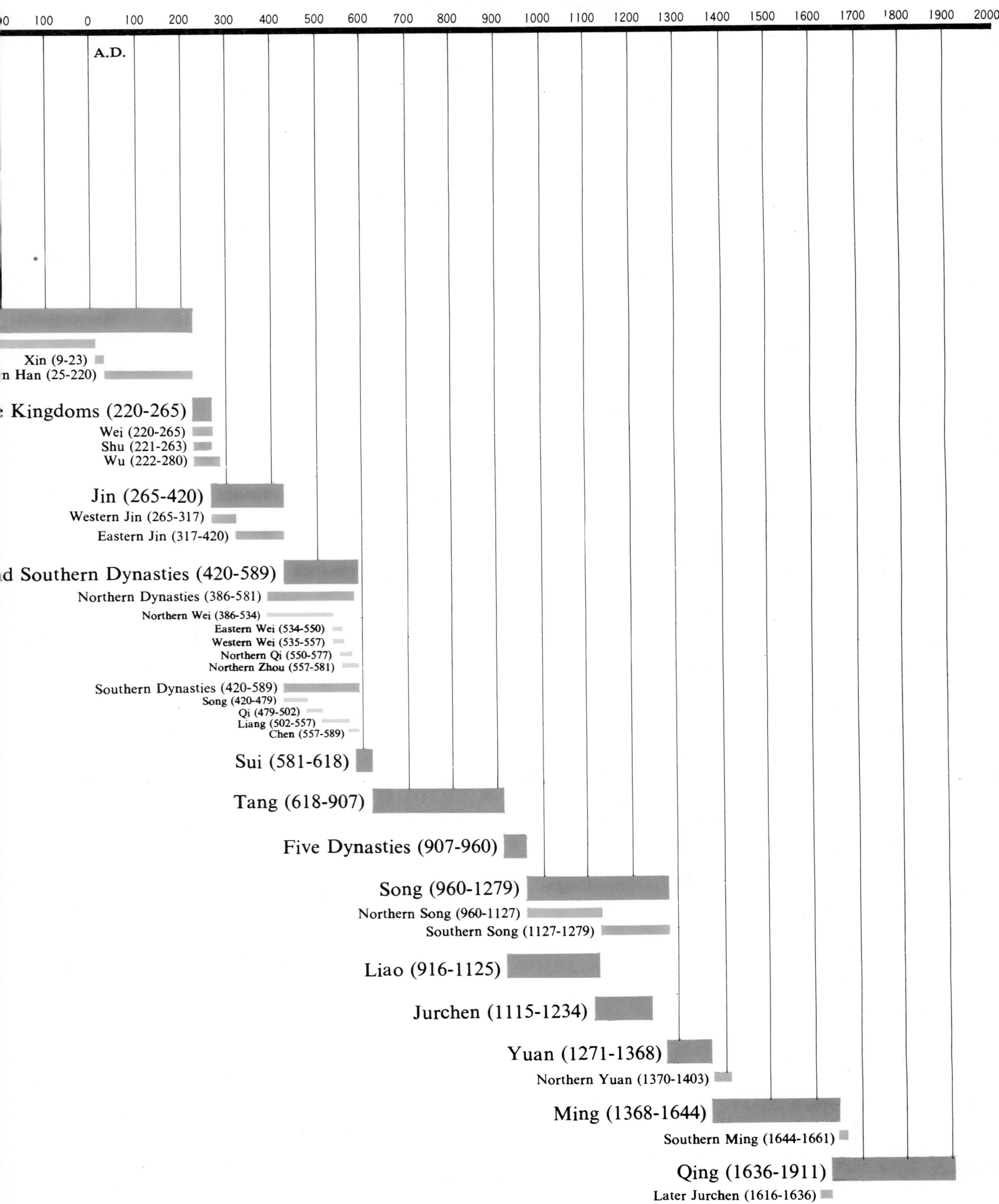

A Brief Chronology of Beijing

c.700,000 B.C.   Peking Man appears in the Beijing area.

c.1027 B.C.   King Wu of the Zhou dynasty makes Duke Shi of Zhao the prince of Yan. City walls and moats first appear in Beijing.

226 B.C.   Qin conquers the state of Yan and occupies its capital Ji or Jicheng near present-day Beijing.

350 A.D.   The state of Former Yan attacks and occupies the city of Jicheng and soon moves its capital there.

756   An Lushan proclaims himself Emperor of Great Yan and changes the name of the Beijing area from Fanyang to Yanjing.

911   Liu Shouguang declares himself Emperor of Great Yan and makes Jicheng his capital.

938   The court of the Liao dynasty upgrades Youzhou (Jicheng) as its auxiliary capital, renaming it Nanjing (Southern Capital).

1153   Prince of Hailing of the Jin (Jurchen) dynasty moves its capital from Huiningfu in present-day Liaoning Province to Yanjing and renames it Zhongdu (Middle Capital).

1215   The Mongolian army occupies the Middle Capital of the Jurchen dynasty.

1272   The emperor of the Yuan dynasty renames the Middle Capital Dadu (Great Capital) and moves its capital from Shangdu in present-day Inner Mongolia to Dadu.

1285   Construction of Dadu is in the main completed.

1368   The Ming troops attacks and occupies Dadu, renaming it the Peiping Prefecture.

1403   The Ming government elevates Peiping Prefecture to Beijing (Northern Capital).

1406   The Ming emperor announces the removal of his capital from Nanjing to Beijing.

1407   Construction starts for the city walls, moats, palace buildings, altars and temples in Beijing.

1420   Construction of the above projects is completed.

1421   The Ming government formally moves its capital from Nanjing to Beijing.

1564   The wall of the Outer City of Beijing is partly completed.

1644   The Qing government moves its capital to Beijing.

1911   A revolution breaks out under the leadership of Dr. Sun Yat-sen.

1912   Emperor Xuantong of the Qing dynasty abdicates.

INDEX

283

编　　辑：王燕荣　马　悦
英文翻译：赵一鹤　潭爱清　王行正　方振亚
英文定稿：赵一鹤
摄　　影：严钟义　胡　锤　刘志岗　孙贵奇
装帧设计：魏　明
绘　　图：俞美尔

古　都　北　京

编辑、出版：朝华出版社
　　　　　　北京车公庄西路21号
印　　刷：北京新华彩印厂
　　　　　　北京车公庄大街 3 号
总　发　行：中国国际图书贸易总公司
　　　　　　北京车公庄西路21号，北京第399信箱
编　　号：8·297—62（英）　84—E—645D　12500（精）
　　　　　　ISBN 7—5054—0092—4
1987年第一版

中华人民共和国印刷